reticent son, the original General Lee emerges from this book if not 'first in war' and 'first in peace,' at least deservedly restored to the pantheon his later indiscretions denied him."

—**HAROLD HOLZER**, author, co-author, or editor of more than fifty books; the Jonathan F. Fanton Director of Hunter College's Roosevelt House Public Policy Institute; and winner of the 2015 Lincoln Prize

"Ryan Cole's new biography of Henry Lee—the daredevil cavalry master of the American Revolution and the father of Robert E. Lee—provides us with a portrait nearly as headlong and fast-paced as 'Light-Horse Harry' himself. Lee was the George Custer of the Revolution, and like that ill-fated general, his life blazed in a heroic beginning, but spluttered to an agonizingly sad and tragic ending. Never was the American nation more 'slowly wise or meanly just' than to the man who immortalized Washington as first in war, first in peace, and first in the hearts of his countrymen; never did an American hero deserve better at America's hands. Perhaps, in the hands of Ryan Cole, some of that justice can now be done."

—**ALLEN GUELZO**, Henry R. Luce Professor of the Civil War Era, Director of Civil War Era Studies at Gettysburg College, and author of the bestselling *Gettysburg: The Last Invasion*

# LIGHT-HORSE HARRY LEE

# LIGHT-HORSE HARRY LEE

## THE RISE AND FALL OF A REVOLUTIONARY HERO

### RYAN COLE

REGNERY
HISTORY

Regnery History™ is a trademark of Salem Communications Holding Corporation
Regnery® is a registered trademark of Salem Communications Holding Corporation

Cataloging-in-Publication data on file with the Library of Congress

ISBN 978-1-62157-697-6
ebook 978-1-62157-860-4

Published in the United States by
Regnery History
An imprint of Regnery Publishing
A Division of Salem Media Group
300 New Jersey Ave NW
Washington, DC 20001
www.RegneryHistory.com

Manufactured in the United States of America

10 9 8 7 6 5 4 3 2 1

Books are available in quantity for promotional or premium use. For information on discounts and terms, please visit our website: www.Regnery.com.

*For my parents,*
*to whom I will always owe everything.*

# CONTENTS

# PROLOGUE

## THE WEST INDIES, 1813–1818

*No, not a word; what can a moment's space profit a wretch like him to death devoted? Quick let him die & cast his carcass for the dogs and vultures; they will best perform fit obsequies for him; by this alone we can be free and happy.*

The words were inscribed in a small mahogany-colored leather book; the hands that held and scribbled in it were tired and worn like the body they belonged to. The only other items its owner could claim were a battered old trunk and a drum of Madeira. The man's skin had tightened around his bones, and the clothes covering them were frayed and dangling from a body that bore little resemblance to the distinguished figure it had once been.

To those he passed, the man seemed little more than an aged vagabond.

But as he drifted among the Caribbean islands in search of health, running from his obligations, there were still men and women who enjoyed his charming conversation, who knew his name, even if they had trouble reconciling it with his now withered form. Yes, this was the famed warrior who had once been a counselor to presidents, who had basked in the admiration of great governing bodies and legendary generals. His bravery had won a people their freedom; his once golden voice had played a crucial role in their earliest political debates; his eloquent prose had comforted them in a time of great grief.

But bad judgment had brought on poverty and political isolation. Unpopular opinions had ignited the fury of his countrymen, whose knives and fists had lacerated his body. Disease was slowly eroding his being; fate and a flaw in his nature were conspiring in the pitiful final act of his life's drama.

Across an ocean, a wife and children wondered about the fate of this drifter. The only love he could show them was in rambling letters and little curios picked up as he limped along white beaches and sailed on turquoise water: the backbone of a shark, a lone pearl found in Bermuda, a few pieces of Irish linen.

There were those who took pity on him, who fed him, nursed him, and gave him money and shelter, with no compensation other than his perfervid gratitude. There were government functionaries who helped him, and captains of frigates who gave him passage.

But he was alone, this little book his only confidant. Scrawled across its pages in disordered writing that slipped between English and Latin, French and Spanish, were a lifetime of thoughts, opinions, learning and scholarly observations on history, ancient and recent. There were fragments from Sophocles, quotes from Cicero, recollections of the reigns of Persian emperors and Russian czars, distillations of the wisdom of ancient Asian and Arab prophets and the early followers of Christ. There were passing reflections on American politics and worshipful references to the man who had stood atop them like a colossus, his friend and hero, "the great and good" George Washington.

Incongruously, items such as a recipe for ginger-infused mead—the only drink his sickly constitution could tolerate—interrupted. So did spiteful observations on unfulfilled financial promises, baffling details of business transactions, constant mentions of illness and pain. He wrote of the divine importance of virtue, the harmony of harmonies—perhaps an admission that his own life had not always been so virtuous or harmonious. And there were lofty hopes expressed for sons, including one named Robert, whom he hardly knew and would never set eyes upon again.

It was the dark record of a once renowned but now miserable man, his tragic life nearing its terrible conclusion.

# 1

# FREESTONE POINT

It was an auspicious spot from which to go out into the world.

The house no longer stands; only a few brittle foundation stones remain, offering the faintest clues to its appearance. The manicured garden is gone, but the daylilies and daffodils still bloom in spring. Farmland that sloped down to the water is now forest. Family fisheries that lined the shore have been washed away, along with much of the sandy beach that curved across the land.

Visitors can still make their way up the craggy hills to a jutting piece of land called Freestone Point, though—a cliff named for the porous locally quarried rock, standing high on the property's eastern edge. There, on a clear day, it is not difficult to imagine the boy galloping his charger up the hill to take in the commanding view. From its crest he could watch the Potomac River wind its way into the horizon. The history of his family followed its path.

The first of the Lees had set foot in the new world in 1639. Richard Lee was barely twenty years old when he arrived in Virginia's capital, Jamestown, from western England. The boy, his father a clothier, brought little with him that would suggest future fortune. He had set sail with Sir Francis Wyatt, Virginia's first colonial governor. Through this connection, the Immigrant, as he was known to later generations of the Lee family, prospered quickly in his new home. Two decades after his arrival, Lee was a wealthy fur trader, a colonel of Virginia's military, and a planter with vast land holdings and scores of slaves. He was also a politician of note, serving as the colony's attorney general and then as a member of the House of Burgesses, its primary legislative body, which administered the colony in tandem with a governor appointed by the Crown.

By the time he reached middle age, Lee could claim title to more land in the colony than any other man—close to fifteen thousand acres. With his eight children and his wife Anne, who had been a ward of Governor Wyatt, Richard Lee moved around the western edge of the colony before anchoring at Paradise, a plantation on the Poropotank River near the community of Gloucester. Several years later, probably in 1655, the family moved to the wilderness of Virginia's Northern Neck, the northernmost of three peninsulas jutting off of the Old Dominion's western shore, sitting between the Potomac River to the north and the Rappahannock to the south. There Lee built another home, Cobb Hall, on Dividing Creek near the town of Kilmarnock. Then in his final years, he took the family back to England. There he secured a home in Stratford Langhorne in Essex, a suburb of London. But Lee ultimately had a change of heart and stipulated in his will that his heirs return to Virginia upon his death in 1664.[1]

Henceforth the pattern was set.

For generations to come, Lee men were to follow the precedent established by the Immigrant, pursuing and padding their fortunes through farming and the relentless acquisition of land, rising to prominence via politics and military service. And they would do these things for the most part in Virginia.

The mantle of family leadership fell on the Immigrant's son, known as Richard II, who at the time was seventeen years old and a student of great promise at Oxford. Returning to America, the younger Richard inherited and took up residence at Paradise and subsequently claimed ownership of yet another Lee land, Machodoc on the Potomac River in Westmoreland County. The tract had been purchased by his father and then lived on by his brother John, who died heirless. Richard II served in the House of Burgesses and on the King's Council, was appointed a naval officer of the Potomac, and raised a family with wife Laetitia Corbin. When not attending to public or economic matters, he amassed one of America's great collection of books and manuscripts, injecting an intellectual strain into the family blood.[2]

Upon Richard II's death in 1714, the Lee family fortune was split between his three sons—the eldest, Richard III, who was heir to the family estate at Machodoc, and his two younger brothers, Thomas and Henry. Richard detached himself from the family affairs by moving to England and prospering as a tobacco merchant. He leased Machodoc to his younger brothers for "annual rent of one peppercorn only, payable on Christmas Day."[3] At Machodoc the younger siblings made their contributions to the Lee empire: raising and selling tobacco, and of course holding public office. Thomas, like his father, grandfather, and great-grandfather before him, sat in the House of Burgesses; and briefly, before his death in 1750, he was Virginia's governor.[4]

Henry, meanwhile, held office in Westmoreland County and eventually built his own home, Lee Hall, on a lot inherited from his father near the community of Hague, also on the Northern Neck. Together the brothers purchased countless swathes of land, including many in northern Virginia. In early 1728, felons broke into, burglarized, and set flame to Machodoc. Thomas built a grand Georgian plantation on another piece of Lee property, naturally on the Potomac—known as the Cliffs for the 150-foot bluffs standing between the land and the river—and moved there in 1738. He would name this house Stratford Hall.[5]

Henry Lee had five children with his wife, Mary Bland. Her lineage was worthy of a Lee: she descended from both the Bennets and Randolphs, two of the colony's other preeminent families. Five of their children survived to adulthood—three boys and two girls. Eldest son John settled in Essex County, on Virginia's middle peninsula.[6] So Lee Hall fell to the second son, the eccentric Richard, known to acquaintances as "the Squire." As was family custom, he too served in the House of Burgesses and as a naval officer—before marrying past the age of sixty.[7] Henry and Mary's youngest son, Henry II, who was born at Lee Hall in 1730, had just begun studies at the college of William and Mary in Williamsburg, where Virginia's capital had been moved in the final year of the seventeenth century, when the elder Henry died in 1747.

The original Henry's will, written in 1746, stipulated that Henry II attend college for two years and thereafter serve as a "writer in the Secretary's Office, till he be twenty-one years of age."[8] It also bequeathed an immense amount of land to the boys. Henry II received "all my plantations and land in Prince William

County which I have at Free Stone Point and at Neapsco and Powells Creek." In addition to these properties, amounting to 2,000 acres, young Henry also took title to an additional 3,111 in neighboring Fairfax County, plus twenty slaves,[9] all of his father's cattle and hogs, two guns, and a watch. As the younger Henry was eighteen at the time, his inheritance was watched over by sister Lettice until he turned twenty-one.

After serving as a writer, or clerk, in the Secretary's Office, Henry II remained in Westmoreland County and practiced law. His mother attempted to steer the boy, whose friends playfully called him "Buck," towards marriage.[10] In a letter to her young son, Mary Lee reasoned that "the felicity that holy state can admit...is certainly one of the happiest this side of the grave." Eventually heeding his mother's advice, Henry Lee II ended up marrying—spectacularly. On December 1, 1753, he wed Lucy Grymes, a girl so fair that history has given her the nickname "the Lowland Beauty." The groom was twenty-four, the bride nineteen. Golden-haired, soft-skinned, and blue-eyed, she was a renowned beauty. Her bloodlines were impeccable, her wealth notable. Lucy's grandmother, Francis Corbin, was the sister of Henry II's grandmother Laetitia Lee, wife of the Scholar. Her father, Charles Grymes of Morattico, who died during the previous decade, was a landowner, a sheriff of Richmond County, and later a member of the House of Burgesses.[11]

Winning her hand was a remarkable coup for Henry, for she was the object of many prominent young Virginians' marital aspirations. Among her unsuccessful suitors is said to be a boy by the name of George Washington. In the final years of the 1740s, the lanky, red-headed Washington, just a teen, was receiving his initial taste of the American frontier, surveying western lands for the powerful Fairfax family. His diaries from this period wistfully mention a "former passion" for a "lowland beauty." Some historians have suggested that the object of Washington's affection was Grymes.[12]

Henry II's family and acquaintances heartily approved of the union. "It was a great surprise to me and a pleasure equal to the best surprise when your brother told me the success of your amour, My Dear Buck (for the last time that I must dare to call you so)," wrote one friend.[13]

The wedding was officiated by William Preston, the minister of James City Parish, at Green Spring, a plantation just west of Williamsburg and the former home of Governor William Berkley.[14]

Henry Lee had come into his majority and taken ownership of the property left him by his father. While the Lees had always clung to Virginia's coast—the family inseparable from the Potomac—Henry II now extended their reach northward along that river, clearing land in Prince William County. Construction of the new estate, Leesylvania (Lee's woods), which was on land inherited from the original Henry Lee in Prince William County, was completed by 1753.[15] The site, a forested peninsula projecting into the Potomac, was known as Freestone Point; the local Doeg Indians called it "Neabsco"—Point of Rocks.

For his new plantation house Henry Lee had cleared a singular spot: a rise affording a stunning panorama of the river. Soon it was surrounded by fields of corn and tobacco tilled and tended to by the slaves inherited from the elder Lee. The cultivation of the latter crop was particularly lucrative, as Lee moved shipments en masse to market in London from the wharves at Dumfries, a town just three miles below Freestone Point and the commercial center of Prince William. On the banks of the river below Lee's house were rows of fisheries where ships were cast out and returned with nets full of shad. And then there were the grand stables, housing Henry Lee's great passion: prized horses named Diamond, Roan, Gimrack, Ranter, Flimack, and the bay mare Famous.[16]

The home burnt in 1797. No contemporary images of Leesylvania exist. Perhaps the estate was similar in appearance to nearby Ripon Lodge, a house built in 1747 by the Blackburn family and overlooking Neabsco Creek, which also bounded Leesylvania. The Lee home was two and a half stories tall, capped by a gabled roof with twin brick chimneys on top of a stone foundation, with double-tiered porticos wrapped around the front and rear of the building. While comfortable, it was modest in comparison to other plantations on the Potomac.

Part of the land the home sat on was bulldozed in the middle of the twentieth century to accommodate a service road, and few tactile clues about Leesylvania remain. A portrait from this era does survive, showing the lord of Leesylvania as an impeccably dressed, handsome man with an aquiline nose, full lips, and a light-colored shock of hair nearing his shoulders. Henry II exudes a confidence befitting the leader of his community, a wealthy squire, and a son of his colony's first family.

Henry Lee, appointed in April 1753 by Virginia Lieutenant Governor Robert Dinwiddie as Prince William's County attorney general to "personally attend and to prosecute all offenders against the laws of Great Britain,"[17] quickly launched the requisite military and political career. Serving as commander of the Prince William militia, he became the first citizen of the county.

In his capacity as militia commander he dealt often with George Washington, who by the 1750s was lodging at and managing Mount Vernon, the estate established by his brother Augustine, just thirteen miles upriver from Leesylvania.

Washington, who had been captivated by military regalia as a boy, was now in his early twenties and at the outset of his career as a soldier. With the outbreak of war between Great Britain (and her colonies) and France (and her North American possessions), Washington, with no previous military experience, was commanding Virginia's volunteer militia corps and venturing into the wilderness of western Pennsylvania. When General Edward Braddock led a combined force of British and colonists to capture Fort Duquesne, he brought along Washington, who had been in the area the year before as an aide and guide. When the expedition was routed by the French and their Indian allies, and Braddock mortally wounded, Washington buried the general, donned his ceremonial sash, regrouped the scattering British force, and executed a successful retreat. The exploit created an early aura of valor around the young Virginian.[18]

Washington pleaded for reinforcements from Prince William County during the conflict. In October of 1755, for example, while posted in Fredericksburg, Washington pressed Lee to supply one hundred men on horseback from Prince William County to "assist in the protection of our Frontiers." He asked that they bring provisions with them to remedy the "scarcity of Bread" among his troops.[19] Though Lee was a friend, Washington was unimpressed by the militia under his command, decrying their "superlative insolence."[20]

After Henry II and Lucy relocated to Freestone Point, they started their own branch of the Lee family tree. In 1755 the couple welcomed their first child, a daughter who died ten months later. Their grief was lessened on the evening of January 29, 1756, when Lucy gave birth to a blue-eyed baby boy, who was named after his father and grandfather. A biographer two centuries later, using a dash of creative flair, wrote that the child had arrived amidst a hailstorm[21]—a likely apocryphal but utterly appropriate detail. The third Henry Lee may not have been born in a tempest, but he lived his life in one.

In the years following the birth of the boy who would be known to posterity as Light-Horse Harry Lee, his father's attention turned to practical matters: finding a tutor for the child— and perhaps even more important—selecting a suitable foal to be trained specifically for his son. Riding was in the blood of aristocratic Virginians. From an early age the boys across the colony were on horseback riding to and fro to perform domestic chores. By adolescence they were expert horsemen.[22]

Henry Lee III, most often referred to as Henry Jr. at the time, was joined by a succession of siblings—most immediately brother Charles, who arrived in 1758, and then another brother, Richard Bland, in 1761. Mollie, Theodorick, Edmund, Lucy, and Anne followed.[23] Life at Leesylvania provided the perfect milieu for the upbringing of the young Virginia aristocrats. The estate's acreage provided a venue for young Lee to roam on horseback and to raise ponies; the wild fields and thick forests were the perfect venue for practicing marksmanship and fencing. Tutors provided the foundation of an education. Then there was the river, whose waters had been a constant in the life of the Lee family since their arrival in America. The Potomac was the boy's primary vista. And the river, along with the King's Road—just miles away and linking the thirteen colonies—brought a regular line of guests to Leesylvania.

Because of Leesylvania's location along the Potomac and Henry II's military and political connections, notable relatives, and acclaimed hospitality, Virginia's most influential citizens were constant presences in the young Harry Lee's formative years.

In 1758, the elder Lee was elected to a term in the House of Burgesses, the first of many. Joining Lee in Williamsburg was a crop of budding statesmen[24]—George Mason, whose home, Gunston Hall, was visible from Leesylvania, representing Fairfax County; the eccentric Richard Henry Lee, one of Henry's cousins from Stratford Hall, a former justice of the peace for Westmoreland County and the political leader of the Lee clan; and Lee's neighbor George Washington, representing Fredericksburg, where he was stationed during the French and Indian War. On his trips back and forth from Mount Vernon to Fredericksburg and Williamsburg, Washington regularly lodged and dined at Leesylvania. Beginning in 1768, Washington's diary entries mention stops there along his travels, usually for dinner and a warm bed, occasionally with wife Martha in tow. At the time of Washington's first known pause at Leesylvania, Henry Jr. was twelve years old.[25]

As the boy entered his teens, the conversations around the Leesylvania hearth were increasingly animated by an ardor slowly spreading throughout Virginia and her twelve sister colonies. In March 1765, two years after the conclusion of the French and Indian War, Parliament, looking for a means to finance Britain's military presence on America's western frontier, passed the Stamp Act, which levied a tax on all printed products used across the colonies: licenses, newspapers, and legal documents, all of which had to be printed on paper produced in London, and affixed with a revenue stamp.[26] Taxes of many varieties had been previously collected across the colonies, but the Stamp Act— though the levies charged were small—signified a troubling development for Americans. Never before had Great Britain imposed a direct tax on its American subjects. Across the colonies, outrage boiled over. Broadsides were composed, protests staged, mobs formed, and for the first time candid conversations held about the relationship between America and England, between freeborn man and monarchy.[27]

In Virginia's House of Burgesses, where Henry Lee II sat, a newly arrived legislator from Louisa County introduced a set of radical resolutions that openly defied Parliament. Patrick Henry fumed, "Caesar had his Brutus; Charles the First his Cromwell; and he did not but doubt some good American would, stand in favor of his country."[28] The fiery rhetorician had an ally, if perhaps one less radical than himself, at Leesylvania. The Lees were previously loyalists and loyal members of the English Church. But Henry II's sympathies lay with his countrymen, and from this point forward countrymen meant fellow Americans. His cousins at Stratford Hall, Thomas Ludwell and Richard Henry Lee, were also galvanized by the Stamp Act, organizing a meeting at Leedstown on the Rappahannock River to stage a formal protest. The result, the Westmoreland Resolves of February 27, 1776, promised that Virginians "with no regard to danger or to death" would "exert every faculty, to prevent the said Stamp Act."[29] The seeds of revolution were planted.

A month later Parliament repealed the Stamp Act but further outraged Great Britain's American subjects with the passage of the Declaratory Act, asserting Parliament's authority to pass laws governing the colonies.[30] Another set of taxes, on items such as glass and tea, arrived the next year in the form of the Townshend Duties.[31]

More American indignation followed, particularly in the colony of Massachusetts; in 1768 British troops arrived in Boston Harbor to attempt to quell a growing uprising. On the night of March 5, 1770, these soldiers shot and killed five colonists outside of Boston's Custom House in the midst of an angry colonial protest. Little time remained now before an explosive separation of Britain and her colonies.[32]

Henry Lee Jr. entered young adulthood amid this turmoil. His gifts were evident at an early age. The boy was handsome; he had inherited blond hair, fair skin, and blue eyes from his mother. He was also intellectually precocious, much like his great-grandfather Richard the Scholar, far outpacing his parents in this respect. "Two negatives make a positive," was his alleged explanation of the incongruity, later in life.[33] He had already accumulated a small library and a taste for Greek and Roman literature. And of course he was a Lee, and could count on the connections that came with membership in one of Virginia's "first families." Harry Lee's potential was limitless. And his rise came in perfect confluence with history—his with a revolution on the horizon.

Atop Freestone Point the future looked as brilliant as the sun beaming on the ripples of the Potomac. Looking back over half a century later, a distant relative remembered—with justification— a young man who, "in his outset of life bid fairer for a glorious termination of it than perhaps any man in America."[34]

# 2

# ALL SONS OF LIBERTY

**V**irginia's state capitol was large enough to hold the House of Burgesses, but not large enough for this crowd. Nor was Bruton Parish Church, the city's primary place of worship, despite additions to accommodate the growing population of Williamsburg.[1] In fact, no house or building was large enough. For this occasion, only the open expanse in front of the capitol could accommodate the crowd. There the townspeople pressed into the cobblestoned courtyard to hear and be held rapt by a sermon delivered in an impenetrable Scottish burr by an "intolerably homely" preacher.[2]

John Witherspoon was not entirely unfamiliar with rebellion. The son of a corpulent and demanding Presbyterian minister and a minister's daughter, he had been born in Gifford, a village outside of Edinburgh, in 1723. By the age of four he was reading and memorizing passages from the Bible. Having earned a master's of arts from the University of Edinburgh in 1743, Witherspoon went on to study divinity and was ordained on April 11, 1745. He then found work preaching in a nearby parish.[3]

In 1745, Charles Edward Stuart, Bonnie Prince Charlie, ignited the Jacobite Rising by sailing from France to Scotland, intent on claiming the British throne he considered his hereditary right. When calls went out from local parishes for Scots to raise arms and monies to repel Stuart and his men, Witherspoon complied, gathering militia and dutifully raising funds. In the aftermath of the Battle of Falkirk Muir, a rout for the Jacobites' opponents, Witherspoon was imprisoned in Doune Castle, a decrepit fortress near Stirling. The uprising fizzled shortly afterwards, so Witherspoon's incarceration was painful but short-lived.[4]

This excitement past, he settled in Beith, a village south of Glasgow, and launched a successful career as a Calvinist minister, writing several treatises, with a particular eye on the evolution of man's moral state. Moral regeneration that transcended man's naturally fallen nature, Witherspoon argued, could only come through reawakening. "What doth it dignify, though you have food to eat in plenty, and a variety of raiment to put on, if you are not born again: If after a few mornings and evenings spent in unthinking mirth, sensuality and riot, you die in your sins, and lie down in sorrow?"[5] He saw his work in a democratic light: preachers, Witherspoon believed, were instruments of the people, who had a say in how they preached.

While his reputation as a brilliant Presbyterian philosopher grew, Witherspoon—awkward, prickly, often sardonic and yet politically savvy—became disillusioned. He bridled at the limited role the Kirk, the Scottish church, was afforded in England to encourage revivalism. He was disappointed in his own place in the church, as well, and in the dwindling global influence of

Great Britain, which he considered "no longer the arbitress of fate" in world affairs. Revival, Witherspoon reasoned, was not affixed to geography; he argued that it "often changes its residence, and leaves one nation, to settle in another."[6]

Across the Atlantic Ocean, the College of New Jersey, situated in the town of Princeton, was in turmoil. Its beloved president Samuel Finley had died in 1766, creating a leadership vacuum in the institution, which had been founded during the Great Awakening two decades before as a training ground for Presbyterian ministers. Presbyterianism was finding increasing favor across the middle colonies, spreading as far south as Virginia. Despite Princeton's success at turning out young ministers, by the time of Finley's death its finances were in disrepair and its curriculum outdated. To remedy these problems, the school's trustees nominated Witherspoon—without his knowledge or consent—as a replacement. A letter of notification was sent across the sea, and prayers went up in hopes that the minister would accept.

Witherspoon, though flattered, initially demurred: his wife, Elizabeth, dreaded relocating to the colonies. The task of swaying the Scots largely fell to two of the college's graduates, Benjamin Rush, a young Pennsylvanian polymath studying medicine at the University of Edinburgh, and Richard Stockton, a dynamic lawyer and landowner who had initially maneuvered to bring the college to Princeton; his grand estate, Morven, was just outside the town.

Through a series of meetings and letters—the latter occasionally dramatic: "O, Sir! Does not your heart expand with unutterable sentiments of love and benevolence when you think that you are to be the means of rescuing so important a Seminar from ruin?" Rush queried Witherspoon in October, 1767—the two men attempted to convince Witherspoon of the great opportunity waiting for him in Princeton and the limits imposed on his ambitions in Scotland.[7]

Witherspoon was eventually persuaded by the chance to build the world's foremost Presbyterian school—in a land just recently fired by revival. On February 4, 1768, he informed Rush that though taking the position and making the move were "against my worldly interest," he would not "draw back."[8] On August 6, 1768, the Witherspoons arrived in Philadelphia and then made their way to Princeton. The campus was aglow for the occasion; his arrival and inauguration, on August 17, generated excitement all across the colony. One observer described Witherspoon's ascension as that of a "prince coming to his throne."[9]

One of his first tasks as president was to shore up the college's finances. To accomplish this, he travelled across the colonies in search of material support. An initial trip in 1768 took him across New England. A second drive the following year brought him to the southern states. Though these trips were ostensibly organized to raise money and seek supplies, they were also a means of convincing colonists to send their sons to Princeton.[10] It was during his southern travels, in October 1769, that Witherspoon addressed the spellbound crowd in Williamsburg. It's very likely that Henry Lee II was in the audience that afternoon.

Thirteen was a tender, though not unheard of, age for boys to commence their formal education in colonial America. In the case of Henry Lee Jr., bright since boyhood, it was old enough. The logical venue for his college studies was the College of William and Mary, where Henry Lee II had studied. Other members of the family, though, such as Harry's cousins from Stratford Hall, Richard Henry Lee and Arthur Lee, had finished their schooling in England. Indeed, their brother William, at the time thriving as a businessman in London, encouraged Henry Lee II to send the prodigy away from the colony. "Your son Harry is a boy of fine parts, and will possess a fine estate, independent of what you may please to give him," he wrote. "Therefore it surely is incumbent on you to spare no pains or cost to give him a complete education. This you know cannot be done in Virginia...."[11] But the College of New Jersey presented another option.

Soon after his arrival in Princeton, Witherspoon had transformed the institution and in the process made himself into a celebrity: a new American "teacher, preacher, politician, lawmaker, and philosopher."[12] Under his leadership the school was no longer merely a seminary to train young men for the ministry but a destination for the colonies' young men to receive a Christian education that could be applied to all manner of professions.

Witherspoon sought not just to tend to his students' souls but to broaden and even challenge their minds and provoke vigorous inquiry. To accomplish these goals he vastly broadened the college's curriculum, introducing secular subjects, filling lectures with history and moral and natural philosophy, finding additional funds to employ a mathematics and philosophy professor while enlarging the school's out-of-date library with hundreds of books from his own collection and a steady stream of new acquisitions. He personally chaired several departments, including English, history, and philosophy, and re-staffed the school, dismissing and replacing instructors deemed ineffective.[13] Witherspoon's active fundraising also shored up the school's finances—to the extent that in 1771 he was able to purchase, at the price of 416 pounds, Philadelphia watchmaker and astronomer David Rittenhouse's orrery, an intricate model of the solar system built of wood and metal to demonstrate the orbit of the planets around the sun and assist in the teaching of natural history.[14]

Ashbel Green, one of Witherspoon's admiring students, later recalled that the president "had more of the quality called presence—a quality powerfully felt, but not to be described than any other individual with whom the writer ever had intercourse, Washington alone excepted."[15] His reputation and reforms brought students from across the colonies to Princeton: by 1770 the student body included just one pupil from the college's home state.[16]

All of this attracted Henry Lee II to the College of New Jersey. But there was also a family connection: the distinguished medical educator William Shippen Jr., husband of Alice Lee, another cousin from Stratford Hall, was a graduate and booster of the school. His father, William Shippen Sr., had helped found it in 1750. The Shippens could not only vouch for the college but also serve as guardians for young Henry from their home in Philadelphia.[17]

This was enough to persuade the elder Henry Lee. By the spring of 1770 the decision was made. Henry Jr. was enrolled at the College of New Jersey. His brother Charles would accompany him north and attend the college's formerly moribund grammar school, which Witherspoon had revived.

The journey to New Jersey, which took Lee away from the luxury and familiar panoramas of Leesylvania for the first time, was across water, over roads, into the wilderness, through Maryland's capital Annapolis and the colonial metropolis of Philadelphia, where he picked up a letter of introduction from Shippen, and then finally to the lush farmland surrounding Princeton, before terminating at the steps of Nassau Hall.[18]

The sandstone structure, built two decades before, was a grand three-story Renaissance-revival building under a cupolaed roof. Inside was the heart of the College of New Jersey: its chapel, library, kitchens and dining areas, and, in the wood-walled and brick-covered basement, student quarters.[19]

If Lee entertained for a moment the thought that he was the lone prince in these confines, he was quickly disabused of that notion. The year before, diminutive James Madison Jr., the brilliant but sickly son of a wealthy Virginia planter and politician, had arrived in Princeton, both to study with Witherspoon and to find a more hospitable climate than that of his Orange County home. His roommate in Nassau Hall was Philip Freneau, a romantic sixteen-year-old from New York City with a budding taste and talent for poetry. Also enrolled was hazel-eyed Aaron Burr Jr., the tenacious orphaned son and namesake of the college's second president; his maternal grandfather, Jonathan Edwards, had been a famed Calvinist minister and the school's third president. There was also Hugh Henry Brackenridge, a nineteen-year-old Scottish immigrant who shared Freneau's literary flair, and Brockholst Livingston, whose father William was one of the colony's grandees.[20]

Lee thrived in his new environs. Rising at five each morning, he headed to the chapel before retiring to study for several hours. After a brief respite for breakfast in Nassau Hall's refectory at 9:00 am, studies and lectures resumed, to be interrupted only by dinner and prayer before continuing until bedtime. There was an almost martial quality to the routine; his clothing, tailored topcoat, satin breeches, white stockings, and silver-buckled shoes had to be immaculate, his quarters spotless, and his superiors respected. Witherspoon punished disobedient pupils by public caning.[21]

In August of 1770, William Shippen visited Princeton and Harry and gave his brother-in-law Richard Henry Lee a glowing report of the boy. "Your cousin Henry Lee is in College and will be one of the first fellows in this country," Shippen gushed. "He is more than strict in his morality; he has a fine genius and is too diligent."[22] The competition with the likes of Madison, whose intense studies had compromised his already frail health, and Burr, who read sixteen hours a day, was stiff. But Lee was every bit their equal, earning the approbation of Witherspoon, who described the boy's progress at Princeton as "in all respects agreeable" in a letter to his father.[23]

As a freshman, in addition to algebra and composition, Harry studied Ovid, Virgil, Horace, and Xenophon. Then, the following year, arithmetic, rhetoric, Roman antiquities, Horace, Homer, and Cicero. As a junior, Locke, surveying, and geometry. And in his final year, logic, "metaphysicks, political economy, and philosophy of the mind."[24] Sessions were held in winter and summer, with vacations in both the autumn and the spring.

Witherspoon's lessons filled with ancient history especially captured Lee's imagination. He pored over the battle plans of generals such as Hannibal and Epaminondas. Aristides of Athens in particular became his hero. Lee also developed a lasting obsession with the English poet Alexander Pope, whom, in another essay, he compared favorably to John Milton.

Excelling in Latin and history, Lee was one of just five students admitted to both of the school's two literary societies, the Cliosophic and the American Whigs, which vied against one another ferociously.[25] By the time of his third year in Princeton, Lee ranked first in his class in Latin and third in Greek.[26]

An anecdote from this time, passed down by generations of Princetonians, demonstrates Lee's pluck. There was, it is said, just one barber in the town, responsible for grooming members of the school's faculty. One afternoon the fresh-faced Lee pounced into the shop. "Shave me, sir," he demanded. The astonished barber sat the boy down and lathered his face. He then stepped out of his establishment and began to walk back and forth in the street. Lee eventually snapped and demanded to know why the barber would not do as he had been told. "Because I am looking for your beard," he replied.[27]

Through the early 1760s, the College of New Jersey remained largely apolitical and unconcerned with the growing tension with Great Britain over colonial rights. In 1762, for example, students staged a musical entitled *The Military Glory of Great Britain*.[28] But as the colonies increasingly chafed under British control, the college and its students followed suit.

In 1765 the school joined New Jersey's businesses and legislature in protesting the Stamp Act. From 1766 forward commencements were full of fiery rhetoric extolling the virtues of American independence; as a sign of protest, graduates wore cloth woven in the colonies. The school's trustees sent letters to King George III expressing their annoyance at the Stamp Act. Honorary degrees, previously given to clergymen, were awarded to radicals such as John Hancock and John Dickinson.

The patriotism and radical fervor had only increased by the time of Lee's arrival in Princeton. In 1770 correspondence between merchants in New York and Philadelphia confirming their resolve to defy the non-importation agreement—a boycott of British goods—was captured and burned in public by Princeton students garbed in black gowns, in order to caution the "betrayers of their country."[29] The level of radicalism grew to the point of intolerance, even. Sons of those who remained loyal to Great Britain were subjected to harassment and chased from campus. "I hope we shall have two or three of the possessed swine turned off when the Doctor comes home," one of Lee's classmates wrote to another while Witherspoon was away on a trip in 1771.[30]

Witherspoon's students were simply following their shepherd. In contrast to many of New Jersey's prominent citizens (William Livingston and Richard Stockton, for example) he had not hesitated to join the cause for independence. Much of what had transpired on campus—the granting of honorary degrees to radical patriots, the activism amongst students—had occurred with at least the tacit approval of Witherspoon. In 1770 his son James even delivered a speech during the school's commencement urging classmates to rebel against Britain. The next year's ceremony featured Hugh Henry Brackenridge delivering "A Poem, on the Rising Glory of America." The ode to America's brilliant destiny, its fate to rank among the great civilizations with Greece and Rome, had been written by Princeton student Philip Freneau, who was ill and unable to attend. Its subject, suggested by Witherspoon, was "greeted with great applause."[31] Brackenridge revived the poem for the following year's commencement, at which an honorary degree was conferred upon astronomer Rittenhouse, who was so caught up in the spirit of independence that his scientific lectures were increasingly including references to self-government and the rights of men. The same graduation also featured a speech on "Passive Obedience and Non-Resistance" and "The Advantages of Political Liberty."[32]

But not everyone was pleased with the politicization of the student body. The following year, after complaints from irritated onlookers, the school's trustees ordered that all speeches to be read at commencement ceremonies were to be submitted four weeks in advance of the actual event, in order to ensure no subject too controversial was broached.[33] Thus at the 1773 graduation of Lee and twenty-eight classmates, the ceremony was a far less political affair, featuring lectures on "Ambition" and "True Honor." A scholarly talk on the "Future Glory of America," did, however, make it onto the program.[34] And in the coming years, Witherspoon would be drawn even deeper into America's battle for independence.

The decision to send Lee to the College of New Jersey was fortuitous. In Princeton he developed a love of classical literature and history and cultivated his gift for rhetoric. Life in Nassau Hall prepared him for the regimentation of military life, and his time with Witherspoon and peers from across the colonies, both North and South, drew him closer to the cause of American Independence and unity. It helped him to see beyond regionalism—to admire men from parts of America beyond his home colony of Virginia, to see them as fellow countrymen with common interests and a common future, and to form friendships that would endure for decades.

When John Adams, an emerging spokesperson for independence in Massachusetts, observed that the young men on Witherspoon's campus were "all Sons of Liberty" he was making no exaggeration.[35] Lee's class was one of the school's most distinguished, producing two senators, three congressmen, a delegate to the Continental Congress, two surgeons in the Revolutionary Army, and five college presidents.[36]

The ceremony that saw these boys turn into men on the last day of September 1773 took place in front of a vast audience that included the governor of New Jersey as well as Lee's father. As was the custom during these events, which were the grand social occasions of the season, there was feasting, drinking, and dancing—as a band imported from Philadelphia played on. "Never was there such a commencement at Princeton and most likely never will be again," remarked an attendee.[37]

On that day Lee, who delivered an oration on the value of the liberal arts, cut a flamboyant figure. "Every mouse hole in the church crammed full—the stage covered with gentlemen and ladies amongst whom was the governor and his lady," a spectator reported, "and that he might not appear singular Lee was stiff with lace, gold lace."[38]

# 3

# THIS STRUGGLE FOR THE RIGHTS OF MANKIND

Few venues offered more gracious hospitality—especially at the dinner table. Set high on a cliff, commanding a scenic view of the Potomac River, surrounded by deer-filled woods, Mount Vernon, the plantation home of George Washington, was renowned throughout the colonies, its elegance and munificence toward visitors known widely.

On April 16, 1775, seated at the bountiful table in the mansion's octagonal dining room under a newly completed ornate plaster ceiling, Henry Lee Jr. was one such guest. Joining him there was George Mason, who had traveled from Gunston Hall, his Potomac plantation, five miles to the south. Also there was General Charles Lee. The British-born Lee, who shared a surname but not blood with the famous Virginia family, was a formidable, though decidedly eccentric, soldier of fortune. A dog lover, he famously maintained a loftier opinion of his canine friends than their human counterparts.[1] His sympathies had most recently taken a turn towards the colonists in their confrontation

with Great Britain: the previous year he had resigned his commission in the British Army and relocated to America. Two other
guests—William Thompson, a merchant from nearby Colchester,
and Angus McDonald, a rent collector occasionally in Washington's employ—were also present.[2]

Across the table—groaning perhaps with roasted pig, leg of
lamb, peas or Washington's beloved rockfish or perch, in the
parlor, or on the piazza, where the river afforded a cool breeze—
talk inevitably turned to the current crisis and the coming war
with Great Britain.[3]

After Mason, Thompson and McDonald took leave, both
Lees remained, continuing their conversation with Washington.
This was heady company. Washington and Charles Lee were
among the most accomplished military men in the colonies.
Henry Lee had known and admired Washington since youth. But
this evening he found the elder Lee, a fluent and opinionated
talker, especially impressive. Lee had fought in the French and
Indian War like Washington and also in the service of distant
kingdoms in Portugal and Poland. Now he was championing
American liberty—if more out of personal ambition rather than
love for the colonial cause.

Soon both Washington and Charles Lee were, separately, to
depart for Philadelphia to attend the second Continental Congress. The latter was attending as a delegate; the former as a
spectator with ambitions set on a military commission. When
Henry Lee went to his quarters for the night, after hours spent
with the two men, decades his senior, both of whom had heard
the cannonball blast and musket fire, he surely dreamt of doing
the same.

Two years had passed since Harry Lee's graduation from the
College of New Jersey. He planned to cross the Atlantic and study

law at London's Middle Temple, one of Britain's four associations of barristers. After completing his education under the tutelage of Bishop Beilby Porteus, a chaplain to King George III and a relative of Harry's mother, he would remain in England to stand before the bar.[4] No doubt a distinguished legal career awaited him. Fate, however, intervened.

Three months after the newly graduated Lee departed from New Jersey, on the night of December 16, 1773, angry patriots had hurled hundreds of chests of tea into Boston Harbor. The gesture was in reaction to the Tea Act, passed by Parliament in May of that year in an attempt to help the British East India Trading Company liquidate its excess inventory of tea at the expense of American merchants and customers. This act of rebellion set in motion a series of measures known as the Intolerable Acts, meant to punish the Massachusetts rebels. Initiated in early 1774, these stripped the Massachusetts colony of many of its rights and forced Americans to house British soldiers.[5] They also enraged Massachusetts' twelve sister colonies. Colonists far from New England, including those in Virginia, seethed.

The previous year Virginia's firebrands—George Mason; Lee's second cousin Richard Henry Lee; a tall, auburn haired lawyer from Albemarle County named Thomas Jefferson; and Harry's father Henry Lee II—had formed a committee of correspondence within the House of Burgesses. The association and others like it around the colonies took up the responsibility of organizing the response to Britain's aggressive actions.[6]

On May 26, 1774, after legislators called for a day of fasting in sympathy with the citizens of Massachusetts, the colony's governor, Lord Dunmore, dissolved the House of Burgesses.[7] Undaunted, that August Virginia's legislators adjourned to a Williamsburg watering hole known as the Raleigh Tavern.

There, during what was to be known as the first Virginia Convention, they endorsed a Continental Congress—a gathering was to take place the following September in Philadelphia and be attended by representatives from each colony—and then selected the seven men who would attend from Virginia.[8]

In Philadelphia, Virginia's delegation, despite agreeing on a ban of British goods, joined with the other eleven colonies in attendance (Georgia did not send delegates) in deferring a separation from Great Britain. They still hoped for reconciliation.

A second Virginia Convention, this one away from Williamsburg at St. John's Church in the town of Richmond, took place on March 20, 1775. Among the attendees were, again, Henry Lee II, Richard Henry Lee, Thomas Jefferson, and a host of other Virginia politicians including George Washington. The atmosphere was electric. On the afternoon of March 23, Patrick Henry rose from his pew and delivered a searing speech declaring, "Give me liberty or give me death!" in the face of English usurpations of colonial rights.[9] The meeting closed with a resolution to arm Virginians for the coming fight for American autonomy. Washington was soon at work training raw militia for the American cause.

"Our Militia of Independents are ordered by the Convention to be armed and well-disciplined, and a great spirit of liberty actuates every Individual," Henry Lee II wrote shortly after returning from Richmond.[10] By this time even Leesylvania itself was on a war footing: the elder Lee halted shipments of hogsheads full of tobacco to Britain. The crop was converted to gun powder: combining the nitro found in rotten tobacco with urine, the planter was busy making "very strong well-grained Powder in the Country therefrom wch ketches quick and shoots with great force so that we shall be able in future to supply ourselves."[11]

With war in the wings, the younger Lee's planned journey to England was impossible. Instead he passed the days at grand galas and elegant gatherings. In the spring of 1774 he attended a three-day soiree at Lee Hall, the home of his uncle, Richard. There the sounds of French horn and violin lilted as the young ladies, their dresses of lace and brocade rustling, swanned across the floor. Refreshments—lemon punch and porter—were imbibed, and toasts were raised to the sons of America. And when the right level of inebriation was reached, the young men pressed their heads together and bellowed out songs dedicated to the cause of colonial liberty. [12]

At these and other gatherings Lee cut an unforgettable figure among Virginia's gentry. A sparkling conversationalist, well versed in the classics, he was also impeccably dressed, with a dashing bearing and princely air. During similar soirees at Stratford Hall, he would have caught the eye of his lovely cousin Matilda. And on visits to Nomini Hall, the poplar-lined plantation of tobacco baron Robert Carter III, the master of the house was impressed. The journals of Philip Fithian, a classmate of Lee's at Princeton and a tutor employed at Nomini Hall, record that Carter, a member of the colony's largest land-owning family, "seemed much pleased with Harry, & with his manner."[13]

With his studies in London shelved, what calling this promising young man would follow was uncertain. Revolution offered a vocation.

Three days after Lee dined at Mount Vernon, British soldiers in pursuit of rebel leaders killed seven American militiamen in Lexington, Massachusetts, and then engaged more American soldiers, known as minute men, in nearby Concord. This time the Americans repulsed the British. Over 125 Redcoats—the name given British soldiers because of the color of their uniforms—were mowed down, shocking news when it reached Parliament. Not only was war at hand, but the number of colonists willing to take up arms against Britain was disturbing. This was no mere mob of angry provincials. Across the colonies local paramilitaries sized arsenals and harassed British officials. "The die is now cast, and a blow [has] been struck near Boston," Henry Lee II observed, only confirming the inevitable.[14]

In June, during meetings of the second Continental Congress, delegates voted to centralize the American war effort, building an army out of of the militia in the eastern colonies, particularly Massachusetts. On the fourteenth of the month they named Washington, who cleverly appeared at the gathering in his old uniform, this new Continental Army's general and commander in chief. By the next month he had arrived in Massachusetts to take charge of a poorly supplied and armed force during a siege on the city of Boston.[15]

Like his kin, Harry Lee was politically predisposed to join the patriot cause. The Lees of Virginia had come to the New World as agents of the Crown; they were loyal British citizens. But the events of the past years had frayed those ties to the point where now the Lees, like so many colonists, saw themselves as Americans rather than Englishmen. Their countrymen were not back across the Atlantic, but in New York, Massachusetts, and North Carolina.

Lee was also a staunch believer in the philosophical justification for American independence—that man was the possessor of God-given rights that no crown or state could take away. These were notions he had been exposed to studying under John Witherspoon.

But there was yet another element to his desire to take up arms. Fascinated by ancient history, he studied the exploits of fabled Greek and Roman generals and soldiers obsessively. Following the history of civilizations and warfare, Lee associated battle with romance. Having imbibed the tales of great conflicts and the brave deeds of soldiers from centuries past, he saw a chance for present-day fame and everlasting glory. Now, with American liberty in the balance, was Lee's chance to satisfy his growing ego and leave his name among the ranks of history's great warriors.

Lee joined Prince William County's militia in April 1775—a humble beginning for the neophyte warrior. With the bulk of the fight taking place farther north, quiet patrol of the Potomac and nearby Quantico Rivers was not exactly the adventure he hoped for.[16]

Lee knew the commander in chief of the rebel army well. But he looked elsewhere to improve his military status. In the months that had passed since Lee's visit to Mount Vernon, his dining partner, Charles Lee, had been made a major general, and—much to his chagrin, given his ambitions—essentially the new army's second in command. "It afforded one the greatest pleasure to see by the public prints that the continental congress had appointed General Lee to act in so high a character in this struggle for the rights of mankind," Henry wrote to the Englishman on July 5, 1775. "The Contention may not be settled for many campaigns," he determinedly continued, "and the familiarity with which you treated me in Virginia has induced me to ask a permit to enlist under your banner in order to acquaint myself with the art of war."[17] But Lee's request to begin a "commencement in the study of Mars" was never answered. The letter was captured by British agents.[18]

Meanwhile, the would-be soldier contented himself by preparing for his moment. "No one proclaims his admiration for the Massachusetts Bay Sons of Liberty more loudly than does Harry…he has so perfected his skill with a sword and pistol that I believe he would run through or shoot to death anyone who mocked him or the cause in which all of us believe," observed George Lee, yet another relative. Indeed, in observing his cousin's fiery patriotism, George Lee glimpsed an element of danger. "He is learned but there is in him a wild and savage humor that neither the gracious living at Leesylvania nor his years at the College of New Jersey have tamed."[19]

Over the next months, the war spread. A series of skirmishes erupted in New England, even north into Canada, and into the rural woods of the American South. The Virginia Convention met once again, this time in Williamsburg, in July 1776, with Lee's father again in attendance, and dissolved King George III's government in the colony.

It then charged its delegates to the upcoming meeting of the Continental Congress with creating language, which Richard Henry Lee subsequently penned, resolving that the American colonies were now wholly independent states. The Convention then concluded by adopting the "Virginia Declaration of Rights." This document, composed by George Mason, declared that "all men are by nature equally free and independent and have certain inherent rights, of which, when they enter into a state of society, they cannot, by any compact, deprive or divest their posterity; namely the enjoyment of life and liberty…."

And, in order to secure these newly asserted freedoms, on May 20 the convention resolved that "Four troops of horse be raised for the better security and defense of this Colony; that the Officers and Troopers, at their own expense, provide their Horses, Arms, and Accoutrements…."[20]

A door was kicked opened.

Theodorick Bland was a physician-planter turned politician from Virginia's Prince George County. He was also, crucially, one of the colony's foremost breeders of horses. His thorough-breds, most notably the black stallion Brunswick, were famous across Virginia and Maryland, where Bland raced them against horses bred by the region's other aristocrats.[21] He was also a Lee relative. A champion of American independence, he had penned sharp-tongued screeds against Lord Dunmore and sounded out Virginia's leaders about a military commission. Though he was a military novice, on June 13, 1776, the Virginia Convention appointed Bland captain of the colony's cavalry, which was soon expanded to six companies.[22]

These regiments were to be stripped down for the sake of mobility and speed, carrying only essential armaments; they were troops of light horse, particularly useful for reconnaissance and skirmishing. Virginia's new units were to have thirty-five mounted soldiers and be supervised by six non-commissioned officers, who would be elected by Virginia's legislature.[23]

By early June Henry Lee, hoping for a commission, made his way south from Prince William County to Williamsburg where the Fifth Virginia Convention was voting on the state's new cavalry leaders. The position of commander was seemingly guaranteed, given his last name, connections, resources, and reputation as a rider. Voting took place on June 13. Bland was nominated to lead the 1st Troop. Several rounds of balloting later, Lee was made captain of the state's 5th Troop of cavalry. On June 18, his commission was signed by Virginia's governor, Patrick Henry. Lee's wish was granted.[24]

There was little time for celebration; Lee had to train his very raw troops. Lee's soldiers, who had signed on for six months' duty with a compensation of three pounds, were barely even

men. The great majority were under twenty; the youngest, Hol-
man Rice, was just sixteen.[25] They had no military experience.
No arms. No supplies. No uniforms. Not even enough horses. It
was on Lee's shoulders to find these things, and do so in haste.

The way he went about that task demonstrated his talent
for military organization, but it also betrayed an unapologetic
willingness to employ his connections and an almost ruthless
aggression.

With the aid of William Lindsay, his lieutenant, Lee quickly
found money for his men: on July 2, the Convention allocated
750 pounds to the 5th Troop for the purchase of horses. They
were the first troop to receive such funds; the name Lee carried
weight indeed. But this wasn't enough to fully equip the 5th
Troop, who were still in need of arms, uniforms and even shelter—the men slept and trained in a Williamsburg park. So Lee
paid from his own pocket and found bonds to scour up needed
supplies. When he caught wind of a store of uniforms housed in
a depot in Fredericksburg, Lee successfully lobbied Virginia's
legislators for access to the clothes. The rest of Virginia's cavalry
would not receive their uniforms for another two months.[26]

While Lee hunted for supplies and pressed legislators for
assistance, away in Philadelphia that summer, the colonies staked
all for freedom and formally declared their independence from
England. King George III, in a message to Parliament, sneered at
the "daring and desperate" spirit of America's leaders and referred
to "My loyal Colonies."[27] With a war for American autonomy
now underway, and attacks on Virginia likely, Lee trained and
drove his men mercilessly.

Many of those who had volunteered saw their service as one
of a limited nature, but Lee believed otherwise. It was generally
understood amongst Virginians that the role of Bland's men was

to protect the colony, not to fight elsewhere. And early in the war, American political and military leaders, including Washington himself, saw little use for cavalry—because of the expense of equipping horse soldiers and the impracticality of maneuvering them across the rocky and heavily forested terrain of the American Northeast. They would certainly not provide much value as the Continental army continued its siege of Boston. But in March 1776, the British abandoned that city and dispatched their fleet.[28]

Washington assumed the enemy would head to New York and dashed off with his army to get there first. Though the British initially reconnoitered in Halifax, Canada, they made their way to New York in July. Now, tasked with guarding the city and its coastline, Washington reconsidered the role of cavalry. The general now saw value in the ability of dragoons—horse soldiers who could also dismount to fight as infantry—"in reconnoitering the Enemy and gaining intelligence." They also would "have it in their power to render many other Important benefits."[29]

Cavalry, including three ragged troops from Connecticut, were put to work patrolling Long Island for Washington's army in July 1776, the same month the colonies formally declared their independence. But this addition ultimately vexed the general when the horsemen refused to perform the tasks of infantrymen, such as garrison duty.[30]

The Continental Army was suffering a string of mishaps. On August 27, the British army, led by General William Howe, executed a flanking maneuver during the Battle of Long Island, killing thousands of Americans and sending those who still stood retreating to their fortifications on Brooklyn Heights. By September the British had control of New York and its ports. A month later Washington was again defeated by Howe at White Plains. There British cavalry pierced and dispersed Washington's ragged infantry. It was now clear that the American army was in dire need of mounted soldiers.[31]

To remedy this need, Washington requested that Congress supplement his army with cavalry, reasoning that "there is no carrying on the war without them."[32] The fledgling nation's legislators obliged, calling for the raising of three thousand men and horses. In early December, Richard Peters, the Philadelphia-born politician named by the Continental Congress as Secretary of the Board of War, the congressional committee overseeing the war effort, wrote to Virginia governor Patrick Henry asking that Virginia's cavalry troops come to Washington's aid.[33]

On December 4, Virginia's General Assembly obliged and commanded three of the colony's cavalry troops to join with the main army. But their departure was delayed because of a continuing lack of supplies. There was also the issue of timing. The cavalrymen had enlisted during the summer for six-month stints, which were due to end in January of 1777. Theodorick Bland was able to convince the men to stay on. In late December of 1776 Lee and the rest of the Virginians began their trek across Virginia and Maryland into Pennsylvania and to the capital Philadelphia, where they arrived on January 20. From there, in late January 1777, four of the companies boarded the Coryell Ferry over the icy Delaware.[34]

The arrival of the new year found the general and his army nestled among the Watchung Mountains, a low-set blue-capped range in northern New Jersey. To their south waited the Redcoats. In November a British force commanded by Howe had chased the rebels away from New York and seized the garrison at Fort Washington, on Manhattan's northern end. The humiliating defeat had sent the Continental Army scurrying south, across New Jersey and then over the Delaware River to Pennsylvania.

But then as the cold winter swept across the east, the earth shifted.

On Christmas night Washington quietly sailed his soldiers back across the ice-jammed Delaware in a fleet of flat-bottomed Durham boats. Once ashore in New Jersey, the men marched to the town of Trenton where fourteen hundred slumbering Hessians, German mercenaries doing Britain's bidding, were easily overrun. Washington sailed back to Pennsylvania with nearly a thousand prisoners.[35]

The surprise victory lifted the sagging spirits of America's soldiers and its citizens alike. Three days later Washington recrossed the river, this time accompanied by two thousand men. Marching north, they encountered General Lord Cornwallis, who, alarmed by the action in Trenton, had come south at the head of superior British force. The armies skirmished before the Redcoats retreated towards Princeton.

Then on New Year's night, in a brilliant bit of trickery, Washington slipped his troops out of their camp under darkness, leaving behind five men to stock burning campfires and to clatter picks and axes, fooling the British into believing their opponents were entrenching for the evening. A drop in temperatures froze the muddy New Jersey soil, making the clandestine move possible if painful for the poorly clothed soldiers—many of whom lacked even shoes.

When the sun rose the next morning, what Cornwallis saw in his spyglass was an empty camp. The rest of the American men had rejoined the main army on its march around and behind the British. In the tenacious battle that followed, the Americans chased their foes towards Princeton, killing 450 of the enemy and losing just thirty-seven of their own.[36]

After a year of military missteps and demoralizing losses, the British in New Jersey were now contained to posts in New Brunswick and Amboy. The rebel army and its leaders, both on the battlefield and in Philadelphia, could point to tangible progress in the War for Independence. But even as these victories were celebrated across the states, they looked likely to be fleeting.

The Continentals were still badly outmanned, outgunned, and out-supplied; chances of ultimate victory against the world's mightiest army remained slim. To a fighting force badly in need of reinforcements, the arrival of the Virginia cavalry, no matter their inexperience, was a godsend.

Rather than rendezvous with the main army, now headquartered in Morristown, the Virginia horse were instantly off to Bound Brook, a northern village situated on the Raritan River, running across the heart of New Jersey.[37] This spot was of considerable strategic importance: to its south was New Brunswick.

A stretch of unoccupied farmland separated the two forces. With winter raging and the British still too numerous for the Americans to engage, Washington formulated a new strategy: in the New Jersey winter, when supplies and nourishment dwindled for the British and their German freelancers, he would deploy men to harass and disrupt foraging runs. This task fell to the Virginians.

Clothed in a blue coat with red piping atop black breeches and boots, on his head a helmet capped by a crest of white horse hair, at his side a double brass-barreled pistol with his initials engraved on the thumb piece, Lee looked the part of a gallant cavalryman, even if his physique was of "light and weakly form."[38] Now began his baptism by fire: weeks of riding reconnaissance south toward New Brunswick, searching for supplies, setting traps for and igniting skirmishes with Hessian soldiers in the bitter cold—all of which quickly took its toll. By March the Virginians were left ragged, in tattered uniforms, and badly in need of supplies.[39]

The majority of the troop was summoned to Morristown, where the foraging was less grueling and provisions more plentiful. In an early instance of his senior officers' approbation of his service, Lee remained in Bound Brook at the behest of the commanding general in the region, Benjamin Lincoln, to oversee the cavalry's missions.[40]

On the morning of April 13, 1777, the British, accompanied by the Hessians and led by Cornwallis, marched north in an attempt to capture the American garrison and officers at Bound Brook. Lee, with Lincoln, posted up at, but then fled from, the home of Philip Van Horne, a gracious local citizen with unclear loyalties. The British looted the outpost and made off with prisoners and cannons; Cornwallis enjoyed breakfast at Van Horne's home before leaving Bound Brook. Lincoln and the Americans had returned to the damaged camp by evening, and Van Horne served them dinner.[41]

Several days later, on April 17, Bland ordered Lee to ride with his men to the town of Chatham, near Washington's headquarters. There was just one problem: Lee was troubled by the threadbare appearance of his men. In this, they were hardly singular. Most of America's army would not even be issued uniforms until the following year. Yet, Lee, upon hearing he was to rejoin the rest of the dragoons, and despite far greater challenges facing the rebels, fretted about appearances.

"How happy would I be, if it was possible for my men to be furnished with caps and boots, prior to my appearance at head quarters," Lee, his ambition and pride on full display, wrote to Bland on April 18. "You know, dear colonel," he continued, "that, justly, an officer's reputation depends not only on discipline, but appearance of the men. Could the articles mentioned be allowed my troop, their entrance into Morris would secure me from the imputation of carelessness, as their captain, and I have vanity to hope would assist in procuring some little credit to their colonel and regiment."[42] Never mind the enemy army, damn starvation and scarcity, Lee was dreaming of a grand and dashing entrance. His request was rejected.

The removal of Lee and his men greatly irritated Lincoln, who wrote to Bland, voicing his displeasure.[43] If this were not enough, Bland was also cross at Lee for failing to submit his regiment's payroll for the month of April. "I cannot but blush," Lee confessed to Bland on April 25, "I have no excuse to plead, but the incessant duty with which I have been occupied, by the order of General Lincoln." Lee enclosed the payroll in his parcel to Bland and explained that Lincoln had asked that he "tarry a day or two" at Bound Brook. "I thanked the general for his politeness," Lee explained, "though I did not require his intercession with you on that head...."[44] Lee remained with Lincoln for several more days, in order to conduct a strike against a Hessian picket, but was on the move by late April.

Unmentioned in the correspondence was that just a week before Lee had purchased saddles, carbines, and pistols for his men with his own money and had then, in another fit of hubris, promptly asked Congress to be reimbursed the amount of $1,116. The Congressional Committee of the Treasury, astonishingly, obliged—and charged the state of Virginia the sum.[45]

Lee's reunion with the rest of the First Continental Dragoons coincided with warming temperatures and a relative lull in the war. Now attached to the larger army, the Virginians were able to re-arm and resupply while continuing to patrol enemy lines. The proximity to Washington, whom he had known since childhood, was important to Lee.

And so too was entry into the small society surrounding the general. From the outset of the war, Washington had recruited a retinue of young men who were charged with carrying out the administrative aspects of the war. They handled the general's military correspondence, couriering his communications. Childless himself, Washington filled these positions with ambitious and talented young men, for whom he often served as a mentor and with whom he established lasting friendships.

Lee was now introduced into the social circle of these aides-de-camp—men such as Alexander Hamilton, the Nevis-born illegitimate and orphaned son of a wayward Scots father and adulterous mother.[46] With a drive that matched Lee's, the slender but authoritative Hamilton had clerked his way to the continent, where he supplemented his self-education with studies at King's College in New York.[47] There, as Lee had done at the College of New Jersey, Hamilton imbibed the philosophical reasoning fueling America's coming revolution, even turning into a fluent propagandist himself before joining a New York militia, the Hearts of Oak. Under Hamilton's leadership the group stole British artillery on Manhattan before joining the Continental Army upon Washington's appearance in New York.[48] Hamilton was with Washington for the crossing of the Delaware; his artillery bombarded the enemy's refuge (and Lee's old home), Nassau Hall, during the Battle of Princeton.[49]

By March of 1777, Lee was becoming familiar with Washington's inner circle of ambitious staff, men such as Hamilton; Tench Tilghman, the son of a wealthy family of Maryland loyalists who had broken with his own kin to join Washington's staff;

John Laurens, the reckless South Carolina–born son of the wealthy planter Henry Laurens, who would serve as a president of the Continental Congress; and Gilbert du Motier, the Marquis de Lafayette, a young French aristocrat drawn to the American cause by idealism and ambition.[50] During the relative calm that sprung in Morristown, Lee formed bonds with these men as he had done during college with the likes of James Madison and Aaron Burr. These relationships would last far beyond the war.

The lull in action would not be long. Washington, encamped at Morristown and commanding an army only half the size of his opponents', was in no position to engage the enemy. Despite a plan to unite the British forces with Generals John Burgoyne in Canada and Barry St. Leger in northern New York and sever New England from the rest of the states, Howe set his sights on Philadelphia. Sacking the American capital would demoralize the rebels and rally loyalists, he hoped.

On June 23, Howe departed from New York and set sail for the Delaware Bay with over fifteen thousand men. It was not until August 22 that the British made landfall: because of faulty intelligence regarding a blockade on the Delaware, Howe pushed on to the Chesapeake Bay, making his way to Philadelphia via Turkey Point, Maryland.[51]

Perplexed about Howe's intentions, Washington moved to Bucks County, in central Pennsylvania, leaving artillery behind in New Jersey. He dispatched the First Continental Dragoons towards Philadelphia but then halted them. When Howe's intentions became clear, Washington withdrew his forces from New Jersey and marched through the American capital and on towards the town of Wilmington in an effort to block the British.[52]

Lee and the rest of the Virginia cavalry followed two days later while the British, seasick from their journey, were recouping their bearings nearly twenty miles away. Soon enough Lee was scouting the areas between the two armies in preparation for a battle—with the fate of Philadelphia lying in the balance.[53]

Over a year before, Lee had been a civilian guest at Washington's table. Now he was a member of his army and a soldier in the struggle for the rights of mankind.

# 4

# A REBEL CAPTAIN BY THE NAME OF LEE

On the morning of August 30, 1777, George Washington dictated a letter to John Hancock, the president of the Continental Congress. As he finished his dispatch, an update on the British position, commotion erupted at headquarters. At approximately 10:00 a.m. a mounted American came galloping into camp, bringing twenty-four Redcoats along with him. Washington quickly appended a note to his letter to Hancock: "This minute twenty-four British prisoners arrived taken by Captain Lee of the Light-Horse."[1] Lee rode off again that afternoon. The next day he returned with another nineteen prisoners of war.

Only a few months before, Henry Lee had never been on a battlefield. Now, at the tumultuous end of 1777 in the stark early months of the following year, he emerged as a hero to an army and a nation much in need of one. Lee's success came with a price, though. While his admiring superiors helped his career along, his jealous peer officers, offended by his ambition and arrogance, plotted to snuff it out. In fact, as the dragoons were riding to Washington's aid in Wilmington on August 24, Lee, for reasons now lost to history, was charged with disobedience of orders. The accusations amounted to little. A court martial found the captain not guilty and labeled the charges, brought by his peers, as "groundless and vexatious." Washington concurred with the acquittal.[2]

There was little time for Lee to stew over the ordeal. Howe and his men, now past the seasickness that both they and their mounts had acquired during the journey from New York, were at last on the march to Philadelphia.

Washington relied on the light horse to shadow and harass the enemy and gather intelligence on their advance. On August 30, Washington wrote to Bland stressing the importance of "a diligent and constant watch being kept on the motions of the enemy." If the British began their march towards Philadelphia, the dragoons were to apprise Washington at once. He instructed their commander to keep "small guards and constant patrols, both of horse and foot, on the flanks and in front of the enemy, as near to them as prudence will permit, so that they cannot possibly move any way, without your having information of it."[3]

The first fight came at Cooch's Bridge, twelve miles southwest of Wilmington. There, on September 3, Howe's men overpowered a force of American infantry and militia.[4] After a short rest, the British force, supplemented by Hessians nearly thirteen hundred strong, continued their northward trek. Washington rushed to cut them off, setting the bulk of his force across the swiftly flowing but shallow Brandy Wine River at Chadds Ford, where the surrounding heights, combined with the breadth of the river, provided a favorable spot for the Americans to stop the British advance. Washington, worried that the enemy might cross the river farther north, deployed his men at passable fords along the river. The information regarding spots where they could possibly cross was provided by Bland. But in his scouting, the major missed one ford, known as Jeffries, seven miles north of the American force. And there, on the morning of September 11, a contingent of Redcoats, led by Charles Cornwallis, swung around the American right flank and across the river.[5]

Upon hearing this, Washington sent divisions north in an attempt to block the British near Birmingham Friends Meeting House, a stone Quaker church just east of Jeffries Ford. From there, in the late summer heat, under clear skies, after six British bayonet charges, the rebels fled. In the following days the armies continued to skirmish. After retreating across the Schuylkill River towards Philadelphia and then crossing back again, Washington was set to reengage Howe near the White Horse Tavern, twenty-five miles west of the American capital, on September 16. But after the fighting began, a torrential downpour intervened, soaking the Americans' musket cartridges, effectively disarming Washington's men and ending the battle.[6]

With a British attack on the American capital now unavoidable, Congress prepared to depart Philadelphia as Howe crossed the Schuylkill, his sights set on the city. Along his path, at Daverser's Ferry along the river, sat several mills stored with flour. On September 18, before the British could seize them, Washington commanded Lee and Alexander Hamilton to destroy the mills. Accompanied by six mounted soldiers, they rode down a long hill then sloped to a wooden bridge spanning the canal which powered the mill's water wheel. Once across, Hamilton commandeered two large flat-bottomed boats; should the British appear, these would provide an escape across the river.[7]

As the Americans set to work, warning shots rang out, fired by two sentries they had placed on the hill. The enemy appeared over the horizon, charging after the guards and towards the rest of the party. Hamilton and four others leapt into one of the boats; during the confusion caused by the surprise appearance of the British, the other craft drifted off. Now Lee made a spur-of-the-moment decision. He and the other two dragoons, rather than joining Hamilton on the river, would charge back across the bridge toward the British and escape via horse. Thus they hoped to draw the enemy's fire away from Hamilton and his cohorts, who at this point had splashed into the river and were fighting its rapid currents. Lee, his fellow dragoons, and the two patrols sprinted past the Redcoats, who opened up a stream of fire from their carbines. Lee and his men escaped unharmed.[8]

But in their absence, the guns were now turned on Hamilton. One of his companions was killed, another wounded. The lieutenant-colonel, leaping into the Schuylkill, was able to swim to safety and escape back to headquarters. Lee was ignorant of his friend's fate. After the danger had passed, he sent a note to Washington informing the general of the failed mission and the probability that his valued aide-de-camp had been lost. As Washington read the letter, an exasperated Hamilton appeared to relay unfortunate news of his own: the British had seized the mills, plus the boats, and Lee was possibly dead. Washington, without saying a word, handed Hamilton Lee's letter.[9]

Any joy brought by this discovery and the reunion of the two officers was short lived. That night Hamilton wrote to Hancock in Philadelphia warning that, "If Congress have not yet left Philadelphia, they ought to do it immediately without fail...."[10] On September 19, the American government departed its capital and fled to the town of Lancaster before eventually moving on to York. On September 26, Howe and his army marched into Philadelphia uncontested, to the ovation of American loyalists.

But Washington would not cede the city easily. Howe had settled the British force, other than a few garrisons, near Germantown, just northwest of the city. There Washington hoped to take him by surprise with a dawn attack in October. But despite a fiercely contested fight, the endeavor, ill-coordinated on account of fog, failed.[11]

Entrenched in Philadelphia, Howe faced a new challenge. Though Congress and its patriot supporters had departed, a surge of loyalists and the arrival of the British soldiers swelled the city's population and strained its resources. In order to feed the occupied capital's population, Howe needed a clear path along the Delaware River for stores to arrive from Britain.

But that waterway was obstructed by a series of jagged wooden defenses known as chevaux-de-frise. And the Americans, who had built these iron-tipped, wooden barriers at the onset of the war, still controlled Forts Mifflin, Mercer, and Billingsport along Howe's would-be supply line. From these outposts they could rake the British with fire if they attempted to navigate or dismantle the obstacles. As a result, the occupying army was forced to transport goods over a circuitous land route. Howe had no choice but to attack and remove the Americans from these forts.

Lee was ordered to cross the Schuylkill and apprise Washington of the enemy's plan, and when possible disrupt it. Riding across the Pennsylvania countryside, he discovered that the British had a small number of men stationed on Carpenter's Island, at the mouth of the river, ferrying cargo in to Philadelphia. If the flow of goods through Carpenter's Island was not stopped, Lee told Washington, "supplies of provision will be as abundant, as if the fleet lay off the wharfs of the city." He also informed the commander in chief that locals near the town of Chester were selling their cattle to the British army in violation of laws passed by Congress. Lee sent dragoons to end this illicit trade and promised, with characteristic confidence, the "endeavors to interrupt this connection, will be effectual."[12]

While Lee continued to gather intelligence and disrupt the trade between Pennsylvanians and Howe's men, he also encountered, pursued, and captured several members of a British foraging party. One of the prisoners, a Marylander, revealed during interrogation that a British attack on Fort Mifflin was imminent. Lee wrote to Washington with this information and appended a bit of advice. If the Americans were to seize Carpenter's Island, Lee suggested, the floating batteries that the British were constructing to attack the rebel outposts could be "totally blasted." With the island in American hands, "we most assuredly can put a stop to their favorite scheme...." and stop the flow of provisions into Philadelphia.[13]

Washington vetoed Lee's plan, and despite a last-ditch effort to save Fort Mercer after Mifflin had fallen, by November 18 the British had cleared the Delaware for transport. Less remarkable than Lee's advice was the fact that he felt free to offer it. After little more than a year of service, the twenty-two-year-old captain had an open line of communication with and was comfortable offering advice to the commanding general of the entire army.[14] And Washington, in a sign of his increasing appreciation for Lee's talents, did not bat an eye.

In the fall Lee and a fellow soldier named Warring passed through North Wales, a Welsh settlement in the woods north of Philadelphia, to which Daniel Wister, a resident of Germantown, had fled with his family when the British army approached the city. He had taken refuge in the farm home of a relative, Hannah Foulke. American soldiers passing through the area often quartered in or visited the house, where Wister's sixteen-year-old daughter Sally, to pass her days in exile, wrote letters to a friend, and—once the mail was disrupted—transferred her observations on the war and the men fighting it to a journal.

Wister jotted down a rare casual and altogether unimpressed portrait of the young captain when he visited on November 2. "Lee sings prettily and talks a great deal," she recorded. He professed his affection for turkey hash and fried hominy, his love for Virginia, and distaste for Maryland. The teenager teasingly mocked the Virginian's accent, laughed at his home state, and disapproved of Lee's insistence on discussing gastronomical matters. Wister snickered at Lee and his companions, "I took great delight in teasing them. They were not, I am certain almost, first-rate gentlemen."[15]

Despite the string of American losses, a ray of hope had emerged in the North. In October, rebels led by General Horatio Gates and a young major general named Benedict Arnold trapped and forced the surrender of a British force in upstate New York. The victory convinced monarchs in France and also Spain to lend their full support to the American cause.[16] In the advance of the move to Valley Forge, Lee was sent back across the Delaware to New Jersey to aid General Nathanael Greene. Reports of British foraging parties there had Washington worried that the enemy was plotting to retake the state. Greene needed cavalry to combat British raids. But after a week of riding patrols, by early December, Lee was on his way back east and once again near the main army in Pennsylvania.

With winter approaching, Howe remained in the comfort of Philadelphia. Washington's selection of a winter camp, on the other hand, was fraught with political and logistical difficulties. The Continental Congress, hoping to return from its exile, had asked that the army remain as close to the city as possible. And the government of Pennsylvania preferred that they keep a safe distance from the lush farmland to the north of the city, while Washington needed to be close enough to keep tabs on Howe's army and contest any raids in the surrounding countryside.

After a debate with his generals beginning in late October, Washington settled on a densely wooded area some twenty miles north of Philadelphia, west of the Schuylkill River. The forests, Washington hoped, would provide the raw materials for the Americans to construct huts in which to wait out the winter. But by the time the eleven thousand American soldiers, with women and children in tow, arrived in Valley Forge, that winter had arrived.[17]

Improperly supplied, the army now faced a great test. Food grew scarce. Paltry provisions of salt pork were barely enough to keep body and soul together. Snows came, and icy winds swept across the hillside area where the soldiers hurriedly threw together their dwellings. What little clothing the men had was in rags. Many were forced to go without boots or shoes, their bleeding feet leaving crimson tracks in the snow. There were not even blankets for the shivering men to sleep under during the frigid nights. Influenza and dysentery swept through the camp; its occupants died by thousands. Morale did not merely sink; the army teetered on the edge of complete collapse. In dire correspondence to Congress, Washington warned that in the absence of "some great and capital change" the army would "starve, dissolve or disperse."[18]

Lee did everything in his power to ensure these things did not come to pass. The 5th Troop, increasingly independent from Bland, would not remain at Valley Forge that winter. Instead they would alert Washington to any attempt by the British to advance on Valley Forge, protect American farmers in the region from any British depredations, and gather as much forage as possible for the starving soldiers back in camp.

Lee initially staged his operations from Randor Friends Meeting House, built by Quakers in 1717, a stone structure that the American army had commandeered in Delaware County, near Philadelphia.[19] The area, and in particular the community of nearby Newton-Square, where the roads to the towns of Chester, Wilmington, and Philadelphia converged, were favorite targets for British scavenging. In the final weeks of 1777, British dragoons made off with over one hundred horses, "robbing and plundering every person they came across" and subjecting those living in the residences of Newton-Square to "barbarity and cruelty."[20] One of Lee's initial responsibilities in the winter of 1778 was to put an end to this.

The 5th Troop was hardly in better supply than their brethren back at Valley Forge. After a year of constant riding and skirmishing, Lee's men were in dire need of new saddles, spurs, boots, and even carbines. With twelve of his thirty-five men in need even of new horses, Lee complained to Washington about the superiority of the British mounts.[21] But none of this hindered their success.

Riding constant patrols on the edge of Philadelphia, swooping in on unsuspecting British detachments, by the end of January Lee and his men had apprehended a staggering 124 enemy prisoners and had only lost a single horse in the process.[22] The officers of the 5th Troop also served as emissaries to farmers living in between the British and American lines. Together they settled on a designated amount of food to be delivered directly to Lee in exchange for protection from unchecked foraging.

Lee posted at Scott's Farm, 250 acres of abandoned farmland west of Philadelphia, in the middle of which stood an expansive stone house. From there he carried on his successful hunts, ambushing British supply convoys and riding off with the Redcoats' food and clothing, redirecting it to the starving and shivering soldiers at Valley Forge to replace their maggot-filled firecakes and self-constructed moccasins of cowhide.[23]

The fifty square miles that constituted the 5th Troop's patrol was a perilous place for Redcoats; the name "Lee" elicited anger amongst the British command and cheers among the American soldiers. By late January 1778, Howe had had enough. "At 11 o' clock at night, 40 dragoons were detached by a long roundabout way to seize a rebel dragoon captain by the name of Lee, who has alarmed us quite often by his boldness and who is stationed fifteen miles from here," Captain Frederick von Munchhausen, one of Howe's aides, wrote in his dairy on the nineteenth of that month.[24]

That night, under Howe's orders, the 17th Regiment of Dragoons, captained by Major Richard Crewe, in tandem with members of the Queen's Rangers, a loyalist dragoon company, set out for Scott's Farm. Once the party, numbering 130 men, reached the outskirts of the property, likely with the aid of an American informant, they clashed with and easily overpowered four mounted guards. Riding on, they reached the stone house as morning arrived and the sun rose. Inside, Lee had only nine men at his disposal, including John Jameson, a visitor from the 1st Dragoons. When the Americans were startled out of sleep by the ruckus outside, one soldier, a panicked quartermaster sergeant, fled the house.[25]

Now Lee, stranded with only eight men, faced a fight against an army. These were odds the captain liked. Hurriedly he rallied his men; they bolted the doors, grabbed their muskets and pistols, and rushed from window to window, giving the impression that there were far more men inside than the few there.

The British charged forward but were blasted back. Those who evaded the musket balls were greeted with slashing broad swords. Finding entry to the house impossible, the startled invaders ran to the nearby stables, where Lee's horses were resting; but this was a failure, too. The Americans, in a coordinated effort, continued to fire; a British retreat was ordered.

During the melee a flamboyant young British cavalry officer named Banastre Tarleton, who had a flair for the dramatic rivaling Lee's own, made a final charge at the house. Ferdinand O'Neal, a French-born member of the 5th Troop, appeared at a window and placed the muzzle of his pistol near Tarleton's head. When O'Neal flicked his firing pan down and pressed back his trigger, the weapon misfired. "You have missed it my lad for this time," Tarleton shouted with a smile as he wheeled his horse around and trotted off under fire.[26]

As disorder set in among the British during their withdrawal, Lee cockily admonished his counterpart, Crewe. "Comrade, shame on you, that you don't have your men under better discipline," he roared. "Come a little closer, we will soon manage it together!"[27] Left behind in the wake of the enemy's retreat were two dead Redcoats and another four wounded. A number of abandoned arms and cloaks were quickly scavenged by the victors. The only American casualty was a slight injury to the hand of Lee's deputy, Lieutenant William Lindsay, though the four privates who had been patrolling the house, plus the fleeing quartermaster sergeant, were unaccounted for, and four horses were lost.

With the smoke cleared, Lee sent a summary of the action to the commander in chief. "The contest was very warm; the British dragoons trusting to their vast superiority in number, attempted to force their way into the house," he wrote. "In this

they were baffled by the bravery of our men."[28] The news of the
gallant little stand thrilled Washington, mired in the gloom of
Valley Forge. In his general orders for January 20, shared with
the entire army, Washington, citing Lee's "vigilance," heaped
praise on the young captain and his companions: "The Commander in Chief returns his warmest thanks to Capt'n Lee &
Officers & men of his troop for the victory, which by their superior bravery and address, they gain'd over a party of the enemy's
dragoons, who trusting in their numbers—and concealing their
march by a circuitous road attempted to surprise them in their
quarters...."[29]

This approbation apparently insufficient, Washington also
personally recognized Lee by letter, noting that although thanks
had been extended earlier in the day, "for the late instance of your
gallant behavior, I cannot resist the inclination I feel to repeat
them again in this manner." Then, hinting at things over the
horizon, Washington continued, "I needed no fresh proof of your
merit, to bear you in remembrance—I waited only for the proper
time and season to shew it—these I hope are not far off."[30]

The exchange at Scott's Farm was tactically insignificant.
It was a minor skirmish in a war filled with great battles. But
the fact that a deeply outnumbered American garrison could
repel the attack of a numerically superior British force provided welcome inspiration and optimism for the continentals
as they weathered that depressing winter in southeastern
Pennsylvania.

It also demonstrated Lee's cool demeanor and ability to
improvise under fire, endearing the captain to his general. It was
the first of Lee's fabled exploits. Meanwhile, across enemy lines,
anger at the rebel dragoon captain raged. "Early in the morning
this captain Lee was indeed surprised by us," Howe's aide

Munchhausen observed, "he himself retreated with a few men into a massive building out of which our men could not force him."[31]

The excitement brought by Lee's exploits, though, did little to relieve the suffering at Valley Forge, where the shortage of supplies had reached a head. Washington himself described it as a "fatal crisis."[32] Broken wagons and incompetent commissary combined with the winter weather had resulted in a scarcity of bread and meat. The suffering was so great and famine seemingly so imminent, the dissolution of the army was approaching, if mutiny did not rend it before then.

In desperation, Washington begged the "virtuous yeomanry" of Americans to prepare cattle for sale to the army and orchestrated a "grand forage," sending Generals Nathanael Greene and Anthony Wayne to scour Pennsylvania and New Jersey, respectively, for supplies.[33] In the middle of February, Lee and members of the 5th Troop joined the campaign, riding south to the areas of Dover, Delaware, and Head of Elk, Maryland. There, Lee was to secure food and forage from the surrounding country with great speed, and to impress wagons when necessary. "If any resources can be derived thence towards the relief of our distresses," Washington implored Lee, "it will be infinitely desirable."[34]

Lee, aided by Colonel Henry Hollingsworth, whose stepbrother was a merchant in Baltimore and familiar with the area, assigned teams of horses to secure any available wagons in the area and send them on to Dover to collect salt provisions. Meanwhile his men scouted the area, collecting "all cattle fat for slaughter, all horses suitable for draught or dragoon service." The operation showed Lee's meticulous attention to detail and diplomacy, as he kept books on his acquisitions and, per Washington's instructions, treated the region's inhabitants with grace, guaranteeing that they were compensated during his efforts to "drain this country of superfluous forage & provision."[35]

The effort met with mixed results. Wayne had little success, but Greene and Lee fared somewhat better. On February 16 Greene sent fifty head of cattle to Valley Forge. Lee, though he had trouble securing wagons, delaying the arrival of salt provisions, dispatched a drove of cattle to headquarters on the twenty-second. But complicating Lee's efforts was his discovery that the southern reaches of Delaware were dotted with loyalists and deserters from the American army. Those living near the marshes he swept were, in his words, "friends to the enemies of America" who, instead of selling their cattle to the army, planned to wait until the spring when the British would offer higher prices.[36]

Months before the crisis at Valley Forge, both Washington and Congress, in a sign of the esteem in which Greene was held across the military and government, had urged him to take the vacant role of the army's quartermaster general. Though he had apprehensions about abandoning a battlefield post for an administrative one, in March Greene eventually relented, bringing an energy and organization to the position that began to relieve the strain faced at camp.[37] With the arrival of spring, the army had lost two thousand men but remained intact. And, incredibly, thanks to the night-time drilling of Prussian General Baron von Steuben, the soldiers who had survived the ordeal of the winter were prepared for the battles to come.[38] Lee, his foraging tasks finished, rejoined the main army at the end of March.

As Lee returned to Valley Forge to prepare for the spring campaigns—rumors were swirling that the British planned to evacuate Philadelphia—Alexander Hamilton sent out a request to Stephen Moylan, the army's captain of cavalry. The commander in chief was in need of a new officer and company of horses. "They are wanted," Hamilton explained, "to relieve Capt. Lee, and perform the duties his parties did."[39]

Influenced by a fondness for the young man dating back years, impressed by his martial skills and daring, Washington had decided that rather than scouting enemy lines or searching for cattle or wheat, Lee belonged in his own inner circle. The duty of transmitting this offer fell to Hamilton, who extended it in person upon his friend's return to Valley Forge.

This was an incredible offer. It meant that Lee, now so accustomed to danger and deprivation, would no longer have to worry about shelter or sustenance. The whiz of bullets and boom of cannons would be replaced by the shuffling of paperwork. It represented a major promotion, and a chance to join a family that included Hamilton and other young warriors. A chance to leave the hardships of the war and join this clique would have been an easy choice for most ambitious soldiers. For Lee, however, it was a difficult decision. The glory he craved would come on the battlefield, not at headquarters.

So he declined.

In a letter composed on March 31, a flattered Lee graciously offered thanks to Washington. Quoting Joseph Addison's Cato ("It is not in mortals to command success"), Lee confessed that the position he had been offered would accelerate his military education, serve as a tutelage in American politics, draw him closer to Washington, and bring "true and unexpected joy to my parents and friends."

But, Lee wrote, "Permit me to premise that I am wedded to my sword, and that my secondary object in the present war, is military reputation." Lee's place in the revolution was in the arena. Glory was in short supply, and penning dispatches was not the way to win it. Laurels were not likely to be won by

delivering messages or treating with Congress and state governments. Lee's destiny, he was convinced, was in combat. "I possess
a most affectionate friendship for my soldiers... a zeal for the
honor of the Cavalry, and [an] opinion, that I should render
m[ore] real service to your Excellency's arms."[40]

Most officers could have only dreamed of a niche in Washington's personal staff. Lee, when offered such an opportunity,
turned it down to pursue his dreams of military fame. And Washington did not begrudge him in the least for his choice.

Responding to Lee's rebuff, the commander in chief effused
that "the undisguised manner in which you express yourself cannot but strengthen my good opinion of you—as the offer on my
part was purely the result of a high Sense of your merit and as I
would by no means divert you from a Career in which you promise yourself greater happiness from it's affording more frequent
opportunities of acquiring military fame, I entreat you to pursue
your own Inclinations as if nothing had passed on this subject."[41]

In the months ahead, Lee would do as Washington suggested.

# 5

# A MOST GALLANT AFFAIR

If Henry Lee would not join George Washington's inner circle, the commander in chief would find other ways to help along his rise.

On April 3, 1778, he wrote to Henry Laurens, president of the Continental Congress since the previous fall, with a proposal. "Captain Lee of the light Dragoons and the Officers under his command," Washington explained, "having uniformly distinguished themselves by a conduct of exemplary zeal, prudence and bravery, I took occasion on a late signal instance of it to express the high sense I entertained of their merit, and to assure him that it should not fail of being properly noticed."[1]

Washington's means of noticing their merits was this: Lee would be made a major and given command over two additional troops of horses, each consisting of fifty men and independent from the Continental Dragoons.[2] These would be led by William Lindsay and Henry Peyton. Such a promotion, the commander in chief reasoned, "would be a mode of rewarding him very advantageous to the Service. Capt. Lee's genius peculiarly adapts him to a command of this nature."[3] The Continental Congress, with Lee's cousins Richard Henry and Francis Lightfoot looking on favorably, approved the request on April 7. The following day Laurens wrote to Lee with news of the advancement and his congratulations. The note reached Valley Forge on the twelfth and was delivered to Washington,[4] who forwarded it to Lee with his instructions; "I shall be glad to see you as soon as possible, that we may fix upon the other Officers for your Corps, and devise ways and means of procuring the additional Men, Horses, Arms and accoutrements."[5] Another step closer to the renown he so desired, Lee began the formidable task of crafting the means to secure it.

Recruitment of men and procurement of supplies for the new independent "Partisan Corps" was underway with the arrival of spring. Members of Lee's Fifth Troop were reassigned. Ferdinand O'Neal, whose heroics at Scott's Farm had perturbed Banastre Tarleton, was made a cornet of one troop, and John Champe of Loudon County, Virginia, was made sergeant of another. New recruits were added. The commander in chief's nephew George Augustine Washington joined the corps along with two brothers from Maryland, John and Michael Rudolph. Robert Forsyth, who had served in another of the Virginia dragoon regiments, became captain of a third troop created in May. The men would be clothed in new uniforms as well, featuring short green coats with crimson linings.[6]

On receiving the news of his promotion, Lee had written to Laurens with profuse thanks. A month later he approached the president of the Continental Congress with a plea. Given the scarcity of resources and the cost of horses, Lee insisted that his partisans must be permitted by Congress to impress horses from citizens along the Chesapeake. And despite strong opposition from the government of Maryland, Congress acquiesced. While suitable steeds for the new corps were rounded up, Lee, for the first time in nearly two years, returned to Leesylvania for a short furlough.[7]

But while Lee rested, the war reignited.

In the fall of 1777, William Howe, facing criticism in England and a war with no immediate conclusion in America, had tendered his resignation, blaming a lack of attention from the government and his superiors. In May 1778 after a grand farewell gala, the general was on his way back to Britain, and the reins of the Redcoat army were in the hands of his deputy, Henry Clinton.[8]

In June, after its leisurely winter in Philadelphia, the British army was once again on the march, headed northeast toward New York City with Washington's newly rejuvenated army in hot pursuit. On June 28, on a smoldering day in Monmouth County in the heart of New Jersey, an advance force led by General Charles Lee attacked the British rear. But the Redcoats, led by Charles Cornwallis, swiveled around and repulsed the poorly executed American attack.[9]

General Lee and his men began a disorganized retreat which smashed into Washington and the advancing American army. In a rare loss of mastery over his fiery temper, Washington verbally eviscerated Lee. His fury released, the commander in chief steadied the retreating Americans and pushed the army forward, giving Cornwallis a furious fight and forcing the enemy back. The battle ended as night fell; by the next morning the British were once again headed north.[10] The Battle of Monmouth was a tactical draw in which both sides claimed victory. For the Americans it demonstrated that Washington's army was indeed capable of holding its own against its mighty British counterpart. The war, now four years old, would go on. But the battle drew the curtain on the military career of Charles Lee. The eccentric general was subsequently court-martialed and dismissed from service to the American cause.[11]

Nowhere to be found at Monmouth was the young Virginian who shared a surname with General Lee and had been so impressed by Englishmen during a dinner several years past. "I have been almost melancholy by my absence from the army. The name of Monmouth reproaches me to the soul," Henry Lee plaintively wrote to Anthony Wayne on August 24.[12]

But Harry Lee's sojourn back home had concluded by September, when he rejoined his partisans in New York. A new assignment awaited, this time under General Charles Scott, a veteran of the French and Indian War, who was commanding a beleaguered force between the American headquarters in White Plains and the British in New York. Lee and his men were set to a familiar task, gathering reconnaissance and stopping British and Hessian foraging in the thick woods separating the two armies. Troubles set in; Lee struggled to gather intelligence; thirty of his men, all part of the original 5th Troop, reached the end of their terms of service and left for home.[13] They were replaced by new soldiers, largely from New Jersey. One of Lee's lieutenants, Patrick Carnes, created a ruckus when he seized oats from New York's militia. Lee refused to punish or reign him in, and New York governor George Clinton sent a scathing letter to Washington criticizing the major; a rare rebuke from the commander-in-chief followed.[14]

But Washington's estimation of Lee did not suffer. With the main army wintering once again in Middlebrook, and Lee's partisan corps in Burlington, the commander in chief invited Lee for dinner on December 14. The major, focused on the coming year, declined. Drilling his men superseded breaking bread with Washington. "Wishing to take the field in the spring with my corps in perfect order, I must procrastinate the honor of waiting on your Excellency at present, as I hasten to Winter-quarters to commence preparations,"[15] Lee wrote in his polite refusal.

In the spring of 1779 Lee had the opportunity to show off the results of his winter work. Conrad Alexandre Gerard, France's first minster to the United States, traveled to Trenton to review the American army. Joining Gerard in the audience were Martha Washington and Nathanael Greene's wife, Catharine. The arrival of the army was announced with blasts from thirteen cannons across an open field; then, parading out in advance of the army appeared a mounted soldier and his men; "A very beautiful troop of light-horse, commanded by Major Lee, a Virginian, marched in front," a spectator, James Thatcher, who was a surgeon with the Massachusetts 16th Regiment, jotted down in his diary. Behind Lee was the imposing figure of the commander in chief, accompanied by his aides.[16]

Lee's men were ready to return to action. Later in the month a fourth troop, this one of dragoons from Delaware, joined their ranks—swelling the Partisan Corps into "Lee's Legion." The new additions were led by Allan McLane, whom Lee had encountered the previous year while searching for horses. Ten years his senior, and with a battlefield resume that stretched back to the opening of the war, McLane was neither impressed by nor fond of Lee; Lee had brought McLane's troop into his Legion as infantry, something that was apparently not communicated to the captain, who bristled mightily at giving up his mounts.[17]

Their differences temporarily put aside, Lee relied on McLane to scout a fortification known as Stoney Point.

Originally established by Americans on a 150-foot hill atop a spur extending from New York into the Hudson River, it had been taken by the British marching north in July, with no American opposition. There they had set to work building a new fort, protected by dozens of cannons.[18]

This gave Clinton control over the river and ended travel across the King's Ferry, the southernmost point across the Hudson, where Washington moved supplies during the war.[19] Determined to take Stoney Point back, the commander in chief assigned Anthony Wayne, in charge of a twelve-hundred-man brigade, to lead an attack. Lee was to gather intelligence in preparation of the maneuver.

During the scouting, in a fit of gory over-zealousness, three deserters—two Irish and one an American—were captured and executed; to set an example, the head of the last was severed. When told of this punishment, Washington gently reprimanded Lee, cautioning that it could "give disgust and may excite resentment."[20]

In the early morning of July 16, with bayonets fixed, the Americans, moving in three columns, silently set out for the outpost and arrived that evening. In a stunning victory, the rebels stormed and took Stoney Point with minimal casualties.[21] Lee and his men who were serving as the reserve, however, missed out on the action. And the glory.

Snatching the fort back from the British gave Americans a success they desperately needed in the summer of 1779. Congress quickly heaped praise upon Wayne. "Resolved, unanimously," their commendation read, "That the thanks of Congress be presented to brigadier general Wayne for his brave, prudent, and soldierly conduct in the spirited and well conducted attack on Stony Point."[22]

A gold medal was struck in Wayne's likeness, and silver ones for two of his subordinates, Lieutenant Colonel Francois de Fleury and Major John Stewart. A stipend of $170,000 was designated for the regiment. All officers lower than lieutenant colonel were promoted one rank. Lee and his men, however, received no praise, despite their meticulous reconnaissance work, which had enabled Wayne's triumph.

During the days that followed, Lee remained largely quiet. The episode generated disappointment. And jealousy. Wayne was a friend, but that mattered little when the major saw the praise he so desired fall to another.

But there was a silver lining. Lee still enjoyed the rare privilege of direct communication with Washington, meaning he was free to float ideas for other military endeavors, new paths to glory. Now, between filing his requests for additional clothing and men, Lee began to plot with an eye on another English outpost on the Hudson River.

Paulus Hook was a piece of land poking out into the confluence of the Hudson and Hackensack rivers. Shortly after the first shots of the Revolution were fired, Americans had hurriedly constructed a rudimentary wooden garrison there. But General Hugh Mercer was ordered by Washington to abandon the fort when the British under General William Howe swept through and claimed New York City. In September 1776, 250 Redcoats under Major William Sutherland had moved into the fort, giving them a strategic toehold in New Jersey.[23]

Most colonials, even a number of Lee's own men, believed the fort impregnable. It was protected by water on three sides. And on the fourth side a muddy creek, two miles of salt marsh, and a flooded ditch stood between the fort and the mainland. The British had placed cannons atop the islet's hills and razor-sharp stakes in front of the fort. Inside awaited six more guns. A loyalist force commanded by Lieutenant Colonel Abraham Van Buskirk came to reinforce Sutherland and his men in the summer of 1779.[24] To top it all off, British frigates patrolled the nearby waters; a signal of two cannon shots and a hung lantern could summon them quickly.

Lee pitched the idea of an attack to Washington sometime in July; the original letter is lost, but on the twenty-eighth Washington's aide-de-camp Richard Kidder Meade ordered Lee to ride from his base at Haverstraw in southern New York to West Point, where the general was headquartered. "By his Excy's desire I wrote to you this morning requesting your attendance here on the very subject mentioned in your letter of this date," wrote Meade. "He still requests you will come on, after making the necessary inquiry's in order that the scheme you propose may be adopted."[25]

Lee was greeted by an intrigued but cautious Washington, who ordered the major to go back and draw up a concrete plan of attack before he would give his approval. Lee returned to Haverstraw and began to plan in earnest. McLane and his rangers were ordered to gather reconnaissance for the mission. They spent days monitoring the comings and goings at Paulus Hook and assessing the terrain. Ultimately they concluded that an attack was impractical: the ground, much of it little more than marshes, was too difficult for either horse or infantry to cross.[26]

Undeterred, Lee drew up his plan: the patriots would march by foot to the fort by moonlight, construct a bridge and cross the Hackensack at Prior's Mill, storm and then destroy the fort after capturing its stores, and then retreat on foot. When Lee's scheme reached Washington on August 9, the general balked, sensing it was likely to fail and not worth the sacrifices involved. "In the present position of the enemy's army, I should deem the operation too hazardous and not warranted by the magnitude of the object," Washington explained in a letter to Lee. "We should lose more in the case of failure than we would gain in the case of success."[27]

But, said Washington, if the major could revise his plan, using fewer than the five hundred men he had requested and approaching Paulus Hook by water rather than over the marshy ground, he would reconsider. "Turn your thoughts this way," Washington urged Lee, "and give me your opinion as to the probability of success."[28] Lee countered with a compromise plan: the Americans would depart from the Hackensack mill town of New Bridge and march twenty miles south to Paulus Hook. Once the fort was breached, Lee and his men would retreat to Douw's Ferry with their prisoners and bounty. There they would board waiting boats, watched by Captain Henry Peyton, and sail across the otherwise impassable Hackensack to safety.

Though Lee would lead the expedition, he would not have total administrative authority over its execution. Washington handed that power to Major General William Alexander, who commanded the Continental Army troops closest to Paulus Hook. Alexander and Washington had been friends since their joint service during the French and Indian War. Alexander, who called himself Lord Stirling in assertion of a dubious claim to a Scottish title of nobility, had shown his mettle during the Revolution, fighting off the British during the Battle of Long Island in 1776 and buying time for Washington's army to escape New York. On August 12 Washington dispatched Lee to deliver a letter to Alexander with the details of the attack. "Success must depend on surprise," Washington warned. The infantry for the expedition, the general stipulated, would come from Alexander's divisions, though he was to "consult Major Lee fully and if, upon the whole, you deem the undertaking eligible you have my consent to carry it into execution."[29]

McLane's intelligence was promising: a deserter reported that a relatively meager force of four hundred waited beyond the fort's walls—two hundred British regulars plus two hundred loyalist militia. A patriot spy, posing as a loyalist seeking news, then visited the fort and reported back to McLane no irregular activities. But at the same time two American letters, one detailing the arrangement with the boats at Douw's Ferry and the other mentioning the recruitment of militia for the attack, were intercepted by a British spy, possibly imperiling the entire mission. Nevertheless, Lee decided that the attack would proceed, despite the risk.

At 4:00 p.m. on August 18, Lee gathered his men at Haverstraw and calmly read the orders for the attack. He was twenty-three years old, dressed in a green frilled jacket, white breeches, gleaming black boots, and a leather cap topped with a flamboyant plume of horsehair. He projected all the authority that his war experience and birthright commanded. And he was just hours away from carrying out his first major operation.

There were four hundred men assigned to the task, Lee's Legion plus additional infantry drawn from Virginia, led by Major Jonathan Clark, and from Maryland, by Captain Levin Handy. The former was a seasoned patriot and soldier, six years Lee's senior and the elder brother of George Rogers and William Clark, fellow soldiers fighting elsewhere in the Revolution and both destined to make their own mark. Many of the men under his and Handy's command had little enthusiasm for a mission they deemed folly.

Before embarking, Lee gave an understated speech to rally the troops. "Major Lee is so assured of the gallantry of the officers and men under his command, that he feels exhortation useless; he therefore only requires the most profound secrecy. Success is not at the will of mortals; all they can do is to deserve it. Be this determination and this our conduct and we shall have cause to triumph, even in adversity."[30]

An hour later the men were on the move. McLane's infantry fanned out across the route to Paulus Hook, clearing the roads and keeping an eye out for boats arriving along the Hudson before reconnoitering with Lee at a wooded point called Three Pigeons.[31] Clark, angered that Lee, a junior officer with less battlefield experience, was leading the expedition, asked when he had been granted his commission. Lee was irritated by the question, especially at a time when he was leading his men towards a major attack. He responded carelessly and untruthfully that he'd been awarded it in 1777—a date that made him Clark's superior. For the time being, Clark let the issue go.[32]

Lee's plan was to travel the twenty miles along New Bergan road from New Bridge village to Paulus Hook, arriving at the fort close to midnight. But his guides suggested a shortcut through a densely forested area that would give the men cover from British sentries. Once they had all filed into the woods, Lee's men quickly lost their way in the wilderness.[33] Their short march morphed into a three-hour ordeal. Soldiers in the rear of the procession were cut off from the rest of the body, reducing the number of men at Lee's disposal for the final attack. Lee and his exhausted troops finally reached Paulus Hook near 3:00 a.m. With dawn approaching, they swiftly improvised a bridge across the Hackensack and scrambled across it to scout out activity in the fort and determine if the canal that fronted it was passable.

It was, although the tide was rapidly rising. The British appeared to be sleeping in their barracks.[34] The time for attack was at hand. Bayonets fixed, the American van rushed forward. At this moment—the most inopportune time—Lee learned that some enlisted Virginians had deserted just as the army reached the marshes. But he remained calm, concentrating on the push forward. His men slipped into the canal and waded forward for a two-mile trek, the swampy water rising to their breasts. They kept their muskets above their heads with cocks down and pans open to avoid accidental fire.[35]

A dozen or so British and German soldiers were in three strategically placed blockhouses defending the main bridge leading into the fort. Behind them lay a redoubt containing five more men as well as the fort's artillery. When the Americans approached the blockhouses, a British sentry fired the battle's first shot, waking his comrades, who rushed out to check the invaders. They were too late. Exploiting openings in the fort's fortifications—there was a large undefended open space to the right of the center blockhouse—the first wave of Americans slipped in, bayonetting everyone in their path. They rapidly captured the redoubt and commandeered its artillery. In mere moments, without firing a single shot or losing one man, Lee had Paulus Hook and its occupants—British soldiers, American loyalists, and Prussian mercenaries—at his mercy.[36]

The original plan, as approved by Washington, had stipulated that Lee would gather up his prisoners, grab their stores, set the installation ablaze, and dash back to safety. With little time to deliberate, however, Lee decided to retreat at "the moment of victory,"[37] without stealing the fort's powder and ammunition or burning it down. In his official report he claimed that his men were unable to find the key to the fort's magazine. But it is probable that they were blocked by a small group of Hessians who had avoided capture and continued to fire on the Americans from one of the blockhouses. Lee also may have scrapped razing the fort because a number of sick soldiers, women, and young children were still inside and he was unable to move all of them. Also figuring in his decision was the fact that dawn was fast approaching. The longer his men waited to withdraw, the more likely an attack from roused Redcoats across the river. The Americans were exhausted from their march, and much of their ammunition was damp and useless after the slog through the canal. Lee also worried that the boats might no longer be waiting at Douw's Ferry for the journey across the Hackensack.

Clark's men gathered up the 250 prisoners—most of the fort's occupants had quickly surrendered—and began the withdrawal. Lee dispatched Captain Forsyth to Prior's Mill to gather men to cover the movement.

Lee's fears were realized. He learned from the officer assigned to coordinate the meeting with Peyton that the boats were no longer at Douw's Ferry. Peyton, assuming that the operation had been cancelled when Lee's men failed to arrive on schedule, had relocated the boats. Lee took his men back onto the Bergan Road in the direction of New Bridge. But they were worn out and hungry. They had marched over forty miles, and their progress now was slowed by the hundreds of prisoners.

And a surprise attack threatened as the light dawned: the prisoners told their captors that a party of British was off to their right. Lee quickly sent off a messenger to Alexander detailing the dire situation, then divided his forces and sent them on three separate routes back to New Bridge—the Marylanders headed off into the hills, Clark and his Virginians stayed along the Bergan Road, and the last group marched north along the Hudson.

Just as the men split up, there was good news. Alexander had dispatched reinforcements: fifty men from the Second Virginia Continental Regiment. Lee assigned part of this force to the troops trekking up the Hudson. The rest joined him, falling in behind Clark. Another round of reinforcements arrived shortly afterwards. But trouble was just up the road: British across the river had heard the shots at Paulus Hook and scrambled into boats to investigate.

Once those British troops reached New Jersey, they were joined by Buskirk's loyalists, who had been off on a foraging run during the attack. The joint force caught up to the Americans along the Bergan Road at a point called Liberty Poll Tavern. Spilling out of the woods to Lee's right, they opened fire. Lee's men turned and faced the enemy, while a detachment dashed into an abandoned stone house. The British, fatigued from their rapid march, melted back into the woods. The Americans moved on and safely rendez-voused at New Bridge by 1:00 p.m. on August 19. The operation was complete. And, despite the difficulties, a success.[38]

Drained, Lee delayed sending his official report to Washington. He did, however, give the news of the raid's outcome to Alexander, who conveyed the information to a greatly pleased Washington. In Lee's description of the raid, he was effusive about the gallantry, honor, and patience of his men, even singling out Major Clark for special praise. Lee had much of which to be proud.

Without firing a shot—the bayonet their "sole dependence," as Lee wrote—and despite an exhausting march through the woods and late arrival, his men had stormed and taken an important British post, one considered impregnable. They had also made it back safely despite fatigue, the burden of prisoners, the missing boats, and a British attack on the Bergan Road. The

Americans had lost only two men. In contrast, most of the British had been killed or captured. In New York, British General Henry Clinton fumed. He would later downplay the affair in his memoirs as a trifling embarrassment, as did the British press, which characterized the attack as bumbling and inconsequential. But the fact that Sutherland, the commanding officer at Paulus Hook, was quickly court martialed betrayed the sharp sting of defeat.[39]

As Lee had hoped, the reaction across America was euphoric. "Major Lee has performed a most gallant affair," General Nathanael Greene wrote to his wife, Catharine. "He has surprised and taken the far greater part of the Garrison at Paulus Hook."[40] Levin Handy described the successful attack as "the greatest enterprise in America." Washington reported to the army that "the enterprise was executed with a distinguished degree of Address, Activity and Bravery and does great honor to Major Lee...."[41] He then forwarded Lee's report to Congress, piling more praise on his protégé and describing the entire operation as "brilliant." The British garrison's flag, which Lee's men had hauled down and pocketed, accompanied Washington's packet to Philadelphia.[42]

As news of the success spread, Lee's list of admirers grew. General Henry Knox noted the young cavalier's genius. And the Marquis de Lafayette wrote to Lee confessing that "the more I have considered the situation at Paulus Hook, the more I have admired your enterprising spirit and all your conduct in that business."[43]

Lee had every reason to believe glory was finally at hand. But when he strained hardest for fame, fortune seemed to frown.

The old resentments resurfaced. A number of the soldiers from the expedition were rankled that so junior an officer had led the expedition. They complained that entire portions of other commands had been detached and given to Lee for the operation without any involvement in its planning.

Lee's brief exchange with Clark soon came back to haunt him: a small cabal of officers argued that he had lied to Clark about the date of his commission, had not in fact been the senior officer on the expedition, and should not have been placed in control of the forces. Letters of complaint were sent to Alexander and forwarded to Washington. Both men privately dismissed their claims. But in early September Lee was placed under arrest and court martialed.

# 6

# GOLD SEVEN TIMES TRIED IN THE FIRE

After the assault on Paulus Hook, General Anthony Wayne, echoing the emotions of many in the army and across the states, wrote of "Our Little Hero Lee."[1] Days later, the little hero was under arrest, awaiting the verdict of a military tribunal. The reversal of fortune was quick and cruel.

William Woodford and Peter Muhlenberg were hardly men of little merit. The former had fought under Washington, a relation by marriage, in the French and Indian War; at the outset of the Revolution he had heroically forced the Tory government out of Virginia during the Battle of Great Bridge; later he took a bullet at Brandywine. Muhlenberg, an ordained minister originally from Pennsylvania, had fought at Germantown and Monmouth. Both were brigadier generals who had participated in the Virginia Conventions. And they had led brigades at Paulus Hook.[2]

In fact, these were accomplished, ambitious middle-aged men. And the sight of a vainglorious princeling leading a charge that they were forced to follow was vexing. Lee was not the only officer in the Continental Army whose successes sparked petty jealousy in the hearts of his peers. The squabbles amongst military men of ranks across the American army were a cause of no small worry to Congress. But Lee presented an especially ripe target. Gifted, opportunistic, and well connected, he had a swashbuckling style of leadership that inspired love amongst his Legion but grated on other aspiring officers. And the American army overflowed with them.

"The pleasure I experience in your Success I can much better feel than express," Wayne congratulated Lee days after Paulus Hook. But, he advised, "be well guarded my friend—I ask your pardon for this unnecessary caution—but believe me that there are not a few, who would not feel much pain on a small disaster happening to either you or me."[3]

Lee arrogantly shrugged off the warning: "I disregard the envy and malice of a certain junto."[4]

But Wayne's words were prescient. In the days following Lee's great triumph, Washington was bombarded by grievances from jealous officers looking to discredit Lee.

The original complaint came from "Lord Stirling." The name of the self-styled nobleman had not appeared in Washington's general orders commending Lee for the successful Paulus Hook expedition. Alexander expressed his irritation to Washington in a letter questioning why Lee had been put in control of the mission in the first place, given his rank—the number of men under Lee's authority, Alexander argued, was far too great for a mere major to lead—and the fact he was a cavalryman, while most of the attack force was made up of infantry. Then Woodford and Muhlenberg piled on, lodging similar complaints with the commander in chief. There was roiling resentment amongst the officers under Woodford and Muhlenberg, as well: Nathaniel Gist, a colonel in the Virginia line and former Indian scout who had fought on the Virginia Frontier, was also stewing.

Washington saw little merit in the complaints. In a letter remarkable for its length and lawyerly logic, the commander in chief refuted Alexander's assertion that Lee had had no business leading the raid on Paulus Hook. In response to the charge that a horse soldier should not have led a force largely composed of infantry, Washington pointed out that whenever the two acted in conjunction, "the officers indifferently command each other with no other title than superiority of grade or seniority of commission."[5] The fact that Lee's own Legion comprised infantry and cavalry was an additional argument for him to lead a force of this nature. "No officer has a claim to the command more than another," Washington argued, adding that "circumstances alone must determine to whom it shall fall; all which in this instance were in favour of Major Lee."[6] Lee, as Washington reminded Alexander, had designed the plan of attack after relentless intelligence gathering, and therefore, "no officer could be more proper conducting it." Washington hoped the storm would pass, telling Alexander, "I think the Gentlemen who have complained on more cool reflection will be satisfied that they have not been injured in this respect, and that the giving the command to Major Lee was agreeable to the strictest military propriety."[7]

Those words were wasted. On August 28, 1779, Colonel Gist formally presented eight charges against Lee. The major was arrested and placed under guard, a jury was gathered, and the date for a trial set. The following day, with their leader incapacitated, Washington informed Lindsay, McLane, Peyton, and Forsyth that for the time being the command of Lee's corps fell to them.[8]

Lee was enraged. In the days leading up to his court martial, he unleashed his fury in a letter to Joseph Reed, a friend, former member of Washington's staff, and now the chief executive of Pennsylvania. "I never conceived myself so important in the army as I find I am," Lee snarled. "Captains and Subalterns used to seek me. Generals and colonels are now barking at me with open mouth."[9]

Of course Lee, ever pugilistic, would not go under without a fight. "I mean to make the matter very serious," he avowed, "because a full explanation will recoil on my foes, and give new light to the enterprise."[10]

This letter offers a window into Lee's character: along with the bravado was a note of self-pity. "I did not tell the world that near one half of my countrymen left me—that it was reported to me by Major Clark as I was entering the marsh—that notwithstanding this and every other dumb sign, I pushed on to the attack," he lamented. "Had I been unsuccessful, I was determined to leave my corpse within the enemy's lines."[11]

Back in Leesylvania, the elder Henry Lee worried. "Your brother's enterprise does him signal honor I flatter myself. It will not be in the power of his enemies to pluck from him those laurels they cannot acquire," the elder Lee wrote his second son, Charles.[12]

Lee's friends and superiors were outraged. "Major Lee has performed a most gallant affair," Nathanael Greene sighed to General George Weedon. "But can you believe it, he has been persecuted with a bitterness by his Countrymen, that is almost disgraceful to mention.... He has been arrested, and brought to trial, on misconduct, but there is not a shadow of evidence against him—on the contrary the more the matter is enquired into, the better he appears. After passing through the furnace of afflection, he will come out, like gold seven times tried in the fire."[13]

The attempt to pluck Lee's laurels rested on eight charges forwarded by Gist and conceived by the other aggrieved officers. He was charged with lying to Clark about the date of his own commission. Some of the other accusations were remarkably trivial—for example, that Lee had placed one of the Legion's captains in charge of one of Gist's though the latter held the senior rank. And some were more dangerous. Allegations were made that he had bungled the initial march to the fort and that a poorly managed retreat placed the attacking force in danger, had it been intercepted by a larger British force, and had it failed to capture a number of enemies hiding in a redoubt or destroy the fort's stores. The last charge accused Lee of "behaving in a manner unbecoming an officer and a Gentleman."[14]

Henry Lee had missed his opportunity to study law in London, but now he made up for it. After he elected to make his own defense before the tribunal, he requested the exact orders as Washington had verbally delivered them before his departure for Paulus Hook. Washington obliged.[15] Lee asked the same of General Alexander.[16] An additional request was made of Washington: Would he make public Lee's original account of the operation? Washington had shared Lee's report with Congress, but the country at large knew little of what exactly occurred on the night of August 19. The commander in chief refused to make the confidential report public.

Lee took what evidence he had to court on September 2 to make his case before a jury presided over by a fellow Virginian, Colonel Thomas Marshall, whose own son John was an infantryman in the Continental Army.

The scene was the small village of Smith's Clove on the west side of the Hudson River, fourteen miles from West Point. Though he had prepared beforehand, Lee's presentation was

extemporaneous. In his short military career Lee had demonstrated a flair for the dramatic and an ability to improvise under
fire. Saving that career would require that he exercise both those
qualities—and his gift for oratory.

Why on earth, Lee asked, was an officer being persecuted
after pulling off a successful enterprise? He turned to Gist. His
motives were sincere, Lee assumed, but why would an "aged and
meritorious officer"[17] like Gist commit himself to such a con-
spiracy? No, this was not Gist's scheme, but rather that of other
officers.

Here Lee took direct aim at Woodford and Muhlenberg.
They were, he said, "men who possess neither candor nor courage
sufficient to act for themselves, but who have basely pushed forward a friend under the perversion of justice to injure character
disgustful to them only from its fairness." Then Lee discharged
his rhetorical pistol. "I view such groveling beings with sovereign
contempt." But the defendant reserved his greatest flourish for
the finale. With what a witness later described as a "becoming
confidence," Lee put the alternatives before the jury. "If I have
misbehaved," he asked, "punish me with severity; but, if it shall
appear that I have done my duty, and that the prosecution is
groundless and vexatious, I trust, gentlemen, you will tell the
world so."[18]

The trial apparently went to Lee's liking. On September 9 he
wrote to Reed once again, exclaiming that "the evidence of the
prosecution throws additional lustre on my conduct." Lee even
expected the conspirators to offer a plea in order to save face.
And he was inclined to entertain such an offer, he boasted, given
that "pity has already got the better of resentment."[19] But no plea
was offered. Instead Lee waited while the jury deliberated. He
still hoped that Washington would make his report on Paulus

Hook, which the commander in chief had sent to Congress, public. But Washington, counseling patience, said that such a measure would be "premature and unnecessary."[20] Justice, he suggested, would come down on Lee's side. And indeed, when the court martial rendered its verdict on September 11, it did.

Lee was cleared on all eight counts. And with honor. When Washington issued his general orders that day, the young major was vindicated: the charges had been unsupported by the evidence. Lee had given the wrong date of his commission simply out of "inattention." Any confusion in the march towards the fort was not his fault. And the retreat had been conducted in "perfect conformity" with Washington's orders. Regarding the allegation that Lee had behaved in a manner unbecoming an officer and a gentleman, the court had concluded that, contrary to the charge, he filled those characters "with honor to his country and the Army."[21]

Lee was vindicated in no small part thanks to his subtle support from Washington. His own spirited defense played a part as well. With the cloud of the court martial lifted, the praise Lee felt was his due arrived. On September 24 Congress passed a resolution praising the victory of Paulus Hook and heaping gratitude on Lee for his "prudence, address and bravery." The sum of $15,000 was to be distributed amongst his noncommissioned officers. And, most amazingly, a gold Medal of Honor was to be struck by the Board of Treasury in Lee's honor and likeness.[22] The other tributes were meaningful, but this reward was extraordinary. Previously only three such medals had been commissioned by Congress for members of the military: the first for Washington after the siege of Boston, another for General Horatio Gates for the victory at Saratoga, and most recently one for Wayne in the aftermath of Stony Point. Only two more, after

Lee's, would be awarded in the remainder of the war, for Generals Daniel Morgan and Nathanael Greene. Of all six men, Lee was the only officer below the rank of general. Given Lee's rank and the fact that the importance of Paulus Hook was far more psychological than tactical, Congress commissioning the medal was proof that for all the envious rivals at his heels, Lee had powerful allies at his back. Still, the trauma of the court martial following the victory at Paulus Hook left an enduring scar on the proud young man.

Observing the ordeal, Alexander Hamilton told John Laurens of Lee's "handsome stroke" on Paulus Hook. "Some folks in the Virginia line jealous of his glory had the folly to get him arrested. He has been tried and acquitted with the highest honor," he wrote. "Lee unfolds himself more and more to be an officer of great capacity, and if he had not a little spice of The Julius Caesar or Cromwell in him, he would be a very clever fellow."[23]

After the excitement of the summer of 1779, the following months were relatively calm. Though the Legion's patrols were dangerous business—"every day we kill and are killed," Lee observed—there was a grand stalemate between Washington and British general Henry Clinton in the east.[24] In October Lee, based in Monmouth, prowled the New Jersey coast on the lookout for the arrival of a French fleet under the command of the prickly admiral Comte D'Estaing.[25] Washington was hoping that with its help he could take back New York. The Frenchman, however, was on his way south, where the locus of the war's action was also headed. There he teamed with the American general Benjamin Lincoln in a bloody and failed attempt to wrest the coastal city of Savannah from British control.

Another brutal winter, this one spent by Washington's army at Morristown, New Jersey, once again dragged American morale down. Snow storms raged across the state, leaving behind drifts as tall as men. Food was once again vanishingly scarce, forcing soldiers to nibble the bark of black birch trees. Spirits plummeted, mutiny rose. It was only the huge unpassable snow banks that kept many Americans from deserting. Lee spent the winter in Burlington planning a successful raid on Sandy Hook, harbor to part of the British fleet. He did not participate in the strike though, as before it commenced he was summoned by Washington to gather cattle and flour for the starving soldiers at Morristown.[26]

In February Lee and many of his men returned briefly to Virginia for rest. On his route—which passed through Philadelphia on March 30—to rejoining the army, Lee and his Legion were ordered south to help General Benjamin Lincoln defend the port city of Charleston in South Carolina. The new assignment "mortified" Lee, in Greene's words; and his march was delayed by sick horses and a lack of supplies.[27]

During his layover in the capital, Lee proved dangerous to himself during a dinner hosted by a doctor named Shields and attended by Anthony Wayne and Thomas Burke, a patriot politician from North Carolina and delegate to the Continental Congress. Lee's strident opinions and long-windedness grated on Burke, who responded by openly disparaging the major, hoping for peace and quiet. But Lee was incensed and challenged Burke to a duel—a challenge the older man rejected.

The following morning the major penned an angry note that Wayne, forced into the role of intermediary, passed on to Burke. "Be pleased to tell me now whether in your conversation at Doctor Shield's table you had it in intention to insult me." The matter was quite serious, Lee warned his dinner companion. "I assure you sir, I cannot but conjecture your reply to an observation made by me on a general matter as a meditated personal affront."[28] Burke explained to Wayne that his remarks had been inspired by a "conversation which was irksome to me and which Major Lee particularly pressed upon me and which in my opinion had already been continued beyond the line of good breeding." After all, politics and other such "serious subjects were not then well timed and were never agreeable to me after certain hours in the day which were then over." Burke eventually convinced Wayne, who in turn was able to persuade Lee, that he had intended no offense "to the most nice and scrupulous honor of a young and gallant soldier."[29]

In May of 1780 British forces seized Charleston and its vital harbor. With newly gained footholds in the American South, the Redcoat leadership hoped to rally the region's loyalists, whom they assumed to be numerous, to the British cause and finally quell the rebellion. For the moment, Lee was unable to move to the southern theatre.

Believing that the Americans, exhausted by the long war, were ready to abandon the revolutionary cause and rejoin the mother country, Baron Wilhelm von Knyphausen, an aged but accomplished Hessian commander, launched an invasion of New Jersey in June with a five-thousand-man-strong force of British regulars, American loyalists, and German mercenaries. His ultimate goal was to seize the Hobart Gap, the pathway to Morristown, running through the Watchung Mountains, and then deliver a knockout blow to Washington, whose army was crippled by their horrible winter. On the eve of Knyphausen's march, Washington had moved north on the basis of faulty information provided by Lee indicating a forthcoming British attack on West Point. Left in charge of American defenses in the commander in chief's absence was Nathanael Greene.

When he learned of the approaching enemy force, Greene threw up defenses near the town of Springfield, dividing his forces and concentrating on the bridges spanning the Rahway River. On the morning of June 23, Lee's men gallantly defended the Vauxhall bridge to the north of town before being over-whelmed by superior numbers and falling back into the hills beyond the river and joining other regiments. Rather than con-front the Americans, Knyphausuen set fire to Springfield and retreated towards New York. Greene, despite being vastly out-numbered, had held the day and blocked the enemy. New Jersey would never again be contested; major operations in the North-ern theatre were at an end.[30]

But soon enough the rebels were hit with a psychological shock. On the morning of September 23, a trio of New York militiamen apprehended Major John André, a British intelligence officer, near Tarrytown. Stuffed in his stocking were documents providing evidence that Major General Benedict Arnold had conspired with the British to surrender the post of West Point, then under his command. For this he would receive twenty thou-sand pounds.

When the papers connecting André to Arnold were presented to Washington, the commander in chief's facade remained stolid, obscuring his boiling blood and the personal betrayal he felt. Since their first encounter in 1775 Washington and Arnold had developed a firm bond. The commander in chief had recognized in the wealthy merchant with no military experience a soldier of great perseverance and enterprise. His estimation was borne out time and time again, even in defeat during the unsuccessful American attacks on Quebec and Valcour Island on Lake Cham-plain. Arnold had played the part of the hero during the rebel victory at Saratoga, where his horse and leg were shot. The former crashed down upon the latter, smashing it into several pieces and leaving him with a lasting limp. But Congress never properly honored Arnold for his sacrifices; the slow pace of his promotions was a constant source of frustration. He even contemplated resigning his commission. But Washington, playing the familiar role of mentor, talked Arnold back from the brink and continued to champion his prized soldier.

After the British fled Philadelphia, the widowed Arnold was appointed the military governor of the city. There he fell in love with and married Peggy Shippen, a beautiful British loyalist and acquaintance of André. When Arnold was accused of using his military assignment in the capital for personal gain and subsequently court martialed, Washington could only bring himself to offer a mild reprimand. This was followed by overtures by the commander in chief to give Arnold command of the left wing of the American army. Arnold preferred the post at West Point, which, after months of secret negotiations, he intended to hand over to the enemy.

Washington's initial hope was that the British would exchange Arnold, who had escaped to New York to take command of his own regiment, for André. When Henry Clinton refused, Washington set to work on an outlandish scheme to bring justice to the turncoat. To execute it, he called on Henry Lee.

When Lee stepped inside Washington's tent, he found the commander in chief sedate and seated at a desk writing. He motioned for Lee to be seated; a packet of papers was on a nearby table awaiting the major's eyes. Their contents indicated not only Arnold's guilt but also a possible connection between the traitor and another major general in the American army who had enjoyed Washington's confidence: Arthur St. Clair. Lee suggested that the connection could be a ruse, constructed by Howe to sow paranoia in the rebel army. Not ruling this possibility out, the commander in chief meditated for a moment before the silent Lee and then continued. "I have sent for you, in the expectation that you have in your corps individuals capable and willing to undertake an indispensable, delicate, and hazardous project." What Washington then proposed was that one of Lee's men feign desertion, cross enemy lines, join with the British under cover of this pretense, and then find his way to Arnold, apprehend him unharmed, and haul him back to Washington and justice. This operation, it was hoped, would also confirm or rule out the guilt of Arnold's possible co-conspirator.[31]

This was a mission that offered little chance of success or even survival. But Lee didn't hesitate; among his men were many daring enough to see it through—or die trying. None more than John Champe, a sergeant major in his early twenties from Virginia's Loudon County, who had fought alongside Lee since 1776. Champe was broad-shouldered and reserved, his courage unquestionable. Champe and Lee conferred on the night of October 21; Lee elucidated the plan, considering its risks. Though Champe had reservations about deserting, Lee appealed to his honor. How would his fellow cavalrymen react, he asked, if Champe refused and a soldier from some other corps took up the assignment, bringing glory to his comrades?[32]

This was enough to finally persuade Champe. With little time to burn, Champe and Lee synchronized their watches. The latter then gave the former three guineas and his best wishes. Lee repaired to his tent in search of sleep. Champe donned his cloak, gathered his valise and orderly book, mounted his horse, and spurred it out of camp.[33]

Before his departure, Lee had warned Champe that there was little he could do to prevent or even stall pursuit once members of the Legion discovered his desertion—lest Lee be seen as abetting the act. Sure enough, as Lee tossed and turned in his tent, Captain Patrick Carnes appeared outside. A dragoon had just rushed out of camp, he exclaimed. Lee, feigning grogginess and exhaustion from his long ride to and from headquarters earlier, made Carnes repeat himself, then dismissed the notion that a member of the Legion had left camp without permission. But the captain persisted. He quickly counted the Legion's horses and soon enough identified who was missing: John Champe. A party was assembled to pursue the deserter, its departure waiting on Lee's orders. Stalling for time to help in Champe's escape, Lee asked if it was not possible that the sergeant had left camp for "personal pleasures" rather than abandoning his mates. Then, in a final play for time, he told Carnes that he was needed at camp for a delicate task in the morning. Cornet John Middleton was sent for and told to lead the search party. This took an additional ten minutes, which was the last bit of extra time Lee could manage to give Champe. Once Middleton arrived, Lee gave the final orders: the men were to follow Champe on the road towards Paulus Hook: "Bring him alive, that he may suffer in the presence of the army; but kill him if he resists. . . ." Lee commanded.[34]

As they galloped off at midnight, rain fell. The plan to capture Benedict Arnold was now in great danger: as the showers turned the ground to mud, Champe's tracks became clear—all the more so because the shoes on his mount's two front feet bore a mark made by the Legion's own farrier, to help them recognize one another's tracks. As day broke, the men were closing in on Champe as he rode past the Three Pigeons Tavern and on toward the village of Bergan. This was familiar ground to all of Lee's Legion; Middleton knew of a bridge leading into the village and, assuming Champe would cross it, broke his party in two, sending half of it to block the bridge. But foreseeing this, Champe diverted his path, riding through nearby woods and finally swinging into Bergan.

A wild chase through the village followed, with Champe galloping hard toward Elizabethtown Point, a spot on the Hudson River where British galley ships were frequently docked. Riding towards it, he lashed his clothing and orderly book to his shoulder, drew his sword, and discarded his scabbard. Now with Middleton only two hundred feet behind him, Champe leapt out of his saddle and splashed into the marsh and then into the river, calling for the nearby British. In response, the ships fired on and dispersed Champe's pursuers. A boat was sent to retrieve the seemingly wayward American, who was then whisked away to New York. Middleton and his men rode back to camp with Champe's horse. This sight excited the rest of the men, who at first were led to believe the deserter had been dealt with. Lee, emerging from his tent, was distraught. But soon enough he realized, by the look on Middleton's face, that Champe had made it to relative safety.

This news much pleased Washington when it was relayed to him. Four days later Lee received a coded message from Champe, who was in New York and had been interrogated by the British. His defection, Champe explained to his inquisitors, was a symptom of a larger fever among Americans. Arnold's actions had inspired his compatriots to abandon the cause of liberty and want to reunite with the mother country. This news delighted Henry Clinton, who met with Champe and then sent him off to Arnold, who was in the process of forming his own legion of American loyalists and deserters. Champe was assigned to the quarters housing Arnold's recruiters.

Communicating via spies, Champe kept Lee aware of his progress. By the end of September Champe had made contact with undercover agents in the area and begun preparations to apprehend Arnold. He soon gained enough intelligence to inform Lee that St. Clair was innocent. Saving André, however, was moot: on October 2 a tribunal found him guilty of espionage, and he was executed the following day.

Now all that was left was for Champe to bring Arnold back to American lines. By October 13, the abduction was imminent. Champe had shadowed and studied Arnold's movements and schedule. The general returned home at midnight every night and visited his garden before going to bed. Champe and his contacts would seize and gag him there. Champe removed parts of a fence adjoining the house in order to slip into the adjacent alley more easily. Arnold would be propped on the shoulders of Champe and his companion. Should anyone inquire, they would explain that he was a drunken soldier being carted back to the guardhouse after a long night of merriment. From there they would move on to the banks of the Hudson, where a boat was waiting. Meanwhile Lee, after dinner, departed camp with several dragoons and three spare horses. The party set out towards the town of Hoboken, where they arrived at midnight and lingered anxiously. Lee would personally welcome Arnold back to American lines. But hours passed, and the sun rose with no sign of Champe.

Lee was forced to inform an angry Washington of the disappointing news. Days later, Champe's contacts wrote to inform Lee that on the day before the planned apprehension Arnold had relocated his quarters and sent the American troops to a transport in advance of a supposed expedition. Champe was now sailing south to Virginia—seemingly lost, along with the mission.

Fate had intervened to protect Arnold and deprive Lee, as well as Champe, of the rewards of their enterprise.[35]

But, for Lee at least, another opportunity was at hand. In the midst of his distress over Champe's fate, the major received a letter from Washington dated October 22 informing him that, "I think it more than probable that your corps will be ordered to the southward."[36] The time had come, the commander in chief said, to gather supplies and recruit men. The endgame of this war, now nearly five years long, was approaching, and soon Lee would be on his way to take part.

# 7

# THE GREAT GAME

When America's leaders, both political and military, reflected on the situation in the southern states at the end of 1780, they had precious little to be cheerful about.

The fighting in the Carolinas and Georgia—a tangle of loyalist feeling and patriotic fervor since the Revolution's start—pitted American against American in a brutal backwoods civil war that bordered on outright anarchy. The British had hoped, in partnership with their American supporters, to launch an amphibious assault and subdue the area early in the war. The British army would keep Washington contained to the north while smaller regiments commanded by Charles Cornwallis emboldened loyalists joined in the southern fight.[1]

The British took Charleston in May of 1780, and by the end of that year there was very little in the way of an American army in the South to oppose them. This was evident during the gruesome Waxhaws massacre, when the aggressive Banastre Tarleton, now leading a legion of American loyalists, laid waste to a

Continental cavalry regiment after its commander, Abraham Buford, raised the white flag of surrender near the North Carolina border. Over one hundred Americans were bayonetted to death, establishing Tarleton's fearsome reputation and nickname: "Bloody Ban."

With American General Benjamin Lincoln removed from command after the loss of Charleston, Congress handed the reins in the South to General Horatio Gates, a British-born American general who had intrigued against Washington earlier in the war. Gates rode south with a small continental contingent to meet up with what little rebel military force remained in South Carolina. He promptly marched this army, five thousand strong, to the town of Camden, where it was destroyed by Cornwallis and a British force half its size in the most humiliating fashion on August 16. The aftermath was a scene of total desolation for the rebels; roads were littered with overturned carriages, dead horses, and dying men while Gates bolted two hundred miles north. "Picture it as bad as you possibly can," General Edward Stevens, a brigadier general in the Virginia militia, wrote to his state's governor, Thomas Jefferson, "and it will not be as bad as it really is...."[2] As the rebels reeled, Cornwallis headed to North Carolina to continue recruiting loyalists. All the territory to his south was under British control except for pockets of American militia operating in remote areas.

A chastened Gates lamented that "as unfortunate generals are most commonly recalled, I expect that will be my case."[3] He was correct. In October, Gates was relieved of his command, and the American army was once again in search of leadership in the South. In the past, Congress chose the generals for the southern campaigns, selecting first Robert Howe, then Benjamin Lincoln, and finally Gates. But now the choice was left to Washington.

The commander in chief did not need to deliberate long and hard, nor to search far and wide. In an army where inexperienced generals and soldiers alike had learned the art of war by fighting a war, few men's rise had been as impressive as that of Nathanael Greene.

Born the son of a Quaker anchor maker in Rhode Island, Greene lacked much formal education but compensated with an avid intellect. He had assumed responsibility of the family foundry in 1771, but his career as a businessman was derailed when the colonies declared their independence. In the late summer of 1774 Greene, then a member of his colony's legislature, helped form the Kentish Guards, a sharply dressed Rhode Island militia. As a private in the guards, Greene had zero military experience. But he had feverishly studied every book and manual on the history and craft of war he could lay his hands on.[4]

Politically connected, Greene was named a brigadier general in 1776. He soon matched his theoretical military expertise with actual battlefield experience. He grew close to Washington; they were together during the disastrous early days of the war. Greene maneuvered troops skillfully at Trenton, Princeton, Brandywine, and Monmouth Courthouse. Though he dreaded the duty, preferring a field command, Greene assumed the role of Quartermaster General during the terrible winter at Valley Forge. For two years he imposed order on the army's procurement and transportation of supplies, though the work nearly brought him to blows with Congress and eventually led to his resignation in August 1780. Washington then installed him as commander at West Point, where he ably supervised the trial of John André.

Plump in body, with a sharp wit and steel-blue eyes, an asthmatic cough that interrupted his sleep, and a stiff knee that gave him a pronounced limp, Greene did not quite have Washington's impressive bearing, but the two had confidence in one another. Generals and subordinates had come and gone during the war, but Greene remained close to the commander in chief, serving as his true second-in-command and absorbing the tactical lessons from four years of fighting.

Tellingly, on the very day Congress granted Washington leeway to select a general of his choosing to take control of the southern theater, October 22, he offered the position to Greene. Both men understood the complexity of the task at hand. Before his departure Gates had begun to reconstruct the army, and in an important boon to the American cause, had talked his old friend the seasoned artillery tactician Daniel Morgan out of retirement. But there was no American army to speak of in the South, only the remnants of Gates's force and a number of militias of varying value spread out across the region. "I can give you no particular instructions," Washington gravely wrote, "but must leave you to governor yourself entirely according to your own prudence and judgment and the circumstances in which you find yourself."[5]

Before Greene was a daunting task requiring improvised tactics and irregular strategy. Washington was sending him southward with a formidable weapon: "I have put Major Lee's Corps under marching orders, and as soon as he is ready, shall detach him to join you."[6]

At the time, Lee was in New Jersey, along the banks of the Passaic River with the Marquis de Lafayette preparing for an imminent attack on Staten Island. Thus he was unable to confer with Greene in person before the general's departure. But Lee was clearly itching for the new assignment. "I wish to know whether we go and when," he wrote Greene on October 23. "My anxiety to forward the great game before you, leads me to an inclination of being employed instantly. My troops can follow."[7]

Despite his eagerness, something stood in the way of Lee's departure: the matter of promotion. "I have hitherto contemned rank, I have declined offers made me," Lee wrote Greene on October 25. "If I go south my opinion on this point alters."[8] Lee's reputation across the American army was extraordinary; Lafayette described him as "the best officer of light infantry in the English, Hessian or American armies on the continent."[9] Now was the time to reap the reward for his service in the coin of rank. When Lee did not receive a response from Greene, he made the request again four days later. Though he claimed to scorn titles and their value, Lee complained of the "inattention" that had been paid to his achievements. In the meantime, Congress had approved sending Lee's force south, and Captain Michael Rudulph of the Legion was on his way to Philadelphia to work with the Board of War to gather supplies and horses.

While Lee was imploring Greene for the elevation in rank, the general was on his way south, stopping in Philadelphia and every state capital along his route to make his own plea: more men and material were needed to construct what he termed a "flying army" of cavalry and infantry—for which Greene of course needed Lee and his Legion. Writing to Samuel Huntington, the president of the Continental Congress, he pressed the case for Lee—whose work he described as "generally known and so universally confessed that it is altogether superfluous for me to say anything in their commendation"—to get his promotion. The Board of War debated Greene's request and eventually, on November 6, made Lee lieutenant colonel.[10] The new rank would not erase Lee's insecurities, or cure his suspicion that deficient attention was paid to his heroics.

For four years Lee had roved across the Northwest, bounding between Pennsylvania and New Jersey, enduring icy winters, battling British regulars and German mercenaries in fields and valleys, planning raids along the Hudson River. Now the landscape was low mountains, secluded swamps, and stocky palmetto trees. He had fought against Americans loyal to King George III. But in the South he would confront the face of true fratricide.

Lee's journey south was not a particularly quick or pleasant one. By the seventeenth of November a portion of the Legion departed by boat from Head of Elk, where they had trouble even finding beds to sleep in. Lee dispatched his commanders McLane, Peyton, and Rudulph with letters to the governors of Delaware, Maryland, Pennsylvania, and Virginia, requesting additional men. But there were very few soldiers or supplies to spare in these war-ravaged states. Once again Lee spent from his own his fortune to procure horses and equipment.[11] Still, when Lee finally reached Greene's headquarters near Cheraw, on the Pee Dee River in the upper reaches of South Carolina, his forces had dwindled. South Carolina governor John Rutledge was on hand when the Legion, elegantly outfitted, strode into camp. "Col. Lee arrived yesterday, with his legion about 260," he informed his state's delegates in Congress. "I like him very much and expect great service from his corps."[12] Lee was less sanguine about the situation. "I am confident nothing important can be accompanied by this army in its present state," he confessed to Anthony Wayne.

Lee had been in camp but a single day when he received his first orders from Greene: cross the Pee Dee River—a tributary running from North Carolina into the northeast corner of its Southern neighbor—and ride to a remote spot called Snow's Island to meet with Brigadier General Francis Marion. Since joining the army, Lee had fought alongside and for men who differed widely from him in background and disposition. But none as much as Marion.

Born near Charleston to a family of Huguenots who had settled in South Carolina to escape French persecution, Marion was twenty years Lee's senior. At the age when the Virginian was journeying to the College of New Jersey, Marion was aboard a six-man schooner bound for the West Indies; his parents apparently believed the voyage would toughen the small and sickly child. On its return trip to America the vessel was struck by a whale and capsized. The crew managed to escape into a lifeboat, in which they drifted for five days under a blazing sun subsisting on only the blood and meat of a small dog.

As an adult Marion prospered as a farmer and fought the Cherokee on the western border of South Carolina. With the arrival of the Revolution, Marion joined his state's militia. Fatefully, he avoided being caught in the siege of Charleston in 1780 because a leap from a two-story building to escape a drunken party had broken his ankle and he was recuperating outside of the city.[13]

After recovering, Marion disappeared into the countryside and formed his own band of militia, reappearing to aggrieve the invading British by launching surprise attacks and quick retreats against larger forces. Marion's knowledge of the boggy Carolina terrain and the patriotic leanings of the population of the areas he prowled made him impossible to capture. Banastre Tarleton, sent to end this headache, once chased Marion and his men for twenty-six miles and seven hours before the Americans vanished into a swamp. "As for this damned old fox, the Devil himself could not catch him," Tarleton shrugged. The Englishman's lament gave Marion his nom de guerre: the Swamp Fox.[14]

In the winter of 1781, Lee and his Legion were on their way to the fox's nest. Their progress there was hindered by rains that had swelled the Pee Dee River by nearly twenty-five feet. To expedite the journey, Lee jettisoned his baggage wagons and equipped each of his men with ball and powder to defend himself and hardtack and beef jerky for sustenance.[15]

Lee was traveling towards Marion with a plan: The two of them, he proposed to Greene, would join forces and attack the British garrison in the seaport town of Georgetown. "Be assured of my zeal," Lee wrote the general as he made his way to Marion.[16] Lee and the Swamp Fox did have at least one common trait: they shared a jealousy of status and a sensitivity to perceived slights. Before Lee arrived, Marion wrote to Greene expressing desire that he would command their joint efforts. When Lee dispatched Michael Rudulph to ride ahead, meet with Marion, and pitch the proposed attack, he received a cold reception.

The partnership between Lee, who drank wine from silver chalices, and Marion, who subsisted strictly on a mixture of vinegar and water, seemed ill-starred from the beginning. But when the Legion in their immaculate uniforms finally did arrive at Snow's Island with its towering cypress trees emerging from the green swamp, Marion's scruffy men, many of whom did not even have uniforms, were overjoyed. And Marion and Lee, despite their differences, took to one another. The plan to attack Georgetown was revisited and agreed upon.[17]

On the night of January 24, the Legion and Marion's militia advanced separately on Georgetown. Two of Lee's infantry troops, led by Patrick Carnes and Michael Rudulph, arrived by boat, while Lee and Marion, leading the artillery, came overland. The designated rendezvous time was midnight. Beyond the

Georgetown garrison was a British force numbering over two hundred, led by Lieutenant George Campbell.

Once ashore Carnes seized Campbell in his headquarters while Rudulph positioned his troop to fire on the garrison once the enemy appeared. But thanks to a befuddled guide, Lee and Marion arrived late. By the time the forces were reunited and stormed the town they found the British, now alerted to the attack, barricaded in their quarters. Without battering rams, and fearing that the cost of taking the fort would be too great, Lee and Marion abandoned the attack. By morning they were en route back to Snow's Island. When Lee wrote to apprise Greene of the attack and praise the performance of his men, he omitted any reference to Marion. But the Swamp Fox was impressed by his new partner, telling Greene, "Col. Lee's enterprising genius promises much."[18]

Any future collaboration, though, would have to wait. The day before the attempt to take Georgetown, Greene had written Marion with heartening news. Shortly after taking command in the South, the newly arrived general was plotting a bold move: Greene divided the American army in half, ordering Daniel Morgan southwest to harass the British in the South Carolina backcountry. Cornwallis responded by sending Tarleton in pursuit, and he chased Morgan across the top of South Carolina for several days before their forces clashed on a frigid morning in a pasture used for cattle grazing, known locally as Hannah's Cowpens. Tarleton pushed his men into battle in his usual brash style, underestimating both Morgan and the mostly militia army under his command. Within an hour hundreds of British soldiers and their loyalist allies were killed or captured; those who survived the rout, Tarleton included, were on the run.[19]

The British strategy had failed. In the streets of occupied Charleston, the faces of Tories turned sour with worry. Upon hearing of the debacle at Cowpens, a furious Cornwallis took off after Morgan, who had moved across the Catawba River into North Carolina. Nearing his quarry, the British general burned his army's tents, stores of salts, and wagons to accelerate its advance. Greene rode to reconnoiter with Morgan. Fearing that the divided American army was vulnerable to British attack, he ordered his lieutenant Isaac Huger to guide the main army to the town of Salisbury along the eastern banks of the Yadkin River and give word to Lee to join them at once.[20]

Lee, camping at Port's Ferry, one of Marion's fortifications along the Pee Dee River, balked. Two of his cavalry troops were elsewhere and not expected back for several days. What Lee did not realize was that for his march north Greene was relying on the protection of North Carolina's raw and scant militia; he had only 60 dragoons at his disposal—and Tarleton had 250. Greene desperately needed Lee's Legion to form a rear guard against the advancing Cornwallis as he raced his army towards and across the Dan River, which separated North Carolina from Virginia.

But Lee lingered. Huger wrote again, giving voice to Greene's own anxiety; without cavalry the American army could not fight off the enemy to its rear. Huger, familiar with Lee's character, also tried another tack: he congratulated the lieutenant colonel on his "partial success" at Georgetown but warned him that if he did not rejoin the rest of the army forthrightly, Lee would "lose the opportunity of acquiring wreaths of laurels."[21]

By February 3, Lee had yet to depart. He was fixated on other glorious endeavors. Ever self-assured, he had boldly offered unsolicited strategic advice to Washington, and now he did the same to Greene. If the general would send him additional infantry and cavalry, Lee could drive south, fire up wavering patriots, and liberate South Carolina and Georgia. "Pardon the freedom of this address, it results from zeal for the good of America," Lee added, acknowledging his nerve. But the plan was beyond impractical. The survival of Greene's army, and American independence, depended on a safe retreat to Virginia. And that could not be accomplished without Lee.

It was not until February 7 that Lee began his trek north. By then the rest of the army had reassembled at Guilford Courthouse, in the northern reaches of North Carolina. Lee arrived there two days later. As Greene moved north, the general threw a rearguard between the retreating American army and the advancing British. This bulwark numbered seven hundred men, including Lee's Legion, and was to be led by Morgan. The victory at Cowpens, however, was that general's swan song: plagued by sciatica and rheumatism, Morgan resigned his commission in miserable pain to return home to Virginia. And the command went instead to Otho Holland Williams, a Marylander whose service in the war stretched back to the siege of Boston.

As Greene guided his army towards Virginia, Williams placed his newly organized corps, with Lee in the rear, between it and Cornwallis, who was busy searching for a fordable spot of the Yadkin. Through rain and snow, across alternatively frozen and muddy roads, the armies raced in dramatic fashion towards the Dan River. Initially the British followed Williams, who was intentionally drawing the Redcoats off the path of the rest of the American army while avoiding a direct confrontation. The march was a grueling one; during daylight the British vanguard, led by General Charles O'Hara, was in sight, but by night the Americans had to lengthen the distance between the two forces to avoid an attack under the cover of darkness. Both sleep and nourishment were scarce as half of the soldiers kept watch on alternating nights and the corps resumed their march at 3:00 every morning, meaning that each man slept six hours in two days and had only one meal, breakfast, a day.[22]

With the British less than eight miles to his back, Williams detached Lee and several dragoons with orders to meet the advancing enemy while the rest of the troops crossed over the Haw River. On the morning of February 13, Williams and his men were sitting around their campfires cooking corncakes in a cold drizzle when a farmer named Isaac Wright rode into camp on a mangy colt. He had been burning brushwood in his field when into view came Cornwallis's advancing army—now, Wright claimed, only four miles away.

Not wishing to interrupt his men's breakfast, Williams sent Lee to verify this intelligence. Riding forward with a contingent of his men and with Wright as their guide, Lee saw no evidence of the British and decided to return to camp to resume his breakfast. Captain Armstrong and three other of Lee's dragoons would accompany the farmer the rest of the way to the spot where he claimed to have seen the enemy. But Wright refused to go farther unless furnished with a better horse, lest he fall behind the soldiers and their superior mounts. Lee acquiesced and ordered his bugler, a small, smooth-faced boy named James Gillies, to dismount and trade horses with Wright. Gillies was then sent back to camp to tell Williams that there was no sign of the enemy. Lee and the remainder of the dragoons with him moved back into the woods adjacent to the road and cantered slowly back toward camp. Moments later he heard muskets fire and saw Armstrong and the other dragoons hurtling by, the enemy at their heels.

At once his focus was on the unarmed bugler, Gillies. While Armstrong and the others sped off, the British easily caught up with the young boy, whose only means of defense, a pistol, was with the equipment on the horse he had traded to Wright. The boy was ripped from the saddle, thrown to the ground, and gutted with bayonets. Lee, approaching the scene in hopes of a rescue, arrived too late. Overcome with fury, he lost his composure. Lee spurred his fellow soldiers on to meet the British, many of whom were drunk. Their captain, David Miller, turned to face Lee, but his men were no match for the vengeful Americans. Lee's dragoons, their broadswords drawn and slashing, slaughtered the small party. One of Lee's men, Sergeant Robert Power, killed two Redcoats with his bare hands; another, Thomas Broom, hacked off half the head of a British dragoon, whose sword clanked to the ground along with his body. The bloodthirsty Americans left the ground covered with the dead. The few who did survive, including Miller, were quickly caught and battered and dragged to Lee who, overcome with rage, informed the captain he was about to die. He coldly offered Miller a pencil and ordered him to scribble any last words for the world to read. But before Lee could take vengeance for the slaughter of the boy, shots rang out from the American rearguard warning that the British vanguard was approaching. The Americans hurried back to Williams with their prisoners, and Williams spared Miller's life. Lee's men had left a road littered with eighteen dead Englishmen in their wake, a monument to their leader's unleashed fury. For the sake of speed, Gillies's lifeless body was dumped in the woods to be buried later by a local patriot by the last name of Bruce.[23]

Cornwallis soon marched by this carnage and onward, but not toward Williams. Instead, thanks to intelligence gained from an American prisoner, the ruse was up: Cornwallis now knew that Williams was diverting them from Greene's path. The rest of the American army was preparing to cross the Dan River at a spot called Irwin's Ferry, where every boat available on that body of water had been gathered. Cornwallis was now marching on the road that led directly to them. As fate would have it, Lee too was on this narrow road, having learned earlier that it would provide a shortcut that led back to Williams and the rest of the light corps, on their way to the Dan.

Lee's course was also directed by hunger: he knew of a farm on this route, owned by Andrew Boyd, where his men could find a meal. Unaware that the British were nearby and traveling the same road, Lee stationed only a handful of sentinels outside the farmhouse. While the Legion were eating their bacon and their unbridled horses chewed oats, the guards suddenly fired their pistols. The British were at hand. Boyd's farm was bound by a creek, much swollen by recent rains and unfordable by any other means than a bridge. A stunned Lee ordered his infantry to rush forward to take this bridge, while his cavalry moved to protect the fleeing guards. Startled to encounter the Americans, the British paused to organize a march. In doing so, they squandered time and opportunity, allowing Lee's men to scramble across the water. The British followed. A mile-long pursuit through farms ensued before the Legion regained the road leading to Irwin's Ferry and eventually rejoined Williams at Harts Old Stores.

The American army had begun to cross the Dan River on February 13; wagons and stores went across first, the men followed. On the next day the light troops, still some thirty miles away from Irwin's Ferry, with Williams in the lead and Lee in the rear, marched hard and fast, in cold weather, through damp air, and across frozen roads. On the evening of the fourteenth, as they continued their breakneck pace, the Americans saw in the distance the fires flickering of what appeared to be a camp.

Lee and Williams feared they had come upon Greene with the British army only miles behind them, and that they would now be forced to square off against the larger force. But this was a false alarm: the camp was indeed Greene's, but it had been abandoned several days ago. After two hours of sleep, they resumed the trek.

Greene, who had not slept for hours and had endured the near total desertion of the North Carolina militia, had written to Williams in the wee hours of February 14 ordering him to come on to the river. By the following afternoon, the army was across and waiting for the light troops. When word that the army had made it to Virginia reached Williams's men the next day, a cheer went up so loud that it was audible to the British still giving chase. At 3:00 p.m. on the fifteenth, Williams pulled up fifteen miles from the Dan. He ordered his men to cross at Boyd's Ferry and Lee to remain behind to cover them in case the British arrived. By nightfall, Williams and his men were across, guided by torches; they had reached Virginia. Lee and his Legion followed. The infantry crossed first and sent the boats back for the cavalry who, with their horses to lead across the water, trailed. The last boat, carrying Lee and Lieutenant Colonel Carrington, reached the Virginia banks of the Dan River with the British not far behind. Thanks in no small part to Lee and his Legion, the American army had dodged Cornwallis and made it to safety. On the sixteenth, Cornwallis, exhausted from the pursuit, repaired toward Hillsborough. A month later, when the British general explained to his nation's Secretary of State, Lord George Germain, how exactly Greene had eluded his grasp and escaped across the Dan, he specifically cited "the enemy's light troops."[24]

Despite their fatigue and famine, the rebels, camped near the town of Halifax, were ecstatic. But as the soldiers shared sustenance and stories, Greene's mind was across the swollen river. The safety it afforded was false, and he knew it. With North Carolina left to Cornwallis, the British would regroup, resupply, and redouble their efforts to recruit loyalists. The American general was in dire need of numbers and pressed Thomas Jefferson, the governor of Virginia, and North Carolina's legislature for reinforcements. He also made a strategic decision: the enemy had given chase, and the Americans had retreated. Now Greene would pursue Cornwallis. And first he would send Lee and the light troops back across the Dan to hound him before the armies finally fought.

Lee, his Legion augmented by two companies of Marylanders commanded by Edward Oldham, glided back across the Dan, camped at Hycotee Creek, and joined forces with a North Carolina militia led by Andrew Pickens, a devout and stern Presbyterian, and that state's answer to Francis Marion. Pickens was a determined guerilla warrior who had fought heroically at Cowpens.

On the night of February 20, Cornwallis arrived at Hillsborough, just twenty miles away. Lee and Pickens, after some delay, finally assembled on the morning of the twenty-third. The meeting was nearly a bloody one: Pickens's men, who had stopped at a farm to rest and forage, were jolted out of their sleep when their rearguard announced the arrival of Tarleton. Pickens hurried his men into formation, but before shots were fired the militiamen realized it was Lee and his cavalry, whose short green tunics were similar to those worn by Tarleton's legion.[25]

Once the two forces were gathered, Greene himself ventured back across the Dan to tell Lee and Pickens of his plans: in the coming days he would bring the entire army back into North Carolina; the confrontation with Cornwallis was coming. Once the general had returned to Virginia, Lee dispatched officers towards Hillsborough; in time one returned with word of a sighting of Tarleton. Off the Americans went in pursuit, along a trail guided by desolation—in their wake, the British had left roads littered with ransacked homes. All the men had fled, with only their wives remaining to greet Lee and his men as they rode by.[26]

Crossing the Haw River, the Americans were informed by a local that Tarleton was close, feeding his troops at a farm three miles ahead. Lee and Pickens dashed forward prepared to attack, but when they arrived at the farm Tarleton had already departed. Here Lee conceived a plan: he would ride forward with two captured enemy soldiers placed in the midst of the cavalry and pass the American force off as reinforcements sent by Cornwallis.

So the Americans, led by Lee, moved on, hoping to overtake Tarleton. Instead they came upon two young men who were overjoyed to see them. They were looking for Tarleton too, but with a much different motivation. They belonged to a militia led by John Pyle, a British-born American loyalist who had trained as a doctor in London. Captured early in the war, Pyle had been forced to take an oath of loyalty to North Carolina in late 1776. But the arrival of Cornwallis had emboldened loyalists, and in the previous months Pyle had recruited four hundred men to his loyalist militia. He was now looking for Tarleton, who would collect and guide them to Hillsborough.[27]

The two loyalists Lee had just encountered believed that Lee was actually Tarleton and he did nothing to convince them otherwise. Instead Lee acted the part. He sent one of the two men back to Pyle with the request that he clear off the main road, so that Lee's force, which the loyalists still believed to be Tarleton's, could pass by on their way to camp for the night.[28]

Pyle obliged. Slowly the Legion marched past his men, who were waiting on the right side of the road with their rifles resting on their shoulders. Along the way a smiling Lee looked on approvingly at the loyalists, complimenting them as he trotted by. When he finally reached the militia's leader, Lee greeted Pyle warmly. But just as the two grasped hands, an explosion erupted near the rear of the cavalry.[29]

To Lee's back were members of Pickens's militia, as well as some of his own officers. Many of the former had originally thought that Pyle's men were actually members of a rebel regiment until they spotted a red stripe on their hats—the mark Tories used for identification. So Captain Joseph Eggleston asked one of Pyle's soldiers whose side he was on. "A friend of the Majesty," he replied. Eggleston responded by smashing the loyalist's head. Now all hell broke loose.

Pickens's men attacked Pyle's. Alarmed by the noise behind him, Lee swiveled and dashed into the action. The loyalists, unable to train and fire their weapons in time, were helpless. The Americans attacked with uncontrolled ferocity, hacking Pyle's men to death, as the confused and panicked loyalists screamed "You are killing your own men!" and "Hurrah for King George!!" Some of Pyle's men were able to grab their rifles and fire at Lee's men, but to little effect: a horse was the only casualty.[30]

The scene eventually deteriorated into total confusion: pausing before they attacked, Lee's men asked of their victims "which side are you on?" before disemboweling them. The scene was savage; broken and bent swords were scattered among the bodies of ninety dead loyalists. Remembering the Waxhaws massacre, where Abraham Buford's men had been slaughtered while surrendering to Tarleton, six prisoners were hacked to death as their executioner screamed, "Remember Buford!!!" Lee attempted futilely to wrest control of the chaos, screaming at his scattered men to form a line.[31]

This was unlike anything Lee had witnessed before. It was civil war, Americans hewing Americans.

He had been sent back to North Carolina to dissuade loyalists from joining Cornwallis to support the King's cause. In horrifying fashion, Pyle's Hacking Match, as it would be known, did exactly that. Americans contemplating casting their lot with the British would remember this massacre and think twice about doing so—frustrating Cornwallis's push to carry the war farther north and keep the South under his thumb.

Once Lee was able to regain control of his men, it was soon discovered that Tarleton was only three miles away. Hoping to find details of the surrounding terrain, he demanded that one of Pyle's soldiers be brought to him for questioning. A middle-aged man named Holt was dragged from the disorder, blood dripping from his wounded head. When the questioning came to a pause and Lee was lost in thought, Holt spoke. "Well God bless your soul, Mr. Tarleton," he said confusedly, "you have this day killed a parcel of as good subjects as ever his majesty ever had." At which point Lee broke his silence: "You dammed rascal, if you call me Tarleton, I will take off your head," he roared. "I will undeceive you: We are the Americans and not the British. I am Lee of the American Legion, and not Tarleton." Holt looked at him in shock.[32]

Lee and Pickens continued to chase Tarleton but eventually abandoned hopes of that prize when the pursuit brought them too close to Cornwallis. A bigger fight was imminent, in any case. On February 23, Greene and the American army, having secured promises of direly needed reinforcements from Virginia, came back across the Dan. Word of their return prompted Cornwallis to recall Tarleton. For the following two weeks, Lee's Legion, part of a larger screening force commanded once again by Otho Holland Williams and including William Washington's dragoons, constantly patrolled the spaces between the main British and American armies in anticipation of their eventual meeting. Riding hundreds of miles on mud-clogged roads, Lee was in his element, keeping constant tabs on the enemy, providing intelligence, and—as was his custom—offering unsolicited advice to Greene.

On the morning of March 2, as Cornwallis moved west of Hillsborough towards the village of Alamance, Lee and the light troops ambushed Tarleton near a mill belonging to a farmer named Barney Clapp. The Americans fired off multiple rounds in woods so thick that twigs and bark flew through the air, hitting Lee's men in their faces, before they retreated in the face of advancing British bayonets.[33]

Three days later, realizing that the Reedy Fork Creek of the Haw River was isolating the American screening force from the main army, the British, led by Tarleton and Lieutenant Colonel James Webster, rushed through a morning fog to cut off access to the only fordable portion of the river, near a mill owned by Adam Weitzel. An alert sentry notified Williams of the coming attack, and the Americans evacuated over the river while Lee's Legion and newly arrived Virginia riflemen were able to hold off the British. Williams guided the rest of the force ten miles ahead to cross the river. Once across he wheeled the Americans around to stand against the British effort to ford the creek; the enemy's initial advance was blocked, but a second one, supervised by Webster, succeeded, forcing the light troops to retreat toward the main army, three miles away.[34]

Instead of pursuing Greene, Cornwallis moved east, toward Bells Mill beside the Deep River. Greene, meanwhile, was waiting on promised reinforcements to arrive from Maryland, North Carolina, and Virginia; he was "vexed to my soul" by disaffected militiamen who, believing they had been used as fodder to protect the continentals, had departed for Virginia.[35] Greene now folded the screening force commanded by Williams back into the larger army, situated north of the Haw River, and replaced it with scouting parties led by Lee and William Washington. On the evening of March 9 Lee reported to Greene that Cornwallis was moving towards Guilford Courthouse, where the Americans had sent their stores and rendezvoused before crossing into Virginia the previous month.[36]

The following day Greene, still waiting to supplement his army with militia, forwarded some four hundred riflemen to join Lee, along with the instructions to guard the British left flank; Washington would take the right. The day after that, Lee, buzzing around the British camps, communicated perplexing news to Greene: Cornwallis had moved towards the American army, then retraced his steps and headed back to Guilford Courthouse. The enemy, Lee speculated, had developed apprehensions about an attack. "If you dare, get near him," the ever-aggressive Lee recommended to his general.[37]

But Cornwallis would be the one to take the initiative.

On the morning of March 15 the British sent their baggage to a mill owned by William Bell on the Deep River, along with a considerable force to protect it, and moved northwest along the New Garden Road toward Greene.

At the time Lee was posted within two miles of Guilford Courthouse. A courier from an officer Lee had sent to scout out the enemy had heard the wheels of the British supply train in motion. Greene ordered Lee forward to verify whether the British army was indeed coming towards his own. At 4:00 a.m. the

Legion was roused and set off towards the British, with Lee and the cavalry leading the way and the infantry and riflemen behind. Two miles into their trek they ran into an American scouting party headed in the opposite direction, in retreat—from Tarleton.

Lee turned his entire force around and galloped it back towards the main army, along a narrow road bounded by long fences, with the British at their heels, discharging their pistols only feet away. Lee ordered his troops to turn, form a column and rush forward, smashing into Tarleton's men, many of whom were dismounted and their horses slain.

Tarleton ordered a retreat back towards the British army, but Lee followed by an alternative route, hoping to cut him off at a nearby Quaker meeting house before he could reach Cornwallis. But the British reached the house before the Americans could and opened fire. A brilliant morning sun was now overhead, its rays beaming off the steel of the British bayonets, and startling Lee's mount, a beautiful but feisty chestnut sorrel. The horse reared, its rider hurled from its back. A nearby dragoon swooped in, jumped off his own horse, and helped his leader back into his saddle.[38]

Pushed back after combating the British and Hessian soldiers, Lee rejoined the main American army at Guilford Courthouse and informed Greene that Cornwallis was close at hand now. In preparation, Greene positioned his army in three lines, separated by hundreds of yards. The North Carolina militiamen were out front behind a rail fence in a clearing cut through by the Great Salisbury road, which led to the Courthouse; to their rear on a ridge, their Virginian counterparts; and lastly, some three hundred feet to the militia's rear, the seasoned Continentals. William Washington's dragoons and a regiment of Delaware Continentals were on the right flank; Lee's Legion and Campbell's riflemen took the left.

In the late morning shots were fired by the Americans' six-pound cannons. The British responded in kind and, their wings led by Alexander Leslie and James Webster, moved forward towards the rebel front line. As they approached, Lee prowled back and forth among the militiamen; one Tar Heel, David Williams, looked up and saw him brandishing a blood-stained sword, in his face a "great rage for battle." Lee exhorted the rebels to "give Tarleton Hell," and reassured them that they had no reason to fear the enemy. He had whipped them three times already that morning and would most certainly do it again.[39]

But his words could not transform the raw militia into reliable soldiers. When the scarlet-clad 71st Highlander Regiment appeared through clouds of gray smoke, the militiamen did fire a deadly first round, mowing down half of the approaching Highlanders. But few fired a second time as the British shot back, fixed bayonets, and charged. Many of the American militia threw down their muskets and ran into the adjacent woods. Lee screamed at the deserters, threatening to turn his cavalry on them, but still they ran. Now the enemy advanced towards the second line; the Virginians fired their volleys and gave fight, some of it desperate and hand to hand. The roar of muskets and rattle of rifles was deafening. After the American right collapsed, the militiamen fell back towards the Continentals, the final line. The British pressed forward, gaining ground but losing men along the way.[40]

Now they faced the most formidable portion of the American army. Irregular fights were scattered across the battlefield, and a rebel volley threw back the enemy's left, tearing apart the leg of their commander, Lieutenant Colonel James Webster. In the hot battle the 2nd Maryland Regiment, a body of largely inexperienced soldiers, was crushed by the British 2nd Guards

Battalion, who seized their artillery. The 1st Maryland Regiment, led by Otho Williams, counterattacked the 2nd Guards, retook the stolen six-pound cannon, and cut the Guards to pieces.

Cornwallis, who had already lost a horse, ordered a spray of grapeshot fired into the confusion, killing many of his own men but repelling the rebels. At 3:30 p.m. Greene ordered a retreat, and the Americans abandoned the field and moved with precision and order up the Reedy Creek Road.

The dead, the wounded, and the blood-drenched survivors were scattered across the field of battle. One Peter Francisco, a hulking Portuguese-born Virginian militiaman fighting alongside Williams's cavalry, stalked off the field soaked in blood, his sword crimson from hilt to tip.[41] But Henry Lee was missing.

When the enemy had confronted the North Carolina militia, British soldiers had pushed off towards the Legion and Campbell's riflemen on the American left, sequestering them from the remainder of the army. Pushed into the woods surrounding the Salisbury Road, Lee's infantry—he was holding the cavalry in reserve in case of a retreat—laid waste to the vaunted 1st Battalion of Guards before the Von Bose Hessian regiment came to their aid. When the Hessians and British fell back, Lee sent his cavalry to rejoin the Continental line and then followed them, battling another regiment of British guards along the way. When the Legion arrived at the courthouse they saw the 2nd Maryland Regiment and what was left of the North Carolina militia in retreat. Assuming the army had been decimated, Lee guided the Legion down the Great Salisbury road before diverting it to a crossroad that connected them with the main army.

Cornwallis, who had only feigned pursuit of the fleeing Americans, held the ground near Guilford Courthouse. But it was covered with the British dead and dying. He had aggressively confronted and beat a foe twice his numerical size. But the truth was that anything short of total annihilation of the American force was a British failure. Before the first shots had been fired, Greene had reasoned that if the Americans carried the day "it would prove ruinous to the Enemy, and if otherwise, it would only prove a partial evil to us." It had cost the British nearly 30 percent of their army to win the bloody Battle of Guilford Courthouse.[42]

Greene, though forced to retreat, was pleased by the pugnaciousness of his only recently constructed army and the damage it had inflicted on the enemy. In general orders issued the day after the battle, he cited Lee's gallant behavior. The Americans, far from defeated, were in high spirits and ready for another fight. Three days after the battle, Greene wrote to the governor of North Carolina, Abner Nash, "The Enemy's loss is very great, much more so than ours."[43]

As the Americans regrouped and prepared to fight on, the gloom that had surrounded their cause in the South was dispelled. The British, exhausted and crippled, remained on the battlefield, two hundred miles away from their stores to the east in Camden. On the night of March 15, storm clouds arrived and unleashed forty hours of pouring rain on their army, making it nigh impossible to care for the wounded. The British had won the Battle of Guilford Courthouse, but it was a victory from which they would not recover.

# 8

# A FATAL STAB TO THE BRITISH TYRANT

At 3:00 in the morning a sentinel's shot pierced the still spring air. The blare of a bugle followed. Troubled sentries hurried to report the muffled sound of an army approaching. The Legion grabbed their arms and prepared to fight. But no enemy appeared. Their leader wondered if, at such an hour, his troops were imagining the sounds.

But then another shot, from another guard, stationed in another part of camp, dispelled that thought. The men reoriented themselves to face the latest warning. Then still another warning shot rang out from elsewhere. One more erupted from the Legion's rear. Now, a horrified Henry Lee, his men camped in an expansive field near a tributary of the Little Pee Dee River, realized that his Legion was facing a likely hopeless fight with the entire British army.

The main American army was at least three days' march away. The Legion was seemingly surrounded. So running was not an option, and help, in the form of South Carolina's militias, was nowhere near. Lee quietly arranged his men into lines of cavalry and infantry and steeled them for battle as the sun rose. But when daylight emerged and the Americans began to move, preparing to encounter British fire at any moment, the enemy was nowhere to be seen. What did come into view were the tracks of wolves. Provisions that had been gathered for the army and left nearby had rotted, attracting the animals, who circled Lee and his Legion.[1]

For a rare moment Lee was prey rather than predator.

It was April of 1781; a month had passed since the Battle of Guilford Courthouse. In the days following that hot and bloody conflict, with the British army triumphant but staggering, Nathanael Greene hoped to stage a rematch forthwith. On March 18, three days after the battle, Lord Cornwallis finally began to move his tattered army away towards Wilmington. They crawled to Ramsey's Mill, a spot on the Deep River, named for its owner, a member of the state's legislature. After two days there, replenishing themselves as best they could, the British constructed a bridge of rocks from the mill's dam to cross the river and move east.[2] But Lee and his Legion were lurking in their shadow, preparing to fight "on the shortest notice."[3]

While the British departed and the bulk of the American army, thirteen miles east of Guilford Courthouse at the Iron Works upon Troublesome Creek, composed itself—tending to the injured, finding provisions—Greene sent Lee to keep track of Cornwallis's progress in anticipation of an American attack. Lee was ordered to destroy the British-built bridge spanning the Deep River, trapping Cornwallis to its west while the rebel army arrived to reengage. But the Americans, in need of provisions and magazines, moved too slowly. By the time Greene arrived at Ramsey's Mill, on March 28, the British had crossed the river and moved on towards Wilmington.[4]

The Americans camped at Ramsey's Mill near the border between the Carolinas, where Greene faced a great strategic dilemma. Earlier in the year, Benedict Arnold, leading his legion composed mostly of American loyalists, had cruised up the James River, landed in the Virginia town of Westover, and marched uncontested into the capital city of Richmond. Governor Thomas Jefferson, hurriedly removing military stores, had fled to Charlottesville, and Arnold had looted and torched the Virginia capital. George Washington, in response, had ordered the Marquis de Lafayette south along with twelve hundred soldiers to pin down Arnold with the aid of a French fleet. A naval battle between the French and British at Cape Henry in the Chesapeake Bay had proven inconclusive, allowing Arnold to be reinforced by two thousand men and continue to terrorize Virginia.

As Greene deliberated on where he would next take his army, one possibility suggested by his officers was to protect the vital state of Virginia, not only as a source of reinforcements, but also as a link between the American armies, North and South. Others, though, proposed that he chase after Cornwallis and provoke the battle Greene had hoped for in the days immediately after Guilford Courthouse.

The American general chose neither.

Rather than attempting to save Virginia or pursuing Cornwallis, Greene decided to return to and liberate South Carolina. The main American army would target the major British strongholds in that state, while Lee, teaming with Francis Marion, would tear into the state's interior and knock out the string of British posts stretching west from the Atlantic Coast and essential to communications and recruitment. If Cornwallis followed him, Greene reasoned, the British general would be abandoning North Carolina; if he did not follow, the British posts would be at the mercy of Lee and Marion. The decision was not reached easily; Greene conferred with his officers, some of whom objected to the plan.[5] By the end of March, his mind was made up, and Greene wrote to Washington to describe the strategy. "The Manoeuvre will be critical and dangerous; and the troops exposed to every hardship," he cautioned.[6]

Of Greene's subordinates, Lee was enthusiastic about the endeavor. "I am decidedly of opinion with you that nothing is left for you," he wrote Greene, "but to imitate the example of Scipio Africanus."[7] The reference was to the Roman general who had diverted his army away from the Italian peninsula and towards Carthage, the backyard of his antagonist Hannibal. As a boy at Leesylvania, and then a student at Princeton, Lee had obsessed over pivotal military strategies from the past and their executors; now he was helping conceive and perform them himself.

The plan was put into action on April 6, Greene marching the American army south, his sights set on Camden, while Lee's Legion, joined by a company of Maryland Continentals, headed across the Pee Dee River in search of Marion, then camped in the swamps of the Black River, a winding waterway in eastern South Carolina. When Lee, having sent two officers to locate his partner, arrived in Marion's camp after a march of eight days, the reaction among the Swamp Fox and his soldiers was euphoric.

The situation in South Carolina was grim.[8] Just the month before, Lord Francis Rawdon, the clever, pug-faced officer commanding the British garrison in Camden, had launched a two-pronged attack led by Major John Doyle and Colonel John Watson to finally exterminate the Swamp Fox. While Marion was busy fighting Watson, three miles away at Britton's Ferry Doyle, led there by a loyalist, raided and ransacked a virtually unprotected Snow's Island, tossing Marion's accumulation of stores and ammunition in a nearby creek.[9] Marion had lost over one hundred men, and many others had been wounded, or their homes burnt to the ground by the British. His force now stood at seventy downhearted and hungry warriors.

As Marion's men ate cold rice out of pots, one whispered to another about the sighting of a large number of Continental troops. The news was transmitted to Marion, and soon the entire camp gathered around, their eyes welling with tears at the arrival of desperately needed aid. The sound of drums was soon heard, and Major John Conyers and Captain Edmond Irby appeared, sent by Greene along with a number of Lee's dragoons to notify Marion of the army's new design and his new assignment with Lee. Later the same day, April 14, the remainder of the Legion arrived. Lee and Marion, happily reunited, now waged their war of posts.[10]

Their first target was Fort Watson.

Named for and built on orders from the British colonel pursing Marion, the outpost sat atop a thirty-foot-high Santee Indian burial mound with a view over both the river named for that tribe and the central road stretching from Charleston to Camden. Along this artery the British funneled vital stores and reinforcements. Wasting no time, Lee and Marion emerged from the woods surrounding Fort Watson on the afternoon of April 15 intending to block this path.

Inside, Lieutenant James McKay was commanding in place of Watson, with a combined force of forty men from the loyalist Kings American Regiment and eighty British regulars. A brief skirmish was followed by demands from Lee and Marion that McKay surrender the post. When this offer was rebuffed, the rebels plotted to make the enemy capitulate. Fort Watson's water supply was derived from Scott Lake, an outlet of the Santee River. Lee and Marion placed riflemen between the lake and the fort to block British access. McKay's men responded by digging a well.

With the siege dragging on, Lee wrote to Greene on the eighteenth, requesting that the general send a cannon so he could "finish the business...in five minutes." Greene declined, citing the risk of expending men to guard the field piece, given that the garrison at Camden, which the American army was approaching, was stronger than he had thought. Frustrated, Lee wrote Greene twice on April 20, restating the request for the cannon and asking for a hundred riflemen and a company of regulars to help conclude the operation. Again on the twenty-third, Lee wrote to Greene, describing himself as "miserable to find...that no field piece is on the way."[11]

While Lee waited, one of Marion's militiamen, Major Hezekiah Maham, suggested a solution: the Americans, putting down their muskets and picking up axes, would fell and chop trees from the surrounding woods and construct a long tower capped with a floor of logs. For two days the rebels worked on the tower, while McKay, lacking any artillery, could do little to stop its construction. On April 23 the Maham Tower, standing forty feet tall and higher than the fort's rampart, was finished and the Americans, led by Captain McCottrey, were atop the structure shooting down into the fort. While McKay's men scrambled to avoid the fire, the Americans dashed around the fort removing the abatis protecting it. The path was now cleared for an assault, and out came the white flag. Fort Watson had fallen.[12]

Meanwhile, to the south, Greene had arrived on the outskirts of Camden. Finally settling his army of some fifteen hundred men on an incline a mile north of the town, he prepared to provoke a fight with the British army, nine hundred men strong and mostly comprising loyalists. When a deserter from Maryland divulged Greene's order of battle and the fact that reinforcements were likely arriving soon in the form of Thomas Sumter and his militia, the British commander Francis Rawdon, his supply lines under assault by Lee and Marion, surmised that an advantageous time for the battle was at hand. In the late morning of April 25, the armies clashed. After initially repelling the British advance, the American army's fortunes fell when a break in its line forced Greene to order a retreat. Looking on from a hole he had carved with a razor blade in a wooden fence was a twelve-year-old boy named Andrew Jackson, then a British prisoner of war.

In the days that followed, Rawdon was reinforced by the arrival of Watson, who tried, with no success, to reengage Greene, now situated several miles to the north. With his stores dwindling and the team of Lee and Marion causing havoc on his supply line, Rawdon withdrew from Camden, leaving it in flames as he moved south.

Unable to block Watson from making his way to Camden, Lee and Marion reunited. But for a spell the future of the collaboration was in jeopardy. Lee had warned Greene that Marion's spirits were low and suggested the general send him a word of encouragement.[13] Months later, matters were worse after Greene had accused Marion of refusing to send horses to the regular army and allowing his men to pillage the property of loyalists. In response, Marion threatened to resign his commission. It was only when Greene, finally following Lee's advice, wrote Marion an eloquent note reminding him of the stakes in South Carolina and the important role he played in the fight there that this issue was diffused.

Now Lee and Marion moved on to their next target.

Rebecca Brewton Motte was, it seemed, haunted by the British army. The child of a wealthy Charleston family, she and her late husband Jacob had been supporters of American liberty from the beginning of the war. When her brother, Miles Brewton, a financial backer of the Revolution, was lost in the Atlantic in 1780, Rebecca inherited his Palladian home on Charleston's King Street and a plantation further inland.

When the British claimed Charleston months later, Sir Henry Clinton used Motte's home as his headquarters, and so did Rawdon once the city was under his supervision. Motte was forced to live in a small space with her three daughters while feeding and entertaining the British officers. When Rawdon permitted the Mottes to leave the city, they relocated to the family plantation, set on the spot where the Rivers Congaree and Wateree merge to form the Santee, in the heart of South Carolina. But the British, seeing the area's strategic importance as a depot for moving supplies westward from Charleston, followed her. Once again her house, a newly built three-story brick mansion situated on a high hill, was seized by the British. And the Redcoats, led by Lieutenant Colonel Donald McPherson, built an installation surrounded by a deep ditch, fortified by over 180 soldiers. The outpost was named Fort Motte; the Mottes, meanwhile, were exiled to an old farmhouse on an adjacent hill.[14]

On the morning of May 6, Lee and Marion arrived to liberate the Mottes' land. The former posted near the homestead; the latter, on the slope leading away from the fort, from which he trained a six-pound cannon, a gift from Greene, on the enemy installation. While Lee's men, with the assistance of local slaves they had impressed, excavated a trench in front of the fort, the Americans demanded that McPherson surrender. The demand was denied, as McPherson falsely believed that Rawdon, who had recently abandoned Camden, would come to his aid.

Lee and Marion grew tired of waiting. When the American ditch was within a few feet of the Motte Mansion, the rebels concluded that if cannons would not bring McPherson out, perhaps flames would. The troops were told to make bows and arrows. But Lee fretted about destroying Motte's home. During their siege, she had sheltered Lee and his officers, fed them well, and even opened her cellar—full of fine wines—to them. On the morning of May 12, Lee met with Motte and, with regret, informed her of his intention to burn the mansion. To his surprise, she was delighted. If sacrificing her home furthered the cause of American liberty, she would happily agree to it. And, as it happened, improbably, in her possession was a stash of arrows brought from the East Indies by a ship captain and presented to Motte's brother.

While the tips of these arrows were then being covered with a combustible wrap, Lee's courier, Dr. Mathew Irvine, went to the fort a final time to seek surrender from McPherson, who politely refused. Then the first arrow was set ablaze and launched from a rifle. When it failed to ignite, another was loaded and launched, with the same result. Then, finally, a third flaming arrow was hurled at the house, piercing and igniting its dry shingles. When McPherson ordered his men to climb to the roof to douse the fire, they were greeted with artillery shots. Out again went the white flag; now Fort Motte had fallen. Another vital link in the chain keeping the British army alive in South Carolina was gone.[15]

Before the Americans moved on to their next objective, Motte hosted the officers of both sides—the American victors and their British prisoners—at a grand dinner. But the conviviality was superficial. When the Americans departed on the thirteenth, they left behind gruesome mementos: the bodies of two loyalists, Lieutenant Fuller and John Jackson dangling from Motte's gatepost. Several American soldiers had been placing a noose around the neck of another loyalist, Levi Smith, when a furious Marion intervened. Who had ordered them to hang this or any man, he demanded to know. Colonel Lee, they replied.[16]

The British were evicted from Forts Motte and Watson. Rawdon, making his way east to Charleston, was reeling. And Greene refused to relent. On May 13 he ordered Lee to demand the surrender of Fort Granby at Friday's Ferry. "I depend upon you pushing matters vigorously." Built in and named—like the town it called home—for a British duke favorable to colonial independence, Fort Granby was a two-story trading post that had been commandeered by the British in 1780. Because of its strategic location on the Congaree River, the fort was another vital link in the British supply line. Behind its trenches were three hundred men, commanded by Andrew Maxwell, a loyalist from Maryland.[17]

Lee would take a new tack at Fort Granby. Hastily constructed towers or flaming arrows would be unnecessary. Maxwell had a notorious appetite for plunder. After Lee's Legion hailed musket fire on the fort, Maxwell was ready to capitulate—with a condition. He must be allowed to leave with his precious booty: horses, two carriages, and two pieces of artillery. Lee blanched at the idea of permitting Maxwell to flee with ill-gotten gains taken from local patriots. But when news arrived that Rawdon was approaching the fort, necessitating a quick end to the parley with Maxwell, Lee relented, and off Maxwell merrily went to meet with Rawdon, his looted treasure in tow. The terms of the surrender so infuriated local militia commander Thomas

Sumter, already annoyed by Lee's presence—"the Gamecock" believed that *he* could have taken Fort Granby, and done so without regulars, and was entitled to the swag behind its walls— that he resigned his commission.[18]

While Sumter was stewing, Lee was blazing across the South Carolina–Georgia border heading for Augusta, site of one of the few remaining British forts in the South, on Greene's orders. (The general, meanwhile was approaching Ninety-Six, the enemy's last outpost in South Carolina other than Charleston.) The ride from Fort Granby to Augusta was seventy-five miles. It took Lee and his Legion three days, riding at breakneck pace. "Your early arrival at Augusta astonishes me," Greene wrote Lee upon hearing the news. "For rapid marches you exceed Lord Cornwallis and everybody else."[19] Once into Georgia, Lee collaborated with Colonel Elijah Clarke, the lynchpin of the Georgia patriot militia. Also on his way to Augusta was Andrew Pickens.

Augusta, situated on the Savannah River, was taken by American loyalists led by Lieutenant Colonel Thomas Brown in 1780. At its heart was Fort Cornwallis, a garrison named after the British general. Two smaller outposts, Forts Galphin and Grierson, sat on the outskirts of the town. These would have to be subdued first. On the morning of May 21, Lee moved on the former, twelve miles south of the city. The Georgia air was dangerously humid, and his men, tired from their long march, had not a drop to drink. Arriving at the fort, which was little more than the two-and-a-half story brick home of an Indian trader named George Galphin, Lee placed the broiling members of his Legion in the pines surrounding it.

Inside the brick walls, a Tory named Samuel Rowarth commanded a force of two hundred of his fellow loyalists. In order to draw them out, Lee ordered members of Pickens's militia to attack and retreat. When they did, Rowarth and the bulk of his men charged out of the house after them. When the gates to the fortress swung open, Lee raced in, forcing the remaining loyalists inside to surrender. Rowarth was cut off from his lair and forced to surrender. Fort Galphin, along with its stores of blankets, ammunition, medicine, and tools, belonged to the rebels.

The following day Lee scaled a hill outside of Augusta and joined with Pickens and Clarke at its summit, gazing down below at Fort Cornwallis, the ultimate objective of this campaign. It was considerably better built and a harder prize to claim; its warden, the loyalist Thomas Brown, was a cagey and stubborn foe who would not easily be persuaded to surrender. Lee had tried just that, sending Joseph Eggelston under a flag of truce to Fort Cornwallis. General Greene's army was approaching, he had informed Brown—untruthfully—and now was the time to lay down his arms. Brown ignored the demand.

With a peaceful resolution foreclosed, Lee, Pickens, and Clarke were determined to isolate Brown by taking Fort Grierson. Constructed around the home of and commanded by loyalist Colonel James Grierson, the fort was connected to Fort Cornwallis, a mile to its north, by a gully. On May 22, the rebels, equipped with axes, swarmed into this ditch, scrambled towards the fort, and hacked away at its stockade. Grierson and his fellow loyalist bounded over the side of the fort and sprinted towards the safety of Fort Cornwallis. To secure their safe arrival, Brown provided a cover of cannon fire. Lee returned the favor, killing several loyalists with his artillery.

Other occupants of Fort Grierson who managed to escape the cannon blasts but did not make it to safety were taken prisoner. Several were in need of medical treatment. Lee sent a loyalist to Fort Cornwallis in order to collect the necessary medicine, reestablishing communication with Brown. (The loyalist commander had refused to surrender when the messenger was Eggelston, partly because he believed him to be a member of Clarke's militia. There was searing hatred between the amateur soldiers in the South, rebel and loyalist.)

This courtesy was short lived. Soon Lee and Pickens prepared to lay siege to the fort. Trenches were dug to its east and west. And, recalling the fit of ingenuity at Fort Watson, a new Maham Tower was built, this one thirty feet tall and stuffed with stones, bricks, mud, and rubbish; and with a six-pounder gun on its top platform, peaking over the fort's ramparts. Underneath, rebel riflemen took aim at the enemy in gaps between the turret's notched logs. Late-night raids launched by the loyalists had led to ferocious fighting in the trenches but did not thwart the construction of the tower.

As the militiamen continued to press towards the fort, some of them rolled up cowhides and draped them on the embankment, forming portholes to shoot through. Tarleton Brown, a captain in the South Carolina militia, looked on in horror as a young soldier named Stafford taking aim through one of the cowhides was blown away by a shot from the fort.[20] Lee and Pickens had again demanded Brown's surrender on May 31, and again he had declined. As the Americans erected their tower he even paraded his prisoners, including elderly men, along the parapets.

But by June 2, the loyalists, trapped by cannonade and rifle fire, were forced to retreat to small pockets of the fort, including caves in the walls, to find safety from the rebel fire. The two artillery pieces in the fort were destroyed. In a last bit of desperation, Brown slipped a Scottish sergeant—posing as a deserter who offered to help the Americans locate and blast Brown's powder magazine—out of the fort to set the tower ablaze. Lee, after initially entertaining the man's proposal, grew apprehensive and placed him under guard.

In one last effort to resist the attackers, Brown set fire to two houses near the fort, left two standing, dug a tunnel under them, and filled it with explosives, hoping that Lee and Pickens's men would take cover there during the attack. If they did, Brown would blow them to smithereens. But Pickens's men inspected the homes in the hours leading up to the attack and the buildings exploded shortly after they left.

On June 3, Lee and Pickens asked for surrender yet again, but Brown would not relent. So the final attack was set for the following day, which happened to be the birthday of King George III. Brown, now with no hope of escape, but desiring not to wave the white flag on the monarch's birthday, finally agreed to surrender—on the fifth. The negotiations may have been aided by a comely young lady[21] whom Brown sent to parley with Lee. Generous terms were agreed upon: Brown and his men marched out of Fort Cornwallis with their arms at their shoulders, drums beating, before heading to Charleston.

Lee's opinion of much of the militia, particularly Clarke's men, was low. "They excel the goths and the vandals in their schemes of plunder, murder and iniquity," he lamented to Greene. He must have known that many of the Georgians and Carolinians wanted nothing more than to extract bloody revenge on their Tory neighbors. To prevent this, at the surrender of Fort Cornwallis, Lee tasked Captain Joseph Armstrong with protecting Brown from would-be assassins.[22]

James Grierson was not so fortunate. James Alexander, one of Pickens's men, stormed into Grierson's home, where he had been sent after the surrender, and shot and killed him in front of his family. His clothes were divided amongst the militiamen, and his body was thrown in a nearby ditch. Lee condemned the murder, but had done nothing to prevent it. Alexander was never punished.[23]

On the morning of June 6, the Legion rode north once again. Lee had loosened the British grip on Georgia, and Greene was in the process of doing the same in South Carolina. Thanks to Lee's successful war of posts, only two British fortifications of any strength remained in the Palmetto State: the occupied port of Charleston, on the Atlantic coast, and to the northwest, the village of Ninety-Six.

The origin of the name of the spot, which Lee mistakenly believed signified its distance from the closest Cherokee settlement, was mysterious. The fort built there by the British in 1780 was stout, star shaped, and manned by 550 loyalists from South Carolina, New, Jersey, and New York. It was commanded by Lieutenant Colonel John Cruger, a New Yorker.

Greene had arrived on the outskirts of Ninety-Six on May 22 and at once set about preparing for a siege. Thaddeus Kosciuszko, a meticulous Polish military engineer whose fortifications had helped beat the British at Saratoga, oversaw the digging of trenches leading to the fort. Another Maham Tower was fashioned as well. But Cruger, upon learning that Greene and the American army were approaching, had strengthened the fort, building a formidable parapet surrounded by a ditch. Nearby were a star-shaped earthen redoubt and a secondary and smaller stockade known as Holmes Fort, enclosing three barns and protecting the loyalists' water supply—both connected to the main fort by covered walks—and several hastily built block houses.[24]

On June 7 Rawdon, who had relocated to Charleston, set out west again—to save Ninety-Six. With the British defenses in the South crumbling, he had gathered three regiments freshly arrived from Ireland. The following day Lee's Legion rode into the American camp, naturally with spectacle. On his approach to Ninety-Six, one of Lee's officers had skirted the town with prisoners collected at Augusta on display. Cruger saw this, believed it a purposeful insult, and opened fire on the Legion, harming none but startling all.[25]

Under Kosciuszko's watchful eye, the Americans were focused on storming the star-shaped redoubt. With the Legion once again at his disposal, Greene assigned Lee to begin approaches to the left of that fortification, where Holmes Fort protected the rested by the side of a spring. Lee's men began digging, built a battery, and positioned a six-pounder—fighting off night-time raids by Cruger's men.

In letters from Sumter, Greene saw evidence—but not yet proof—that the reinforced Rawdon was marching in his direction. While the slow work on the siege works went on, Lee grew frustrated. Focusing on the star fort, Kosciuszko had neglected Holmes Fort. Take this structure, cut the enemy off from his water, Lee argued to Greene, and Cruger will be forced to abandon Ninety-Six. Greene agreed, allowing Lee to send a sergeant and nine privates crawling on their bellies to blow up the stockade. The operation was foiled by Cruger's men, who spotted the small party and killed six of their number.

As the Americans continued to build their entrenchments, a countryman was seen galloping into Ninety-Six holding a letter high above his head. The gates to the enemy garrison swung open, and he disappeared within. The news he carried was good for Cruger, grave for Greene. Rawdon was at Orangeburg, a hundred miles to the east. Greene ordered Sumter to block or slow the British march. But the Gamecock, misreading Rawdon's route, failed to do so. Greene's window for opportunity was inching to a close as Rawdon moved west.

It was time to fight or withdraw. Greene chose to fight. The order was given on June 17. Continentals from Maryland and Virginia targeted the star fort; Lee and his Legion took on the stockade that the smaller party had failed to destroy earlier. The following day, at noon, a tremendous blast from the American battery gave the signal; the rebels sprinted forward, swinging their axes at the abatis protecting the fort and hurling hooks at the sandbags lining its walls.

Lee took Holmes Fort with little contest, the last loyalist inside having fled. But before he could move forward towards the village, Greene ordered Lee to halt. The American right was being greeted with fire and steel from the parapets by Cruger, who sent two contingents of thirty men outside the fort to surround the rebels. Greene watched as his men, bayonetted in the ditches and fired upon from above, quickly sustained heavy casualties. Worried about depleting his army, the general ended the attack and retreated the Americans east across the Saluda River, leaving 147 dead rebels behind.[26]

In his orders issued after the fight, Greene offered the now familiar approbation of Lee. "The General takes great pleasure in acknowledging the high opinion he has of the gallantry of the troops engaged in the attack of the enemy's redoubts," wrote Greene. "The judicious and alert behavior of the light infantry of the legion… and those directed by Lieutenant Colonel Lee, met with deserved success, etc, etc."

On June 21 Rawdon arrived at Ninety-Six and promptly pursued the American army heading east and now across Bush River. The hunt ended when Rawdon realized there were simply too many miles between the two armies; his own, newly arrived from abroad, suffering in the summer South Carolina heat, away from their stores, with foraging a formidable task with Lee prowling nearby, was moving slowly. So he returned to and then abandoned Ninety-Six—its distance from the Atlantic Ocean rendering it too far to be maintained. The British outposts that had once laced through South Carolina and dipped down into Georgia were no longer. The Tories, whose numbers the British had hoped would multiply across the region, were now dwindling and left twisting in the wind. Seeking safety, many attached themselves to the rear of the British army as it marched east.

Before thinking twice Greene, hoping for a rematch, turned around and pursued the enemy army—which though smaller than his, was better equipped and advantageously posted near Orangeburg. Greene's rebels were exhausted, punished by the southern heat, their clothes tattered, many among them wounded or sick. So the general called for a pause in hopes of restoring his fighting force while summer passed in the High Hills of Santee—a twenty-five-mile-long but only five-mile-wide network of sand hills, the tallest standing three hundred feet above the Wateree River, the swampy valley of which lies to their west. The altitude there, among the pines and oak, had for over a century been thought a cure for sickness and fever by South Carolinians. Greene hoped it would have the same restorative power on his army.[27]

Cornwallis, after tarrying in Wilmington, moved north to Virginia to meet up with Arnold's force, the leadership of which had deferred to General William Phillips. But Phillips became ill before the meeting was to take place in the town of Petersburg, which the Marquis de Lafayette was shelling as the general lay dying. Cornwallis was now in control of all the British forces in Virginia, numbering over seven thousand. He raked the state's countryside and sparred with Lafayette's smaller army.[28]

In New York, Henry Clinton, who had never approved of the invasion of Virginia and was now threatened by possible invasion by a Franco-American army led by Washington and the French general Rochambeau, sent a series of contradictory messages to Cornwallis. He ultimately ordered the general to find a secure spot on the Virginia peninsula where British ships could dock in the Chesapeake Bay, presumably to carry away men to open up other fronts. In August the British soldiers began to fortify Cornwallis's chosen port, Yorktown.[29]

The general was sealing his own fate—and Britain's. While Cornwallis occupied Yorktown, Washington and Rochambeau received word that a formidable French fleet led by Comte de Grasse was sailing north from the West Indies. Its twenty-seven ships and thirty-two hundred soldiers were at their disposal. The attack on New York was abandoned, but a small force was left behind so Clinton would think otherwise. The French and American armies began their march south to rendezvous with de Grasse in Virginia.[30]

Whispers from farther north were enough to give even the worried Greene cause for optimism. "The people in that quarter are in high spirits and a defeat and capture of the Earl [Cornwallis] is strongly talked of," he wrote Lee. "But you know this will require hard blows. Some of the southern army is much wished for, I mean the Legi[on] and the gallant Col. Lee."[31]

But Lee was unavailable. Initially he had not joined the army for its sojourn in the hills. Instead Greene had sent him to South Carolina's low country, along the Atlantic coast. There he joined Sumter and Marion in an ultimately futile pursuit of the British 19th Regiment led by Lieutenant Colonel James Coates, before finally heading north in late July to convalesce with the rest of the army in the High Hills.[32]

There the Legion, which had been on the march constantly since arriving in the South, enjoyed clean water, the cool air afforded by high elevation, comfortable quarters, and time to heal its wounded and remedy its sick. In a shock for all but Lee, it was reunited with an old comrade. When Cornwallis had taken command of Arnold's legion, John Champe had deserted, slipped out of Virginia, and drifted southward, eventually finding the American army in South Carolina. Lee greeted Champe warmly while the legionaries looked on in shock—until the entire scheme to capture Arnold was at last revealed. Champe was subsequently sent north to Washington and discharged.[33]

While his Legion rested, Lee was restless. He offered spontaneous strategic advice to Greene. Could he not, with his cavalry, advance on Haddrell's Point, near Charleston, to liberate American prisoners of war held there? Greene was uninterested in the proposal, but allowed Lee to resume his intelligence-gathering activities on August 5, when he rode out of the American camp with the Legion infantry to stalk the British army, whose leadership had changed hands by late summer. Rawdon, exhausted and fighting malaria, had boarded a ship in July bound for Britain. (His arrival was delayed when privateers apprehended the vessel and handed it over to the French fleet.) In his stead, Colonel Alexander Stewart took the reins of the mixed loyalist-British force still camped at Orangeburg. He did not remain there long, though, moving north in late July in search of supplies.

Keeping tabs on the enemy army, Lee pleaded with Greene to venture out of the High Hills and confront Stewart, whose force was smaller and, according to deserters, in terrible spirits. Now was the time for the Americans to thrust "a fatal stab to the British tyrant"[34] Lee pleaded. In a particularly brash idea, he even declared his intention to ride with the Legion cavalry all the way to the gates of Charleston. Greene naturally dismissed such a wild plan. But he did warm to Lee's suggestion of fighting Stewart. Lee, ever optimistic, assured Greene that with the right number of reinforcements the Americans could make easy work of their foes.

Greene dispatched Lee's infantry to join their leader. Then he began to call in all the fragmented parts of the American fighting force, which, after a delay in organizing the junction of the expanded force, began to march south. As Greene moved, his army multiplied: the militias of Pickens and Marion appeared. North Carolina militia commanded by the Marquis de Malmedy, a Frenchman serving the American cause, joined in. South Carolina state troops, non-Continental soldiers signed up to longer terms of service than militia under Lieutenant Colonel William Henderson, were added to the fold. By the time Greene reached Burdell's Tavern on September 7, his army numbered nearly three thousand. Ten miles away was Eutaw Springs, a stream hooking off of the Santee River. There the British army sat, unaware of the Americans nearby.[35]

An initial skirmish between Lee and British cavalry commander John Coffin, who had been sent to confirm rumors of the American presence, began with Greene's order for attack at 4:00 a.m. on the eighth. The rebels rode forward as the sun rose. The day ahead was bloody and boiling. Once Coffin returned to camp to inform Stewart that Greene had arrived, the British army was thrown into one line. On its far right, Major John Majoribanks stood behind a thicket just in front of Eutaw Springs. Cruger commanded the center, made up of both loyalist and British soldiers. To the left, regiments of British infantry were supported by Coffin's cavalry.[36]

The American army deployed in three lines. The first, from left to right, was made up of Pickens, Malmedy, and Marion.

Lee's Legion was positioned on the right flank. In the second line were Continental soldiers from Maryland and Virginia. William Washington and the Delaware Continentals were held in reserve. When the first volleys exploded, the American militia, to Greene's great satisfaction, held their ground and returned fire. But only for a time. Soon Malmedy's men crumpled, and the North and South Carolina militia began to flee. But Greene thrust his experienced second line forward with bayonets fixed. The current of the battle changed swiftly. Lee and the Legion infantry plowed through the British left flank, while Cruger's loyalists dueled, sword to sword, with the American Continentals in the center before falling back. A British rout seemed to be unfolding.

But it quickly folded. As the Americans stormed into the British encampment, the tired, thirsty soldiers began to pillage, unaware of a large and stout brick mansion, owned by Patrick Roche, just beyond the camp. Major Henry Sheridan, commanding a regiment of Tory sharpshooters from New York, following Stewart's orders rushed into the house, barred the doors, opened its windows and began to pick off rebels. Meanwhile, on the British right, behind an impenetrable screen of brush stood Majoribanks, also raking the Americans with fire. Greene's attempt to destroy the house proved futile; the riflemen behind its walls mowed down his artilleryman.

Now the British army began to regroup. Greene dispatched his reserves—William Washington's cavalry and the Delaware regulars—to take Majoribanks. This too failed, as Washington's horse was shot out under him and he was taken prisoner, while many of his men were killed. Greene dispatched his second in command, Nathaniel Pendleton, with orders for Lee to gather his cavalry and make a last effort to charge the British left and Coffin's cavalry. But when Pendleton reached Lee's cavalry, he could not find their leader. Lee was elsewhere, moving across the battlefield, commanding his infantry. The order then went to his deputy, Eggleston, and the charge was made—unsuccessfully. Coffin sent the Lee-less Legion retreating and then attacked the American infantry. With the numbers of dead and wounded growing, the sun scorching, the Roche house unbreakable, and Stewart and Cruger rallying, Greene called for a retreat.[37]

The battle, which lasted four hours, was one of the costliest of the entire Revolution. Over one hundred of Greene's men were killed. Nearly four hundred were wounded. Eighty-five of Stewart's men died; 297 were injured. Lee's Legion lost every fourth man. The American army retuned to Burdell's Tavern. Rain fell the next day, negating any chance for the armies to meet again and soaking the corpses littering the battlefield.[38]

After remaining at Eutaw Springs for two days, Stewart removed to Charleston. For the British, Eutaw Springs was another Pyrrhic victory. Greene, despite his heavy casualties, had been beaten but not dispatched. And the British losses had also been great. The American South, other than the few far-flung towns the British still controlled, was liberated. There was not, nor would there be, a great loyalist uprising.

From the day he had arrived in the South, Lee had done so much to bring this about. He had deflected Cornwallis during the race to the Dan, allowing the American army to escape into Virginia intact. He had fought gallantly at Guilford Courthouse and been commended for it. And he and his Legion had been the burning fuse that had detonated the forts so vital to the maintenance of the British war effort. And yet cruelly, during the climactic final major confrontation in that theater, at the moment of greatest need, he had been absent.

His place in the Battle of Eutaw Springs would torment Lee and haunt his legacy. Fellow officers grumbled that he had cost the Americans a total victory by freelancing on the battlefield and not attending to his cavalry. Lee was a vain man—and especially sensitive after the court martial-stained triumph at Paulus Hook. Naturally he was distraught over the missed opportunity to hand-deliver "the fatal stab" to the British. This despite the fact that his "great address, gallantry and good conduct" were singled out on Greene's summary of the battle to the latest president of the Continental Congress, Thomas McKean.[39]

Nearly a month after the battle, Lee wrote an unaddressed letter to a friend. To the recipient, whose identity is lost to time, he narrated the events of the recently ended battle. "You will feel for our mortifying disappointment," Lee wrote, "after carrying victory for two miles by an intrepidity never before exhibited so generally, during the war." The long letter concluded with an admission: "I have been exceedingly ill of a fever which took me while below."[40] After five years of constant fighting, disappointment and fatigue were overtaking Lee.

But he did not have much more war left to wage. Days before the battle at Eutaw Springs, de Grasse's French fleet had defeated and dispatched a British naval force in the Chesapeake Bay, eliminating any means of escape or reinforcement for Cornwallis. Weeks later, Washington and Rochambeau arrived in Yorktown and began their siege.

With Cornwallis trapped, Lee remained in the High Hills of the Santee, sending Michael Rudolph to Virginia in a vain search for men and supplies to fortify the Legion. In October, Greene presented Lee with a new mission. Washington wanted a full appraisal of the state of affairs in the South. Greene hoped to convince the commander in chief to supply the South with the necessary manpower to finally clear the British from the region once Cornwallis capitulated. To ensure better and more comprehensive communication, Greene sent Lee north to Yorktown to liaise with Washington. The choice was natural given the bond between the two Virginians. Carrying a letter to the Marquis de Lafayette on his person explaining the assignment, Lee departed his Legion and headed to his home state, arriving in Yorktown by mid-October.[41]

In the American camp, old friends and acquaintances abounded. Alexander Hamilton, after a brief absence from the army, was no longer an aide-de-camp but now commanded a battalion of light infantry. On the night of October 15, in the twin pursuits of victory and glory, he personally led the American attack on one of the two last redoubts blocking the advancing American trenches, leaping over the parapet, calling for his men to follow. John Laurens, another of Washington's protégés, was there blocking the retreating British. Lafayette and his fellow Frenchmen took the other redoubt. Anthony Wayne was there too, commanding his Pennsylvanians in unrelenting bombardment of the British.

His fortifications pummeled, his army surrounded on all sides, escape impossible, Cornwallis sent out an officer waving a white handkerchief on October 17. Two days later, after terms of surrender were negotiated, the siege ended.

On the morning of the nineteenth, the French and American soldiers spread out on opposite sides of a road, stretching in line for over a mile. Washington and Rochambeau were mounted and at their respective heads. The Frenchmen were resplendent, their uniforms crisp, their bands playing tunefully. The Americans, though less elegant, their musicians less grand, were to a man beaming. Beyond the armies, hundreds of civilians had congregated nearby to watch. When representatives of the vanquished army appeared, Cornwallis, claiming sickness, was not with them. Instead the sword of surrender was presented by his second, General Charles O'Hara, who mistakenly addressed Rochambeau before being directed to Washington. The sword was then handed to General Benjamin Lincoln, Washington's second. The British soldiers tramped onto an open field and abandoned their arms. American independence, while not formalized, was won.[42]

Henry Lee was looking on. As a spectator.

# 9

# YOU CANNOT CEASE TO BE A SOLDIER

ornwallis had capitulated, but there were likely other campaigns to fight. Cities were left to liberate. The British still controlled New York. George Washington was returning to the Hudson in order to take it back. To the south, Charleston and Savannah remained occupied. The commander in chief was sending Arthur St. Clair with much needed reinforcements to aid Nathanael Greene in freeing them.

Washington was eager to convey these decisions, as well as the particulars of the recently concluded terms of surrender, to Greene. But his emissary was absent.

Correspondence between the two generals was postponed for a time. Lieutenant Colonel Henry Lee had vanished. After a year of constant marches, sieges, and battles across the southern states, Lee was resting. He was touring the town of Port Royal at the head of the Rappahannock River—or so Washington had heard. And perhaps on his way there he had ventured to the Northern Neck to visit his cousins at Stratford Hall, one of whom caught his attention as he looked, at long last, towards life beyond this war.[1]

It was two months after he had left South Carolina—a short span of time, but an eternity for so dedicated a soldier to be absent—that Lee returned south and rejoined Greene's army, reaching headquarters in late November 1781.

Only days after his arrival, in another sign of his value to the army and importance to its general, he was placed in charge of all cavalry of the South.[2] There was an irony here, though. The end of the war was in sight, but it was not over. And yet Lee's own enthusiasm for the endeavor and the energy he needed to carry it to conclusion were waning. His health was a continuing concern, his pride suffering. As operations to liberate Charleston began, Lee was sidelined. He was, in his own estimation, recovered enough to return to action by early December. Greene's aide Lewis Morris, though, was skeptical, telling the general, slyly, that Lee's health was restored or "at least he thinks so."[3]

By this time Greene had swung the American army into the South Carolina low country, and after a skirmish before the British fort at Dorchester, pushed back and pinned the enemy down in Charleston. Still, the American army was in need of supplies, its numbers were dwindling, its morale falling yet again. The British force, which Alexander Leslie was soon to take command of, remained formidable if contained. Greene fanned the elements of his army out around South Carolina. Lacking naval support, Charleston could not be liberated. Major battles were now replaced by skirmishes and raids across the country.

Lee and his Legion were ordered to the area between the Ashley and Edisto Rivers to fend off British marauders. There, in the first weeks of 1782, he fixed on St. John's, an island to the south of Charleston whose fields provided pasture for the cattle that sustained the British army occupying the city. After reconnoitering the enemy's strength at St. John's, Lee determined that the force there, commanded by Lieutenant Colonel John Harris Cruger, could be easily overcome. And then, he predicted, the citizens of Charleston, weary of the British, would rise and take the city back.[4]

Throughout January Lee harangued Greene for approval of a strike on the island, pestering him for feedback on the "propositions of an interesting nature" he had suggested.[5] The general was skeptical of the enterprise, suggesting that Lee was "too confident" of his strength. Any attack on an island, he wrote, was inevitably dependent on the coming and going of the tide. Nevertheless, as usual, he gave Lee discretion to stage the attack if he believed it could be carried out.[6]

In John Laurens, Lee had an ally in his fervor for the attack on St. John's. Laurens had been assigned to Greene's army after the siege at Yorktown. Now he was placed in charge of the Legion's infantry for the operations on St. John's Island. The addition of Laurens to the southern army was both political—he was one of Washington's most esteemed aides and the son of a powerful politician—and impolitic; his appointment inspired resentment among soldiers in the South, who grumbled that he had been foisted on them by higher powers to further his ambitions, which had not yet been satisfied despite his participation in the war since its beginning.[7]

Laurens was a particularly cosmopolitan soldier, the son of a wealthy South Carolina planter. He had been educated in Europe and broken into Washington's inner circle in part because of his fluent French. He was also a grand idealist. Though his father's fortune had been built on the labor of slaves, the younger Laurens could not reconcile human bondage with the American

Revolution and its emphasis on liberty. He turned against the institution, arguing with all who would listen, including Washington, and even lobbied Congress to allow him to lead a regiment of freed slaves.[8]

Laurens was a dashing and romantic figure cut from the same cloth as Lee and Alexander Hamilton, with whom he developed a deep friendship. And like those two warriors, his conduct was governed by a deep patriotism—and an unbridled ambition. But whereas Lee and Hamilton were prone to accept risks for both causes, Laurens was utterly reckless. He racked up injuries whenever he set foot on a battlefield; the Marquis de Lafayette remarked after Brandywine that "it was not his fault that he was not killed or wounded, he did everything that was necessary to procure one or t'other."[9]

Lee's ego was already aggrieved, and the arrival of a soldier with ambitions as outsized as his own did not help his state of mind. Nevertheless, the two men cooperated on the proposed attack of St. John's. Lee, recognizing that Laurens's commission pre-dated his own, even offered to serve as second in command on the enterprise, but they eventually shared command. It ultimately mattered little which man was in charge; in the end, Greene's skepticism was warranted.

With no boats, the attack depended on the successful fording of a canal that was traversable only late at night when the water receded to waist level. And the canal was guarded by two British galleys on either side of it. The Americans had a limited window in which to slip between the British ships and onto the island.

The attack was originally scheduled for December 29. The day before, Lee mentioned to Greene that afterwards he wished to discuss a leave of absence from the army. Both this conversation and the operation itself were postponed when Lee and

Laurens learned that British troops were posted on nearby St. James Island to the north. Two weeks later, late in the night of January 12, the attack unfolded.

For the crossing, Laurens divided the force into two columns, one led by Lee and the other by Major James Hamilton. The first made it to the island without incident, but the second one was soon lost. An hour passed before Laurens relocated it. By then the tide was on the rise. The operation was abandoned, Lee forced to trek back across the canal in the cold rain, his men slipping and sinking in its muddy bottom. The debacle was an embarrassment and disappointment for both Lee and Laurens[10]—and, as it turned out, a thudding conclusion to Lee's service in the war.

Lee had been soldiering, in one form or another, since early 1776, when he had joined his home county's militia in Virginia. Nearly six years of struggle had now passed, with scarce respite. There had been moments of glory—his exploits at Scott's Farm outside of Philadelphia, the raid on Paulus Hook, the war of posts. And there had been approbation—from his generals, from his fellow officers, and from the fledging country's government. But it was not enough. Lee's dreams of glory were still unrealized. And his fatigue magnified the disappointments. It clouded his judgment and exaggerated slights and criticisms.

There were many in the army and in Virginia who resented Lee's connections and family name, who were jealous of his rise and rubbed raw by his arrogance and ambition. But the influence of his champions—including his own general, Greene, not to mention Washington, the commander in chief—carried far more weight than that of envious soldiers. Lee, though, could not look past the haze of disappointment and self-pity. He was still seething over Greene's official account of the action at Eutaw Springs, which he viewed as insufficiently praiseworthy. The arrival of Laurens, the frustration over St. John's Island, these too surely compounded his unhappiness.

On the twenty-sixth of January, Lee wrote to Greene requesting leave from the army. "Disquietude of mind and infirmity of body unite in giving birth to my request," he explained. The letter was a masterpiece of self-pity, with petulant complaints of "the persecution of my foes" and "the indifference with which my efforts to advance the cause of my country is considered by my friends."

Demonstrating his signature flair for the dramatic, Lee revealed his plans for the future. "However disgusted I am with human nature, I wish, from motives of self, to make my way easy and comfortable. This, if ever attainable, is to be got only in an obscure retreat."[11]

The letter kicked off a startlingly frank and emotional correspondence between the two men. Greene responded immediately after receiving Lee's letter, acknowledging that for some time he had suspected that the lieutenant colonel's desire for leave was motivated by melancholy as much as malady. "Whatever may be the source of your wounds I wish it was in my power to heal them," Greene commiserated.

But he would not accept Lee's assertion that he had in any way failed to do justice to his subordinate's contributions. On the contrary, Greene asserted, he had done everything in his power to promote them. He disagreed with Lee's belief that the public was not giving him credit for his deeds: "I believe few Officers either in America or Europe are held in so high a point of esteem as you are." Hoping that Lee would reconsider, he pleaded with him to "let me entreat you not to think of leaving the army." And displaying a depth of feeling that clearly transcended the thought of the army's losing a valuable officer's service, Greene expressed his personal concern, confessing to Lee that "you know I love you as a friend."[12]

Lee carried on with his responsibilities in the next few days, scouting out and communicating about possible British reinforcements to Charleston for Greene. He did not acknowledge the general's attempt to lift his spirits and keep him near until January 29. In a letter sent that date, Lee complained again about Greene's public reports, saying that he had read them with "distress because some officers & corps were held out to the world with a lustre superior to others, who to say the least deserved equally."

But he confirmed his devotion to the general and explained that his desire to return home was motivated by "imbecility of mind." Attempting to reconsider his decision would only tear open the wounds. The young man who had turned down Washington's invitation into his inner circle to pursue military fame was abandoning the American army to seek anonymity. "At present my fervent wish, is the most hidden obscurity. I want not private or public applause."[13]

The anguished correspondence continued, Lee increasingly overcome with heartache, Greene growing frustrated. Both poured regret and pain over the dissolution of their partnership into words. In a particularly lengthy note written on the eighteenth of February, an exasperated Greene addressed the perceived slights regarding Eutaw Springs. He reminded Lee that he had been praised in every public report during the Southern campaign. Then he turned the tables and compared his own career in the North, and how little public praise he, by contrast, had received for it. In the end, he wrote, all he wanted was for Lee to give himself "time to cool, and to take a general view of the Southern operations and see how important a part you have played in them."[14]

Lee regretted the trouble that his "stupid conduct" had caused Greene, but his decision was made.

Laurens was placed in command of the light corps. And Lee offered a parting shot, warning Greene against putting the Legion into the hands of an irresponsible officer. "If he is an experimenter," Lee predicted, "he will waste the troops very fast."[15] Laurens was dead by the end of the year, shot from his saddle in a rice paddy during an immaterial attack on British foragers.

Greene offered to introduce Lee to the Comte de Rochambeau if he wished to visit the French army and inform the general on the Southern campaign. Lee declined. Overcome with emotion, he also refused a farewell ceremony. In late February, after a delay caused by the lack of a carriage to convey him, with fifteen guineas in his pocket, Henry Lee left his Legion and the cause to which he had devoted all his exertions for so long. "You are going home; and you will get Married; but you cannot cease to be a soldier," Greene wrote Lee upon his departure.[16]

So the weary warrior returned home. He did not remain there long, though. As a youth Lee had visited Stratford Hall, the grand Lee family plantation on the Potomac, where there were balls to attend, relatives to call on. And he may have visited again in late 1781 and seen a woman who changed his plans for the future. In any case, in the spring of 1782 Lee returned there with a new purpose. At twenty-six, he was still a young man. No matter his frustrations, he was a war hero whose name was known across the continent and beyond. The months riding in the southern sun had agreeably bronzed his skin. And the depression that had consumed him so recently had done nothing to diminish his allure.[17]

His was a striking figure making his way down roads lined with poplars and cedar trees, passing before a grove of sugar maples, their lime-green flowers sprouting, and wheeling into Stratford Hall's wide lawn on a gorgeous spring afternoon. Beyond this lay the great H-shaped mansion with its Flemish-bond brickwork, its wings crowned with constellations of chimneys, its rooftop promenade gazing out on the Potomac. And up its sharply inclining stone steps, behind its lofty front door, waited the Divine Matilda.

Matilda Lee was the second child and eldest daughter of Philip Ludwell Lee. Colonel Phil, as family called him, was the eldest child of Thomas Lee, brother of Henry Lee's grandfather, Henry Lee I. So he was first cousin to Lee's father, Henry II, and Harry and Matilda Lee were second cousins. Colonel Phil, educated in London, had hoped to remain abroad but had been called back to Virginia upon the death of his father Thomas in 1750 to execute his estate and assume the lordship of Stratford Hall, the Georgian house that Thomas had built in the 1730s on the tract of family property called the Cliffs.[18]

Snobbish and prickly, Colonel Phil chafed at living amongst the yeomanry of Virginia.[19] But Matilda's father willingly did his part for the colony, serving as a judge, lieutenant of militia, member of the House of Burgesses and the governing council. It was Colonel Phil who transformed Stratford Hall, relatively modest in his father's time, into a truly luxurious home. With his wife and former ward Elizabeth Steptoe, whom he married in 1763, Colonel Phil modernized the house itself, opened its doors to fine social gatherings, expanded its stables and filled them with fine horses (including Dotterel, an English racehorse), and cultivated the shores beneath its cliffs.[20]

He was a parsimonious businessman, a dedicated gardener, and, perhaps most of all, an admirer of music. The echoes of violin drifted out into the Virginia night as bands summoned visitors to the mansion's epicenter of socializing, its great hall, or serenaded them as they took in the panorama atop its promenade. Colonel Philip's love of music was so great that he even toured the countryside with woodwind players, whose instruments announced his arrival at the homes of friends and relatives.[21]

Colonel Philip was thrust into a parental role for his younger siblings, including Richard Henry and Francis Lightfoot; he welcomed his first daughter, Matilda, in 1764. A second, Flora, arrived in 1770. The girls had little choice but to take up their father's interests. A skilled German violinist named Charles Leonard was frequently present at Stratford, performing and training Colonel Philip's daughters. Another tutor, a harpsichordist named Lomax, promised to make "Matilda sing and play finely." As Colonel Philip wrote to his brother William in London, "He is fond of her ear and voice." He also requested that William source the complete works of composers Carl Friedrich Abel, Carlo Antonio Campioni, and Domenico Scarlatti in hopes, no doubt, that Matilda could add them to her burgeoning repertoire.[22]

Matilda was a regular attendee of grand dinners and soirees at which the children of the Virginia gentry learned to dance. There she and her sister, elegantly outfitted, moved effortlessly through minuets and country dances.[23] As she grew into maturity, so did her beauty and poise. When Colonel Philip died suddenly in 1775, Matilda became the mistress supervising Stratford, and her new responsibilities increased her independence. When a brother named Philip, born on the day of his father's funeral, died in 1779, Matilda also became the teenage heiress to the property. A compelling combination of attractive qualities—her lithe and long form, her musical accomplishments, her quick mind, and her strong spirit—earned her the sobriquet "Divine."

When Henry Lee returned to Stratford Hall it was to take her hand. They had known each other since childhood, and the courtship had commenced over the previous year. By the standards of the era and their class standards, it was an impeccable match. By virtue of her thousands of inherited acres, she was a wealthy woman. She was also lovely and engaging. He was heroic and handsome; George Welden, his effusive English valet, whose affection for Lee impressed Matilda, saucily told the bride that her husband's brown complexion was restricted to his face and hands; the rest of his skin was "fair as a lily."[24] Together Harry and Matilda Lee united two wings of one great family. It was a union based on both pragmatism and love.

"My ambition might have been very great once, it is not so now, and I rest contented with my crass future," Lee had pouted just months before.[25] But on an April day in 1782—standing in the airy salon of Stratford Hall, the landscape that rolled to the Potomac River visible from its northern entrance, the portraits of his ancestors peering down from its high walls—Lee abandoned his ambition for what seemed a rather comfortable obscurity. His future was anything but crass.

He stood atop a hamlet of agricultural activity, spread out over 6,595 acres.[26] Tobacco, Stratford's original crop, had injured the soil, and in its place were fields of wheat, corn, and barley. Cattle, sheep, and hogs roamed the grounds. They and smaller gardens yielding peaches and pears, apricots and apples, provided much of the family's food.

The Potomac, which brought and took goods and crops to and from the plantation, also surrendered its own harvests—baskets of blue crab and oysters, seines full of fish. In workrooms spread across the property were shoemakers, blacksmiths, and carpenters. Mills ground corn and flour, small copper stills brewed alcohol. The unheralded engine of all the industry was, of course, African American slaves. In 1782 there were eighty-three enslaved men, women, and children toiling in Stratford Hall's fields and shops.[27]

A farmer Henry Lee was not. He had been born and grown up on a plantation, but had not lived there since the beginning of the war and, other than spells when his father traveled for business, had not managed it. George Washington, absent so long now from his own farm Mount Vernon, was passionate about cultivating his land and applied all manner of ingenuity and experimentation to do so. He rotated crops, used new plows, tested various fertilizers, and kept exacting records of it all along the way. He was genuinely fascinated by agriculture and was by nature an entrepreneur. Lee, by contrast, merely flirted with farming, and he had far more energy for business than understanding of it.[28]

For a while he tried to fill the role of the country squire, tending to his fields. Colonel Phil's estate was formally partitioned the month Harry wed Matilda. Twenty thousand pounds were distributed to its executors, Matilda's uncles and her mother, who had remarried in 1780. Her new husband, Philip Fendall, a wealthy banker from Maryland and a Lee cousin, took up residence at Stratford, whose main floor was crowded with the newlyweds and in-laws. Early in their marriage Henry and Matilda made adjustments to Stratford Hall, enlarging their bedchamber.

Around this time, likely during a trip to Philadelphia to resign his commission, Lee sat for the painter Charles Willson Peale.[29] A renaissance man and occasional soldier in the American Revolution, Peale had come to Philadelphia in 1776. There he painted the likenesses of the leading figures of the nascent nation and its government and housed them in his museum alongside objects of natural history. Henry Lee was an ideal addition to Peale's collection. His portrait of the renowned young warrior captured a man with rose-tinted cheeks, dark brows over clear blue-gray eyes, a broad nose over full lips. His hair—long, fair, and full— was powdered, pulled back and pinned down behind his head in a barely visible bow. That masculine style, known as a queue, was popular among military men—a calling connoted by Lee's buff tunic with its green edging,[30] a single gold epaulette on its right shoulder, and the black stock around his neck. The portrait projects a curious mix of youth and experience and, naturally, an undeniable self-assurance. It is also the image of a man who was still in his soul a soldier.[31] In 1785 Lee sat for Peale once again. This sitting yielded a miniature, an almost sedate and far sweeter likeliness of its subject. Another portrait generally believed to be from this same period, by Englishman Robert Edge Pine, showed a less flattering likeness.

Soon there was no war left to wage. The surrender at York-town had set in motion the events that would bring the American Revolution to its successful conclusion: the collapse of the British government presided over by Prime Minister Lord North. Its replacement was a Whig government open to parleying for peace with the Americans. Henry Clinton was recalled back to Britain. His replacement, General Guy Carleton, suspended military operations.

Peace negotiations, conducted in Paris, began in earnest in April 1782. In July the British civil and military authorities abandoned Savannah. In November, preliminary articles of armistice were agreed upon. The following month Charleston was abandoned. The Treaty of Paris, granting American independence, was signed on September 3, 1783. A month later the last remaining elements of the British army, along with their loyalist allies, evacuated New York. Once the last Union Jack was torn down and replaced with the Stars and Stripes, General George Washington marched through Manhattan at the head of his victorious army. On December 23, standing before Congress in Annapolis, Maryland, the commander in chief, fighting back emotion, relinquished his commission. He then took a seemingly final bow to public life and returned to Mount Vernon.

A new nation was truly born. And along with it arrived the attendant political debates and business opportunities. These would have to suffice as Lee's substitute for warfare.

Populations would inevitably migrate, waterways would open to commerce, cities and towns would rise. There were fortunes to be made in the purchasing and selling of land in this embryonic empire. Catching a fever for speculation that was setting in amongst his fellow citizens, Lee began to acquire property. His hope, common amongst his countrymen, was that the land he purchased for little in these early years of the emerging republic would, as America grew and prospered, be easily sold for a handsome profit in the future.

But there was a wild, starry-eyed nature even to Lee's business ventures, a frenzied eagerness in his entrepreneurship that brushed aside principles and practicality. He offered, for an exorbitant price, mills upon the Occoquan River to a group of Quaker investors predicated on the promise—one he plucked out of thin air—that a road was soon to be built connecting the ports in Dumfries and Alexandria and increasing the value of the property.[32]

Early on Lee acquired and sold parcels near Alexandria, Virginia, with some success. He purchased acres near Stratford, broadening his estate out along the Potomac. There were plots in

Prince William County leased to his brother, Richard Bland. And there were lands beyond the Appalachian Mountains. Settlers, navigating the Ohio River and crossing the Cumberland Mountains, were pouring into this territory, part of Virginia, and into the distant Kentucky territory, where Lee also invested. He also began to lease portions of Stratford's vast acreage to small farmers.

While he attempted to acquire fortune through land, Lee also began a family, as Matilda gave birth to an heir, Philip Ludwell Lee, in 1784.[33] That same year, when several officers of the late American army founded the Society of the Cincinnati, an organization formed to perpetuate memories of the recently ended war and keep strong the bonds between the men who had fought it, Lee naturally joined. He even extravagantly commissioned a set of china bearing the society's insignia.[34]

The family's fortunes waxed and waned. In the spring of 1785 Henry and Matilda were ordering French wines, olives, anchovies, and hair powder. Lee had reconnected with George Washington, now resuming his role as gentleman farmer at Mount Vernon, and he sent chestnut trees, boxwood clippings, and Italian barley to his hero. But by the following year Lee was forced to write to Matilda's uncle Richard Henry, then the president of the Continental Congress—the body that had been organized to oversee the rebellion and was now feebly governing the nation—in distress. "I would not in your present station, ask a moments attention were not my circumstances so straightened, as to demand very pointed attention to matters of money," he wrote, pleading for assistance in collecting monies owed by a Mr. Hall.[35]

Lee's behavior during this period of domesticity suggests a difficult transition from military life, validating Greene's prediction that Lee would not be able to "cease to be a soldier." Despite a new family and his responsibilities at Stratford, he was once again on the move—rushing away from Westmoreland, leaving Matilda and her baby behind, galloping across the wild Virginia landscape, a pack of dogs trailing. There was a restless element in Lee's temperament that served him well in war but proved problematic in peace.[36]

The affairs of the new nation and the fortunes of his men in peacetime increasingly occupied his time. Former members of his Legion, familiar names such as Patrick Carnes, corresponded and visited. As their commander, Lee had paid special attention to the needs of his men, often using his own money to meet them. In peace he did what he could to make sure that the promises that Virginia had made to the veterans were honored. The pay that had been assured to members of the Legion, like all of America's soldiers, had depreciated on account of inflation. When Virginia's government—the House of Burgesses having been replaced by a two-chambered general assembly at the onset of the war—offered promissory notes to the veterans in lieu of the promised wages, Lee was quick to do his part to help his old comrades obtain the warrants.

He had pledged to seek obscurity, but he would not stay out of the public sphere. In the fall of 1785 Virginia's General Assembly elected him to a one-year term representing the state at the Continental Congress, now meeting in New York. He was on his way north in December. Matilda, feeling unwell, remained at Stratford with little Philip.

Lee's formal introduction to politics proved frustrating. From the outset of his time in Congress, the body itself was dysfunctional. The American government continued to labor under the Articles of Confederation, a constitution that had been constructed to unite the thirteen states during their war for independence. It granted little power to the central government, and its legislature was a unicameral house requiring supermajorities to pass laws and total agreement among delegates for any type of amendment to the Articles themselves.

The greatest inadequacy of the federal government, though, was in regard to fiscal matters. The Articles of Confederation granted it no authority to levy taxes. It was left to the states, each of which had its own currency, to contribute revenue voluntarily. There was no money to fund the government, no money to pay down the massive debts to foreign nations incurred during the war, and no money to finance an army should another war arrive or a rebellion erupt.

Lee arrived in New York City in February 1786,[37] when only eight of the thirteen state delegations had gathered.[38] There were no accommodations provided, so he took rent of a comfortable home. Matilda, who early that year gave birth to a baby girl named Lucy for Lee's mother, arrived in New York along with Philip in April.[39]

Lee proved an active legislator, writing motions for a formal celebration on the anniversary of the signing of the Declaration of Independence and for the creation of an Indian Department to help secure the nation's western frontiers.[40]

Amidst this activity, sad news reached Lee in Philadelphia. His dear general, Nathanael Greene, had died in Georgia at the age of forty-three after a short fever. "Universal grief reigns here," he wrote to Washington, conveying the news, "how hard the fate of the U. States, to loose such a son in the middle of life—irreparable loss—But he is gone, I am incapable to say more."[41] Even now, with the Revolution still fresh in minds, Lee fretted that the great men who had won it, men he called friends and mentors, would someday be forgotten. Dotted across Europe were statues to kings and warriors, enduring markers of their fame. America should throw up monuments to its own men, Lee thought, starting with Greene. Accordingly, in July, he introduced and helped pass a measure providing for the creation of a monument to Greene in the federal capital. Emblazoned across its base would be this inscription: *Sacred to the memory of N. Greene, esqr., who departed this life on the 19 of June 86, aged—, late Major General in the service of the U.S. and commander of their army in the Sou. Department.*[42]

But these were merely trifling projects. Lee had barely taken his seat in Congress when he was caught up in a conflict that pitted the interest of his state's leaders against his own. The Treaty of Paris had seemingly granted Americans rights to navigate the Mississippi River. But in 1784 Spain brought an end to this regime, angering the Americans who had rushed west from Virginia, North Carolina, and Pennsylvania. Sailing their crops down that river was essential to the fortune these pioneers sought.

When Spain's emissary, Don Diego de Gardoqui, made his way to America in the spring of 1785, he began negotiations with John Jay, the nation's Secretary of Foreign Affairs, on a commerce treaty. When negotiations faltered, Jay broached the idea of an accord that would delay the opening of the river to American cargo for three decades. The southern states rejected this idea vehemently. Virginia's government, in particular, feeling the pressure from its citizens now settled on the western frontiers, objected. In the middle of this firestorm stood Lee, who privately opposed opening the river to American navigation but was instructed to push for it.[43]

His position on the question was motivated both by self-interest and by a genuine concern for the future of the Union. Lee, like Washington, viewed the opening of the Mississippi to

American commerce as competition, a threat to his own financial interests. And should these western settlements prosper and grow, there was the danger they would break away and form their own nation. Lee, echoing Washington, favored a system of canals cutting east and west along the nation's waterways, such as the Potomac, as a preferable means of linking the nation and its economic interests—and his own.[44]

The issue pitted North against South, as the states of New England argued against the opening of the river, lest it jeopardize a commercial treaty with Spain that stood to help their ailing economies. But the southern states opposed any pact that excluded navigation rights, without which their western inhabitants were threatening an uprising or an eventual war with Spain. In the end, Lee ruefully capitulated.[45]

But his feelings on the matter were well known in Virginia. In the fall of 1786 Lee was cautioned that his position jeopardized his future in Congress. "Mr. Madison tells me that my congressional conduct relative to the Mississippi navigation, or rather the proposed treaty is carped at," Lee explained to his brother Richard Bland. "A community ought to be tender of the reputation of her servants, I expected delicacy as well as justice from my country, or I never would have risked a reputation dearer to me, than rise on the precarious tenure of a democratic assembly."[46]

And, indeed, on November 7 the assembly recalled Lee from New York. To make matters worse, it was sending James Madison as a replacement. Lee and Madison had been classmates at the College of New Jersey; their paths diverged after Princeton. While Lee did his part for independence on the battlefield, Madison did his in politics, becoming a political philosopher and master parliamentarian. Whereas Lee was hot-blooded and passionate, Madison was cool and bloodless. Yet the two had rekindled a friendship upon Lee's election to Congress; Madison was serving in Virginia's legislature at the time.

But when Lee received the news that his term was ending after one year—three was the typical length—he was furious at Madison. In typical rash fashion, Lee gathered his family and headed home just as winter storms swept across the North. After a three-week journey with both Matilda and Philip trembling from the cold, the family reached Georgetown. From there they boarded a ferry to cross into Alexandria. The hour was late and the river clogged with ice that endangered the family, nearly destroyed their carriage, and left them stranded on the water for four excruciating hours.[47]

Once safely in Alexandria, Lee dashed off a furious missive to Madison, on whom he placed the blame for his "disgrace." "I am frank to declare to you," he pouted, "that the opinion I had formed of your deriliction of the friendship which existed between us rendered my affliction doubly severe." The letter was typical Lee: emotional and overwrought. "Your abandonment of a man who loved your character to excess & who esteemed your friendship among the first blessings of his life connected with the circumstance of your election to the office from which he was dismissed, together with many other considerations which are unnecessary to repeat wounded me deeply, & has given me many melancholy hours."[48]

Madison, calm and reasonable, was able to soothe his distraught friend. Another Virginian assigned to the congressional delegation, Joseph Jones, ultimately declined the assignment, and on the first of December the assembly voted to return Lee to Congress to fill this absence, rendering his hasty return to Virginia and his antagonism towards Madison all unnecessary.

Lee went back to New York in the spring of 1787, and Matilda—after giving birth to another boy in May, this one named for his father—joined him there, this time bringing the two youngest children with her but leaving Philip at Stratford Hall. Lee's domestic life during this period was turbulent. When Matilda's uncle Arthur Lee visited New York, he described a troubling scene in the family's home: "Vexation—torment torture...Matilda crying..Harry Lee ranting—delightful group for a social party...."[49]

While in Congress Lee continued to acquire land wildly and rack up debt in the process. In a typical transaction, he was forced to offer twenty-six thousand acres as security for an obligation incurred to a William Glassell in the town of Fredericksburg. There was more land purchased in Alexandria, including a tract he promptly mortgaged—later in 1787, his most ambitious acquisition yet—of twenty lots at the cost of two thousand pounds, which he sold to family members and deeded to creditors.

It was increasingly clear to those around him that Lee's ventures were risky and ill-conceived and that he was not to be trusted when it came to financial matters. In September Lee's father, Henry II, died at Sully, the plantation of Richard Bland Lee. In his final years Henry II had himself been pestered by his son to help pay off debts. In his will, the elder Lee bequeathed some of his land and a small number of slaves to his namesake and eldest child, particularly acres in Kentucky territory, as well as some in Westmoreland County. But, tellingly, he chose sons Edmund and Theodorick to serve as executors and divided the bulk of the estate between his wife Lucy, who retained ownership of Leesylvania, and the remainder of the children.[50]

But Lee had other matters on his mind. The states were at each other's throats over commercial disputes and, as in the case of Virginia and Maryland, the rights to rivers. There was no doubt that the Articles of Confederation were insufficient to unite the thirteen states in the absence of a common cause or enemy. Cash was scarce. Veterans went unpaid; farmers were unable to pay debts, their land snatched up by collectors. Violent uprisings, such as the lengthy one led by veterans of the Revolution, Daniel Shays and Luke Day—the latter a member of the Society of Cincinnati—in western Massachusetts, transpired. There was no federal army to subdue such rebellions, only state militias.[51]

Delegates from five states had met in Annapolis in September of 1786 searching for some solution to the nation's economic woes. The suggestion was forwarded that all the states convene to take up the task of properly reforming the Articles of Confederation. The following summer, delegates from the thirteen states made the trek to Philadelphia, where George Washington, a reluctant attendee, was elected head of the proposed convention.[52]

In the preceding year Lee and Washington had corresponded frequently. They discussed domestic matters: Lee offered Washington a bargain on dinnerware bearing the Society of Cincinnati insignia, Washington asked Lee to purchase a bricklayer on his behalf, as long as the purchase did not tear the slave's family apart. The two men discussed literature: Lee was studying the work of famed agricultural theorist Sir Arthur Young in hopes of acquiring knowledge to apply to his farm. He forwarded Young's *A Tour through Ireland* to Mount Vernon.[53]

And of course they also talked politics: from his perch in New York City, Lee kept Washington abreast of the tension over the treaty with Spain, and sent reports regarding the disturbing tumult in Massachusetts. In May 1788, settling quietly into a seat crafted by a Philadelphia furniture maker, a gilded sun carved on its back as the Constitutional Convention convened, perhaps Washington recalled an admonition in one of these letters from his protégé. "The period seems to be fast approaching," Lee had predicted, "when the people of these U. States must determine to establish a permanent capable government or submit to the horrors of anarchy and licentiousness."

"How wise would it be, how happy for us all," Lee had said, "if this change could be made in friendship, and conducted by reason."[54]

# 10

# ONE PEOPLE

A top Shockoe Hill in the heart of Richmond, the khaki clouds of dust were visible from all directions. Horse hooves plodded along the drought-dried roads leading into town. From all points they came, traveling over Virginia's primitive byways in gigs, carts, or phaeton carriages—their destination the state capitol, a hastily constructed three-story wooden building sitting at the intersection of Carey and 14th Streets.[1]

Some were the grand old men of Virginia, whose oratory a decade before had been the kindling for the Revolution. Others were the youthful warriors who had fought it. Together they had won Virginia and her sister colonies independence. Now the question at hand, the one that brought them all to this city on the James River, was would these former colonies remain united? Would they coalesce at last around a government capable of guiding the young nation into a splendid future?

In June of 1788, Henry Lee came to Richmond determined that indeed they would.

When the Constitutional Convention had convened eight
months before, its goal was to amend the Articles of Confederation into an operable system of government. A plan sketched by
James Madison, the first delegate to arrive in Philadelphia,
morphed into a wholly new form of government. It would feature
three branches—a bicameral legislature, an executive, and a
judiciary. Once these were agreed upon, the delegates debated
the details before agreeing on a grand compromise. Washington,
naturally, was the first to sign the document. The responsibility
then fell to the states to approve the new system.

Four members of Virginia's delegation—the old lion of liberty
George Mason, the scholarly George Wyeth, the famed physician
James McClurg, and Edmund Randolph, a member of one of the
state's distinguished families—had declined to endorse the new
government. Some had contributed little or left early. But others
had objected to the lack of a bill of rights and were deeply suspi-
cious of the executive, or president, created by the Constitution.
Another of Virginia's leading politicians, Patrick Henry—skeptical
of the entire enterprise and fearing a federal government empowered at the expense of the states—had simply refused to attend the
gathering.[2]

Lee sat in Congress while the Constitution was created and
debated and did not leave New York until October 29. On his
route back to Stratford Hall he made a familiar stop: for two days
at the end of November, he rested at Mount Vernon and conferred with George Washington.

In regard to the Constitution, the general, Lee later told
Madison, was "firm as a rock."[3] Lee and Washington had been
commiserating on the loathsome state of the American government for several years; this sentiment was hardly newly arrived
at. During the war Lee had chafed at the inability of the loose

confederation of states to properly sustain their army; in peace he, like Washington, lamented the states' dysfunction, worried it would jeopardize his future financial success, and looked on in horror at the uprisings against the federal government in Massachusetts and elsewhere.

While states organized their conventions to approve or reject the new government, papers and pamphlets were filled with arguments for and against. Politicians and the public alike weighed its virtues and flaws. Lee's old friends Madison and Alexander Hamilton (and fleetingly John Jay), using the pen name Publius, composed the most persuasive arguments on behalf of the Constitution in a series of essays sent to New York newspapers. Those who opposed the strengthening of the federal government, men such as Patrick Henry and Richard Henry Lee, responded with their own propaganda. Those in favor of adoption and a stronger central government were often called cosmopolitans, though history has labeled them federalists. Those against, more likely to support an agrarian economy and to harbor suspicions of a stronger central power, were localists and later anti-federalists.

States scheduled their own conventions and called elections to nominate delegates; the debates began in some states as early as the fall of 1787. On October 25, Virginia's legislature met and scheduled elections to be held the following March; two delegates would represent each of the state's eighty-four counties. The convention itself would meet the first week of June. By December, Lee had declared his candidacy and pleaded with Madison to do the same. But given the number of other contenders in Westmoreland County, Lee was skeptical about his prospects. His fears were unfounded: the following spring, both men were nominated to the convention. Lee would be the only member of his family to attend, and an outlier on account of his support for the Constititution. With the exception of Francis Lightfoot Lee, the Stratford wing of the family, Matilda's uncles, were opposed to the Constitution.[4]

There was considerable antagonism towards the Constitution in the counties below Richmond; the state's legislature, influenced by Patrick Henry, now a delegate, was also hostile. But the people of Northern Neck, where Stratford Hall sat, were in favor.

"Three sets of men are to be found on the question of government," Lee observed, "one opposed to any system, was it even sent from heaven which tends to confirm the union of the states—Henry is leader of this band—another who would accept the new constitution from conviction of its own excellence, or any federal system, sooner than risk the dissolution of the confederacy, & a third who dislike the proposed government, wish it amended, but if this is not practicable, would adopt it sooner than jeopardize the union—Mason may be considered as the head of this set."[5]

In early 1788, in the months before the gathering in Richmond, Lee was suffering rheumatism while Matilda, complaining of "burning and tingling," traveled to western Virginia seeking relief in the region's mineral springs.[6] Lee made yet another major investment in land: the purchase, for four thousand pounds, of over five hundred acres in northern Virginia adjacent to the Great Falls where the Potomac River splashed over a jagged crop of rocks and into an unnavigable gorge below. The Potomac Company would soon build a set of locks to open the spot for passage. There Lee dreamt of building a thriving town catering to the traffic sailing by on the river. When he arrived in Richmond in June, it was to help guarantee the nation not only a secure government, but also one that would allow projects such as this to flourish.

At 10:00 a.m. on the second day of June, Lee took his seat in the wooden capitol building in Richmond along with 167 other delegates. It was a blisteringly hot summer, the air indoors stifling. Sentiment for and against the Constitution was evenly divided across the delegates. The stakes were dramatically high: out of the nine states required for ratification, eight had already voted yes. The creditability of the document, even if passed by the necessary number of states, would be tainted without the support of Virginia, the largest of them.

The attendees sweltered as Edmund Pendleton, the esteemed jurist-politician who had played an outsized part in the state's fight for independence, was nominated president. Once other officers and a chaplain were chosen, the gathering agreed to reconvene the following day in a more suitable location, the New Academy on Shockoe Hill, a spacious wooden building ambitiously built two years before as the town's cultural center.[7] On the morning of June 3, the convention formally commenced. The proceedings were open to the public, attracting spectators and reporters alike. Doorways and hallways were crammed with curious citizens drawn to the deliberations from all over Virginia. Among the delegates they watched and listened to, distinct divisions, roughly contouring to Lee's categories, became evident.

One faction featured George Mason; William Grayson, a one-time aide-de-camp to Washington who had led his own regiment during the war; and Benjamin Harrison V, a former member of the Continental Congress, a signer of the Declaration of Independence, and most recently the state's governor, who all viewed the Constitution as a dangerous usurpation of Virginia's rights. The Articles of Confederation, at most, had needed adjustments, not replacement by a Constitution authorizing a new, larger, and more powerful form of government.

As Lee had observed, their unquestioned leader was Patrick Henry. Silver-tongued and acerbic, he stood a thin six feet, his hair curling to frame a face with Grecian figures and deep set hazel-blue eyes. He was a master of emotional political rhetoric whose voice had been heard at almost every junction since the colonies began their quest for independence. "Much will depend on Mr. Henry," Madison had forewarned Washington, realizing what a formidable foe the man from Louisa County would be.[8] Henry had made the journey from his plantation home Pleasant Grove to Richmond to fight the adoption of this new form of government, and he came prepared to do the bulk of the labor necessary to defeat it.

Challenging Henry and his fellow anti-federalists were a band of younger Virginians. Among this group were Lee, Madison, and John Marshall, a budding politician and fellow veteran of the Revolution. Aiding the federalist cause, much to the chagrin of Mason and Henry, was also Edmund Randolph, who had refused to vote for the Constitution in Philadelphia before having a change of heart late in 1787. Madison was the unquestioned leader of this group. Diminutive and soft-spoken—listeners strained to hear his voice in the hall—he did not have Henry's presence. Nor was he capable of his fiery oratory. Instead, he relied on reason and logic, relayed respectfully, to parry Henry's thrusts. The work of sparring with the old spellbinder in rhetoric would fall to the likes of Lee in the long and hot days ahead.

On the opening day of the convention, Lee immediately displayed his usual aggression, introducing a petition alleging that one of the delegates, William White, had been nominated illegally. Once the substantive debate was underway, Mason offered an opening gambit: why not scrutinize every single clause of the Constitution rather than rushing to a quick vote? Madison raised no objection. To little avail, an impatient Lee argued that the convention should not waste time in clause-by-clause discussion. Mason and Harrison countered that the members of the convention ought to have time to properly consider the document. Lee protested. Virginia's General Assembly was set to meet on the twenty-third, and the matter would have to be settled before then. He called the anti-federalists' bluff: for months every man present had been considering this Constitution; they knew its contours in detail. No one needed weeks to come to a decision.[9]

The actual debate did not begin until the following day, the fourth of June. The attempt at a clause-by-clause discussion of the Constitution was interrupted repeatedly. While the delegates contemplated the Constitution's preamble, Patrick Henry rose from his seat time and time again to thunder against the entire document. "A year ago the mind of our citizens were in perfect repose," he intoned, commanding the attention of all the delegates. "Before the meeting of the late federal convention at Philadelphia, a general peace and a universal tranquility prevailed in this country—but since that period they are exceedingly uneasy and disquieted...it arises from a proposal to change our government—a proposal that goes to the utter annihilation of the most solemn engagements of the states...."[10]

But what most offended Patrick Henry was the language of the document itself. "What right had they to say, we the people?" he queried. "My political curiosity...leads me to ask, who authorized them to speak the language of we the people, instead of we the states? States are the characteristics and the soul of a confederation."[11]

On the following day, June 5, Lee rose to respond to Henry. He professed nothing but respect for the elder statesman, speaking of the "respect and attention" he had paid to his speech the day before. But then he rejected Henry's histrionic attack on the opening of the preamble. "This system is submitted to the people for their consideration, because on them it is to operate if adopted," Lee contended.[12]

Next he accused Henry of rank demagoguery. "The worthy character informed us of the horrors which he felt, of apprehension in his mind, which made him tremblingly fearful for the commonwealth," Lee recalled before asking "was it proper to appeal to the fear of this house?"

And Lee was not yet done. Now he began his own brand of fearmongering. Henry had painted a picture of domestic tranquility and prosperity disrupted by the introduction of a new government. But "let him go to our seaports," Lee cried, "let him see our commerce languishing…let him ask the price of land, and of produce in different parts of the country: to what cause shall we attribute the low price of these?" Lee wove an image of the nation under the Articles of Confederation as exaggeratedly bleak as Henry's was rosy. "And the impossibility of employing our tradesmen and mechanics? To what cause will the gentleman impute these and a thousand other misfortunes our people labor under?" Lee inquired. "These, sir, are owning to the imbecility of the confederation; to that defective system which never can make us happy at home nor respectable abroad."[13]

Lee's attack ignited a marathon rebuttal from Henry, who, veering away from the subject at hand, predicted that the chief executive, or president, created in the Constitution would eventually enslave America. An exasperated Randolph commented, "If we go on in this irregular manner, contrary to our resolution, instead of three or six weeks, it will take six months to decide this question."[14]

In the days that followed, the Convention addressed the Constitution's contents, at last digging into its articles. Randolph and Madison coolly spoke at length regarding the new system. Henry meanwhile wailed that the central government would eventually "absorb" those of the states, in a "great consolidation of the government." He lamented the lunacy of trusting to amend the document after its ratification, as had been proposed, and warned of the danger that the president would transform into a monarch: "Look for an example of voluntary relinquishment of power from one end of the globe to another: you will find none."

One of Henry's harangues also took aim at the Constitution's empowering Congress to raise and regulate armies. A standing army, he maintained, would ultimately be a tyrant's weapon to terrorize the people. The responsibility of protecting the states should fall to their militias, he argued.

As Henry returned to his seat, Lee took leave of his. At thirty-two, he was two decades Henry's junior. His political career—two terms in Congress—paled in comparison to his antagonist's storied past. But on this issue Lee spoke with authority and experience that Henry, for all his rhetorical pyrotechnics, could not match. While Henry had attended the Virginia Conventions, had twice been governor, and had even ridden to the first Continental Congress with George Washington, Lee had been with Washington at Brandywine and Germantown, and during the agonizing winter at Valley Forge. He had fought at Guilford Courthouse and Eutaw Springs. Henry had not.

Now he enlightened Henry on the impracticality of using the militias as a primary form of national defense. "Without vanity, I must say I have had a different experience from that of the honorable gentleman," Lee began. "It was my fortune to be a soldier for my country. In the discharge of my duty, I knew the worth of militia...I saw what the honorable gentleman did not see. I have seen incontrovertible evidence that militia cannot

always be relied upon." Now he shared his memories of Guilford
Courthouse, where the North Carolina militia, standing on the
front lines and faced with the advancing Redcoats, fled. Memories danced by of Lee chasing after the scared soldiers, threatening them, pleading for them to return to the field as the American
front caved. "Had the line been supported that day Cornwallis,
instead of surrendering at Yorktown, would have laid down his
arms at Guilford," he lamented.[15] No, the only practical means
to defend the nation was for the new government to employ both
regulars and militia.

Now Lee invoked an experience that only the other veterans
present shared. He had been born and raised in Virginia, though
he was educated in New Jersey. But he had left home at the end
of 1776 and spent the following six years fighting in the Northern
and Southern states and alongside Northerners and Southerners
alike. He had established enduring friendships with men from
New York and Pennsylvania. His Legion of Virginians had even
been augmented by soldiers from Northern states, such as New
Jersey. These were his countrymen, his brothers.

Lee grieved that "from the terms in which some of the
Northern states were spoken of, one would have thought that
the love of an American was in some degree criminal, as being
incompatible with a proper degree of affection for a Virginian."
And then, the delegates' attention at his command, slicing
through the sultry air in the Richmond Theatre, Lee made a
definitive appeal to a lasting union of the states. "The people
of America, sir, are one people," he declared. "I love the people
of the north, not because they have adopted the constitution but
because I fought with them as my countrymen, and because I
consider them as such. Does it follow from hence that I have
forgotten my attachment to my native state? In all local matters

I shall be Virginian: in those of a general nature, I shall not forget that I am an American."[16]

There were still many days of arguing and speechifying to come. The debates dragged on. Henry continued to harangue wildly; Madison, with an eye towards persuading the wavering delegates to the Federalist cause, continued to push the convention to order, to keep it on the task of weighing the merits of each section of the Constitution.

Lee played his part, decrying a nation whose government could not recompense its veterans or provide for their widows and orphans. When his conduct during the debate over a treaty with Spain was raised, he dug in. "The public welfare was my criterion," Lee confessed. "In my opinion, I united private interest, not of the whole people of Virginia, but of the United States. I thought I was promoting the real interests of the people."

On the sixteenth, Madison received a letter from Alexander Hamilton, who was preparing to defend the Constitution in New York's ratifying convention. The news was discouraging: antifederalists held a majority at the meeting. Hamilton hoped that if Virginia approved of the new government, it could sway New Yorkers; he asked to be notified at once if Madison could carry the day in Richmond. Madison replied immediately, informing Hamilton that the vote would be close—if the federalists triumphed it would be by only a handful of votes. He then folded the sheet and wrote "turn over" on its bottom. On the other side, Lee wrote a note to his old friend, "We possess as yet in defiance of great exertions a majority, but very small indeed," a moment of uneasy optimism shared between three members of the founding fraternity.

But as the convention reached its crescendo the anti-federalist cause crumbled. Madison's calm reasoning, teamed with the

rhetorical firepower of Lee and Marshall, persuaded the wavering. Mason resorted to demagoguery, warning of a popular
uprising against the new government. Lee dismissed this as
beneath the venerable old statesman. "If the dreadful picture
which he has drawn be so abhorrent to his mind as he had
declared, let me ask the honorable gentleman if he has not pursued the very means to bring into action the horrors which he
depreciates."[17]

With ratification approaching, on June 24 Henry attempted
to introduce forty amendments to the constitution, which would
then be reviewed by the other states—a desperate stalling tactic.
Madison swatted this proposal away, arguing that such a process
would lead to permanent disunion, and it was rejected by the
majority the following day. Then on the twenty-sixth, after making a host of concessions, the friends of the Constitution carried
the day, as the delegates voted in favor of ratification: eighty-nine
yays to seventy-nine nays.[18]

On June 21, while the Virginians debated, New Hampshire
had ratified the Constitution at its own convention, formally
bringing the new American government into being. But Virginia's
endorsement of the new system was crucial nevertheless. Like
New York, which would ratify the following month, Virginia
was one of the nation's most populous and prosperous states.
Without its inclusion, the union would be incomplete, fractured,
and illegitimate. Madison, in his quiet manner, had led the way.
But Lee's soaring, confrontational rhetoric, motivated by a love
of union and sense of nationalism fired by war, and his fearless
confrontations with legendary statesmen many years his senior
played a part as well. He had helped win American independence
on the battlefield. Now he had helped to guarantee a form of
government that would unite the land he loved.

The month after Virginia ratified the Constitution, Lee returned to New York to attend the final session of the Continental Congress, which was gradually less active in the months leading up to the time when the new Constitution would come into effect and the new legislative bodies would meet, beginning in March of 1789. Meanwhile, debate in the old legislature turned to the permanent location for the national capital. In its final years the Continental Congress had called New York home, only because other proposed locations—near Trenton in New Jersey, for example—had failed to win the approval of different sections of the country. There was clamor to bring the government back to Philadelphia, but a stalemate had set in.

During Lee's final moments in Congress, the body resolved to establish a capital city at Germantown, on Pennsylvania's Susquehanna River. Until it was built, though, the government would remain in New York. This plan was postponed and eventually scuttled, leaving the location of a permanent capital in the hands of the incoming Congress. Lee realized that the placement of the federal city on the banks of the Susquehanna would help commerce in the Chesapeake region, but he, like other Virginians, preferred a capital on the Potomac[19]—particularly now because Lee was placing an incredible amount of dependence on the land he had acquired on the Great Falls.

There was also the matter of who would fill the new executive position created by the Constitution. As conceived, this position was naturally designed for Washington. The general, though, facing various financial pressures, was not sanguine about leaving Mount Vernon once more. But his wishes were irrelevant. In late 1787 the newspapers were already publishing articles about his assumption of this new office. Before the first national elections, scheduled for the fall of the following year,

Washington was beseeched by old friends and comrades to accept the presidency to which he would certainly be elected.

Predictably Lee lent his voice, which commanded Washington's respect, to this chorus. Anxiety about the launch of the new government was great. Much depended on a successful beginning. Washington's leadership was necessary to ensure it. "To effect this and to perpetuate a nation formed under your auspices," Lee wrote to his old friend in September, "it is certain that again you will be called forth." He urged his old commander in chief, "Without you the govt. can have but little chance of success, and the people of that happiness, which its prosperity must yield."[20]

Washington's response, written in late September, was frank, confidential, and prolonged, giving a clue of his own difficult deliberations and the trust he placed in Lee. He was attached to farming, he explained, and treasured the life of a private citizen. "You are among the small number of those who know my invincible attachment to domestic life," he wrote, "and that my sincerest wish is to continue in the enjoyment of it, solely, until my final hour."

But there were also other reasons he was disinclined to be the first president. Why could not some other man, with "less pretense," do the job every bit as capably? "You will perceive, my dear Sir, by what is here observed…that my inclinations will dispose and decide me to remain as I am," Washington concluded. There was a caveat, though: "unless a clear and insurmountable conviction should be impressed on my mind that some very disagreeable consequences must in all human probability result from the indulgence of my wishes."[21]

Lee and Washington continued the conversation in person at Mount Vernon, where the former visited at the end of October on his way home from New York. Lee was lending his voice to a chorus to which Washington would eventually relent. The anti-federalists were continuing to work to undermine the new government, even after ratification. Despite his defeat in Richmond, Patrick Henry still held sway over Virginia's legislature, which sent members to the upper house of the new national legislature and drew congressional districts. He would do everything he could to deny Madison and the federalists access to power.

No matter Washington's wishes, the national electors responsible for picking the president voted for Washington unanimously. By the time this outcome became clear, in the spring of 1789, he was resolved to accept the task. Debts were paid, transportation to New York was prepared, a final visit to his ailing mother, Mary, was made. There was also the conclusion of a transaction: Washington agreed to sell Magnolio, a magnificent chestnut-colored Arabian stallion, to Henry Lee in exchange for five thousand acres in Kentucky.[22]

Once the outcome of the election was verified, a messenger was sent to Mount Vernon. Notified that he had been elected, Washington declared his intention to serve. Lee, who had been called back to Stratford Hall, was unable to bid him good-bye. But when asked by Colonel Dennis Ramsey, the mayor of Alexandria, to compose a farewell from the city to the departing hero, Lee dashed off a stirring adieu. "Again your country commands your care," it read. "Obedient to its wishes, unmindful of your ease, we see you again relinquishing the bliss of retirement, and this too at a period of life when nature itself seems to authorize a preference of repose!" The people, he said, would "be doubly grateful when they contemplate this recent sacrifice for their interest."[23]

Washington departed Mount Vernon on April 16, 1789. On the thirtieth he became the first man sworn into the American presidency.[24] "I anticipate with delight our approaching felicity and your new glory—they are entwined together and I hope will never be cut asunder," Lee wrote to the president-elect before his departure.[25]

In the spring of 1789, Henry Lee had every reason to be a contented man. Though he did not seek a seat in the new Congress, and was for the time a private citizen, his great hero and good friend now governed the nation they had both freed. His allies, led by Madison, were a majority in the first Congress. Another old comrade, Alexander Hamilton, was addressing the nation's dire finances as Secretary of the Treasury. And soon the land Lee owned on the newly navigable Great Falls on the Potomac River might be upstream from the nation's new capital city, and the new nation's commerce, moving to and fro from the Atlantic to the Alleghenies, would surely help create a thriving community, enriching him in the process. Then in October 1789 he was elected to Virginia's House of Delegates and arrived in Richmond to participate in that body's debate over amendments to the Constitution that had recently been proposed by Congress.

Lee's ascent in prominence and prosperity had so often moved in tandem with that of his county. But now, at this moment of glory for the United States of America, Lee's fortunes took an abrupt and terrible turn.

The five hundred acres he had acquired at the Great Falls of the Potomac was, at least for the moment, unusable. There were quitrents, or past due rent, on the land that Lee had bought from Bryan Fairfax. This meant that on top of the four thousand pounds he had already paid to Fairfax, Lee was obligated to pay an additional 150 pounds a year. Until this money—which Lee did not have—was tendered, he could not take deed to the land.

At once he contrived schemes to raise the funds, wrangling Madison into the project and pestering Thomas Jefferson to solicit European investment to help underwrite it.

Matilda, after a brief recovery, was deteriorating. In the summer of 1788, there was a return of "burning and tingling." Her beloved mother, Elizabeth, stricken with breast cancer, died in May. The loss devastated Matilda and taxed her already failing health. "Poor Mrs. Lee is particularly injured by it, as the affliction of mind adds to the infirmity of her body," Lee wrote to Madison in June.[26] Despite every effort, there would be no recovery. "Mrs. Lees health is worse and worse, I begin to fear the worst," her husband concluded, ominously. "My long afflicted Mrs Lee is now very ill & I fear cannot be preserved," he sighed to Washington some months later

While Matilda faded and Lee agonized, Alexander Hamilton moved. In a grand bargain struck with Jefferson and Madison during a dinner in New York in the summer of 1790, the Virginians achieved the relocation of the capital city to the Potomac River, and Hamilton won their agreement to his controversial proposition that the federal government assume the debts incurred by the states during the war. This would mean purchasing bonds, many of which—once thought worthless—had been sold at discount to speculators at full value, and establishing an excise tax on whiskey and a tariff on imported goods.

Lee was eager to hear of Hamilton's plans, even hoping for an early confidential preview. "From your situation you must be able to form with some certainty an opinion concerning the domestic debt—will it speedily rise, will the interest accruing command specie, or anything nearly as valuable, what will become of the indents already issued?" he asked the secretary in the fall of 1789, confessing that the "queries, asked for my private information, perhaps they may be improper." Hamilton sagely demurred, explaining that giving any such information to a friend might indeed be "misinterpreted" as improper.[27]

While Lee was originally enthusiastic about Hamilton guiding the nation's finances, he was horrified when he learned of these plans for the federal government to assume the states' debts. Speculators who had swindled impoverished soldiers out of bonds after the war were now to be rewarded by the government. States such as Virginia, which had paid off their debts, would now be forced to pay for the outstanding debts of Massachusetts and others. And by Hamilton's design, it was a plan for boosting American manufacturing, much of which was located in the North, at the expense of the agrarian South.

Lee railed against the plan. He wrote a screed to Madison outlining his objections, which were shared by many in the South. "I am confident it is abhorrent to political wisdom & not strictly consonant to justice," he proclaimed. The idea of the government's paying full value for bonds bought from starving soldiers he found "inadmissible."[28]

The government's shouldering the burden for all this debt would just encourage additional debt and discourage frugality: "political tricks of this kind are abominable & dangerous in their effects," Lee warned Madison. There was also the matter of industry versus agriculture. Lee wondered "how can America expect to flourish under a system calculated only for commercial society." Americans' goods came from the earth, and the process of cultivating them nurtured its citizens. God forbid the government ever subverted this in favor of manufacturing and mercantilism. "If this should not be the case," Lee prophesied, "a change may be worked in our national character which will debase us as men, and destroy us as a people."[29]

The Constitution and new government that Lee had placed so much faith in was now creating policies he conceived to be harmful to his country. And, doubly painful, a dear friend was ushering them in. Public sentiment in Virginia turned against Washington's administration, and Lee, from the floor of the general assembly in Richmond, emerged—in an incredible about-face—as a fierce and eloquent critic of federal policy. He grew increasingly bitter, his language progressively subversive. He spoke of a "monopoly" being imposed from "northern hives," and an effort to "depress the south and exalt the north," with talk amongst those in the government that the natural role of the South was "to be slave to the north."

In a dizzying turn, Lee now viewed Patrick Henry's opposition to the Constitution as prophetic: "his predictions are daily verifying," he told Madison. Dramatically and dishonestly, he declared an end to all his political ambitions. "I wish to be done with govt.," Lee proclaimed. "On the score of tranquility and peace I am also desirous to be quiet, for every day adds new testimony of the growing ill will of the people here to the govt."[30]

The policies that Lee believed were the cure—and an end to this "gambling system of finance"—were unlikely to be implemented. So Lee even broached the subject of rending the Union, with all the carnage it would bring: "I had rather myself submit to all the hazards of war & risk the loss of every thing dear to me in life, than to live under the rule of a fixed insolent northern majority."[31]

The man who was once so attached to union, who had argued so eloquently on its behalf, now strode up to the line of civil war. "But we are committed & we cannot be relieved I fear only by disunion," he wrote. "To disunite is dreadful to my mind, but dreadful as it is, I consider it a lesser evil than union on the present conditions."

Lee asked Madison, "How do you feel, what do you think, is your love for the constitution so ardent, as to induce you to adhere to it tho it should produce ruin to your native country. I hope not, I believe not."[32]

Meanwhile, Lee's project on the Potomac was still stalled. Jefferson communicated from France that interest in investment was nil. And the Potomac Company, in order to clear way for canal construction, seized part of the Fairfax property. Lee desperately attempted to scrounge up the necessary funds to pay off the quitrents on the Great Falls property by selling and leasing land in far flung parts of Virginia.

In the summer of 1790 Lee traveled to Ballston Springs in southern New York with Matilda. There it was hoped that mineral springs would once again provide a tonic for Matilda's ailments. The couple went from there to Albany, where Lee reported that his wife had indeed made some minor progress in the restoration of her health.

There was a new danger though: Matilda was once again pregnant. If her health allowed it, they would return to Stratford in September. At that point, it should be clear whether Lee's "afflicted wife" would "acquire the strength to go well thru her delivery." Lee had spent the previous eight months largely focused on her restoration. The dips and small rises in her health vexed him greatly; his political disenchantment and financial troubles compounded the melancholy.[33] In July Matilda gave birth to a boy, Nathanael Greene Lee, named for his father's old general; the child died in early infancy at Stratford, on the twenty-eighth of that month.[34]

On August 10, alarmed at her husband's efforts to finance his schemes by leasing and selling land she had inherited, Matilda arranged and, along with Lee, signed a trust deeding Stratford Hall to their children, effectively safeguarding it from future depredations by her husband. Surely she realized the end was drawing near. On August 16, the Divine Matilda died; she was twenty-five years old, a wife for merely eight years, and mother to three living children.[35]

Weeks later, an old friend offered Henry Lee his sympathy.

"I... very sincerely condole with you on your late, and great losses," Washington wrote from the house of Samuel Osgood, which was the temporary executive residence in New York, "but as the ways of Providence are as inscrutable as just, it becomes the children of it to submit with resignation & fortitude to its decrees as far as the feelings of humanity will allow and your good sense will, I am persuaded, enable you to do this."[36]

Lee, mindful of posterity, scribbled "the deaths of my wife & son" at the bottom of the letter.

# 11

# INDIFFERENT DESTINY

There was bloodshed in the Northwest. White settlers flooding into the land north of the Ohio River were killing and more often being killed by Shawnee and Miami Indians, on whose land these Americans were intruding. In the autumn of 1790 a mixed force of militia and regulars led by Josiah Harmar made their way to the area to stop the violence. They were promptly routed in a series of battles with a confederacy of tribes.[1]

Looking on from Virginia, Henry Lee saw the humiliating defeat as an opportunity to escape his own agony.

"If the events of war should render a change in the command of your troops necessary, and you should consider me equal to the charge," he wrote to Washington at the end of 1790, "such is my miserable condition from the vicissitude attendant on mortals, that I should esteem it a happiness to be called to military service."[2]

On December 16, 1790, Virginia's General Assembly approved an act formally creating a town at the Great Falls of the Potomac. Its name: Matildaville.[3] A melancholy tribute from a heavy-hearted husband to his absent wife.

The land was divided by its trustees into half-acre lots; streets were plotted and named, and still the ground remained untouched. The plan was still nothing more than a dream, as Lee continued to mortgage other property—two thousand acres in Berkeley County, another twelve hundred in Loudon County—hoping somehow to gather the money so it could at last move forward.

As winter arrived, finally bringing an end to Lee's miserable year, the young widower remained at Stratford Hall, surrounded by his three motherless children, Philip, Lucy, and little Henry. The specifics of Matilda's death are unrecorded. It is unknown if her remains were interred at Stratford Hall. If they were, they would have rested alongside her father's in the family's red-brick burial vault just east of the great house, visible from a window in Lee's bedchamber.

When the spring arrived, the offer he had hoped for, the one that would lift his spirits and at last mean a return to his true vocation, arrived. But not in the form he desired. General Henry Knox, heading Washington's War Department, offered Lee the command of a Virginia battalion being sent into the Northwest for an expedition against the Miami and Shawnee. But the expedition, made up of soldiers from Maryland as well as Virginia, was to be led by General Arthur St. Clair. So Lee, if he accepted the appointment, would be a subordinate to St. Clair. He declined.[4]

When summer arrived Lee, escaping from the gloom of the Matilda-less Stratford Hall, journeyed to Philadelphia, where government offices and agents had established a temporary home. He dined with President Washington and Thomas Jefferson.[5] He continued to scrounge up resources to move forward with the construction of Matildaville, telling Madison he planned to have the money raised when he returned to Virginia later in the summer.[6]

In Philadelphia Lee saw firsthand the speculative boom running wild as the price of securities spiraled upwards during the summer before falling back to earth in the fall—a result of Hamilton's financial program.[7] When he made his way back to Virginia in August, he saw stock gambling all across the route.[8] "What is astonishing in this business," he wrote Madison, "is that all orders of people seem to reckon this appreciation of the public paper a positive proof of wisdom & integrity in govt."[9]

Lee continued to train his eloquence against the administration, winning him allies in Virginia, where the federal government had grown unpopular. And in November the state's legislature, then charged with appointing governors, selected Lee as its chief executive. A week after his inauguration, congratulations arrived from Washington. "An anxiety to do well, which is inseparable from high Offices, generally increases with the importance of the trust committed to our charge," the president advised the new governor.[10]

Lee had sworn the oath of office and begun a one-year term on December 1, 1791.

It was a relatively powerless and not overtly partisan position, but it did require Lee to relocate to the governor's mansion in Richmond. In the final weeks of December Lee left for Richmond along with his eldest son Philip. The two younger children, Lucy and Henry IV, were taken care of by Helen Gilmour, a relative of Lee and the widow of a Scottish shopkeeper living in Lancaster County on the Northern Neck.[11]

Richmond, originally little more than a village on the James River, was something short of cosmopolitan. An abundance of fresh-water springs ran along its savagely rutted streets. Traveling across these gravelly roads was perilous by any means other than horseback. On Shockoe Hill, where the recently finished state capitol stood—a not-yet-stuccoed columned temple conceived by Thomas Jefferson and French architect Charles-Louis Cléris- seau—cattle and hogs wandered. A shabby wooden building nearby housed the public guardsmen and their families. Laundry waved on clotheslines while children and chicken scurried around the grounds.[12]

Lee's new home, the governor's mansion, was the piece de resistance: a modest wooden structure two stories tall, its walls bereft of paint, its furnishings Spartan. Only two rooms, both of average size and on the first floor, were suitable for any form of hosting or even inhabiting.[13] Years later one of Lee's successors, Governor John Tyler Sr., described the dwelling as "intolerable for a private family."[14] In the front yard, goats, climbing up the hill, grazed on the overgrown grass.

The man bounding through the shabby mansion's front door provided a stark contrast with his surroundings. Henry Lee turned thirty-six in January 1792. As he headed towards middle life, no matter his financial vexations and personal tragedies, he remained a figure to behold. The gift of language, the love of literature and banter, the clear eyes and ruddy complexation— they all remained. Still associated with the romance of the Revo- lution, he had a legendary past. And now, as the chief executive of Virginia, he was experiencing an improbable renaissance in his political career: the loyal friend of Washington who had helped ratify the Constitution was now amongst the federal gov- ernment's most notable opponents, allying himself for the time with the political movement that would eventually coalesce around Jefferson. He "was at the head of everything in Virginia," it was recalled decades later, braving Richmond's primitive byways in a polished chariot pulled by six fine horses.[15]

Lee's political position was odd, in opposition to a government whose heights were peopled by old friends and heroes. "No man loves and venerates the P[resident] more than I do, and to hurt his feelings would be doleful to my heart," he wrote Madison, who was now in Congress and increasingly his political sounding board. He then turned around and chided him for not fully rebuffing one of Washington's speeches during the legislature's formal response.[16]

Jefferson and Madison were alarmed by the influence of the *Gazette of the United States*, a pro-administration journal. In search of a counterbalance, they tapped Lee and Madison's old classmate Philip Freneau. Freneau was hired as a State Department clerk, but the appointment was in truth a means to anoint the skilled writer the editor of a new publication, the *National Gazette*, which would critique Washington's government, often vehemently. Jefferson, Madison, and Lee all eagerly leaned on colleagues and friends to buy subscriptions.[17]

Lee's anger at Hamilton's scheme had not abated, though he kept up cordial relations with the secretary of the treasury. "No man is more warmly attached to his friends than I am; among the first of whom my heart places you," Lee wrote to Hamilton. There was no anger; he did not chalk Hamilton's policies up to nefarious intentions. And yet he would not endorse them. "I am solicitous for your encreasing fame," he continued, "and yet cannot applaud your system." This was his civil tone with an old and treasured friend.[18] Lee was even in the process of procuring a well-gaited riding horse for Hamilton amidst their political disagreements.[19]

To Madison he described Hamilton's financial plan as "imitative of the base principles & wicked measures adopted thro necessity in corrupt monarchys." He lamented, "I cannot cease to lament the fatal project introduced and carried by my friend Hamilton of whose head & heart I entertain the highest sentiments of respect."[20]

The year before Lee had talked of destroying the union if it meant protecting his and Virginia's interests. Now he backed away from such incendiary talk. "I deeply lament the sad event," he cried, "but really I see no redress, unless the govt. itself be destroyed. This is risking too much because great evils indubitably must flow from discord & the people must suffer greatly whatever may be the event of such an experiment."[21]

Perhaps he remembered the massacre of John Pyles's men in 1781, or the savage vengeance loyalists and rebels had exacted upon each other in the South—or any grizzly memories from the six years of a war that was at its heart a civil conflict, a people turned against themselves. To resist the policies of America's government, no matter how grievous to Lee's home, in anything other than words or through politics, was to invite destruction. "Sir that funding system will undo us," he warned Madison. But forbearance was preferable to fighting. "While we deprecate & lament the obnoxious event we must submit to it, because effectual opposition may beget civil discord & civil war."[22]

And besides, there was already war elsewhere. In the expedition that Lee had longed to lead to the Northwest to subdue the Indian alliance, General Arthur St. Clair's force was overpowered by an army of Miami, Delaware, and Shawnee near the Wabash River. For the Americans it was not merely a defeat but a humiliating rout, in which nearly all of St. Clair's men were killed or wounded. When news of the debacle reached Philadelphia, the president and Congress were outraged. The legislature opened an investigation into the army's plight—the first such inquiry in the government's history—and at Washington's urging began to gather a more formidable force, a new Legion, to send into the Northwest to at last subdue the coalition of tribes. Lee badly wanted to lead it.

A return to military service could provide a cathartic escape from his troubles and his continuing grief for Matilda. The chaos in the West was on his mind, as he urged the government investigation into the disaster and warned that whoever took St. Clair's place was sure to meet many more Indians. But Lee expressed only polite interest in a personal role in any future expedition. "Was I called upon by the president to command the next campaign," he claimed, "my respect for him would induce me to disregard every triffling obstruction which might oppose my acceptance of the office; such as my own repose the care of my three children & the happiness I enjoy in attention to their welfare, and in the execution of the dutys of my present station."[23]

But in a letter to Madison, Lee sketched out a campaign. The Indians, he believed, were "a gallant desperate people who understand the use of their arms perfectly." The army would have to be retrofitted and properly equipped with better officers and abundant supplies if it was to meet this challenge effectively. And to have a chance of success the campaign would have to begin in the early summer.[24]

Allies in Congress promoted his name for the job—not just Madison, but also Richard Henry Lee, then one of Virginia's two senators, who acquainted his cousin with the ongoing deliberations over a new commander of the western expedition in late March.[25] "I am indifferent as to my destiny," Lee cavalierly responded, "and therefore war suits me as well as peace."

On March 9, Washington met with Hamilton, Jefferson, and Knox to ruminate over possible replacements for St. Clair. What

about Daniel Morgan? Too infirm. Thomas Sumter? Too insub-
ordinate. Andrew Pickens? Talented but not capable of such a
task. Charles Pinckney? Too busy with his business interests.
Anthony Wayne? Brave, but little else.

And then there was Henry Lee. "A better head and more
resource than any of them," the group observed. But there were
two problems. Lee's string of foolish investments and financial
troubles had not gone unnoticed. He had "no economy," it was
devastatingly observed. Plus, there was the matter of rank. When
Lee rode north from South Carolina and away from the army,
he was still a relatively junior officer; those with higher ranks
would be reluctant to serve under him: "being a junior officer,
we should lose benefit of good seniors who would not serve under
him," the cabinet concluded.[26]

Ultimately, after much deliberation and political calculation,
Washington selected Wayne.[27] Lee, naturally, claimed he had
never expected the commission in the first place, but he was stung
by the decision. All that was left was to offer his hopes for
Wayne's prospects. "I sincerely hope the new general may give
peace to our country, and restore the honor of the American
name,"[28] he declared to Madison.

So he remained in Richmond as an exceptionally beautiful
spring arrived, tending to the duties of his station. The lunatic
asylum in Williamsburg was in need of funds; there was little
in the state coffers to spare, though. There were petitions from
citizens ranging from aggrieved shop keepers to destitute soldiers to consider. The state capitol's roof had cracked; rain was
flooding into the building; repairs were needed. The stove and
windows in Richmond's courthouse were in need of replacement. There were disputes over malfunctioning flues and fireplaces in the various government officials' offices to adjudicate.

An infamous horse thief, William Towe, had escaped from prison; Lee was compelled to issue an award for his apprehension. There were pleas for stays of execution to consider, and boundaries, such as those between Virginia and North Carolina, to be established. Fisheries had to be regulated, and there were solicitations for the governor to pay Virginia's past due contributions to the construction of the new capital city on the Potomac River.[29]

"I have withdrawn myself from continental politics," Lee breezily informed Hamilton. "My indifference has begot an ignorance and both together have established an uninterrupted calm in my breast. The State business furnishes me with employment and ease & innocence accompany my execution of the dutys of my station."[30]

But larger matters intruded on Lee's supposed calm. On Virginia's southeastern coast, in the port towns of Norfolk and Portsmouth, citizens were fretting. Beyond the Atlantic Ocean, there was a troubling revolt on the French island of Saint-Domingue. Inspired by the revolution underway in Paris, as well as by the ethos of America's own struggle for independence, free blacks and slaves led by a romantic figure named Toussaint Louverture rose up in search of freedom, sending French colonists scurrying. Many set sail with their slaves and landed on Virginia's Chesapeake Bay.[31]

This development was unwelcome to slave owners who feared that their property, seduced by word of the rebellion, would seek their own freedom by force. Beginning in the summer of 1792, Lee was receiving panicked letters from Norfolk and Portsmouth, carrying word of the "insolent and troublesome" behavior of slaves, as well as rumors of midnight meetings attended by liberty-seeking blacks and their white allies. There were no weapons or ammunition to fight off a slave insurrection, the governor was continually warned.

Of course Lee was a slave owner through inheritance and marriage—as were most members of his family, though Richard Henry Lee's opposition to the institution pre-dated the American Revolution. Henry Lee's views on the matter were similar to those of Virginia's other planter-statesmen such as Washington, Jefferson, and Madison. They cursed slavery as an awful quandary bequeathed to them by previous generations. And yet—despite their passion for liberty and remarkable intellectual gifts—they were sadly content to leave it to a future generation to resolve the dilemma. The state's laws regarding slaves were staggeringly cruel. During his time as governor, Lee regularly received pleas to spare the lives of slaves who had been condemned to death—in one case, for stealing corn and bacon.[32]

Unsurprisingly, Lee saw the rumors of insurrection as a threat to be dealt with in the harshest terms, directing the county lieutenants in the regions that feared rebellion to "crush the mad attempt."[33] Arms were dispensed—though one official complained that the muskets were in disrepair, their bayonets rusty. But when Lee travelled to Norfolk to take stock of the situation, he discovered that the alarm was overblown. The number of slaves plotting rebellion was miniscule. And one of the great causes for any potential uprising was, according to Lee, "the practice of severing husband, wife & children in sales."[34]

A more formidable threat raged on Virginia's southwestern frontier, where Cherokee Indians were raiding communities and often killing white settlers along the Kanawha River. Militias were armed, usually at the expense of the federal government, and lieutenants were appointed. Lee scheduled a tour of the state's western frontier to inspect fortifications firsthand in the summer of 1792. Before that journey, in July, Lee traveled back to the Northern Neck, likely to see Lucy and his son Henry IV in Lancaster County, at the home of Helen Gilmour. After a week's absence Lee returned to Richmond to receive awful news.

In Lee's absence, Little Philip Ludwell Lee, his oldest surviving son, had died following a sudden illness on July 17, 1792.[35] Lee, who was still grieving the boy's mother, was devastated. A miniature of the child, who was said to resemble Matilda, was painted by Charles Willson Peale around 1790. The watercolor, on ivory, depicts a sweet-faced boy with dark hair and light eyes. Lee carried the portrait for the remainder of his days.

"I am still depressed in my mind & continue to be the subject to unavailing woe," he wrote Hamilton. "My son on whom I chiefly counted for future comfort was suddenly deprived of life during my absence, which event on the back of what took place two years past has removed me far from the happy enjoyment of life."[36] To Madison he simply wrote of "my late domestic calamity which stings me to the quick."[37]

Shortly before this latest blow, Lee had begun to ameliorate his ennui with a new pastime. Arguably the most eligible bachelor in Virginia, if not the country, Lee was contemplating romance once again. He described himself as "in love with every sweet nymph but not so far gone with any one yet as to think of matrimony." One lady in particular, Anne Penn Allen, the daughter of Philadelphia loyalist James Allen and one of the most gracious and stunning beauties of the era, enchanted Lee. "The beautiful Miss Allen I hear is still unpossessed," he wrote to Hamilton.[38]

Love, though, had to battle war for Lee's attention. An ocean away the revolution in France, inspired by many of the same lofty philosophies as America's, was raging. Lee's old friend the

Marquis de Lafayette, whose portrait hung in Stratford Hall's parlor, played an early part in the revolt, sitting in France's national assembly, commanding the French National Guard and drafting, in collaboration with Jefferson, the Declaration of the Rights of Man, a grand statement of human rights and liberties.

Nathanael Greene's prediction that Lee could never cease to be a soldier was proving prophetic. Lee still longed to return to battle; he desired to once again experience the euphoric fury of combat. He also saw a resumption of his military career as a way to restore purpose and direction to his life, a means to escape his sorrow. Sometime in 1792 he wrote to Lafayette wondering whether there was some way he could join France's revolutionary cause. But the timing was unfortunate. Lafayette, a relative moderate in a revolution far more savage and convulsive than the one he and Lee had fought in, was attacked by radicals, chased from France, captured, and imprisoned in Austria. He could be of little help to Lee.

But Lee also wrote to William Stephens Smith—who had served on Lafayette's staff in America and was in France in 1792—wishing to know about "the real state of affairs" there. Were the violent convulsions jeopardizing the revolution? "I very much wish to cross the Atlantic and offer to that illustrated Nation my humble services as a soldier," Lee wrote, "this line of life, my friend, suits me, for an addition to the loss of my wife, I have lately lost my eldest son, the Chief remaining source of my comfort...."[39]

Smith shared Lee's letter with Venezuelan freedom fighter Francisco de Miranda, who was for a time a general in the French Revolutionary Army. Through these channels, Lee was tendered an offer of the military commission he coveted.[40] As 1792 wound to a close, he deliberated over departing for France. But in

October Virginia's General Assembly, satisfied with Lee's performance as governor, returned him for a second term, to begin the first of December. The influence of an older generation of Lees on American politics was waning, though. That fall Richard Henry Lee, citing infirmity, resigned his Senate seat. His brother Arthur, a diplomat during the American Revolution, died two months later.

As the year turned, Lee still planned to leave Virginia for France, but new considerations came to mind. He had fallen deeply in love with Maria Farley, a twenty-three-year-old woman who had grown up at Nesting, a plantation on the Charles River, and was kin to the Carter clan, another of Virginia's grand families. Years before the Revolution, Robert "King" Carter had been one of the colony's wealthiest and most powerful men. Farley was a ward of Carter's grandson, Charles, a wealthy politician-planter in his own right, and the lord of Shirley, a gracious plantation on the north banks of the James River, southeast of Richmond and north of Williamsburg.

Lee made repeated visits there in hopes of winning Maria Farley's hand. While he courted the young woman, her cousin and companion Anne looked on achingly. For it was Anne, Charles Carter's daughter, not Maria Byrd Farley, who was overcome by the handsome governor, mesmerized by his conversation, impressed by his station and storied past, charms that were lost on Maria. When Lee offered her marriage, she declined. Stunned, Anne Carter, pleaded with her cousin to reconsider— "O stop stop Maria—You do not know what you are throwing away!"[41]

But Farley's loss was Anne Carter's gain. Spurned by the object of his desire, Lee looked to the girl who would requite his love. She was seventeen years his junior, the first child of her father's second marriage, and one of twenty-one siblings. Nick-named Nancy, she was especially dear to her father, who was advanced in age at the time of her birth. Her manner was sweet but solemn, matching her severe beauty: her raven-colored hair matched her dark eyes, offset by olive skin. She was educated, a fluent raconteur and a fine writer—skills not common amongst Virginians of the fair sex in the eighteenth century. She was also musical, a talented harpsichordist with a honeyed voice. Growing up among her family on the great plantations of the James River with loving and generous parents, her youth had been happy. But she was prone to idolatry. And his excellency Governor Lee, bolting up Shirley's lawn on horseback, was too much to resist.

In the spring of 1793 he was still contemplating a place in Paris, but Charles Carter, already dubious about seeing his young daughter united with Lee, would not consent to the marriage if he was to leave the country. In the end, searching for advice, Lee turned to the man whose judgment carried more weight than all others.

"Bred to arms I have always since my domestic calamity wished for a return to my profession, as the best resort to my mind in its affliction," Lee wrote Washington on April 29. He informed the president that a major generalship awaited him abroad. If it was a "fair war on terms of honor, with certainty of sustenance to the troops and certainty of accord among the citizens," Lee would "embark." But he wished for Washington's advice. "I am consequently solicitous for the best advice, and this I am persuaded you can give," he explained.[42]

Washington's response, written little more than a week later, was brimming with subtle and disinterested wisdom. "As a public character, I can say [nothing] on the subject of it. As a private man, I am unwilling to say much," the president wrote. If he were in Lee's place, Washington advised, "I should ponder well before I resolved...." How would it look, he wondered, if the leader of one of America's largest states wandered off, like a soldier of fortune, to fight in a war an ocean away? Given Lee's position as "first Magestrate of a respectable State, much speculation would be excited by such a measure; and the consequences thereof not seen into at the first glance." Besides, Washington continued, the state of affairs in France was dangerous and in disorder, her citizens on the verge of tearing each other to shreds.[43]

The words dissuaded Lee from this military adventure. By early May 1793 he had abandoned the idea. "I have to thank you from my heart for your late letter—It has had I hope a happy effect, for I feel myself yielding to its weight of reason," he answered Washington, "and begin to think that the pursuit of my plan would in the present condition of things be madness."[44]

Lee's cooling ardor for the French Revolution mirrored larger events in American politics. When that war, sprawling across the European continent, drew England in, Washington—after his cabinet deliberated the matter—issued a public statement of American neutrality between France and England. The United States were neither strong nor established enough to engage in such a conflict. The outlier among Washington's cabinet on the issue was Secretary of State Thomas Jefferson, who supported the French Revolution, opposed the declaration of neutrality, and was increasingly estranged from Washington. Lee praised the proclamation and considered it wise.[45]

His flirtation with France over, Lee now focused on matrimony. "I mean now to become a farmer & get a wife as soon as possible," he wrote to Hamilton.[46] In early May he proposed to Anne Carter and promptly informed her father of his intentions.

The elder Carter relented. "The only objection we ever had to your connexion with our beloved Daughter is now entirely done away," Carter told him, "...you have given over all thoughts of going to France, and we rest satisfied with that assurance." But, perhaps aware of Lee's impetuousness or doubting his dedication to Anne, Carter made one request: "as we certainly know that you have obtained her consent you shall have that of her parents most cordially to be joined together in the holy bonds of Matrimony, whenever she pleases....Inclinations and sincere affections of all the Friends as well as the parties immediately concerned we think the sooner it takes place, the better...."[47]

The pair wed in Shirley's Great Hall, on a torturously muggy Tuesday evening, June 18. The joy of the family and friends crowding around to hear the vows recited was diminished only by their soaked clothing. Washington sent congratulations, expressing his joy that Lee had abandoned "the rugged & dangerous field of Mars, for the soft and pleasurable bed of Venus."[48] A locket, inside it a miniature of the president, was sent as a gift.

The *Virginia Gazette* called the groom "Virginia's favorite young soldier," described the bride as "amiable and accomplished," and labeled the occasion "an event which promises the most auspicious fortune to the wedded pair."[49] Indeed, it was, by appearances, a splendid match—a pairing of prestige, prosperity, and power that portended a joyful future for both bride and groom. And it was seemingly an end to Lee's gloom, an answer to his aimlessness.

# 12

# POINTING THE BAYONET AGAINST THE HEARTS OF OUR COUNTRYMEN

The French frigate *L'Embuscade* docked in Charleston Bay on the afternoon of April 9, 1793, and off stepped a self-assured young diplomat to a rousing reception. South Carolina's governor, William Moultrie, was at the head of a cheering crowd that awaited him with warm greetings. Impeccably connected, with a gift for languages, Edmond-Charles Genêt was France's newly minted minister to America. He arrived with orders to fire up enthusiasm for France's Revolution among Americans and to tilt their government's stance in its favor. There were also the loans lingering from America's own Revolution, which Genêt was ordered to collect.

So instead of heading quickly to Philadelphia to present his credentials to the president and his deputies, Genêt embarked on a prolonged mischief-making tour on his way north. Calling himself "Citizen Genêt"—to underline his revolutionary bona fides—he was greeted on his journey by cheering crowds and feted by politicians at public dinners. Also, in direct violation of America's policy of neutrality that Washington declared, he freely handed out notes authorizing privateers to apprehend British vessels with the full authority of the French government.

On May 9, Genêt arrived in Richmond to meet with Henry Lee, notorious critic of the central government. To the seemingly sympathetic American, Genêt spouted his reliable argument against neutrality: should the French Revolution fail, the great monarchies of Europe would come to squelch the democratic experiment underway in America, he warned. But Lee was unaffected. Washington's policy was in the best interests of both America and her friend France, he retorted.[1] "Peace to America is in one word, our all," he wrote to Hamilton, defending the policy.[2] It was also politically sound: in his travels across Virginia, soliciting the perspectives of the state's planters, Lee found the neutral stance popular.[3]

Genêt's arrival and Lee's changing attitude came as American politics, cracked during the first years of Washington's presidency, fully ruptured—something the president's decision regarding France made inevitable. Across the country, egged on by Genêt, clandestine clubs called "Democratic-Republican Societies" coalesced. Members, many from the American yeomanry, celebrated agriculture over manufacturing and wished to empower the states at the expense of the central government. These men admired France's increasingly radical revolution, loathed Great Britain, and detested the policies of Washington's government. They fixated on Alexander Hamilton, who was seemingly always at the president's elbow, covertly driving the nation's policies.

Thomas Jefferson, who had hoped to resign from Washington's cabinet in early 1793 but had been coaxed by the president into remaining, was the leader of this emerging faction in American politics; his friend James Madison, its legislative workhorse in Congress. Propagandists such as Philip Freneau, whose scribblings Lee had once promoted, spread the faction's message and spat malice at its enemies. Despite his own histrionics in the preceding years, and the history and principles he shared with members of this coalition, Lee, like Washington, viewed the formalization and intensification of America's factional partisan divide with alarm.

In 1793 Lee, remarried and sharing the modest governor's mansion with his new bride and his two surviving children, was occupied once again with the minutia of his office. The Richmond Literary Society sought his permission to use the Senate room in the state capitol for its meetings.[4] There was an outbreak of fever on the Caribbean island of Grenada; at Virginia's ports sailors were screened to prevent any potentially sick men from setting foot on her soil.[5]

There was an ongoing lawsuit that had been brought by the Indiana Company, which claimed ownership of lands in Virginia. When ordered to appear before the Supreme Court in August, Virginia blithely refused; in December the state adopted a resolution asserting that Virginia was not obligated to appear before any federal court.[6]

There was the matter of Angelica Barnett, a free black woman who had murdered a white man, Peter Franklin, when he stormed into her home screaming accusations that she was harboring fugitive slaves. Fearing for her life, Barnett drove an axe deep into Franklin's skull. She was well known and esteemed among Richmond's elites, and, in a curious twist, she became pregnant while in prison. Prominent Virginians, including John Marshall, petitioned for her pardon, which Lee granted.[7]

Alarmed notes from the frontier still arrived reporting attacks by Indians and decrying the lack of government assistance. But, with a peace conference scheduled with the western tribes on the Lower Sandusky River in Ohio, Secretary of War Henry Knox ordered that no more incursions onto Indian land be made by militia or settlers. Knox also asked Lee to seek no further federal reimbursements for arming Virginians.[8]

The state of Lee's finances continued to disintegrate. In the spring he joined a syndicate with John and James Marshall, their brother-in-law Rawleigh Colston, and Philadelphia financier Robert Morris, who had played a central role in creating the nation's financial system during the Revolution and also happened to be James Marshall's father-in-law. The group purchased 160 acres of Northern Neck land from the Fairfax family for $20,000.[9]

And at long last, on September 3, 1793, Bryan Fairfax granted Lee the lease of 500 acres at the Great Falls of the Potomac for 900 years at the cost of $666.66, with the first installment due in December, finally clearing the way for Lee to lease Matildaville's lots. He hired an English farmer to live at the Falls and supervise work there.[10] By the fall the Potomac Company was making some headway in its work at the Great Falls, though the state still owed the organization much-needed money.[11]

Scrounging for ways to fund this enterprise, Lee received a visitor from the national city being built farther east on the Potomac. The Irish-born architect James Hoban had met with and impressed Washington and been christened the victor of a competition to design a new house in the capital city for future presidents. In search of materials, Hoban trekked to Stratford Hall, where he contracted with Lee for the purchase of a number of large oak trees to be used as timber to raise this new executive mansion. The builders of the federal city to be named in tribute to Washington continued to pester Lee about "the delay of payments from the state": Virginia remained delinquent on her contributions.[12]

When the Virginia legislature reconvened in the fall, Lee addressed the problem of Genêt and the Democratic-Republican Societies. Washington's government had eventually requested the minister's recall after he personally insulted the president and threatened to appeal over his head to the American people to side with France against Great Britain. But the party organizations remained. One of these in particular, the Society of Philadelphia, was advocating loudly on Genêt's behalf through circular letters.

Observing that "I ever attributed the mad conduct of a certain foreigner to the insidious & malignant councils of some perverse ambitious americans," Lee still worried that Genêt's antics would entice Americans to flout their own nation's policy and side with France, at the risk of great dangers. The society in Philadelphia was the greatest offender. "This was intended as a standard for the people to rally under," Lee angrily wrote to Washington, "and menaced from its very nature the destruction of the constitution and government under which we live."[13]

Some governors, including Maryland's Thomas Sim Lee, had issued their own proclamations praising the federal government's course of action and pledging to prohibit any violation of it. Virginia's governor took this a step further, seeking to make an even grander display in favor of the policy of neutrality. With Washington's approval, Lee nudged Virginia's legislature to issue their own resolutions in support of Washington's neutrality proclamation.[14]

But this gave birth to a vitriolic legislative session character-ized by partisan divides not before seen in Virginia's government. On the first day of November 1793, the House of Delegates, the lower body of the legislature, passed the resolutions—only to see the Senate reject them a week later. Lee was reelected for a third term on the fifteenth of that month, and—assuming that his stance on the issue had played a part—he thanked both chambers for their "commendation of my prompt and decided support of the President's Proclamation." This sentiment was not shared by all. Madison, puzzled by the governor's speech, described Lee's conduct as "curious" in a letter to Jefferson.[15]

In the spring of the following year, Lee's fears about the subversive influence of the partisanship fanned by Genêt and the Democratic-Republican Societies were proven true: an enraged Norfolk crowd turned on and tarred and feathered a dissenter in the midst of a pro-French demonstration.[16] Then in June events forced Lee to take action. The *Unicorn*, a boat docked in the river town of Smithfield on the eastern coast of Virginia, was equip-ping in order to privateer. Its captain brushed off any inquires by the local marshal, even threatening him with violence in the face of a search warrant. Militia were gathered, but the conduct of the ship's captain, a man named Sinclair, grew increasingly threatening. Finally, Lee ordered the state's cavalry to Smithfield. Their arrival ended the matter quickly. The ship was appre-hended, along with muskets with which to capture British vessels. The *Unicorn* was guided out of Smithfield and on to the Bahamas by armed guard. "Events of this sort excite universal attention, and I trust will receive universal detestation," Lee wrote to Knox, apprising the secretary of the "wicked effort."[17]

"The zeal, love of order, and determination to support the civil authority, which animates the militia in every quarter," Lee continued, "manifests in the strongest colours their sense of the indignity offered to their government...."[18] When Knox passed this news on to Washington, the president received it with "great satisfaction."[19]

Lee was never a partisan in the truest sense. He had found certain policies offensive to his personal interests and dangerous to the country. But his relations with Washington and Hamilton had remained cordial even as he lambasted their government. These were simply spirited and principled disagreements; Lee had never had a desire to see the Constitution and government fall or the president fail. So it was not surprising when he was drawn back into the Federalist orbit and used the threat of force against his own countrymen in order to maintain peace and order and enforce the government's laws. Shortly he was called on to do the same beyond Virginia's borders.

Reports of restlessness in the western regions of his state in response to Hamilton's excise tax on whiskey production had crossed Lee's desk. Zachariah Johnston, a farmer-orator who had attended the Virginia Ratifying Convention, informed Lee of the unpopularity of the levy in the Shenandoah Valley, where stills were lying idle and the inhabitants, to a man, detested the law. And though it was seemingly just rhetoric, some were talking openly of petition for redress or even a repeal by force.

Madison and Jefferson had gritted their teeth and agreed to Hamilton's economic scheme in order to secure the Potomac location for the national capital. And part of his plan to repay the debts of the nation (and of the states) involved this tax on goods produced and consumed across America, including fees on items such as snuff, lump sugar, and—most consequentially— whiskey. Producers and refiners of the first two products could cope with the fines by raising prices. But the tax on whiskey was far more problematic.

Western farmers and frontiersmen used their crops—oats, wheat, and rye—to distill the spirit, and not just to sell or consume the drink. In remote areas where cash was scarce, whiskey served as a substitute currency with which to acquire goods and even pay for services. The salaries of many ministers, for example, were augmented with bottles of whiskey. The economy in remote areas of the nation, far from centers of commerce or population, such as the land west of Pennsylvania's Allegheny Mountains, was monolithically agrarian. As a result, there was not much in the way of a local market for crops. And with customers in Philadelphia too far beyond the mountains and the waters of the Mississippi River still closed to American commerce, where else could they go, infuriated farmers asked. To make matters far worse, the tax was to be paid in cash, at about nine cents per gallon. Producers to the east with bigger capacity and better access to markets could afford the fee. But back-country distillers, producing much smaller quantities than their eastern counterparts, and now forced by the government to register their stills, angrily viewed the law as a direct infringement from a faraway power—one that was not, in their view, doing enough to ward off Indian attacks closer to home.

Protests began in July 1791. Meetings were held at Redstone Fort in Brownsville, Pennsylvania, where the citizens from four western counties in that state with the highest number of distillers in the nation—Allegheny, Fayette, Washington, and Westmoreland—agreed to organize in opposition to the law in their respective homes. Another gathering, attended by prominent citizens and elected officials, was scheduled later in the year in Pittsburg. In September a tax collector in Washington County,

Robert Johnson, was assaulted by a pack of men disguised as women. Pulled down from his horse and stripped of his clothes, he was tarred and feathered, left behind shivering in a forest.[20] Such violence increasingly faced revenue officers attempting to extract taxes.

Both Washington and Hamilton were exasperated as defiance spread from Pennsylvania into Maryland, Virginia, the Carolinas, and even Georgia. In September 1792 the president issued a proclamation, written by Hamilton and edited by Attorney General Edmund Randolph, condemning the resistance, to little avail.[21] The unrest only intensified.

Congress attempted to mollify protestors by amending the law and allowing those in remote areas who refused to pay the tax to appear in courts closer to home rather than to travel to Philadelphia. But before this modification was even codified, David Lennox, a U.S. Marshall, and General John Neville, a federal tax agent in Fayette County, were serving summonses to farmers busy at work during the harvest in Allegheny County. Their rounds included a visit to the farm of William Miller, a typical opponent of the tax: he was a veteran of the Revolution then in the process of selling his farm to relocate to Kentucky. Miller's hoped-for-move was now null, though: traveling to the capital and paying the excise tax would clean him out.[22]

Lennox and Neville came under fire from a posse of angry locals who had stalked them across the countryside. Unscathed, the two agreed to split, with Lennox riding off to the town of Pittsburg and Neville returning to Bower Hill, his fortified home. That night, the posse multiplied into a militia, deputized a marshal and headed to Neville's house in hopes of arresting Lennox. There a confrontation ensued. Neville and his slaves opened fire on the group, striking and killing Miller's young nephew

Oliver.[23] The following day the rebels returned to Bower Hill in greater force, led by James McFarlane, another veteran of the Revolution, who was killed while attempting to call a cease fire. This loss of life escalated what had begun as a series of defiant gestures against the government into a real rebellion. Sensing the escalation at hand, one excise collector resigned his post explaining that the "opposition" had changed from a "dignified rabble to a respectable party."[24]

Now with David Bradford, a prominent local lawyer, at their head, the rebels seized mail leaving Pittsburg bound for Philadelphia in search of any communications hostile towards their cause. On August 1 Bradford called for a gathering of militia at Braddock's Field, eight miles outside of Pittsburg. The city itself was the closest thing to urban sophistication in the region, which made it a target for the farmers' rage; many of its citizens feared that the approaching rebel army was coming to pillage and burn. But with some seven thousand men behind him, Bradford led his flock peacefully into Pittsburg, in large part on the advice of another local politician, Hugh Henry Brackenridge, who also urged the citizens of the city to banish several of their number who were vocally opposed to the rebels. On their march back west, though, the army set fire to the barn of Major Abraham Kirkpatrick, who had brought soldiers to aid John Neville, his brother-in-law.[25]

To Washington, this signified the first major challenge to the authority of the young government. On August 7, 1794, he issued another proclamation, enumerating the misdeeds of the rebels, decrying their "dangerous and criminal purpose," forbidding Americans from lending them aid, and finally, under the authority granted him by an Act of Congress two years before, warning that federal militia were to be raised in order to finally end this rebellion should it not cease its exertions against the laws of the U.S. government.[26] But in hopes of avoiding a violent confrontation, peace negotiations were scheduled in Parkinson's Ferry in central Pennsylvania, a hotbed of anti-excise sentiment.

When Secretary Knox sent copies of the proclamation to the governors of Pennsylvania, Connecticut, Maryland, and Virginia, he included orders to raise and equip militia prepared to stand ready to "march at a moments warning," to a yet-to-be-disclosed rendezvous point.[27] While the president still hoped the situation could be diffused by peaceful means, Hamilton, eager to meet the rebellion with a show of force, propagandized against the rebels in Philadelphia's newspapers.[28]

Anger against the excise tax in Virginia's rural areas did not match that in western Pennsylvania. And though the state's Democratic-Republicans had welcomed Genêt and hailed the creation of the Democratic-Republican Societies, they quickly condemned the insurrection.[29] This, however, did not stop some of the rebels from other states from crossing into Virginia and raising hell. On the night of August 9, a pack of thirty Pennsylvanians slipped south across the border and surrounded the house of the federal tax collector in Morgantown, on the Monongahela River, and chased him off, forcing Lee to issue a proclamation that decried the "evil doings" of these "banditti."

These Pennsylvanians, Lee declared, were part of a deluded combination, "forgetful of obligations human and divine." They "seem only intent on rapine and anarchy and therefore endeavor by their emissaries and other illegal means to seduce the good people of this Commonwealth inhabiting the country bordering on the state of Pennsylvania, to unite with them in schemes and measures tending to destroy the tranquility and order which so

happily prevails, and thereby to convert the blessings we so emi-
nently enjoy under our free and equal government into the most
afflicting miseries which can possibly befall the human race."[30]
Virginia's civil and military officers were, the governor wrote,
empowered to bring these villains to justice.

Lee's original instructions from Knox ordered the governor
to raise 3,330 men. They were followed up, though, with an
additional directive. Should this army, made from the combined
militias, be forced to march against the rebels, Lee was to be at
its head. "The President anticipates," Hamilton wrote, "that it
will be as painful to you to execute, as it is to him to direct, measures of coertion against fellow citizens however misled." Nevertheless, Washington planned to march west to meet with the
army; if it inspired his confidence, he would return to the capital
leaving Lee to direct it onwards to quell the rebellion.[31]

Lee had longed for a return to military service for some time.
Chances for this had passed him by, or in the case with his fling
with a commission in France, second thoughts and outside advice
had convinced him to turn down the offer. Now he was to be a
major-general; no higher rank was obtainable. He would lead a
force of many thousands into the field to arrest a rebellion that
threatened national harmony. It was a task he naturally accepted,
though not without distress.

"I consider this insurrection as the first *formidable* fruit of
the Democratic Societies," Washington wrote to Lee on August
26.[32] True, egged on by Genêt, they had given rise to something
seemingly pernicious: a segment of the citizenry who, as a result
of "party spirits," were bent on undermining their union. And
no doubt this contagion had played a part in giving life to the
unrest in the West. "All good citizens," Lee told Washington,
"deplore the events which have produced this conduct on your

part, & feel but one determination to maintain inviolate our happy government at the risk of their lives & fortunes...."[33]

But to end this insurrection might very possibly require bloodshed—making war on fellow Americans. As Lee began the task of raising Virginia's militia, he suffered from "agitation of mind." As he confessed to Washington, "My grief for the necessity of pointing the bayonet against the hearts of our countrymen is equaled only by my conviction of the wisdom of your decision to compel immediate submission to the authority of the laws...."[34]

Hamilton's plan to pay off the country's debt—the very policy that had given birth to the tax these Whiskey Boys were rebelling against—appalled Lee. But no matter any personal sympathy Lee had with their grievances, the authority of government, the restoration of order, the maintenance of peace, all required that the uprising be put down. Union and peace trumped partisanship and factionalism.

The peace negotiations in western Pennsylvania faltered. The rebels had one nonnegotiable condition, which the government would not concede: that the tax be repealed. "The crisis is now come, submission or opposition," Bradford bellowed.[35] A grand show and threat of force was now the government's only recourse. It was either that or a society governed by, in the words of the *Gazette of the United States*, "tar, and feathers, a guillotine, or riots."[36] On September 3, Hamilton informed Lee that the militia would likely be called to march and that he should be ready to muster as soon as possible.[37]

The work of raising and arming soldiers from across Virginia went forward. Thomas Nelson from Yorktown and George K. Taylor from Petersburg were named Lee's aides-de-camp and Otway Byrd his quartermaster general. Daniel Morgan, the hero of Saratoga and Cowpens, aging but again in passable health and full of rage against the rebels, would recruit and command part of the force.[38] Arms, stores, tents were all gathered from the state and federal government. Uniforms were designed and donned. Virginia's cavalry would wear the short green coats and bear-skinned caps that Lee of the Light Horse had once worn. Now a general, he donned a coat of navy, its buttons yellow, its cuffs and lapels buff, golden epaulettes draped across its shoulders, and polished black boots, on his head a black hat punctuated by a cockade.[39]

In late September Lee reluctantly left Virginia. Both Anne and his son Henry IV were ailing at Shirley. And sickness had so recently claimed another wife and a son. As he left them behind, he feared the farewells could be final. "The day which blessed you cursed me," he wrote James Madison, who a week before had wed a voluptuous young widow named Dolley Payne Todd. "I left my family to join the troops destined to restore order in Pennsylvania."[40]

Training in the northern Virginia town of Winchester was pleasant for the green soldiers: "We have mountains of beef and oceans of whisky," a young militiaman named Meriwether Lewis wrote his mother.[41] There were difficulties, though. Because of a want of supplies, everything from muskets and bayonets to reams of cartridge paper to screwdrivers to camping equipment had to be shipped from Philadelphia, lent by the federal government to supplement the state's stores.

The gathered force from the four states was to reach nearly thirteen hundred. But organizing it proved problematic as many Americans, particularly those from rural areas, refused to fight their countrymen and attempted to avoid the service by fleeing from home. Draft riots erupted in Maryland and Pennsylvania.

Pockets of Virginian resistance, in Norfolk and Dinwiddie County in the heart of the state, resulted in court-martials and imprisonments. In Surry, a local militia captain was able to compel only eight men to join his force; offended locals formed a short-lived counter militia that, rumors said, was bent on attacking one of the state's arsenals.[42] Worried that this sentiment would spread to other parts of the state, Lee pleaded with Bilby H. Avery, a colonel in that region, to do what he could to lift spirits. "I beg you to tell your worthy lads," Lee wrote, "that I am drafted as well as themselves, and I mean to march hand in hand with them, leaving behind me a sick wife and a very sick only son."[43]

"If we permit our laws to be violated with impunity," he continued, "farewell to order, farewell to liberty and all the political happiness we enjoy, and for which we so prodigally bled and paid."[44]

The army's original destination was Fort Cumberland, which the British had built during the French and Indian War on the confluence of the Wills and Potomac Rivers. There the Virginia and Maryland forces would converge before moving east. Regiments from New Jersey and Pennsylvania were marching towards the town of Carlisle, under the supervision of Washington and Hamilton. The latter, to avoid political fury, had retained the rank of lieutenant colonel. But as Secretary of War Knox had been granted a furlough in order to return home to Maine to tend to his estate, Hamilton assumed administrative control over the entire endeavor.[45] The army itself was a sloppy amalgamation of raggedy outfitted raw recruits drafted from the American underclass and stylishly clad affluent volunteer soldiers; the latter naturally sneered at the former.[46] Westerners, deriding this amateurish rag-tag fighting force, labeled it the Watermelon Army.[47]

Lee headed east into Maryland as the regiments departed Winchester. The combined forces, which would make up the left wing of the army, arrived at Fort Cumberland by October 10. The president, announced by the firing of artillery and escorted by three troops of light dragoons along stone roads men under his own command had opened in 1758, arrived there on the sixteenth. The soldiers scrambled out of their encampments and regiments were drawn up, as Washington passed by and bowed to all the assembled officers. He remained there for two days, planning the army's movements with Lee. Then he rode back east to Bedford, where the right wing of the army, made up of the troops from New Jersey and Pennsylvania, was gathering.[48]

When he arrived at Bedford, Washington strutted three thousand of the militiamen up the streets as awed and anxious westerners looked on. At the tiny town's courthouse a giant transparency in Washington's image was set ablaze. On its reverse was a clear warning: the words "woe to anarchy." Satisfied with the strength of the army, Washington, through Hamilton, sent word to Lee that the entire force was now under the Virginia governor's authority, with Pennsylvania Governor Thomas Mifflin the second in command.[49] Along with these orders, the president sent a farewell note to the soldiers before riding back to Philadelphia. "No citizens of the United States can ever be engaged in a service more important to their country," it read. "It is nothing less than to consolidate and preserve the blessings of that Revolution, which at much expense of Blood and Treasure constituted us a free and independent Nation."[50]

On October 24, with Lee at their head, the left wing of the army began their ascent up the Allegheny Mountains. Their path took them through a spectral and dark forest known as the Shades of Death. As the autumn sun sank, cold rains arrived, drenching the soldiers as they climbed; finally, they rested on the very spot where doomed British General William Braddock had camped and Washington had made a valiant last stand against the French and Indians so many years before. Marks from the campaign still remained, lingering like ghosts. In the following days the rain continued, turning the ground into sludge, soaking feet and wagon wheels, which slipped in the mire as the hungry troops marched up to nineteen miles a day. Sickness plagued the army; dysentery and diarrhea ravaged the troops; hundreds of sick men were treated in makeshift hospitals.

To many of the men in the army, the Americans living in this wilderness were strange creatures, disturbing to behold. Robert Wellford, the army's surgeon general, wrote that the impoverished countrymen who glowered at the army as it passed by "appeared...to be in strict alliance with everything that can be called filthy and undesirable."[51]

Washington had warned Lee and Hamilton that this army should not engage in pillaging and that its treatment of the people in these remote regions should be nothing but civil and legal. But the inability of stores to keep pace with the soldiers marching up mountains resulted in thefts of food and clothing. Then Hamilton authorized the impressment of property from terrified farmers along the army's path.

Lee pointed his wing of the force across the deep, fast-flowing Youghiogheny River and then over Laurel Hill. From this vista, three thousand feet high, the soldiers could see miles of mountains spreading behind them. But lying before them was the fertile green land of Uniontown, Pennsylvania, situated at the foot of the Alleghenies, with its manicured and prosperous farms. Organized in three columns, Lee's men pushed forward towards Brownsville—and finally into Parkinson's Ferry, the seat of so much of the rebellion. The full army, 12,950 men strong, finally coalesced there in early November.[52]

Even before the troops came together, rumors had spread that the resistance, faced with this federal army, had already begun to disperse. The soldiers had seen liberty poles—the sign of anti-excise resistance—as they marched west, but encountered little in the way of armed opposition. A few suspected rebels were rounded up along the way—many of them scruffily clothed, poorly fed, and petrified.

On November 8, Lee issued a proclamation—a measured threat to the inhabitants of the four counties where the cauldron of rebellion boiled. The residents of this region would soon notice, he informed them, a powerful army camped near their homes and farms. These soldiers had left behind their families and journeyed through inclement weather to answer a "sacred...call." Now the rebels and the poor neighbors they had roped into their foolish endeavor were witnessing the might of the government and the determination of the American people to defend it. "The scene before your eyes ought to be an instructive one; it ought to teach many useful truths, which should, for your happiness, make a deep and lasting impression on your minds."[53]

The citizens in the counties beyond Laurel Hill, Lee urged, should give every indication of their respect for the government, remain peacefully in their homes, and provide for the army in whatever way possible. And they should take an oath of loyalty to support the Constitution and obey its laws. Then the threat would be lifted.

In Parkinson's Ferry, there was no sign of rebellion, not even a man who would voice his support for the insurrection. The presence of this giant army arresting impoverished malcontents for trial in Philadelphia was enough to cool the ardor for resistance and to bring about a swift submission.

"We are here in the center of the country," Lee wrote to John Fitzgerald, a former aide-de-camp to Washington. "Resistance which was once contemplated very seriously," he continued, "has yielded to submission and flight. A people by situation capable of every happiness have been duped by artful leaders to sacrifice it and now depend on the mercy of the very government they have vilified and abused."[54] Lee met with delegates from the four counties, who now wished to make peace. Regardless of their desires, Lee informed them that he would take the army to Pittsburg. But, he assured them, "On my part, and on the part of the patriotic army I command, assure your fellow citizens that we come to protect and not destroy..."[55]

The rebellion, such as it was, was at an end.

When the army began to file into Pittsburg, the leaders of the insurrection were nowhere to be found. Bradford, the figurehead, had boarded a coal barge and sailed south down the Ohio, eventually reaching New Orleans. Others were in hiding. Hamilton and Washington had hoped to haul a number of the primary fomenters of this rebellion all the way to Philadelphia for instructive public trials. Once he arrived in the city, Hamilton launched an investigation aimed at landing a number of these conspirators. He longed for evidence implicating Albert Gallatin and William Findley in particular, two members of Congress from the region who had opposed his financial policies. A Pittsburg resident named John Powers was brought before Hamilton and asked if he had information implicating Gallatin. When he said he did not, Hamilton had Powers escorted to a prison cell to give him ample time to refresh his memory. Richard Peters, a judge who had traveled west with the army, began interviewing suspects. Many men, though, were tossed in prison without hearings. Or into frigid barns. Or even outhouses.[56]

One man who fell under suspicion was Hugh Henry Brackenridge. A local lawyer and politician, he had been a chaplain in the Continental army before launching a literary career in Philadelphia as the founder and editor of the short-lived *United States Magazine*, a publication notable for labeling General Charles Lee a "fluctuating weazel."[57] Brackenridge later relocated west of the Alleghenies and became involved with politics there. He had opposed the excise tax but at several points—most notably when the rebel army, at its apex, marched on Pittsburg—had pleaded for moderation.[58]

But now Brackenridge heard rumors that he would soon be arrested—or even assassinated. And he arrived at his home one day in the middle of November to see a sign affixed on its front door: "The Commander-in chief's quarters." Entering his parlor, Brackenridge encountered a face from the far past. Two decades before, as a senior student at the College of New Jersey, he had met a blue-eyed boy from Virginia, and served as his tutor for eloquence and composition courses. Now that same Virginian stood before him in his buff-and-blue uniform, the commander in chief of the army occupying his city, and—Brackenridge, feared—the man who would sign his death warrant. Their initial encounter was icy. Brackenridge moved his entire family into a single small room in the house, leaving the remainder for Lee and his staff. There he awaited his fate. To Brackenridge's surprise, Lee extended invitations to join him for dinner on numerous occasions, and eventually—after offering apologies to his wife—removed from Brackenridge's home to find a new headquarters elsewhere.[59] Brackenridge, following a series of torturous interviews with Hamilton, was eventually cleared of any wrongdoing.

By the middle of November, all that remained was administrative and legal work. Lee began to dispatch the various parts of the army back to their points of origin, but he left a small force under the command of Morgan behind in Pittsburg. His conduct during the campaign found general approbation, even among those Hamilton wished to drag back to the capital. "There are no complaints of governor Lee having been inexorable or inhumane," Findley recalled.[60] Lee had answered the government's call and raised an army whose march through the wilderness alone had been enough to snuff out this challenge to the young government, without firing a shot. Now he prepared again to ascend the Allegheny Mountains, ride over the rocky hills and ragged roads, across snow covered vales and over chilled waterways, back home to Virginia. But if he was anticipating a hero's welcome there, Lee was sorely mistaken.

# 13

# CRACKED

Long before the march to Pittsburg, even before the political tussles over the Constitution, Lee had been promised a golden medal. It was for his exploits during the raid on Paulus Hook, now part of the lore of the American Revolution.

In 1780, the creation of this award, along with six others, had been tasked to Benjamin Franklin, who was to have them struck by Parisian artisans.

But Franklin was only able to commission one medal—for the Frenchman François-Louis Teissèdre de Fleury—before passing the project along, first to David Humphreys and then to Thomas Jefferson. Mysteriously, at some point along the way, Lee's name was shaved from the list of medal recipients. So when Jefferson returned stateside in 1789 with the finished set, there was no medal for Lee.

Annoyed, Lee approached Jefferson about the omission as early as 1792. Eventually Joseph Wright, the engraver at the newly established U.S. Mint, was tasked with and paid for striking the promised and long-delayed medal. Lee sat for the engraver, who produced a robust profile portrait. But when Wright made the medal, the dye cracked, likely during the hardening process or the actual minting.[1] The entire cursed project foreshadowed the coming star-crossed years of Lee's life, when fleeting magnificence would give way to cruel misfortune.

Certainly no second medal or even commendation was coming for his recent military exploits. "I have become an object of the most virulent enmity of a certain political junto," Lee stammered days after returning from Pennsylvania, "who affect to govern the U.S. & belch their venom on every Citizen not subservient to their will."[2] The stress was so great, his soul so broken, that Lee was immobilized for a month with a debilitating cold.

The commander in chief of the American army had marched over the mountains, like Hannibal through the alps, and bloodlessly quelled a rebellion against America's hard-won democratic government. And yet he returned home in the winter of 1795 to find himself a political pariah.

Democratic-Republicans had dared not support the Whiskey Insurrection vocally. Many condemned the rebels, and some, such as John Page, who represented Virginia in Congress, even joined the militia army.[3] But many of them were appalled by what they considered the federal government's grossly disproportionate response. Mustering and marching an army of nearly thirteen thousand into the American hinterlands to squash a pitiful uprising of frustrated and impoverished farmers was the equivalent of exterminating an ant with an anvil. If Democratic-Republicans had not openly supported the rebels, they now criticized the government's excessive use of force to subdue them.

The outrage that Democratic-Republicans felt towards Lee was articulated in heated prose in the *Aurora*, whose editor was

Benjamin Franklin Bache, the namesake of his grandfather whose words Washington described as "arrows of malevolence."[4] The paper, emptying its quiver, contended that Lee's proclamation was a partisan screed vilifying the residents of western Pennsylvania for harboring Democratic-Republican-friendly politics, not for actual illegal activity. After all, the *Aurora* asked, had not Lee himself, less than two years before, "loudly propagated unfavorable opinions of the operations of the general government?" Had his political transformation, the writer wondered, been motivated by Lee's ambition for another military commission?[5]

Even before Lee turned west to guide Virginia's soldiers back to Winchester for their discharge and recompense, his state's legislators had already registered their displeasure with the governor-turned-general. Over the feeble protests of Federalists, Virginia Democratic-Republicans, who were growing in power and angry over the governor's absence, invoked a clause stipulating that the chief executive could not receive a presidential appointment and remain in office and unceremoniously removed him from the governorship. On November 20, by a vote of ninety to sixty, Robert Brooke, a mildly Democratic-Republican lawyer, was elected as Lee's replacement.

Drawn to the Democratic-Republicans in the early years of Washington's presidency, Lee had made an unreliable ally from the start. No longer an erstwhile friend, Lee was now an outright foe. He had supported John Adams for vice president in 1792, firmly endorsed the administration's policy of neutrality, and vigorously enforced it as governor. And finally, while holding that office, he had deserted Virginia to participate in a military endeavor many Democratic-Republicans viewed as little more than a display of federalist chest-thumping.

And Lee had committed another little-noticed but far greater and consequential sin.

In the final month of 1793, Jefferson had at last resigned as Secretary of State. Freed from his position in Washington's cabinet, he now sat atop the Southwest Mountains in his self-constructed Palladian villa, Monticello. This long-threatened retirement to private life, brought on by a discontent with the government's politics, gave Jefferson an opportunity to tinker with new agricultural technology, refurbish his house, and tend to his plantation, which had been overseen by others in his decade-long absence.[6]

It also presented him with the opportunity to fulfill his professed desire to disengage from politics. But though Jefferson avoided newspapers and public proclamations on national affairs for a time, his ally Madison kept him apprised of the actions in Congress, and Jefferson naturally drifted back towards engagement. Privately, he scorned the government's reaction to the Whiskey Rebellion. He defended the Democratic-Republican Societies– what right did the members of the Society of Cincinnati have to ridicule such organizations? He also encouraged Democratic-Republicans in congress to oppose John Jay's Treaty. Despite his talk of an idyllic retreat from politics, a partisan movement was uniting around the Sage of Monticello, and his return to the stage, and eventually to power, was inevitable.[7]

Hitherto, Lee and Jefferson had been acquaintances with common friends, little more. Their paths had crossed, and Jefferson solicited potential European investors for Lee's project at the Great Falls, though at Madison's behest. They had shared dinner at Washington's table in New York and had communicated frequently and formally while Lee was governor of Virginia.

But in the summer of 1794, shortly before he marched off to Pennsylvania, Lee ensured that what little connected the two men was blown to pieces.

That year Major Robert Quarles, the superintendent of Virginia's arsenal at Point of Fork, was a dinner guest at Monticello. During the course of his conversation with Jefferson, Quarles wondered aloud whether Washington, as the Democratic-Republicans alleged, was vulnerable to British influence. No, the host responded. As long as the president was plied by wise counsel from his advisors, there was no danger of this.

Quarles reported this dialogue back to Lee, who was in disbelief. When he requested Quarles "to reflect and reconsider and to repeat again the answer," Quarles stuck to his story. This was an outrage: Jefferson, sitting atop his mountain, archly observing that the judgment of George Washington—like an old and infirm man leaning on a young one to stand and walk—was only as sound as the men surrounding him. Lee, rumor-mongering, ran to Washington to report the entire affair. "Now as the conversation astonished me and is inexplicable to my mind as well as derogatory to your character," Lee reported, "I consider it would be unworthy to me to withhold the communication from you...."[8]

The president reacted calmly to Lee's gossip. "With respect to the words said to have been uttered by Mr. Jefferson," Washington responded, "they would be enigmatical to those who are acquainted with the characters about me, unless supposed to be spoken ironically; & in that case they are too injurious to me, & have too little foundation in truth, to be ascribed to him."[9]

In this matter Washington was, as always, levelheaded and magnanimous. Jefferson was less so. Somehow, over the course of the next year, he was made aware of Lee's snitching and reacted savagely. The gossip, Jefferson informed Washington, was "the slander of an intriguer, dirtily employed at sifting the conversations at my table." Lee, he sneered, was nothing more than a "miserable tergiversator, who ought indeed either to have been of more truth or less trusted by his country."[10] In a few short years, the alignment of American power would incline towards Jefferson and his disciples. Lee had now made mortal enemies of both.

In the spring of 1795, after returning from the expedition to Pittsburg, he dined with a Democratic-Republican Congressman named William B. Giles. "Political hostility immediately ensued," Giles reported to Madison. "I observed that his feelings are hurt beyond description from the late political occurrence in this country." Lee was wounded, isolated, and hypersensitive to slights. After dinner was eaten and wine decanted, Lee lifted a glass and offered a toast to Madison. But then Lee added a curious remark: he had heard from reliable sources that Madison had "made frequent remarks upon his reputation." It fell to Giles to tell Lee that his information was exaggerated, and that his old friend had not in fact uttered such insults.[11]

During this period of angst, Lee and his brood lingered at Shirley; in the spring new family member Algernon Sidney Lee, the first child of his union with Anne Carter, was born. The choice of the child's namesake, the seventeenth-century English political theorist who had been put to death for his anti-monarchical views, was telling. The old revolutionary fervor still burned in Lee's breast.

Despite his alienation from politics, Lee took no pause from it, returning to Virginia's legislature as a delegate. Lee could not disengage, could not be Cincinnatus and quietly return to his farm. And as Washington looked for men to fill vacancies in his cabinet, Lee served as an informal advisor. He convinced the president that the old lion Patrick Henry, although a Democratic-Republican who had originally opposed the Constitution, now adhered to it and disdained the Democratic-Republican Societies and would make a wise appointment. Lee served as an emissary extending Washington's invitation to join the government, either as Secretary of State or as a Supreme Court justice to a flattered but uninterested Henry.[12]

The bond with Washington did not diminish, but the president's estimate of Lee's acumen and reliability began to suffer. In the summer of 1795 the president, much to his dismay, discovered that the land in Kentucky for which he had swapped the horse Magnolio to Lee had previously been sold to General Alexander Spotswood. Washington's patience with his protégé, which dated back to the war, was once again on display: he could not believe Lee's mistake was driven by duplicity. "To suspect Genl Lee of fraud in this transaction I cannot," he wrote to George Lewis, a former aide who had traveled west to investigate the land, "and, as it is almost as improbable that it should be the result of forgetfulness, I conceive...that the two sales cannot be for the same land."[13] Lee, mortified, was forced to give Spotswood another set of parcels.

Lee and Anne expanded their home's northwest staircase and covered its parlor walls with vibrant verdigris green paint, an expensive shade found exclusively in the homes of early America's affluent. Carelessness with finances and business was eroding Lee's own fortune, and slowly degrading his reputation as well. In the fall of 1795, Timothy Pickering, the Massachusetts soldier-politician who had replaced Knox as the head of the War Department, shifted over to lead the Department of State. When Pickering consulted with Washington about a replacement, Lee's name was inevitably discussed. But his financial escapades, as well as his recent political troubles, proved disqualifying. "With ample military talents, General Lee is conceived to want others essential to a secretary of war," Pickering related to Hamilton. "Embracing some great objects, the department comprehends a multitude of details, and demands economy in its numerous expenditures," he explained. "This appointment would doubtless be extremely unpopular: it would be disapproved by the enemies of the government, without acquiring the confidence of its friends."[14]

Amidst his financial turmoil, the town at the Great Falls was once again stalled. Nevertheless, like an addict, Lee kept speculating in land. In 1763 Washington had joined a project to drain the Great Dismal Swamp, a two-thousand-mile morass of murky wetland stretching from Virginia's southwest to North Carolina's northeast. Investors hoped to drain the swamp, clear and sell its timber, and then market the fertile land. Work had slowed greatly during the Revolution, but Washington revisited the scheme in peace; as the construction of canals began in 1793, his interest waned. In need of cash, Washington offered his four-thousand-acre shares, dotted with glorious cypress and juniper trees, to Lee. Two years later, the two reached an agreement: Lee would give Washington $20,000 for the land, to be paid in three installments due the following years.[15]

Lee made his first payment on the Great Dismal Swamp land. The second one, however, he was unable to front. Instead he offered Washington seventy shares of stock in the Bank of Columbia, worth $2,800, a $1,000 endorsement note, and thirty barrels of corn. The president accepted begrudgingly, his patience tried once again.[16]

Lee had lent $10,000 to James Wilson, the intellectual driver of the American Revolution: he was the only man whose imprint graced the Declaration of Independence, the Articles of Confederation, and the Constitution. Despite his brilliance as a lawyer and legislator, Wilson was a poor businessman—a combination regular amongst the founders. He had overextended himself with land acquisitions, fallen deep into debt, and landed in prison as a result. Lee would never see the $10,000 again: Wilson died in 1798, stricken with malaria, without repaying his debt.[17]

There was also a costly entanglement with the Blake family of Boston, who had given one of Lee's partners, a man by the name of Glassel, a sizable promissory note. Glassel turned around and employed Blakes's guarantee as security for an investment in partnership with Lee, who then goaded several associates to contribute towards it, even to stake their homes as collateral. This was folly. When the Blakes refused to honor their debt to Glassel, the men Lee had roped into the project risked losing their estates. Lee, fearing disaster, pelted his agent, William Sullivan with desperate pleas. "How must I feel?" he wrote. "If your expectations fail, I am gone!" A settlement was eventually reached, at Lee's expense.[18]

Then there was the matter of Robert Morris. Lee had resigned his spot on the consortium buying the Fairfax land on the Northern Neck. But Morris, facing his own economic difficulties due to unwise land investments, asked him for and received a considerable loan—some $40,000—which Lee was to spend the following years attempting to reclaim from him.

Lee's addiction to land speculation and his ambition for fortune raged out of control while the value of land in early America was pushed down from its apex by the collapse of credit markets, which triggered deflation, dragging down the fortunes of those who had amassed land in the previous years. Lee was among them. His eldest siblings, Richard Bland Lee, several times a congressman representing northern Virginia, and Charles Lee, now the nation's attorney general, were dragged into the morass and forced to loan their beloved but profligate brother capital to subsidize his schemes.

Anne Lee quickly developed a bond with Elizabeth Lee, the wife of Richard Bland Lee. She was a frequent visitor at Sully, the couple's elegant plantation in Fairfax County, in northern Virginia, during summers. The two couples had welcomed babies simultaneously: Algernon Sidney and his cousin, Mary, were born just a month apart. At Sully the families would join hands and stage a playful marriage of the two babies, a prelude to a real, hoped-for union to come in the future. There was to be no future for either child, though. On June 27, 1795, after a short illness, Mary Lee died. Algernon Sidney followed his cousin into the grave two months later while visiting Sully with his mother. The children were buried together just beyond Elizabeth Lee's bedroom window in a spot, she would wistfully recall, "that contains two of the loveliest babes that ever breathed."[19]

Early in 1796, Washington resolved to take a final bow, vacate the presidency, and conclude his decades-long service to the nation. He was weary of the violent partisanship generated by the disputes over the conflicts in Europe and the Jay Treaty. He was saddened to be estranged from old friends and allies—his relationship with Jefferson was irreparably torn. After an exchange of letters in July 1795, the two would never communicate again. Washington's hair had turned from auburn to gray; the prime of his life had played out on the public stage. Now he wished to take leave of it. Washington reasoned, echoing words drawn up by Madison for a potential valedictory speech in 1792, that his retirement would be "an early example of rotation in an office of so high and delicate nature" and "accord with the republican spirit of our Constitution."[20] In correspondence during the summer of 1796, he declared the intention to "close my public life on the 4th of March, after which no consideration under heaven that I can foresee shall again with draw me from the walks of private life."[21]

He would return to Mount Vernon to live out his remaining years, and, by doing so bequeath the country, if not the world, a parting present, the opportunity for the will of a nation's people to determine their leader.[22] As Washington, with help from Hamilton, prepared a farewell plea for national unity, the contest to replace the great man began. Presidential electors encouraged Jefferson to descend from his mountain; Vice President John Adams, uninterested by his current office, sought elevation himself. Vain and independent, with no love for Hamilton, the vice president, though favored among Federalists, was not sufficiently pliable to make a successful head of his party. Hamilton concocted a scheme to steer the presidency towards South Carolinian Thomas Pinckney, but this backfired, handing the presidency to Adams and the vice presidency to Jefferson.

In Adams, the Federalists had a president with only a loose allegiance to their cause, though he continued Washington's refusal to engage in Europe's war. Both the French and the Democratic-Republicans raged at this, even more so when Adams began to bulk up the nation's military. The Democratic-Republicans had wanted America to weigh in on the side of the French revolutionary government, but Adams was now preparing for possible war against France, freely apprehending and impressing American vessels suspected of engaging in commerce with Britain. A disastrous and humiliating peace parley in Paris turned the American public against France, despite America's emotional debt to her former ally. Retaliation on the high seas followed, and a new American army was prepared in the event of an invasion. In the summer of 1798 an ageing Washington was placed at its head. After a torturous deliberation on rank, Hamilton, who longed for command of the affair, was at his side along with Knox and Pinckney. Lee was commissioned a brigadier general, but ongoing and eventually successful diplomatic efforts to avoid war would prevent him from actually donning the buff and blue once again.

When the French Revolution reached its bloody zenith, political disharmony in America touched its own apex, with hints of disunion and even civil war coming from Democratic-Republicans. In November 1798, Federalists in Congress passed the Alien and Sedition Acts, a quartet of bills enabling the government to escort French immigrants back across the Atlantic and to imprison critics of its policies. Predictably, this outraged Democratic-Republicans, who viewed the laws as outright violations of the Constitution.

In Virginia's General Assembly, where Lee continued to serve as a delegate, resolutions—from the quills and under the guidance of Jefferson and Madison—were introduced decrying the acts as unconstitutional and asserting the rights of states to defy them.[23] Lee fought passionately against these declarations, rising to the rhetorical occasion in the cause of the Union, which was once again under the shadow of civil war.

The Alien and Sedition Acts, Lee argued with zeal, were constitutional. If they were not, then by all means Virginia's legislature should voice their displeasure at them. But any man who opposed the laws should do so with a calm response, one that did not threaten to tear apart the government. "Friendship should be the ground, friendship the dress, and friendship the end of his measures," he contended.

The soundest argument Lee leveled against Virginia's resolutions rested with the Revolution. Decades past, in 1776, the precursor of the very legislative body he was now addressing had declared that any citizen who sided with King George or Parliament was liable to punishment, even imprisonment. Many of the men who penned that resolution had also helped craft the Constitution. "They must have understood their own work," Lee postulated, "they could not mean to violate the constitution." Then he took aim at Jefferson. The very man behind this resolution had helped write that older declaration, which argued expressly that punishing those who put falsehoods in print, "ought not to be inhibited."

And Virginia's resolution was a danger to national unity, an invitation to anarchy, a summons to violate America's laws served by Virginia herself. "Insurrection would be the consequence," he warned. Lee reminded his colleagues of another rebellion, one he had helped subdue, one he now described as a "comedy." The revolt Democratic-Republicans were now inviting would be far less farcical. "We have had one insurrection lately and that without the patronage of the legislature. How much more likely might an insurrection happen, which seemed to be advised by the assembly?"[24]

As Lee finally asked, "Was the government worth preserving? If not, let it be annulled. If it is, deny not to it, the means of preserving itself."[25]

The Democratic-Republicans, greater in number, carried the day, ultimately approving the Virginia Resolutions. Lee, writing pseudo-anonymously as "a Member from Westmoreland," penned the minority's dissent, which was printed piecemeal in the *Virginia Gazette and General Advertiser*, a Federalist broadsheet. Charging back into politics headlong, he followed this up with "Plain Truth," a manifesto in defense of the government. This too appeared in print, and it was subsequently packaged into a pamphlet. The flurry of rhetorical activity presaged Lee's candidacy for Congress for Virginia's 19th District, which represented his own Westmoreland County, as well as Northumberland County, its neighbor to the south.[26]

Despite his financial misfortunes and the anxiety they generated, Lee remained optimistic as the century ended. Offering lots in the rising federal city as payment for debts past due to Washington, he acknowledged a "present dull period" for his properties, but foresaw that "the time is fast approaching when property like mine must be in great demand."[27]

There was contentment at Stratford Hall. In November 1798, Anne gave birth to another son, Charles Carter Lee. Named for his mother's beloved father, the Lees' second son was a lively brown-eyed boy who brought much joy to the often solitary mistress of Stratford. The removal to such a remote and secluded location, with a husband who was always in motion and rarely present, tested Anne, accustomed to the social hum of her childhood home. She had cheerfully adjusted though. "I greatly enjoy it: when alone my husband and child expected," she wrote to her sister in-law, Elizabeth Lee. "I am not sensible of the want of society—In them I have enough to make me cheerful and happy."[28]

But Lee was increasingly absent from home in early 1799 as he canvassed vigorously in the days leading up to the Congressional elections, scheduled for April 24. His absences were so frequent that letters from Hamilton, addressing recruiting in Virginia for the newly revived army, went unanswered.[29] With the conflict between Federalists and Democratic-Republicans at a fever pitch, the scene at polling stations in Virginia verged on chaos. The picture in Westmoreland County must have been much like similar scenes across Virginia, as each district's land owners appeared to cast their votes: communal barrels of whiskey stood under shade trees near the courthouses where the contest was settled; an array of venison ribs, shucked oysters, and glazed hams were offered and consumed; eligible voters either arrived of their own volition or were escorted to the polling station. Supporters of the two contenders, fueled by liquor, argued at the top of their voices and then settled the disputes with their fists before declaring their votes aloud to the county justices seated at an expansive table, with the candidates seated to their sides. When the final tally was accumulated, Lee had thumped Jones, 233 votes to 47.[30]

Several days later, when Lee wrote anxiously to William Sullivan regarding his finances, and "money long due and much wanted," he also mentioned promising news for the Federalists. Empowered by a brief spell of popularity for Adams and a fall from favor for the Democratic-Republicans connected to the public's anger at France, both chambers of Congress remained in Federalist control. "Our elections to Congress give 10 out of 18 'members' supporters of government…among them Marshall and myself," Lee crowed.[31] (Fellow Federalist John Marshall had been elected to represent the state's 13th Congressional District, to the west of Lee's own 19th.)

Lee had won the election, but he was in financial peril. The consequences of his years of improvident buying, selling, borrowing, and lending were a deluge advancing toward a cracked levee. However, Lee's seemingly dormant political career had revived. In their best performance since 1793, Federalists had gained seats in Virginia. The Federalists were seemingly ascendant; Jefferson and his party, for the moment at least, in retreat.

"The congressional elections, as far as I have heard them, are extremely to be regretted," Jefferson wrote from Monticello. "I did expect [Leven] Powel's election; but that Lee should have been elected...marks a taint in that part of the state which I had not expected."[32]

But Americans' anger against France was diminishing. And though Federalists continued to command the national legislature, their power was fading. The victories by Lee and Marshall were the result of the popularity of the individual candidates in each district, rather than of their party. State-level elections indicated the trend of the future. Democratic-Republicans retained control of the Virginia General Assembly and governorship. Marshall warned Washington of the "very considerable changes" that had been wrought by the election.[33]

# 14

# FAREWELL GREAT AND NOBLE PATRIOTS

On the morning of June 6, 1799, Patrick Henry was administered liquid mercury by a physician in an attempt to ease a painful intestinal infliction. The dosage proved fatal.[1]

The patriot's accomplishments were singular. His arguments and principles had sustained the cause of American liberty from its infancy. Word of his death ricocheted around Virginia and across America.

Henry Lee, who heard the news during a dinner, hastily solicited a scrap of paper and scribbled off a stirring tribute.

"Your Henry is no more! Ye friends of liberty in every clime, drop a tear!" it began.

"Farewell great and noble patriot, farewell," wrote Lee. "As long as our rivers flow and mountains stand so long will your excellence and worth be the theme of our homage and endearments; and Virginia, bearing in mind her loss, will say to rising generation, IMITATE HENRY."[2]

This eulogy, which appeared in the *Virginia Gazette*, was archetypal Lee. Over two decades had passed since the Revolution. Many men who had waged it—Nathanael Greene, for example—were already gone. Now, with more of them growing gray and dying, the epoch receded further into the past. Washington himself was just three years away from his seventh decade. Because of his eloquence, understanding of history, and reverence for its heroes, Lee more than any of his contemporaries was supremely suited to console and stir his countrymen as time's curtain came down on the founding generation.

The months following Lee's election to Congress were consumed with the usual chaos: promissory notes signed to creditors, inherited land sold, executors attempting to collect money that Lee owed. The coming relocation to Philadelphia, though, would be a welcome respite—not just for the new congressman, but also for Anne, freed from her exile at Stratford Hall. After a visit to the medicinal Sweet Springs in western Virginia, the Lees arrived in the capital and settled into their rented rooms in the fashionable Franklin Square in the first days of December. It was the first time Anne had left Virginia's borders in her twenty-six years.[3]

Little more than a week later, on the frosty Virginia morning of December 12, clouds brought a succession of snow, hail, and finally freezing rain upon Mount Vernon. George Washington had never let inclement weather obstruct his plantation chores. He rode out into the chill to scrutinize several buildings on the property. When Washington returned to his office in the afternoon, his greatcoat was soaked and snow hung from his hair. Without changing from his damp clothing, he ate dinner—then went to bed as usual. The following day the old general complained of a sore throat, but as was his custom, took no medicine to remedy it. Despite a lingering hoarseness, he seemed to be in good spirits as he spent the evening in the mansion's parlor reading and commenting on newspapers. "Let it go as it came," Washington told his personal secretary, Tobias Lear, who urged him to take some medicine before bed that night.

Sometime between the hours of two and three the following morning, Washington awoke barely able to speak or breathe. When his wife Martha suggested sending for help, the general stoically demurred. The following day, a concoction of molasses, vinegar, and butter was mixed to sooth his throat. When it touched Washington's lips, he convulsed. Doctors arrived. Blood was drawn repeatedly. To no avail. One of the three doctor's present surmised that the membranes of Washington's throat were inflamed and that, short of an emergency surgery, the patient would die.

But the other two physicians would not risk performing the dangerous procedure on such a prominent patient. Instead they continued the bleeding and administering of purges. Soon both they and Washington knew that the end was at hand. He asked to see copies of his will, to be assured that final chores had been attended to, and finally—with gratitude for their efforts and apologies for their inconvenience—that the doctors let him go.

"I die hard, but I am not afraid to go," he whispered. That evening, December 14, with a group of afflicted friends and family near his bedside, never bothering to look at the clock to record the precise time, George Washington breathed his last. [4]

Word of the hero's illness and death traveled from Mount Vernon. By the sixteenth, the news appeared in the Alexandria city papers ten miles south. From there stage carried it east to Baltimore, leaving grieving citizens, shuttered shops, and ringing church bells in its wake. In the early hours of December 18, a

passenger traveling on the stage from Baltimore arrived in Philadelphia, where he encountered an acquaintance on the street and
transmitted the news, which spread rapidly, eventually reaching
Congress Hall, where the House of Representatives was gathering
for the day's legislative session. Shocked legislators conferred as
John Marshall rose, announcing that though not yet confirmed,
there was strong reason to believe the news. When he suggested
adjournment for the day, the body unanimously agreed and
arranged to meet again the following morning.[5]

Lee had not yet reached Congress Hall when the bulletin
broke. Instead, he heard of Washington's death as it spread across
the city. Stricken, he retreated to his rooms, reached for parch-
ment, and poured his aching heart out into a statement and set
of proposals he intended to read when the House reconvened the
next day. Because Marshall had moved for the adjournment, it
was expected that he would be the one to offer resolutions guiding the government's response to the death of its first leader. His
writing at an end, Lee went to Marshall's nearby quarters, presented his composition, and then asked that Marshall read it in
the House.[6]

The next morning, the nineteenth, Marshall read from Lee's
script in a low, mournful voice. "Our Washington is no more!—
the hero, the sage and the patriot of America," he began, "the
man on whom in times of danger every eye was turned and all
hopes were placed lives now only in his own great actions, and
in the hearts of an affectionate and afflicted people."[7]

Four resolutions followed. The House would, at an appropriate time, wait on President Adams; its Speaker's chair would be
shrouded in black; its members would form a committee to determine an appropriate expression of the national grief generated
by the loss of this great man. Having adopted all four resolutions,

the House agreed to once again adjourn and gather four days hence, on the following Monday.[8]

A letter detailing Washington's death arrived from Mount Vernon. The Senate concurred with the House's resolutions; a delegation visited with Adams at the executive mansion; the joint committee was named, with both Lee and Marshall as members, and made its recommendations: a marble monument was to be raised in the new capital city bearing Washington's name. If his family consented, his body would rest underneath it. For the time being, he had been interred at Mount Vernon.[9]

And on December 26, America's first state funeral would leave in procession from Congress Hall and end several blocks north at the Zion Lutheran Church on Fourth and Cherry Streets. Built three years before, the huge brick structure was one of the largest houses of worship in all of America, ideal for the giant crowd expected. (An earlier incarnation of the church, built to accommodate the city's German immigrants, had been fashioned into a hospital for British soldiers during the Revolution and hosted memorial services for Benjamin Franklin in 1791, before being destroyed by a fire three years later.)[10]

Once both chambers of Congress approved of the funeral, the details were planned. Speaker of the House Theodore Sedgwick and President of the Senate Samuel Livermore (standing in for Vice President Jefferson) were each to select a member of his chamber to deliver an oration at the funeral before Congress.[11]

Naturally, one of Virginia's delegates would be selected. And of those thirteen men, none could match Lee in his intimacy with Washington. From boyhood, when the formidable figure had sat at Leesylvania's fireside, to manhood, when Washington's example had inspired him to the life of a soldier and his patronage and patience had propelled his career and ambitions, they had been mentor and apprentice, patron and protégé. With American independence won, Lee never ceased looking to Washington as an exemplar and seeking his guidance, even as he grew into an advisor and ally. And despite strains in their relationship—Lee's anger at Washington's government, his irresponsibility in business—the bond never broke.

No man was more strongly suited than Lee to articulate the nation's sorrow, to offer it solace. When Sedgwick and Livermore asked Lee to prepare and deliver the eulogy, he agreed.[12] Lee knew that Washington's legacy would last long after his life. Now was his time to hang the hero in the heavens for generations of unborn Americans to gaze upon.

For two days Lee shut himself up in his rooms fashioning an appropriate lamentation. As he sat scribbling during Christmas, the formal signs of grief spread across the city and beyond. Black crepe bands were slipped onto arms (Congress requested mourning citizens to leave them there for thirty days); the bells of Christ Church, where Washington had prayed when president, were silenced, his former pew draped in black.[13]

As the sun ascended on the morning of December 26, the blasts of sixteen guns rang out in the chill air; a single shot followed every thirty minutes until night fell. At noon a line of soldiers—arms presented, colors unfurled, drums beating—formed at the steps of Congress Hall, lifted the ceremonial bier, and began their promenade.[14]

A trumpeter led the way, somberly filling the air with George Frederick Handel's "Dead March." Platoons of soldiers followed, their arms reversed, their standards covered in black. Brigadier-General William MacPherson, overseeing the ceremony, appeared near the head of the procession. More men followed, as a band, their drums hushed, playing a dirge. Grenadiers and riflemen, dismounted, their swords drawn, followed. Members of the clergy came next, their white scarves matching the white horse, led by two marines, behind them. It was covered in black crape, an eagle upon its breast, an empty saddle upon its back, pistoled holsters at its side, reversed boots in its stirrups. Alexander Hamilton, another of the fallen president's disciples, trailed with his suite.[15]

Behind him were members of Congress and officers of the government, wearing white scarves tied in bows marked with roses of black ribbon on their shoulders. The procession wound its way up a path crowded with crestfallen citizens, up Fifth Street and over to Walnut, and then finally came to a halt in front of Zion Lutheran Church, with the deep and solemn notes of the organ trilling out of its doors.[16]

As bells tolled and minute shots rang, the bier was placed in the center of the church's middle aisle. The Reverend William White, an Anglican bishop, opened the ceremony with a homily, observing that "it has pleased the Almighty God, in his wise providence, to take out of this world our beloved brother in Christ, and our ever-honored fellow citizen."[17]

The sermon was followed by a short pause.

Then Henry Lee appeared before the four thousand men and women in attendance.

His remarks opened with apologies for his inadequacy to his task. Lee was but a "humble organ" rising in obedience to the public's will. "Desperate indeed," would be any attempt to "meet correspondingly this dispensation of heaven." No matter Lee's words, the lamenting would not cease over this "heart-rending privation."[18]

Now came the flourishes. "The founder of our federate republic—our bulwark in war, our guide in peace, is no more!"

he mourned. "Oh, that this were but questionable! Hope, the comforter of the wretched would pour into our agonizing hearts its balmy dew. But, alas! There is no hope for us; our Washington is removed forever!"[19]

Lee retraced the sad events that had brought the nation such grief. Washington, stout in health, had—as was his custom—neglected himself, and paid the price with his life. But his death was by no means a finale. "An end, did I say?" Lee queried. "His fame survives! Bounded only by the limits of earth, and by the extent of the human mind." He would live on in hearts, and in the minds of rising Americans. And on the day "when our monuments shall be done away; when nations now existing shall be no more; when even our young and far-spreading empire shall have perished; still will our Washington's glory unfaded shine, and die not, until love of virtue cease on earth, or earth itself sinks into chaos."[20]

Where to even begin, to chronicle the days of "a character throughout sublime"?[21]

Then Lee's words formed a portrait of a now distant past, pulling all those present to the banks of the Monongahela, where they saw a young Washington rescue the remains of Braddock's injured army. Then they moved to the eve of Revolution, when Washington risked all to command his country's legions. "Will you follow him," Lee asked "to the high grounds of Boston," to Long Island, York Island, New Jersey, to Trenton, across the icy Delaware? "His country called; unappalled by surrounding dangers to the hostile sore; he fought; he conquered." And then on to Morristown, Brandywine, Germantown, Monmouth. Always, he "upheld our tottering Republic."[22]

But it was not during war alone that this man's greatness and goodness were proven, that his gifts to a grateful people were given. He was a statesman as well as "our shield and our sword." His "parental advice," which Lee himself had so often solicited, was still sounding.[23]

In sweet peace, "mindful only of the common good," Washington surrendered "his power into the hands from which he had received it, converted his sword into a ploughshare." His mind was "clear and penetrating," his judgment "strong and sound," his integrity "incorruptible." He was a man for the ages. "The finger of an over-ruling Providence, pointing at Washington, was neither mistaken nor unobserved...."[24]

And when Americans, stretched across a vast continent, formed a union and framed a Constitution, it was to this man they turned. And always, rejecting his own interests and bliss, he answered and "brightened the path of our national felicity." Then Lee detailed the trials of Washington's presidency, the battles on the frontiers won, the wars in Europe avoided, all before finally showing the great man happily "returning to the humble walks of private life," even though his countrymen clamored for him to lead them still. "When before was affection like this exhibited on earth?—Turn over the records of ancient Greece—Review the annals of mighty Rome—Examine the volumes of modern Europe; you search in vain." And even when time had taken its toll, when the man had grown gray, he once again answered the call to service in the face of another potential war.[25]

Now the coda.

"First in War, first in peace, and first in the hearts of his countrymen," Lee pronounced Washington, refashioning a passage from the resolutions that he had composed but Marshall had delivered. He "was second to none in the humble and endearing scenes of private life."[26]

Washington himself seemed to speak through Lee's words. "Methinks I see his august image, and hear falling from his venerable lips, these deep thinking words: Cease, Sons of America, lamenting our separation." There remained common dangers to be confronted, knowledge to diffuse, arts and sciences to patronize, party spirit to resist, peace to cultivate, religion to revere. Only by doing these things would the union—"the constant object of my terrestrial labors"—be perpetuated.[27]

Lee fell silent and stepped away. The grief of those gathered swelled. The organ resumed. "Angels ever bright and fair, take, oh take him to your care," caroled a choir. The bier was removed from the church and three volleys fired above it; drums at last were unmuffled as soldiers marched and spectators filed away.[28]

Similar services were held elsewhere. Gouverneur Morris delivered a eulogy in New York on the last day of the year at St. Paul's Chapel. Fisher Ames, a Federalist politician from Massachusetts, did the same at the Old South Church in Boston.[29] But whatever contemporary acclaim these and others received, it, and they, soon faded. Lee's oration, which the *Pennsylvania Gazette* described as delivered with "emphasis and elegance," would endure, cementing in death the connection that the two men had shared in life.

The following day both the Senate and the House issued public notes of thanks to Lee, commending his eloquence and requesting that he provide Congress with a copy of the oration so that it might be printed and circulated across the land. Even though he could have printed the document himself, and possibly reaped a desperately needed windfall, Lee obliged.[30]

The acclaim over the eulogy only lent further luster to the figure that Lee cut in Philadelphia during the winter of 1800. Henry and Anne Lee's union represented beauty and gallantry, with impeccable bloodlines to boot; the two were dazzling lights on the Philadelphia scene. Though its time as the center of American government was nearing an end, the city was humming, full of recently arrived French immigrants who had fled the bloodshed in their own country, giving the city "the appearance of a great hotel." Streets were filled with the sounds of violin and clarinet; vibrant shops along the Delaware River stocked exotic goods and garments; sumptuous dinners and balls were staged; theaters featured thrilling performances. And for Lee, friends too abounded. It was a period of short happiness that belied the growing strain put on the family by the recklessness of its patriarch.[31]

Amidst the gaiety, politics raged on in a session of Congress characterized by conflicts between the Federalist majority and their Democratic-Republican opponents. Lee, while firmly aligned with the former, played the part of a moderate, prioritizing national interests over partisan ones.

In January of 1800 the Democratic-Republicans, led by Albert Gallatin, proposed stripping away the standing army that had been organized in case of a possible war with France. The Federalists proclaimed that the proposal was another example of the opposition party's determination to unravel the federal government, paired with a naïveté regarding the trustworthiness of France. Lee, as he had done during debate over the ratification of the Constitution, testified from his war experience to the unreliability of militia. Reducing the army in pursuit of savings while peace negotiations continued, he argued, would project the image of a weak-willed nation in the throes of "fiscal debility," which would only "encourage aggression, and invite an attack even on our independence."[32]

Lee declared to his colleagues, "As much as I wish to see our militia placed on a respectable footing, much as I count on their aid whenever danger approached, yet I never can be brought to trust the defense of the country solely to them."[33] Gallatin's argument rested on the national deficit—then at six million dollars. But the nation's security was hanging in the balance. And Lee was certain that the states would be willing to provide their share of the funding to sustain the national army via taxation. "Whenever money is wanting for the public good, it will be readily given."[34]

During this session of Congress, a free black Philadelphian named Absalom Jones submitted a petition to Congress. There were seven hundred thousand black men, women and children chained in slavery in America. On the shores of Maryland and Delaware slave traders were apprehending free blacks, ripping them from their families, and dragging them deep into the South, snuffing out their freedoms and throwing them into slavery. A law, passed by Congress in 1793, permitted local governments to snatch escaped slaves and ship them back to their owners. Jones did not ask for total emancipation, but rather that some measures would be taken by the government to address the inhumanity of the slavers and the fugitive act.

Lee responded predictably. He "was not second to any gentleman in a genuine attachment to the rights of humanity." And yet he denied that granting Jones's supplications would do anything but harm. The representatives, after all, had been "sent to that house to protect the rights of the people and the rights of property." And the property, he continued, "which the people of the Southern States possess consisted of slaves, and therefore Congress had no authority but to protect it, and not take measures to deprive the citizens of."[35]

It was the familiar refrain of the planter. Let the slave trade "be entirely obliterated," Lee argued, but he hoped sincerely that the government "would never intermeddle with the property of any of the citizens." Slavery contradicted the principles of liberty lovers such as he. But the steps he was willing to take to end it stopped short of surrendering his own interests and "property."[36]

On May 15 Congress adjourned. Its business in Philadelphia was at an end. On that day President Adams ordered the federal government to begin its move to the new and as yet unfinished capital city on the Potomac. Cabinet members and government employees, numbering 125, gathered their belongings and departed; official documents and archives were packed and sent via waterways, though the president himself would remain until November.[37]

Another election was at hand, and the states, permitted to schedule polling at their own pleasure, would soon vote for the president in piecemeal fashion. Jefferson, though he was Adams's vice president, sneered at the president's policies, as he planned to contest the presidency in 1800. In a harbinger of the coming electoral swing, New York Democratic-Republicans organized by Aaron Burr routed their Federalist rivals, captained by Hamilton, in elections to take control of the state legislature and guarantee the state for Jefferson.[38]

Meanwhile, during visits home to Monticello, the Republican majordomo plotted with his deputies Madison and James Monroe, unleashing a muscular political operation that flooded newspapers with pro-Democratic-Republican editorials. Some, like those penned by James Thomas Calendar, savagely attacked Adams, articulated a platform descended from Jefferson's own dictums, and organized political action in states and cities.[39]

Before leaving Philadelphia for Virginia, Lee dined with Adams and Jefferson. Astoundingly, the president talked unguardedly of political matters with his rival. After the vice president took his leave, Lee delivered a warning to the president: Jefferson was intriguing to replace him in the presidency. A greatly irritated Adams retorted that Jefferson was among his closest friends; far closer than men of his own political party or administration. Jefferson's only ambition, Adams assured a stunned Lee, was to serve as the president's deputy.[40] Disaster was pending for Federalists, and Adams was apparently unaware.

With Congress adjourned until the fall, the Lees returned to Stratford Hall and their now familiar troubles. A promissory note to one John Porter went unpaid; Porter sued. Lee attempted to sell land in Alexandria, but Anne, whose dower rights lent her co-ownership, refused to sign the deed. The sheriff of Westmoreland County apprehended a case knife in order to fulfill a debt owed to John Washington. To meet other debts—now growing alarmingly in number—Lee sold off slaves, bartered cattle, and deeded lands, all the while still acquiring property.[41]

Now away from the excitement of Philadelphia, Anne, who gave birth to a daughter, Anne Kinloch Lee, in June, took time to resume correspondence with family. "Many of my friends (and you among others I find) have supposed that when in Philadelphia I ought to have loved, thought of, and written to them as usual," she waspishly wrote Elizabeth Lee, "but my dear you must all learn to know me better when I visit gay City's; it was unreasonable to imagine I could find leisure to remember Country friends while immersed in the pleasures of a City life."[42]

When Lee returned to Congress on the seventeenth of November, he and his colleagues met in the half-complete, frigid, leak-riddled, dome-less Capitol building mounted on Jenkins Hill, which extended eastward in the center of Washington. The village itself was little more than a collection of shanties connected by terrible roads; a dreadful contrast to the cosmopolitan charms of Philadelphia. Construction on the Capitol, which had begun in 1793, was impeded by a lack of resources; only a single wing, designated for the Senate, was complete; the House and Supreme Court were forced to fit into this space as well until their own quarters were complete.

Beginning in October, electoral tallies from across the country had been flowing in. The results were uncertain in a contest that pit Jefferson, along with Aaron Burr, the Democratic-Republican vice presidential candidate, against Adams and Pinckney. Hamilton, irked by Adams's independence, hoped to throw the election to the theoretically more malleable Pinckney, creating chaos among the already poorly organized Federalist party.

With Congress in session, the outcome of one yet-to-be-decided state, South Carolina, was left to determine the next president.

While the nation waited, Lee returned to a familiar subject. The previous year, after Washington's death, he had put forward the idea of a suitable monument for the fallen. The House had approved of the idea, but the Senate had not taken it up. Even in the wake of Washington's death, Lee had encountered unforeseen difficulties in securing funding for the project, describing the process to Tobias Lear as "a difficult business, infinitely more so than you or I thought."[43]

In the poisonous climate of the Sixth Congress, even a proposal to erect a monument to Washington had sparked a partisan brawl, with Republicans hesitant to grant Federalists this favor. In December Lee urged the House to approve this tribute—now restyled as a granite and marble pyramid, one hundred feet across by one hundred feet high, designed by architect George Dance—again, as they had done in the previous Congress.[44]

But after a year of reflection out of the storm of national sorrow, Democratic-Republicans in the House had had a change of heart. How would this heap of stone, they wondered, enhance Washington's reputation? And at what financial cost? Such talk astounded Lee. After all, he argued, "there was not a rich man in Europe who loses his mistress that does not raise a trophy to her memory; and shall it be said that we, who have sustained the most irreparable loss in the death of our Chief—shall it be said the we refuse to pay him those honors which are lavished so liberally upon such inferior objects?" True to form, he brushed aside concerns over the cost, pondering, "can there be a greater, a more patriotic purpose than this?"[45]

In this debate, Lee encountered a man who was his opposite in every way. True, North Carolina's Nathaniel Macon had studied at the College of New Jersey, arriving three years after Lee's graduation, and fought in America's Revolution. But there the similarities ceased. Macon, who had started his career in the Tar Heel State's General Assembly, had refused to serve as a delegate to the convention that created the Constitution in 1787; instead, he had battled against its ratification. Defeated in this endeavor, he won a seat in the new Congress in 1791 and dedicated himself to the strictest possible interpretation of that document. Both personally and publically he was parsimonious; there were few federal projects he would approve of. A standing army or navy, or a national mint, for example, were ideas he fought and ridiculed. He abhorred debt, both his own and his nation's. So great was his fear of it, in fact, that in the hours before his death in 1837 Macon summoned an undertaker and insisted on paying for any bills relating to his funeral lest he owe a single cent from the grave.[46]

Naturally, Macon argued that the cost of the tribute to Washington that Lee had proposed was not to be taken lightly; he did not consider seventy thousand dollars a "trifling sum." It was a great expenditure. In any case, the seventy thousand dollars was only a starting point; the total sum would no doubt mushroom. Macon, in a nasty and personal jab at Lee's own financial difficulties, brushed aside reassurances about reasonable costs and promised that he would "not be carried away by the visionary notions of speculation."[47]

Apart from the cost, though, Macon, speaking for the Democratic-Republicans, objected to the monument on other grounds as well.

Virtues, Macon insisted, could sparkle without shrines; monuments did not themselves impart morals. "I have heard of a place called Westminster Abbey," he said, that was full of monuments to men now forgotten to time. This debate was about a larger question facing the young American republic. When Macon urged Congress to "make a stand against this monument mania," he was eyeing the precedent. "If we decline raising a mausoleum to Washington, no man who succeeds him can expect one reared in his memory," he predicted. "On the other hand, if we now raise one to Washington, every pretender to greatness will aim at the same distinction."[48]

Constructing ostentatious tributes to men, any men, even the great Washington, ran contrary to the spirit of this new nation. Raising reliquaries to leaders, dead or alive, transformed mortals into deities.

A decade before, during the last days of the Continental Congress, Lee had proposed a monument to honor the late Nathanael Greene. Ever mindful of the sweep of history, always admiring the men who commanded it, he saw monuments as valuable markers. They were a means for those mourning to show gratitude and an example for future generations to imitate.

264 LIGHT-HORSE HARRY LEE

"The grandeur of the pile we wish to raise will impress a sublime awe in all who behold it," he predicted. "It will survive the present generation. It will receive the homage of our children's children; and they will learn that the truest way to gain honor amidst a free people is to be useful, to be virtuous."[49]

It was a seminal and important debate, with implications for centuries to come—and no easy answer. In the end, politics settled the matter: the memorial was approved, with all of the chamber's thirty-four Democratic-Republicans voting nay and forty-five of its Federalists voting yay. The project, though, was considerably scaled back in the hands of the Senate, which reduced the appropriation for it to $50,000.

On December 16, 1800, South Carolina announced its tally in the presidential election. Nationwide Jefferson had narrowly defeated Adams, but ended up in an electoral college stalemate with Burr, his own running mate. By order of the Constitution, this tie threw the decision to the House, where the Federalists were still in the majority—though the next Congress would be Democratic-Republican, the voters having turned dozens of Federalists out of office to hand both chambers to Jefferson's foot soldiers. It would take thirty-six ballots before the results of the presidential election were finally decided.

Federalists made the most of their remaining months in power before the new Congress arrived in 1801. Lee supported and added an amendment to a bill to flesh out the federal judiciary, creating circuit courts and expanding the number of district courts as well. Conveniently, this allowed Adams to fill the judiciary with Federalists in his remaining days in office; the party would cling to power in one branch of the federal government.

The Sedition Act, which was set to terminate in March 1801, was renewed with Lee's support, though the Senate would allow the law to expire in the new year. And even though negotiations with France seemingly promised peace, Federalists pushed for a law prohibiting American commercial intercourse with that nation. Lee, breaking from his party, fought against this ultimately successful act. Lee's votes on two other bills in the last weeks of the Sixth Congress also showed his independent spirit: he supported a bill to improve the nation's post roads and vehemently opposed another that would have hamstrung the incoming president by prohibiting the Secretary of the Navy from participating in the civilian maritime trade. Making the executive a supplicant to the other branches of government, no matter who the executive might be, was a betrayal of the Constitution in Lee's view.

On February 11, 1801, the House gathered to settle the matter of the presidential contest. The Federalists were badly split. Though Jefferson was his rival, Hamilton respected him—at least compared to Burr. Jefferson, he argued, was the less dangerous of the two men, and even had "pretentions to character." Burr, on the other hand, was "bankrupt beyond redemption." Should he take the presidency, "he will certainly disturb our institutions and to secure himself permanent power."[50] Thus Hamilton scrambled to urge his fellow Federalists to cast their votes in Congress for the Virginian, while writing pamphlets and opinion pieces decrying Burr as "an embryo Caesar."[51]

Lee begged to differ. "But really my friend," he wrote to Hamilton, "after much deliberation on the business I am decidedly convinced that our best interests will be jeopardized should Mr. J[efferson] succeed."[52] His position is easy to understand. His personal animosity towards Jefferson still burned; Burr, on the other hand, had vaguely redeeming qualities. He was a former classmate at the College of New Jersey and a veteran of the

Revolution. And besides, Lee explained to Hamilton, should he rise to the presidency, Burr would be held in check. He was not the preferred candidate of his own party; Democratic-Republicans would desert him; he would be forced to cooperate with Federalists. Either way, though, Lee was willing to live with the result. "In any event I feel disturbed for our poor country, but in every vicissitude I shall hope for the best, resign to the public will...."[53]

For over a week the House cast ballots until, on February 17, Delaware's lone Representative, James Bayard, after negotiating with Jefferson's subordinates, ended his opposition to the Virginian. So too did Bayard's Federalist associates in Maryland and Vermont, flipping those two states to Jefferson and handing him the presidency.[54]

The Federalists had been routed; Lee decided not to seek another term representing Virginia's 19th District. Instead, when Congress adjourned in March and Jefferson settled into his quarters in the unfinished Executive Mansion, Lee returned to Stratford Hall. His lone term in Congress was consequential. He had been a voice of moderation among Federalists, a spirit of independence in a fiercely partisan period, and, as always, an advocate for national interests. He had also shown himself to be a grand eulogizer and hopeful monument maker for America's founding hero.

But with the ascent of Jefferson, this was all at an end; Lee now bid adieu to the arena.

"On politics I will not even whisper," he wrote Harrison Gray Otis, a fellow ostracized Federalist in April, "dead as is my heart from the late events to a subject at once mortifying and ominous."[55]

# 15

# UNCEASING WOE

As the eighteenth century turned to the nineteenth, Henry Lee sat for Gilbert Stuart, the era's preeminent and most prolific portraitist. The artist's painting of George Washington is among the most life-like and penetrating wrought of that visage. He could tell, Stuart said to Lee, that the general had a tremendous temper. Only days later, over breakfast, Lee shared Stuart's observation with the Washingtons. "Upon my word," Martha exclaimed, "Mr. Stuart takes a great deal upon himself, to make such a remark." But Lee, soothing his hosts, explained that Stuart had also claimed that the president had his temper "under wonderful control." A slyly smiling Washington remarked, "He is right."[1]

Stuart's painting of Lee, likely done around 1800 in Philadelphia, is equally perceptive. Two decades had vanished since Charles Willson Peale had captured Lee's likeness. The cool young soldier was now a rosy-faced middle-aged man, fuller in face and body. The green-trimmed tunic had been replaced by a frockcoat of buff and blue. The air of aristocracy remained, but the self-assurance of the younger man was gone—in its place a strained look of worry. Here Stuart clearly hit his mark.

As the new century began Henry Lee's political career was at an end; his personal life, slowly unraveling. The heavy bill for years of rashness in business, of over-eager speculation, was soon to come due. Angry creditors and betrayed business partners were growing impatient. Lee would be transformed from hero to desperado.

In 1801, while Lee was away from Virginia, John James Maund, who served as his agent, wrote to Lee's brother-in-law Robert, who had inquired when he might return. "No man knows when that will be, and the most gloomy aspect hangs over all his affairs here," Maund pessimistically observed.[2]

Still, Lee was indulging in new schemes. There was a project in the Bahamas, and Lee carelessly gave another agent, Thomas Rowand, the deed to a Northern Neck property known as Cabin Point as collateral; he would not get it back.

Lee was stripping his estate of any property not locked down by the trust he had signed with Matilda near her death. Tracts of land at Chantilly, the old home of Richard Henry Lee, were sold to pay debts, as were lots in the town of Alexandria, in order to repay Lee's brother Charles.[3]

Still more suits were filed and more subpoenas were served, as the walls slowly closed in on Lee. His desperation mounting, Lee pursued the $40,000 he had lent to Robert Morris years prior. But the old financier had hit the skids. In a familiar pattern, extravagant borrowing, ceaseless speculation, broken promises, and misbegotten ventures had left the once richest man in America among the most in debt—and, eventually locked away in a cell in Philadelphia's Prune Street Prison. In 1800 Congress narrowly approved the nation's first bankruptcy law, created in part to liberate Morris. It relieved imprisoned merchants from their debts and set them free, with the consent of a majority of their creditors. The following year Morris was free again, and Lee was once again in pursuit of the elusive $40,000.

In vain. Morris simply didn't have the money. A bankruptcy court, Morris explained, in August 1801, had "restored to me to my home and family which I hope, (notwithstanding your sufferings) you will be pleased to hear," in a piece of news that offered Lee little succor. "I am now my dear friend at liberty to walk in the open air but I have not one single solitary dollar that can be called my own.... You will clearly see by this my actual situation that my good wishes is all that is left in my power."[4]

That door closed, Lee packed his family into their coach-and-four and hauled them off for a tour of the Northern states in 1802. The trip was likely undertaken so that Lee could recoup debts and seek loans. In September, during a stopover in Camden, New Jersey, Anne gave birth to another son, Sydney Smith, whose name was an honor to the family's hosts at the time. The children were oblivious to their family's growing worry. Lee carried little Charles Carter, now four, everywhere he went, including to the theatre; decades later the boy would vividly remember sitting next to his father at a performance of Thomas Otway's *Venice Preserv'd.*[5]

But when the Lees returned to Stratford Hall, their troubles were still with them.

In 1803 Lee's elder daughter Lucy, now a temperamental black-eyed teenager whose beauty recalled that of her mother, married Bernard Carter, her step-mother's brother—perhaps in an act of spite. Carter's father Charles gave the newlyweds a home, Woodstock, in Fauquier County. The patriarch of the

Carter family farsightedly altered his will to safeguard Anne's inheritance from Henry and his creditors. It would be a loveless and miserable marriage; according to family legend, Lucy threatened to burn down the home unless Bernard relocated her to Philadelphia. Woodstock did eventually burn down, though not by Lucy's hand.[6]

There were still tender moments for Anne and Henry; the two played chess under the swaying candle-lit chandelier in the mansion's lofty parlor, and the parents' love of the game was passed on to their children. To the younger Lees, life at Stratford Hall was an unceasing adventure. Charles and his sister Anne devotedly tended to the chicken coop built for them by their mother and delighted when the white pullet inside gave birth to tunefully chirping chicks. They watched as nets of fish and crabs hauled out of the Potomac were emptied under the shade of a pear tree outside the kitchen and a family hound scampered off with a crustacean dangling from its tail. And there were visits from fascinating family members, often from Shirley.[7]

But these happy moments belied the decay setting in at Stratford Hall. As complaints and lawsuits multiplied, Lee was becoming a faded version of his old self.

John Rose, in a suit against Lee for money owed with interest in Westmoreland County, complained that he had "removed himself out of the country, or so absconds or conceals himself that the ordinary process of law cannot be served upon him." Robert Sanford, who also claimed Lee owed him money, alleged the debtor no longer even lived in Virginia; when a subpoena was filed, Lee was nowhere to be found.[8]

Years behind in his payments to Bryan Fairfax, with the interest accumulating, Lee lost control of Matildaville, the manufacturing hub he had dreamed of founding at the Great Falls, when the land there was repossessed. There was $15,000 owed to Alexander Spotswood.

Lee spent years evading the estate of William Ludwell Lee, to which he owed 5,000 pounds. His refusal to pay only compounded his woes: as the years passed, an additional 5,550 pounds in interest accrued to his debt. In an increasingly familiar scramble, when the executor threatened to take Lee's land as collateral, he promised to sell a separate tract instead to generate the owed money, but eventually passed the debt on to his harried brother, Richard Bland, who after years of helping his older brother was now deeply in debt himself. "I remain disappointed by him," wrote another of Lee's brothers, Charles, no doubt speaking for many members of the family.[9]

Elizabeth Lee strained to see good in her brother-in-law, complaining, "Mr. Lee's business with him for the last five years has produced to us anxiety and unhappiness. I must confess I thought when she [Elizabeth's mother] was with me the case was a desperate one and that Gen. Lee kept himself from his friends because he did not mean or had not the means of releasing them—since which I have had reasons to believe and hope for better that Gen. Lee is a better and more honorable man than might some time ago be suspected I have no doubt tho' we have suffered so many inconveniences from his embarrassments I believe he wishes to do justice."[10]

In this, Richard Bland Lee's wife was correct. Lee's trail of ruin, which was littered with dear family members, was not the result of malice or perfidy. Rather, it was the manifestation of an unchecked fever for speculation and a poor head for management. So dizzyingly confused were Lee's own holdings, debts, and arrangements that by the early 1800s he was confessing that in one case "the thing is so obscured and so mixed with my other transactions that I cannot speak with any precision therein."[11] The hurt spreading from his own mess only caused Lee further anguish. "I am vastly unhappy in being the instrument to such deep injury," he admitted.[12]

Lee was now truly desperate to evade his creditors—and they to recoup their losses. He became embroiled in a long-running legal feud with his former agent, Thomas Rowand, to whom he had given the deed to Cabin Point as security. Another of Lee's agents, John James Maund, a well-known lawyer in Westmoreland County, had opened the doors of Stratford Hall during one of its owner's frequent absences and allowed Ransdell Piece, a deputy sheriff, to claim household goods, including furniture and even slaves, as payment for Lee's debts.

In an exceptionally berserk episode, Lee retaliated. He frenziedly stormed into Rowand's property, tore down his fences, dashed across his yard, trespassed into his home, and—in a wild free-for-all—grabbed bedding, tables, chairs, knives, forks, dishes, meats and liquors, anything he could lay his hands on. Lee even rounded up several slaves and gored an ox, for good measure, on his way out. Rowand sought damages for $5,000 for Lee's incursion.[13]

The prospect of arrest threatened. Nathaniel Pendleton, a jurist and Revolutionary War veteran, claimed that Lee owed him $25,000. Pendleton was caught up in a legal morass regarding land he had taken possession of after it passed from Lee to Baldwin Date. He wrote to Lee's agent, pointing to evidence that "will clearly show he is speculating upon me."[14] When Pendleton learned that Lee was passing through Fairfax Courthouse, he offered $250 for Lee's arrest.[15] Failing this, he proposed to follow Lee to and from his various hideouts to collect the money.

Anxiety made Lee ill. "I am very sick and looking over my papers," began a typical letter from him.[16] And the health of his wife—deserted at Stratford Hall, which was now decaying as a result of years of neglect, abandoned by her husband—was in decline. Anne Lee longed to be with family to ease her loneliness, but she had no transportation—the family carriages had all been repossessed or wrecked. "I consider you among the number of those dear friends whom fate has probably for ever severed me from," she wrote to Elizabeth Lee in 1803. "I am much of an invalid," she lamented a year later. "But having been so often an invalid, I imagine myself adequate to judging of the feelings in a similar situation,"[17] she wrote her beloved brother Robert, who had returned to Virginia unwell after time abroad.

In the scorching summer of 1806, after months of longing to visit Shirley, Anne finally wound her way back to her old home along with her children—including the sickly Sydney Smith Lee—traveling towards the James River in the middle of a heat wave. When the familiar pineapple atop Shirley's roof came into sight, though, heartache was only moments away. Anne's beloved father, whom she had traveled across the scorched Virginia landscape to lay eyes upon, was dead.

"Before I arrived at this place, the arms which had ever received me with so much delight, were folded in death!" she wept to her husband. "The eyes which used to beam with so much affection on me, were veiled for ever! And the cold grave was closed on my too dear and ever lamented father!"

In this moment of sharp grief, she vainly tried to stir her husband to responsibility. "Oh! my dearest Mr. Lee remember, that your poor afflicted Fatherless wife, can now, only look to you, to smooth her rugged path through life, and soften her bed of death!"

With her grieving mother's health now failing, Anne hoped to leave Shirley and return to Stratford before summer's end. "I trust Mr. Lee you will certainty bring a conveyance for me by that time, do not disappoint me I conjure you...." Two of the children, Carter and Smith, were now sick; the latter in desperate need of skillful medical attention. Anne was worried about her husband's well-being as well. "Let me hear from you immediately," she continued "and forget not my dearest Mr. Lee, to guard your health with more care, than you have for several years past—your life is more important to your poor wife and children now, than ever it was: their other protector is taken from them, for ever and for ever!"[18]

But the family's carriage was broken, and Lee was not able to find another one to carry Anne and the children back to Stratford Hall for months. After so much delay, when they finally made the voyage in an open-topped carriage, it was winter and Anne contracted a lingering cold during the trip. While she sat in her decaying mansion, its closets still full of Matilda Lee's gowns, huddled around the fire with her brood, there were whispers too about her husband's fidelity. During a dinner in Alexandria, after Lee joked about allegations of infidelity among his relatives, female guests quietly snickered. "Now did you ever hear of such a man as General Lee?" Portia Lee, a cousin, wrote to Lee's sister-in-law Elizabeth. "I could not help laughing heartily to think of his interrogating a gentleman on such a subject."[19]

In January of 1807 Anne learned that Elizabeth, in Philadelphia at the time, was expecting a child. "You have my best wishes for your success my dear, and truest assurances, that I do not envy your prospect, not wish to share in them." But Anne was concealing a secret. In her poverty, desertion, and illness, she too was pregnant once again. On January 19 she gave birth to another boy, whom she named Robert Edward in honor of her two beloved brothers. His father was predictably absent when the boy entered the world.[20]

Astonishingly, as the noose tightened around his neck, Lee found time and energy to indulge in a favorite pastime: antagonizing the president. Conflating his personal misfortune with his political frustrations, Lee made Thomas Jefferson an all-purpose scapegoat for his misery. And much to the president's enduring irritation, Lee managed to interpose himself into a particularly embarrassing and delicate matter pressing on the chief executive.

John Walker was a patriot, a politician, and a classmate and dear friend of Jefferson, who had been a groomsman at Walker's wedding and even the designated executor of his will. In 1768 Jefferson and his wife, Martha, paid a visit to Belvoir, Walker's estate in Albemarle County, Virginia. The Jeffersons slept in the home's upper story in a bedchamber across a passage from that of Walker and his wife Elizabeth. At some point during the visit, Jefferson slipped into the corridor dressed only in his shirt, apparently "ready to seize her"—his hostess and friend's wife, that is—"on her way from her Chamber—indecent in manner."[21]

These advances, Elizabeth later alleged, persisted until 1779. But fearing a duel between the two men, she explained, it was not until Jefferson departed for Paris in 1784 that she informed her husband of his friend's impropriety. Walker removed Jefferson from his will, and the couple seemingly buried the issue.[22] But then in 1802 James Callender, a scurrilous journalist who had once been Jefferson's pet, splashed word of the entire episode—along with the rumor of an affair with a slave named Sally Hemmings—across the pages of the *Richmond Recorder*.[23] Jefferson having barely begun his presidency, his Federalist opponents were feeding frenziedly on the salacious news. Walker's honor now demanded soothing, and Jefferson's political reputation required that the scandal be quieted.

Into the middle of this mess sauntered, of all people, Henry Lee. Elizabeth Walker, as chance would have it, was one of Anne Lee's nieces. So Lee took it upon himself—likely in hopes of compounding Jefferson's headache—to serve as an intermediary between the two men. Visiting Monticello twice in 1803 and again in 1806, Lee—improbably, given the animosity between the two men—negotiated with Jefferson, then composed a statement for the president to sign to satisfy Walker. Lee helped wring out of a greatly chagrined Jefferson the concession that long ago, when "young and single I offered love to a handsome lady."[24]

But Jefferson was soon causing trouble for Lee, in turn. While Lee was finishing his troublemaking negotiations with Jefferson, he was informed that the president had passed along the rumor to a visitor to Monticello that Lee had knowingly offered a potential client farmland he had no title to or right to sell. Now it was Lee's honor that was injured. "This description of conduct," he wrote Jefferson, "conveyed a character which my soul abhors and which never with justice can be applied to me." It was up to the president, Lee insisted, "to restore my misrepresented character."[25]

Later Lee caught word that Jefferson had drawn a connection between himself and Aaron Burr. In the years after he had lost the presidency to Jefferson, Burr had fallen into deep disgrace. He had mortally wounded Lee's old friend, Alexander Hamilton, in a duel in 1804; the fallen patriot's second in that affair, Nathaniel Pendleton, was among those to whom Lee owed money. After vacating office in 1805, Burr immersed himself in a complex plot to establish a breakaway republic in the American Southwest. Any insinuation that he was in league with such a disgraced character enraged Lee. He demanded an explanation from Jefferson, who claimed innocence in the matter.[26]

But it was not until 1809, when Jefferson was preparing to hand the presidency over to James Madison, that Lee fully unloaded his fury. Lee's anonymously published thirty-eight-page screed was titled "A Cursory Sketch of The Motives and Proceedings of the Party Which Sways the Affairs of the Union." It was the inverse of his eulogy for Washington. Its opening paragraphs alone were studded with references to the "dreadful condition to which our country is reduced," "lost happiness," the "cause of our present difficulties" and talk of a nation recently "tumbled from the summit of prosperity."[27]

Lee charged, "The present chief magistrate is confessedly the author and promoter of that system of that policy, be it good or be it bad, the deplorable effects of which are so sensibly felt by all." He recalled Jefferson's time as secretary of state, claiming that he had undermined Washington and duped and betrayed John Adams and Alexander Hamilton, the former a "victim to political treachery" the latter "marked for sacrifice."[28]

Jefferson was an "arch fabricator" who forced love of France and hatred of Great Britain upon the American people as a litmus test for political righteousness. After deserting Washington's government, Jefferson "had retired to his unfinished grotesque mansion on the top of a spur of a mountain" where, "perched on this craggy mountain," he plotted his successful deceit of the American people and takeover of their government. "The name of liberty was prostituted to consecrate personal exaltation," Lee sneered.[29]

The pamphlet was ostensibly an effort to dissuade the nation from another war with Great Britain, then a growing possibility. And Lee was able to exercise one of his preferred arguments against the president: that his contributions to the American Revolution, such as they were, had not occurred on the battlefield. He went so far as to paint Jefferson as a coward: "war, however necessary," Lee wrote, "never can be acceptable to him whose envious mind sickens in observing merit rising to eminence; unless in a man too young to rival his superior self, and too obsequious to dare to do so."[30]

The potential war with England that Lee decried had come close to reality back in 1807 when a British warship, the *Leopard*, overtook the *Chesapeake*, an American frigate, and apprehended four of its sailors, eventually hanging one. Outraged Americans had called for retaliation, leading Jefferson to impose an embargo on Great Britain. Lee, amidst all his personal tumult, had risen to the occasion, once again prioritizing patriotism over partisanship and exhorting Virginia's militiamen to prepare for war with Great Britain. He had penned yet another stirring broadside, promising that Virginia's young warriors would "manifest to the world, that the bright example of our dear, and great Washington, and his sage maxims, have sunk deep into our hearts, and we shall present to our unjust foe, a front of bayonets, in the hand of freemen, estimating peace with honor, as the highest national good."[31]

The preparations for a potential war and the forays back into politics—both conducted amidst his scurrying from place to place to avoid bills—likely gave Lee some catharsis. But it was only temporary.

The creditors circled. Sheriffs appeared at the now chained doors of Stratford Hall. Lee's health continued to sink. So too did Anne's. Both complained of respiratory ailments. He looked desperately for an escape. The family could sail to South America, preferably Brazil. A friend had offered the Lees use of his home there, and the warm weather and dry air there would afford some relief—and remove Lee a safe distance from his creditors. But the voyage was impossible. In a cruel twist of fate, Jefferson's embargo forbade the trip.

Lee pleaded with James Madison, then secretary of state and soon to be president, for an exemption. "The state of my own health my physician considers imperiously requiring a sea voyage,"[32] he wrote at the end of 1809. When Lee, in Washington, received word that Anne had taken a terrible turn, he pressed his case once again to Madison. "The last letter from my family commands me to make the only effort in my power to preserve a life, the loss of which will bear me to the grave with unceasing woe."[33] But there was nothing Madison could do.

When Madison secured the presidency, Lee, holding no grudge, wrote a lengthy note of congratulations and recommendation. "My state of health continues precarious and I have seized an interval of ease from pain to tell you what I conceive best...." he concluded.[34]

Ben Stoddert. John Porter. William McCleery. William Franklin. Lawrence Muse. Jasper & Davenport. The list of men attempting to collect money from Lee, or filing suits against him, went on and on. He owed money to his brothers and to friends living and departed, including Patrick Henry and George Washington. There were outstanding debts for hats, gun powder and flints, and even for the paper on which he had scribbled his angry screed against Jefferson.[35]

His correspondence now revealed the frantic urgency of a man watching the last few grains of sand falling into the bottom of the hourglass. In a complicated scheme, he prodded a young attorney named Robert Goodloe Harper to help collect money owed to his first wife Matilda's long-dead father, Philip Ludwell

Lee. "My necessities are such that every days gain in time, is momentous to me," a typical letter to the lawyer began.[36]

There were fleeting respites. A creditor from the county of Rockbridge arrived at Stratford writ in hand, and Lee, jocular as usual, treated the guest to "a delightful social hour." The man left Westmoreland County empty-handed, never even pressing the purpose of his visit.[37]

Lee turned to two friends and fellow veterans of the Revolution, James Breckinridge and James McHenry, for loans, offering the sale of iron ore. It was a final attempt to avoid the inevitable. "I am miserable indeed as I must prepare for jail," Lee confessed to Breckinridge.[38]

Under the law, he faced a choice: proclaim bankruptcy and avoid incarceration, but hand over all of his remaining property and assets to seizure by creditors. Or try to hold onto his property by refusing to declare bankruptcy—and leave himself open to imprisonment at the demands of his creditors.

Many of Anne's own belongings, protected from her husband by her father's will, were even now in jeopardy of being apprehended to satisfy his debts. In 1808 Henry IV, studying at William and Mary College, turned twenty-one and took ownership of Stratford Hall. His father began transferring property across Virginia, parts of Matilda's estate, to his eldest surviving son.[39]

By the spring of 1809, though, Lee's flight was at an end and a decision was made: the shackles beckoned, a cell awaited. He would go to jail, a sacrifice for his family: "the pain and sufferings I undergo...for the good of my children," he informed Harper.[40] On April 11, Edward Herndon, the sheriff of Westmoreland County, presented a writ for 5,436 Spanish dollars and interest. On the twenty-fourth Lee yielded. He was ushered to Montross Courthouse and locked in a twelve-by-fifteen-foot room.[41]

Stratford Hall, where Lee had for so long been little more than an apparition, stood wasting away. Inside, his wife sheltered her small children; all that remained of the patriarch of the family was the weary face hanging on one of the mansion's cracking walls.

"I have your picture here executed by Stuart," Henry Lee IV wrote to his father. "It affords Mrs. L. the pensive satisfaction of paying to it, that adoration, which she has so constantly and sweetly done to its original."[42]

# 16

# WHEN FUTURE GENERATIONS SHALL INQUIRE

The hero of Paulus Hook, the leader of Lee's Legion, the eulogizer of Washington, sat alone in a dank cell. "This depot of misery," he described it to his son-in-law Bernard Carter.[1]

Henry Lee was isolated, humbled, and destitute. His name was in ruins. And despite his attempts to shield them from the consequences of his own actions, his family was left with little. Originally imprisoned in Westmoreland County, after a few months Lee was hauled north to Spotsylvania Courthouse to serve time for yet more debt.

The bars and chains keeping him from freedom provided no sanctuary from the hounding creditors. William Brock, representing William Augustine Washington, appeared at Spotsylvania Courthouse curious to know when Lee would settle his debts, but the prisoner shrugged him off, saying that he was "too much indisposed to attend to any business."[2]

There was another matter preoccupying his mind.

Remarkably, as he languished in his cell, Lee had conjured a way to transcend the despair, to find release, not in body but in mind. He had returned to the central epoch in both his and the country's formation.

Though a soldier, a politician and a planter—to varying degrees of success—Lee was at heart a historian. He had argued for the creation of monuments to Greene and Washington as a means to elucidate their deeds for future Americans. He had used his soaring rhetoric to the same purpose in his eulogy for the second of those two great generals. Even his diatribe against Jefferson in 1808 was in essence a chronicle of the era. Now, to cut through the prison gloom, to revisit long-past days of grandeur from his squalid present, and perhaps most important, to enshrine his own place in the saga of America, Lee set out to sketch a record of the Revolution.

The idea of the project was conceived before his incarceration; in its original iteration it was to be a biography of Greene. But Lee soon realized that he knew far too little about the Rhode Islander's life prior to the Revolution to fill an entire book. So his focus shifted. He would compose a memoir of the conflict, centered on the campaign in the Southern states, where he had spent the final years of his service and played such a crucial part in the climactic battles at the war's conclusion.

Initially he drew upon his own memories. But in some cases these had grown dim. Nearly thirty years had passed since Lee rode home to Virginia, leaving his Legion and Greene's army behind. So as he proceeded with the project, he filled the gaps in his recollections with the memories of old comrades.

"The books extant upon our war deal so much in the general as to overlook all individual," he wrote to Charles Simms, a veteran of the Virginia Line who helped Lee gather firsthand accounts from other offices, "which can only be sought for in the memory of living actors of the manuscripts of the dead, thus I am very troublesome where my wishes are indulged in by my brother officers."[3]

In fact, word of the endeavor heartened Lee's old comrades. John Mercer, another Virginian veteran, happily lent his first-hand account of the Battle of Brandywine. "Whatever General Lee writes on this subject will most probably from his genius and reputation bear a value with distant posterity," he enthused.[4]

William R. Davie, the commissary general of Greene's army and, like Lee, a cavalry officer turned politician, lent his own memories of the Battle of Charlotte, which had been committed to paper "while circumstances were fresh in my memory." Davis wrote to Lee, "I rejoice that you have imposed on yourself the task of writing the History of the Revolutionary War, by which you will add a claim to the gratitude of your country, perhaps even more important, than the brilliant services you have rendered her in the field."[5]

Revolutionary pamphleteer William Goddard, thrilled by Lee's project, wrote to express to the author his delight that "Brother Officers dear to your heart, many of them beloved friends of mine would, through your sympathy and generosity be rescued from the Gulph of oblivion."[6]

Christopher R. Greene, a young relative of the general, whom Lee had never met, wrote reverently to Lee, sharing materials at Goddard's urging and buoying the old hero with flattery: "when time shall have enforced on you, the immutable law of Nature, your memory may never be obscured."[7] Phebe Champe, the widow of John Champe, whom Lee had dispatched to apprehend Benedict Arnold, shared her husband's papers. Even Nathaniel

Pendleton, who had so recently sought Lee's arrest, eventually lent his diaries from the era.[8]

These materials provided the missing pieces of his story, while the enthusiasm and encouragement pushed Lee to consecrate the shared past. Lee's *Memoirs* answered the question he raised in their pages: "When future generations shall inquire, Where are the men who gained the highest prize of glory in the arduous contest which ushered in our nation's birth?"[9]

Lee's own role in the pivotal events, his connections with key players, his knowledge and love of history, and his rhetorical genius all made him the perfect author for the story. As Davie declared, "this work seems to have been reserved by Providence by your pen."[10]

Lee submerged himself in the project, sitting on the grassy lawn outside the Spotsylvania Courthouse or in his damp cell, escaping from his present troubles, passing the days. Letters and documents arrived, and the writing went on. The result was both sprawling and intense, littered with vivid details that had lingered in his mind for so many years. "The determination of the mind to relinquish the soft scenes of tranquil life for the rough adventures of war," the manuscript began, "is generally attended with the conviction that the act is laudable; and with a wish that its honorable exertions should be faithfully transmitted to posterity."[11]

The story began in 1777, as Ticonderoga fell under the boot of Burgoyne; it ended only when Leslie sailed away from Charleston in 1782. Between these were exciting episodes featuring the faces of old friends now long gone: the hair-raising escape on the Schuylkill River with Alexander Hamilton, Champe's daring spy adventure, the American army's dash across the Dan, and the journeys through South Carolina's swamps with Francis Marion.

Ancient heroes strode across the pages, mingling with those of the current age. Quintus Maximus and Publius Scipio rubbed elbows with George Washington and Nathanael Greene. The Battle of Brandywine recalled the Battle of Cannae.

The embellishments were poetic, the details vivid. Lee painted the scorching sun and foggy morn that preceded the attack on Fort Granby; the hissing of flaming arrows descending on Fort Motte; the worn shoes, tattered clothes, and threadbare blankets during marches; the British muskets glittering in the sun before battle; and the bodies of the dead rotting in the pouring rain after. "This night succeeding this day of blood was rainy, dark and cold; the dead unburied, the wounded unsheltered, the groans of the dying and the shrieks of the living, cast a deeper shade over the gloom of nature," he wrote of the hours following the conflict at Guilford Courthouse. His pen conjured to life the defeated British army, marching at Yorktown with their colors cased, drums beating.[12]

To a manuscript swelling in size to hundreds of pages, Lee appended letters and statistics and, true to form, many opinions: General Charles Lee, whom he had admired since their dinner at Mount Vernon so long ago, had been needlessly maligned in the wake of Monmouth; he was "guilty only of neglect," rather than disobedience.[13] The Siege of Ninety-Six had failed because of the blunders of Tadeusz Kosciusko, who was, Lee wrote, an "extremely amiable, and, I believe, a truly good man, nor was he deficient in his professional knowledge; but he was very moderate in talent."[14]

There were topical asides. Lee labeled slavery a "dreadful evil, which the cruel policy of preceding times had introduced," and rued that the Constitution had not stipulated its gradual prohibition.[15] And he defended America's original inhabitants.

"I could never see the justice of denominating our Indian border-ers savage," he observed. "They appear to me to merit a very different appellation, as we well know they are not behind their civilized neighbors in the practice of many of the virtues most dear to human nature."[16]

There was also history to set straight. Charles Stedman, a British soldier who had fought in and later penned a history of the war, had castigated Lee and his Legion over the brutal encounter with Colonel John Pyle and his men in North Carolina. As he had written in 1794, "humanity shudders at the recital of so foul a massacre." It was not foul, Lee asserted, but unintentional. "The fire commenced upon us, and self-preservation commanded the limited destruction which ensued."[17]

And there were scores to settle. Thomas Jefferson had risen to the presidency, and Lee's political fortunes had faded. Narrating the course of the Revolution, in which the former had been a spectator, the latter a solider, presented Lee with a chance to dent the legacy of his nemesis.

When Benedict Arnold had sailed up the James River and sacked Richmond early in 1781, Virginia, governed by Jefferson at the time, had wilted. Surprised that the traitor and his legion would set their sights on the capital, the state's chief executive had failed to take proper precautions—a restoration of the state's militia, Lee estimated, would have easily snuffed out Arnold's expedition.

"But unfortunately we were unprepared, and efforts to make ready commenced after the enemy was knocking at the doors," Lee charged. "The government which does not prepare in time, doubles the power of its adversary, and sports with the lives of its citizens."[18]

Though Lee scarcely mentioned Jefferson, this was an attack on the Sage of Monticello—and one that stung sharply. After

Arnold had burned and left Richmond, Jefferson's actions were investigated by Virginia's General Assembly. The investigation cleared him of any wrongdoing, but he was not retained for another term. He later admitted that he had been "unprepared by his line of life and education for command of armies."[19] The taint of the retreat from Richmond remained with Jefferson; when he sought the presidency, critics, referencing the summit he traversed to escape from Monticello when the British approached, branded him "the coward of Carter Mountain."[20] Now Lee chiseled this embarrassing episode into history, to Jefferson's horror.

"It will scarcely be credited by posterity, that the governor of the oldest state of the Union, and the most populous," Lee disdainfully concluded, "was driven out of its metropolis, and forced to secure personal safety by flight, and that its archives, with all its munitions and stores, were yielded to the will of the invader...."[21]

Lee made sure to underline his connections to and shower praise on treasured friends and heroes. Greene was a "Soldier of consummate talents," Washington constantly striving to "perfect his army in the art of war."[22] But the hero of the *Memoirs*, mounting his horse and dashing across the pages, was, naturally, Lee.

There was no mention of the court martials, or the wild ambition that had led him to turn down Washington's offer of a promotion. Nor did he write of the fit of pique that had ended his participation in the war. Instead he took the opportunity to embellish his significant contributions. This was most clearly evident in his sly suggestion that he had not merely endorsed but rather proposed that Greene take the American army south after the Battle of Guilford Courthouse—the strategy that eventually carried the day in the Southern campaign.

*The Memoirs* were classic Henry Lee: self-serving, discursive, flamboyant, erudite, provocative, and—as time would reveal—a definitive account of the subject.

The book, Lee told Simms, was largely completed by January of 1810. But, he explained, it was "written with too much freedom for the times and will appear without my name." Its commentaries were sure to be controversial. He hoped to have the final product perused and edited by friends—though this was impossible at the moment—and that it would be printed in two volumes and available via subscription.[23]

By the spring Lee had begun to see the light at the end of the tunnel. Taking advantage of Virginia's bankruptcy laws, he compiled a lengthy list of his possessions, which would be dispersed to pay off remaining debts. This was not an easy thing for him to do; it meant trading his children's inheritance for his own freedom. To Bernard Carter, he confessed how difficult it was "for a man whose property is large to bring himself to deprive his family of it." Straining to preserve something for their future comfort, he had Carter shelter $4,000 worth of furniture as well as six hundred acres of land in Loudon County.[24]

The rest of his assets, though—a collection of land staggering in size, ranging across Virginia, Pennsylvania, and Tennessee—were dispersed to meet the multitude of financial obligations. On March 20, after over a year in prison, Lee was freed, "discharged from the custody of the Sheriff or Keeper of the jail of the said County."[25] His manuscript in hand, Lee returned to Stratford Hall to reunite with Anne and their children.

Anne Lee had to strain to see the traces of the dashing governor she had long ago fallen in love with in the man who returned to her from prison. During his absence Carter Berkeley, who had married her now dead sister, had offered his spacious Fredericksburg home to Anne and her children. But Lee had pleaded with her to wait for him at Stratford Hall. "Mr. Lee constantly assures me, his intention is, to live with his family: after his release from his present situation," she informed Berkeley.[26]

So the family was at last reunited in the spring of 1810. Lee's book was not yet completed, despite his earlier claims. He continued the labor, the profits of which would now be put towards helping his family. Richard Bland Lee had lent his older brother $7,000. Now the elder Lee conveyed the rights to his memoirs as payment of that debt and convinced his younger brother to buy lots in Alexandria with the proceeds of the book and hold them for Anne and her children. Lee had dragged his wife and children to the brink of destitution, but he did what little was in his power to aid them.[27]

In May, Richard Bland Lee was busy soliciting potential publishers and distributing a prospectus for the work, which would be titled *Memoirs of the War in the Southern Department of the United States by an Officer of the Southern Army.*[28]

Despite his infamy, Lee was able to still dip a toe into politics, serving as a judge on the Westmoreland County Court shortly after his return to Westmoreland County. But his time in the Northern Neck was coming to an end.[29] He passed his life interest in Stratford Hall on to Henry IV, in order to pay yet another debt. Lee's oldest son had dutifully supported his father, even writing letters following up on his still-not-yet-awarded congressional medal while he languished in jail.[30]

Anne had agreed to wait for his release, but she would no longer gamble her family's fate on his reckless behavior. Instead she exerted her own will over their destiny, seeking out a new and at last stable home.

With a new master at Stratford, her family would move north to Alexandria. The bustling port town was bounded in two directions by "Washington": the growing capital city was to its north, across the Potomac. And to its south was Mount Vernon, whose dead master's memory lived on in the hearts of the town's Federalist denizens.

The Lees had family in Alexandria. William Henry Fitzhugh, a cousin of Anne's, owned property there. Edmund Jennings, Lee's pious younger brother, was a local politician and served on the vestry of Christ Church. Richard Bland Lee, Lee's harried brother, also soon arrived in Alexandria after selling his plantation, Sully, a consequence of the financial troubles brought on by his elder brother.[31]

The city was buoyant, full of culture, home to a theatre and a firehouse, and filled with friends. And the quality of the schools and doctors was what Anne desired for her children—and had not been available on the Northern Neck. The new home Anne secured in Alexandria was a modest two-story Federal affair built, like so many dwellings in the town, of red brick, sitting quietly at 611 Cameron Street. Its owner, John Bogue, a prosperous local cabinetmaker who had participated in George Washington's funeral procession, leased the home when he moved to a larger residence.[32]

In the final weeks of 1810 the family gathered their scant remaining belongings—a few books, a clock, and a cradle—and headed to their new home. Left behind were the dark memories of Stratford Hall; the only marker remaining there was the growing horse-chestnut tree that Anne had planted in the garden under the eyes of her youngest son, Robert.[33]

# 17

# THE SAD CATASTROPHE OF BALTIMORE

James Madison made an unlikely commander in chief—a diminutive five feet, six inches tall in unfashionable black pantaloons, his face "shriveled with care." Travel was problematic for him because of painful hemorrhoids. He was shy and stumbling, and often inaudible when speaking in public.[1] And yet in the summer of 1812 he found himself the president of a nation at war.

For years Europe's conflicts had threatened to wash upon America's shores. During Thomas Jefferson's presidency, battles between Great Britain and Napoleon's France had obstructed American commerce as the two European nations waged economic war against one another, prohibiting trade and blockading ports. The Orders in Council issued by Britain in November 1807 forbade even neutral nations from trading with France without permission from the Crown. They also, insultingly, encouraged the seizure of America's ships and the impressment of her sailors, many of who

293

were Irishmen or Englishmen seeking naturalization, a concept—Britons becoming Americans—that Britain refused to recognize.[2]

A second generation of American statesmen newly established in Washington now began to press for retaliation and reclamation of American honor by force. Among these young war hawks were two South Carolinians: the eloquent Langdon Cheves and the fiery nationalist John C. Calhoun. Kentucky's Henry Clay, who as Speaker of the House had called for members to wear only American-spun garments, beat the drums in the Senate.[3]

They lit a fire under Madison, who in June 1812 forwarded a message to Congress enumerating Britain's misdeeds; both chambers, controlled by the Democratic-Republicans, subsequently voted for a formal declaration of war. Federalist members voted in unison against the measure. Support and opposition followed the same partisan divide across the nation. While another fight with Britain found favor in the South, northeastern states peopled by anti-war Federalists approached open rebellion against the government over Mr. Madison's War.[4]

Madison presided over a woefully unprepared army with decrepit arms and planners more adept at politics than combat. Commanding generals, men such as Henry Dearborn and Thomas Pinckney, were long in the tooth.

While Madison stewed in the Executive Mansion, across the Potomac an old friend indignantly stumbled along the cobblestone streets of Alexandria.

The Lees had come to their new home in the last weeks of 1810; once arrived, they had welcomed another child, their last, a girl named Catherine Mildred. Their stay at Cameron Street was brief. Within a year of their move to Alexandria they relocated to another, more spacious home at 607 Oronoco Street.

The dwelling, with its Georgian facade, was originally built by John Potts Jr., the first secretary of the Potomac Company; purchased by William Fitzhugh, a planter, politician, and friend of George Washington; and eventually rented by his son to the Lee family. Situated on a block bound by Washington and St. Asaph's streets, where Lee relatives congregated, it was on the city's edge, the nation's capital visible across the nearby Potomac.[5]

While Lee worked on his manuscript, he did what he could to adjust to this new life—his reputation forever soiled, his dreams of prosperity entirely dashed, his restless existence dependent on his wife's inheritance from her father. He took up a regular chess game with a merchant on King Street, the town's main commercial drag, which stretched to the wharfs on the Potomac. During the matches Lee fell into the role of the old soldier, haranguing his opponent with reminiscences about the Revolution and Washington.

One afternoon his chess partner was nowhere to be found. Lee questioned the store's young clerk, who explained that the owner was out of the shop. Lee furiously accused him of lying. The man was avoiding him, Lee suspected. The clerk fired back that if Lee did not leave at once he would be forcibly removed. Lee "folded his military cape about him and walked slowly but majestically out the store."[6]

With a vacuum of military acumen and leadership in Washington, Lee should have been a logical choice for a commission. But long before the beginning of hostilities, he had viewed another conflict with Great Britain an unwinnable folly, one whose root cause—the fate of immigrant sailors impressed by the enemy—was not worth fighting over. In the early months of 1809, before he was imprisoned, Lee had encouraged Madison to pursue peace with Great Britain. "It is not worth fighting in our infant condition with her for a principle," he reasoned.[7] "For 50 years We ought to Cultivate peace with zeal, that our girls & lads surrounded with the Comfort, of the plenty & bliss of our country may think first of love & next of its fruits."[8]

But should war come, Lee had encouraged Madison to wage it skillfully and win it decisively. Call on the governors, he had suggested, to raise the proper number of militia to supplement the regular army. Train them well, keep them healthy, and fortify ports and other points most likely to be attacked by Britain. "Doing things by halves in War, is inviting disaster," he counseled.[9]

Yet three years later, on the eve of battle, Lee was still encouraging Madison to do everything in his power to avoid bloodshed, suggesting the president hold back his warships in hope that the recent assassination of Prime Minister Spencer Perceval and sentiment against the Orders in Council, which Parliament was considering lifting, might obviate the need for a fight. "Believe me my dear sir you could by no act so widely gratify the majority of yr. Country as by standing still awhile," Lee wrote. "You immortalize yr. name too by shewing yr. deep reluctance to wade in human blood."[10]

Blood would flow, though for Lee it would not be on the battlefield.

By the end of 1811 he had finished his memoirs. And by the next year he had found a publisher, Bradford & Inskeep. The imprint had been founded in Philadelphia in 1808 by Samuel Fisher Bradford, scion of an established publishing family, and his brother-in-law John Inskeep. They had previously printed volumes on ornithology as well as Washington Irving's *History of New York*.[11] Lee's work would appear in two volumes bound in brown "tree calf" leather, printed by Fry and Kammerer Printers, available in late 1812. And Lee had had a change of heart;

the author's name would appear. Lee optimistically continued to "indulge a hope that it will take a great run when published."[12]

But continuing health concerns and lingering debts led Lee to again contemplate distant shores. In the spring of 1812 he encountered James Monroe, now secretary of state, and learned of an earthquake that had leveled the Venezuelan city of Caracas. Congress had appropriated $50,000 in humanitarian aid to be sent to the victims of the disaster, and Lee hoped to catch a ride away from the Unite States on the vessel carrying this relief. "I suggested the hope that I might be entrusted with its present-ment," he wrote to Madison, recalling their meeting. "I wish no emolument for so doing being satisfied with the welcome which it will be sure to attach to my visit." Congress was then in the process of crafting a law allowing for exceptions to the embargo currently blocking boats from leaving American ports. Lee hoped to take advantage of it and present the flour and other supplies headed to South America.[13] But Madison and Monroe never acted on his appeal. Escape eluded Lee.

In the early weeks of the War of 1812, the nation was endur-ing a domestic war as well. The political conflicts between Fed-eralists and Democratic-Republicans were spilling out into violence in America's streets, particularly those of Baltimore. The Maryland city, its population swelling towards fifty thou-sand, was the third largest in the nation. Peopled by immigrants freshly arrived from Germany, France, Scotland, and Ireland, it was rapidly growing, its population dynamic and socially strat-ified and its commerce tied to the maritime trade obstructed by Britain. The city's political culture, largely Democratic-Repub-lican, was at odds with that of the genteel plantation-owning Federalists of southern Maryland, creating a political schism in the state.[14]

Baltimore was not entirely bereft of Federalists, though. Alexander Contee Hanson was a notable exception to the Democratic-Republican political culture in the port city. Originally from Montgomery County, the grandson of a president of the Continental Congress and the son of a former chancellor of Maryland, Hanson had established a broadsheet in Baltimore, the *Federal Republican*. Exceptionally pugnacious, he filled it with virulent anti-Democratic-Republican and anti-administration insults. The publication had merged with another newspaper, the *North American and Mercantile and Daily Advertiser* in 1809, and set up shop in the wooden home of Hanson's partner, Jacob Wagner, on the corner of Second and Gay Streets. From there it blasted venomous denunciations of Democratic-Republican politics and politicians. As a consequence, Hanson was challenged to duels and subjected to lawsuits. Even the city's Federalist minority grew weary of his constant provocations.[15]

On June 20, 1812, days after Congress's declaration of war with Great Britain, Hanson uncorked a particularly wild manifesto assaulting "the patrons and contrivers of this highly impolitic and destructive war." It boasted, "We are avowedly hostile to the presidency of James Madison," and promised to "hazard everything most dear, to frustrate anything leading to the prostration of civil rights, and the establishment of a system of terror" that was sure to flow from "the measure now proclaimed."[16]

Such statements did not sit well with the people of Baltimore. Two days later an angry crowd congregated under the moon before the offices of the *Federal Republican* armed with axes and hooks. They proceeded to smash their way into the house, tossed Hanson's printing presses, types, and paper into the street and destroyed them, then tore down the house they had been taken from. The city's mayor, Edward Johnson, did little to interfere with the horde, but Hanson and Wagner managed to scamper off to safety.[17]

The *Federal Republican* was not the only target of such violence in Baltimore. Angry Democratic-Republicans had destroyed vessels alleged to have engaged in commerce with Britain and demolished the dwelling of a free black man named James Briscoe for reportedly declaring his affection for that loathed nation and its people. A church housing a black congregation was also in the crosshairs before the city assigned a horse patrol to protect the building.[18]

Hanson temporarily retreated to the town of Georgetown, near the national capital, and resumed production of the paper, mailing editions to Baltimore. These, though, were captured at the post office and destroyed. "We shall cling to the rights of freemen, both in act and opinion, till we sink with the liberties of our country, or sink alone," he had declared. And indeed in July, spoiling for a fight, Hanson ended his exile.[19]

Sneaking back into Baltimore, he set up shop in a two-story brick dwelling at 45 Charles Street. From there the *Federal Republic* resumed its defiance.[20] On July 27, the day that the newspaper, as he put it, "ascend[ed] from the tomb," Hanson took aim at Baltimore's mayor and police for permitting the earlier attack, exposing the paper and its property to the "fangs of a remorseless rabble."[21] This edition of the paper had actually been printed in Georgetown, but it was distributed in Baltimore; zealously exercising his constitutional rights, Hanson was begging for a return engagement with the rabble. And he got exactly that.

Many of Baltimore's Federalists, who had armed themselves after the original round of riots, viewed Hanson's risky behavior as madness. Accordingly, when Hanson settled into the house on Charles Street he had to find friends from elsewhere to man his new headquarters.

Chief among them was James M. Lingan, a grizzled veteran who had been bayonetted and imprisoned on a British ship, the *Jersey*, during the Revolution. He was later appointed the collector of the port of Georgetown and commissioned a general. When Hanson had retreated to that town, Lingan gave him shelter.[22] Lingan was a fierce Federalist and an equally staunch champion of a free press. The supporting cast were younger men: Captain Richard I. Crabb, John Howard Payne, Charles J. Kilgour, Otho Sprig, Ephraim Gaither, John Thompson, Dr. Peregrine Warfield, Major Musgrove, Henry C. Gaither, and William Gaither.[23]

One more man joined the party on Charles Street, serving as its informal commander in chief.

Later he would explain that this was merely a business trip to Baltimore, that he had visited the city on matters relating to his memoirs and called at the house on Charles Street on the evening of the twenty-seventh to visit old friends and play a game of whist.[24]

But as Hanson assembled a small army to defend his business, he recalled the mythology of the American Revolution. In the dire winter of 1778 a young rebel captain, aided by only a handful of soldiers, had repelled a larger British force from a house in the Pennsylvania countryside. Hanson wanted the hero of that episode to come to his defense. He had invited him for that purpose. Never mind that nearly forty years had passed since that fabled morning or that the young revolutionary was now aged and ailing, his youthful lust for battle dissipated.

Every indication suggests that Lee went to Baltimore on a military mission, and that he passed over Hanson's threshold determined to defend the house and the freedoms he had fought to win another war ago.

On July 20, he sent an unsigned letter to Hanson, outlining how the house on Charles Street could be defended. He wanted two men posted at each window and the stairway just beyond the front door barricaded. A stockpile of stones and logs on the home's upper level should be ready to be dropped on invaders.

"Should the iniquity of the mob render it proper for you to implement my advice," Lee cautioned, "remember that you ought not to provoke their action, that you ought to require in time the aid of the civil authority, and that you having begun defense, must never ever think of concession—Die or conquer."[25]

Sixty men, at a minimum, were necessary to defend the home. And they were to approach their mission with military regimentation. Roll call was scheduled for 6:00 p.m., after which no man was permitted to leave. Lee even wanted a spy ring, with men leaving the house during the day to gain intelligence on the plans and movements of the enemy.[26]

As the sun receded and the sky darkened on the evening of the twenty-seventh, a crowd began to gather around the house on Charles Street. It consisted of young men, laborers, and sailors, many of them immigrants, all Democratic-Republicans. Shortly before 8:00 p.m. a carriage pulled to a halt before them. From it muskets were hurried into the house, only piquing the interest of those gathered outside.[27]

Some of the crowd milling about scooped up stones and chucked them at the house. Soon windowpanes were shattered, sashes and shutters smashed, and a member of Hanson's party, Harry Nelson, injured. Now Hanson showed himself at an upstairs window and addressed the mob. If they would not leave, he explained, they would be repelled by gunfire; blank shots were fired overhead to prove the point. But this only further angered the already angry men below.[28]

There was a rush to bash in the front door, accompanied by screams of "Death!"

Lee had stressed that every measure should be taken to avoid the spillage of blood; a plea for protection should be made to the city's authorities.

But now he was thrown into a defensive crouch. He sent a sentry to the stairs facing the now smashed front door; in its place, chairs and tables formed a makeshift barricade. A stalemate lasted for two hours; then at 11:00 the mob, led by an electrician, Dr. Thaddeus Gale, worked up the will to finally push forward into the building. "I will lead you on, and we will kill every dammed rascal in the house!!" he shouted.[29] But as they entered the home, a hail of fire greeted them. Gale was killed, others injured. The mob retreated, firing shots of their own, wounding one of Lee's party, Ephraim Gaither. Men of the attacking mob tore open their shirts, beat their chests, and screamed, "Fire again!"[30]

There had been no sign of any representative from the city or its police force until 10:00 p.m. Judge John Scott, chief justice of Baltimore's criminal court, arrived on the scene. A loyal Republican, he did little to subdue the crowd. The responsibility for preventing the violence rested with Brigadier-General John Stricker, commander of the Baltimore Brigade of Maryland's militia. But he dithered in his home, just doors down on Charles Street. Stricker was also a loyal Democratic-Republican, a merchant and banker. He had little interest in dispersing a crowd of politically likeminded citizens in order to save a pack of Federalists. Urged by concerned citizens, he did as little as possible, first ordering two justices of the peace to sign a statement enabling him to intervene and then—instead of sending in the entire Baltimore Brigade, the five-thousand-man militia at his disposal—sent Major William B. Barney and a selection of men from his small unit to settle the matter with a mob now numbering over three hundred.[31]

This was barely a half-measure. Barney was a Democratic-Republican candidate for the House of Delegates, and like Stricker had very little political motivation to forcibly remove the mob. When he arrived with thirty of the ninety troops in his unit, he had orders from Stricker not to fire on the crowd. At 3:00 a.m. Barney moved his men into a line in front of the house, forming a blockade between the attackers and their prey. Soldiers, their swords held aloft, were stationed by the windows. So riled was the throng that Barney was approached by a drunken Irishman who accused him of protecting the Tories and punched him in the chest.

Once he managed to enter the house, Barney conferred with Lee and Hanson. There was little he could do, the major explained. He had not been ordered to disperse the crowd. His men did not even have pistols. When he asked for a drink of water and Lee walked with him to a cupboard to fetch it, Barney pleaded with Lee not to stand near him, lest those outside think they were in league and kill him. "I know your situation, it is a delicate one. I am sure you are doing all you can," Lee charitably responded.[32]

Once again outside, Barney explained to the crowd that he was there only to secure the property and those in it. Many happily assumed this meant he was there to apprehend and jail Hanson and his comrades. But still they lingered, growing impatient and eventually breaking into a nearby armory and dragging a cannon to the house. However, the men didn't know how to fire or even aim the weapon.[33]

Finally, as the sun began to rise, Baltimore mayor Edward Johnson and General Stricker appeared on the scene. The former, yet another Democratic-Republican, had been mayor for four years and was in pursuit of a second term in that office. He entered the house and delivered a rebuke to Hanson: his conduct was inviting civil war. But this was his house, and he had every right to defend it, Hanson countered. Ultimately Johnson and Stricker could not and would not protect the party; the only recourse was to surrender to the city's authorities and be escorted off to jail. There, Stricker promised, they would be safe.

Hanson vehemently objected to this proposal. "To Jail? For what? Protecting my house and property against a mob who assailed both for three hours," he cried.[34] Lee inquired why the entire Baltimore Brigade had not been called out. That is the brigade, said Stricker, pointing to the crowd outside.[35]

Lee, many years Hanson's senior and no longer the quarrelsome young soldier who had beheaded deserters and challenged congressmen to duels, recognized the odds. Supplies were dwindling; there was little food or water left in the house. Only twenty-three of the defenders remained; the rest had escaped during the night. Every single authority in the city, Jeffersonians all, was predisposed towards the mob. If another confrontation came, the men in the house would have little chance of survival.[36]

Surrender was the only means to end the stand-off without further violence. Lee parleyed in the home's parlor with Johnson and Stricker for terms of surrender. Could they be allowed to leave the home bearing their arms, on horseback, surrounded by the militia? This was not permissible, replied Johnson and Stricker.[37]

Hanson protested bitterly. The promises of these Democratic-Republicans could not be trusted. If they could not dismiss the mob, they could offer no real protection. He repeated over and over that to surrender was to be sacrificed. But eventually Lee convinced Hanson and the others to submit. He believed the assurances from Stricker, a fellow veteran of the Revolution, were trustworthy. At 9:00 a.m. the party exited the house, marching a mile to their destination in a protective square formed by militiamen. The home was ransacked shortly after its inhabitants departed.[38]

Upon hearing of an unexecuted plot to stone the prisoners to death on their way, Johnson and Stricker ordered a brigade of militia to guard the Baltimore City jail, a two-story stone structure with no perimeter wall. But these militias would be furnished only with blank cartridges. Rightly fearing they would be torn to shreds by a bloodthirsty mob, barely fifty soldiers appeared at the militia headquarters on Gay Street.[39]

After their hour-long journey to the jail, during which they were pelted with rocks, Lee and the others were crammed into a barely finished room, off a long corridor sided by cells in a section of the building reserved for "negroes and rogues."[40] A stout door secured the prisoners, its thick iron bars forming a grate.[41]

In the afternoon both Johnson and Stricker arrived at the jail, along with other city officials, to guarantee the prisoners would be safe. But two leaders of the mob slipped in behind the mayor's party and carefully studied the faces and clothing of the prisoners.[42]

As the city leaders left the jail, they encountered a gathering crowd outside. When promises were proffered that no bail would be posted for the prisoners, the gathering seemed to disperse. Satisfied, Stricker rode home, intent on finally catching some sleep. On his way he dismissed the militia. Lee's trust in a fellow warrior was badly misplaced; he later cursed the "base perfidy of General Stricker's un-kept promise of protection."[43]

Word that the militia had been recalled filtered back towards the jail. The mob, construing this as tacit approval of a massacre, regrouped and stormed the building. When the entrance to the jail would not give, they moved around to an opening on the east side of the building. Now three doors separated them from their prey. The first they labored to take down for fifteen minutes before finally passing through. The second door they bashed open quickly. The mob then entered the corridor in search of Lee and Hanson's cell. Initially they hit on the wrong room, but a Frenchman inside pointed them towards the right one.[44]

Watching the scene unfold through the spaces between the iron bars of their door, the prisoners hurriedly debated a course of action. Armed with only a handful of pistols and daggers, they wouldn't be able to fight off the mob. Lee suggested they use the pistols to kill themselves, sparing themselves from the coming torture and depriving the would-be murders of the pleasure.[45]

John Thompson, one of the youngest and strongest of the prisoners, welcomed the fight. As the mob searched for the cell, he shouted, "You are at the wrong door, we are in here!" When they arrived at the right door, they opened it with its key, likely procured by the butcher Mummua, one of the men who had scoped out the prisoners when Johnson and Stricker visited the jail. At that point Thompson, along with Daniel Murray, burst out, pistols pointed forward, warning, "My lads you had better retire, we shall shoot some of you." Members of the mob replied, "How will you do it, you can't kill all of us!" Then in an instant Thompson and Murray sprang forward, extinguishing the torches of their unwanted visitors, sprinting towards the jail's front door.[46]

In the ensuing darkness and confusion, the prisoners proceeded out the door of their room, rushing for safety. Thompson was the first to pass the door, but as he exited he was bashed on the head, and tumbled twelve feet down the stairs leading out of the jail. Surrounded, he begged for his life, only to be tarred and feathered and then put in a cart and wheeled away, his face slashed with rusty swords. John Hall and George Winchester were also beaten on their way to freedom. In minutes the jail's floor had turned red with blood.[47]

As Hanson made his dash for the door, Mummua recognized the arch-Federalist, knocked him senseless, and tossed his limp body down the stairs. When the crowd beat the crusty old Lingan, he chided his attackers. He had fought for their freedoms, after all. In his last moments he ripped off his clothing, exposing the scars he still carried from the war. Where had his attackers been during the Revolution, "in France or among the bogs in Ireland"?[48] As he was bludgeoned to death, a member of the mob declared that "the dammed old rascal is the hardest dying of them all!"[49]

This was not technically true. As Lee made his way from the cell, he was apprehended, his head pummeled with clubs, his body hurled outside, bounding down the steps before finally coming to a rest atop the shoulders of a John Hall. The bodies of others were quickly piled on top of those two, forming a macabre monument to the throng's bloodlust.[50]

Lying on the ground, unable to move, Lee quietly groaned. This only excited the crowd. As more men arrived, he was singled out as "the dammed old tory." One of them snorted, "He died true game—huzzaing for King George to the last," seemingly unaware that the mob's victim had long ago helped pry that monarch's grip off of America.[51]

An assailant approached Lee's wounded body, drew back his blade and began to slice off his nose. Unable to sever the entire thing, he left Lee with a gaping gash in the middle of his face. Now another knife was thrust at his eye; as it approached, Lee sat up, blocking the blow, which instead ripped through his cheek, covering his face in blood. He collapsed, his head falling on the prostrate Hanson's breast. He was promptly kicked off, leaving a crimson splotch on the younger man's chest. "See Hanson's brains on his breast!" enthused one of the monsters, mistaking Lee's blood for Hanson's. To measure if any life remained, Lee's eyelids were peeled open and scalding candle wax dripped over his pupils.[52]

Lingan was dead; Lee, seemingly so. Others, such as Hanson, feigned death. As he lay still, a member of the throng booted him square in the genitals. There were women present too; they chortled at the violence, crying "Kill the Tories!" The scene only grew more ghoulish. Children clapped and skipped, and all present joined hands, dancing around the heap of writhing bodies, singing, "We'll feather and tar every damn British Tory. And this is the way for American glory!" Tributes to Madison and Jefferson followed.[53]

Then came the exciting matter of disposing of the bodies. One voice suggested dumping them in the jail sink. Another suggested tar and feathers. Another advocated for dissection. A mass hanging was proposed. While the debate went on, Richard Page, the prison's primary physician, alerted to the chaos, arrived. Though a Democratic-Republican, he was appalled by the carnage. He appealed to the mob, worn out from their evening of gory mischief, to go home and leave the bodies under his care. After all, he reasoned, most were dead and the rest would soon be. Satisfied, they merrily moved on. As Page spirited the prisoners back to their jail cell, one spectator asked where they were being taken. To which another responded, "To Hell."[54]

With the assistance of the jail's other resident physicians, Page cared for the survivors, dressed their wounds, and provided brandy. An attempt was even made to sew the detached flesh of Lee's nose back into alignment. The doctor then plotted to remove the wounded from the jail. Carriages were called for; Hanson snuck off and away from the city; others were conveyed into the country in carts covered in hay.[55]

Lee's mutilated body was slipped off to the city hospital, where the doctors did what little they could to ease his agony. The following morning he was taken to the home of a Federalist safely away from Baltimore, in York, Pennsylvania. There he lay motionless and speechless, attended by a duo of doctors. His head, crushed with clubs, had swollen and turned black. His face was sliced like a roast. A bloodstained flannel shirt covered his body. The rest of his clothes were ripped to shreds and similarly stained, from "tip to toe." There appeared to be a hole where one of his eyes had once been. When James C. Boyd came to see what was left of Lee, he observed that "when he attempts to stir, he tottered like an infant just commencing to walk."[56]

National newspapers reported his demise. "Two Great men and heroes have fallen in Maryland! Generals Lingan and Lee are no more! Their spirits have ascended on high!" exclaimed the *Maryland Gazette*.[57]

In Washington, D.C., the *National Intelligencer* reported that the mob had "dangerously wounded several, of whom one (Gen. Henry Lee, of Virginia) has since died of his wounds."[58]

In the partisan press, the past three decades of trouble were sheared away—the notorious business dealings, the humiliating stint in debtor's prison all forgotten. In death, Lee and Lingan were Federalist martyrs, convenient symbols of Democratic-Republican savagery. The Baltimore riots were described as "a scene that has never been paralleled since the days of Robespierre."[59] Lee was remembered in glorious terms, as "the celebrated orator, who, selected by the united voice of his country, delivered the funeral oration over the body of the great, the illustrious Washington."

His final moments, according to *Evening Post from New York*, were nobly spent "invoking the spirit of Washington his friend and companion in arms."[60]

Federalists gleefully pointed to the grotesque sacrifice of two old war heroes, Lee and Lingan. Indeed, in coming to Hanson's side, Lee had defended the very rights for which he had fought during the Revolution. And had paid dearly for it. He was no wild partisan; he had come to defend Hanson's right to exercise his views, not to endorse them. He opposed this new war, but he would have fought in it had he been called to. It was another cruel twist in a luckless life.

Only Lee was not dead. The papers were wrong. Confusion spread. From Stratford Hall, Henry Lee IV wrote to William Williams, the son of one of his father's old brothers in arms, Otho Holland Williams. He did not know whether his father still lived, he said, he had only heard rumors; what was true? He begged Williams, a Baltimore resident, to do all in his power to save Lee's life.[61]

This was not necessary. A week after the attack, Lee began to speak again, though with difficulty. His family received word that Lee had survived.

"My father was much hurt," Lucy Lee Carter wept to her aunt, Alice Lee Shippen, informing her of the tragedy in August.[62] "Yes I have heard of the sad catastrophe of Baltimore," Alice responded a month later from Philadelphia. "How melancholy to think or to write of. It is pleasant to report that the worst is over and he is out of danger."[63]

Following weeks of recuperation, Lee was well enough to return to Alexandria in early October. But though he had survived the Baltimore mob, he would never recover from their beating.

# 18

# MY MISERABLE
# EXILE

During Sunday services at Alexandria's Christ Church, parishioners shuffled into the Georgian building and along its bricked floors, taking their seats in the elevated box pews nestled inside.

Customarily, parents faced the parson, children away. As the Reverend William Meade began his services, young Mary Louisa Slacum locked eyes with an elderly man seated with his family across the aisle. His bright black eye cut a startling contrast to the white binding wrapped around his forehead and under his chin. His glance terrified the girl. It struck a similar note of fear in the heart of the town's other children, though they were told that this monster had once been a great warrior in the struggle for independence.[1]

At the conclusion of a sparkling banquet in Alexandria on Christmas night, 1812, the Reverend Dr. John Pierce, a visitor from Massachusetts, spotted a frightening figure. A late arriver joined the party, his head covered by black cloth. His face was decorated with scars; the entire length of his nose was split, his left eye shut. This mangled man, the astonished Pierce learned, had been a Revolutionary War officer and an intimate of George Washington. And indeed when he joined the group, with a charm incongruous to his appearance, he held the company rapt with remarkable tales of that great man.[2]

Years of financial strain and the shame of debt had wounded Henry Lee's spirit, and Baltimore's mob had broken his body. Time and fate had disfigured the dashing cavalier; little consolation came from the whispers of fathers who told their children that there was a hero behind the bandages.

Doctors and the passing of days had resuscitated Lee to a point. But his suffering was still great. His debts lingered, but the memoirs he had so labored on, the ones he had found release in, and through which he hoped to buoy his family's fortunes, were at last published in the fall of 1812. "The patriot will be always delighted, the statesmen informed, and the soldier instructed," declared Bradford & Inskeep. Lee's memoir, they promised, "bears in every part the ingenious stamp of a patriot soldier; and cannot fail to interest all who desire to understand the causes, and to know the difficulties of our memorable struggle."[3]

Appraisals were positive. For seven dollars readers could read a "vindication" of Nathanael Greene, written by a "partisan officer in the War for Independence" who greeted "hostiles" as "honors." Boston's *Repertory* claimed Lee's "felicity at narrative has a signal charm" and described the book as "a durable monument to his own memory."[4]

The *American Review of History and Politics*, though not entirely uncritical, said that "American readers of every description must follow with lively solicitude and unabated interest, the author of these Memoirs, in almost all his details concerning the sufferings, privations, and extraordinary marches of the troops."[5] And in a reference to Baltimore, the reviewer claimed that to "call up a blush into the cheek, of every American not absolutely callous to the national disgrace, he has but to produce these Memoirs. They will, we trust, soon be, on every account, in the hands of all his countrymen."[6]

Lee likely took some solace from the encouraging notices, if he was able to read them; his vision had suffered—the legacy of the hot wax drizzled in his eyes—and the tasks of reading and writing proved laborious. But the reviews did not translate into sales; the much hoped for windfall never appeared.

Apart from his disfigured façade, the beating had also damaged Lee's insides, crushing his organs and causing constant discomfort. In search of some tonic and to evade his ever pressing financial obligations, he made one last attempt to escape. Exchanging the cold of Virginia's winter for the warmth of a tropical sun, Lee hoped, would ease his suffering and provide distance not only from his debts, but also from his unhappy circumstances in America. Absence from his family, from whom he had so often parted, was no deterrent.

In early 1813, Lee approached Secretary of State James Monroe again about passage to some southern spot. The proposition was still complicated. Wartime embargoes blocked the Chesapeake Bay. Lee had no means of securing a ship; "without money, as I am, it will be difficult to execute my object," he warned Monroe.[7] In January, when he wrote to Madison offering another round of military advice, Lee lamented "my painful face & the coldness of the season."[8] His degraded condition tugged at the heart of the president. Despite interludes of political disagreement, his friendship with Lee had endured since they were boys under the wing of John Witherspoon in Nassau Hall. Now, at last, he intervened.

At the behest of the president, Monroe spurred Brigadier-General Robert B. Taylor, who commanded military operations around Norfolk, to remove the obstacles; it was, after all, a personal concern. "Genl. Lee in whose welfare the president takes much interest," Monroe wrote, "is desirous of passing to an island in the West Indies for the recovery health."[9] Taylor did as he was instructed, making arrangements with Admiral John Borlase Warren, then presiding over the British navy in North America, to permit Lee's departure. A passport was produced, along with a note of permission from Warren allowing Lee to "pass without molestation from Alexandria to the West Indies."[10]

He initially intended only to spend a short time away, and then, once he was healthy once more, to return home. There was a wistful tenor to Lee's correspondence in the days before his departure. When he wrote to Ferdinand O'Neal, a member of his Legion, about the pending voyage, he talked optimistically of a homecoming taking him through Savannah, O'Neal's home. There he would once again enjoy the treasured company of his "few surviving comrades."[11]

In May, Lee hobbled out the door and down the steps of 607 Oronoco Street and disappeared. Anne and their children—sons Carter, Smith, Robert, and baby Mildred, objects of his affection but victims of his tragic life story, were left behind. Before leaving, he did what little he could for them, selling the European copyrights to his memoirs to John Howard Payne in hopes the transaction would provide some material comfort.[12] The remaining unsettled debts fell to his stern brother, Edmund Jennings, who had persuaded Lee to meet his obligations before fleeing, to settle. "If I should be obliged to pay this money, it will almost be my ruin," Lee's younger sibling fretted, eyeing the financial morass his brother had pulled so many family members into.[13]

Lee was a destitute traveler, with little to his name but notes for planned biographies of Washington and Greene and a small leather journal. He also carried an effusive letter of introduction from the president "in Hope that it may contribute to secure to him the attention which is due to his services and character."[14]

Lee sped away from home and sailed south, passing through Port-au-Prince, its bay wrapping around the Gulf of Gonave in the Kingdom of Haiti and then southeast through the Caribbean Sea to the island of Barbados, arriving on its pearlescent shores in June. Colonial Governor George Beckwith welcomed the wanderer warmly.

Away from America, Lee could not put the war with Britain out of his mind. Striking up a dialogue with Beckwith that the Englishman "neither sought nor shunned," he shared "reflections on the sad and wanton war, waged by my Country against yours," that "makes me wonder and weak by terms."[15]

Lee, presuming to speak for Madison and Monroe, conducted rogue diplomacy, pressing Beckwith about a possible treaty. The governor wisely viewed Lee's diplomatic initiative with a jaundiced eye, speculating that the president and secretary of state "were pleased to hold a different language" in private conversations with Lee.[16]

In his exile, ending the war became an obsession with Lee. The British sailors and soldiers he met in Barbados, Lee claimed, were uniformly opposed to the conflict. And in his experience, Americans shared those sentiments. "I have never met with but a single individual, who applauds the war," he informed Rufus King, the former minister to Britain and current Federalist senator from New York. The war was unwinnable and would only lead to woe. America's aim in fighting the war—that Britain would cede her maritime rights—was unachievable, a reality that should "induce us to sheathing our swords."[17]

Lee was fixated on extricating his country from this "fatal labyrinth." He persisted in unwanted mediation, writing to Monroe to suggest that legislation forbidding naturalized citizens from serving in the Navy would swiftly end the war and relieve American citizens from fighting for the rights of non-natives. "But really my heart so honestly deplores the war," he confessed to Madison, "that I turn with delight to its only pleasant part—how can its conclusion be most easily effected?"[18]

His efforts to end the war served almost as a form of therapy; "Bitter as are my reflexions on the past and personally uncomfortable as is the prospect before me I forgot my own sorrows in those of our afflicted country," he explained to King.[19]

For a period, his health seemed to improve. "Had I not escaped from my country, the climate must have finished me ere now," Lee told the president. "As it is, I am much bettered & have the agreeable prospect of being restored to my usual health & strength." In thanks, Lee sent Madison a bottle of fine five-year-old Madeira and the largest green turtle he could find.[20]

Before leaving home, he had had "one foot in the grave," and the removal to the islands lifted Lee's spirits—but only for a time. Comforted by the warmth of the sun and vistas of turquoise waves, the initial improvement he claimed in his health was more psychological than physical. It quickly gave way to more distress. "Since that period," Lee wrote Madison in the fall, still at Barbados, "I have successively experienced the ebbs & floods common to continued disease, which confound my hopes & leaves in incertitude the issue which awaits me."[21] Beckwith had a starker appraisal of Lee's condition. "I apprehend he will never recover those wounds and bruises, especially about the head, which he recovered from the Baltimore rioters."[22]

Before the close of 1813, Lee began to pine for another, more restorative venue, such as one of the southern European states.[23] Failing that, he began to roam from island to island—from Havana to Port-au-Prince, zigzagging among the Bahamas, taking temporary refuge in the Turks Islands, then Caicos, then New Providence in search of a relief. He relied on the charity, patience, and gullibility of strangers, who cared for the wilted figure because of his storied past and silver tongue.

In Barbados he struck up a friendship with Thomas Storm, the son of a New York politician working for the State Department. Six months after his arrival in Barbados, he left for Puerto Rico, claiming improvements in health and his intentions to return home in the spring. There he found shelter with a government functionary named Alexander Bininez, an "amiable and learned gentleman" in whose home he claimed to be "happy in my misery."[24] In Caicos he fell in and lived with John McIntosh, a British loyalist banished from his Georgia plantation after the Revolution. McIntosh's daughter helped care for Lee during one of his increasingly frequent periods of immobility; he even hoped to introduce her to his son Henry.[25]

On the island of Nassau, Lee crossed paths with an old foe. During the siege of Augusta in 1781, he had pried the wily commandant of Fort Cornwallis, Thomas Brown, away from his post and mercifully shuttled him to safety in Charleston, lest the American soldiers, seeking revenge, slay the loyalist colonel. Banished to the islands, Brown married well and settled on a vast plantation. Discovering this, Lee sought out Brown, in pursuit of some compensation for his act of kindness so many years before.[26]

When they did meet, Brown was likely startled. Lee had become a pathetic parody of his younger self. While once he had raced across the country in his sharp tunic and plumed helmet, his elegant Legion in tow, improvising sieges, striking fear into the enemy and inspiring love in his men, now he was a threadbare pauper, shuffling from port to port, living off his wits, using what was left of his magnetism to hoodwink those credulous enough to be cast under his spell.

The root of Lee's downfall had been reckless optimism. But when his financial dreams collapsed and he was backed into a corner, his scruples were gradually discarded out of necessity in the desperate attempt to preserve his freedom and protect his family. Now, in this last act of his life's story, he was little more than a scoundrel attempting to survive to see another day.

Few American papers reached the islands, not enough to satisfy Lee's voracious intellect. Makeshift companionship with his new acquaintances was insufficient to sate his hunger for conversation. His thoughts turned tenderly homeward, towards the wife he had forsaken. When word arrived in Puerto Rico in September 1814 that ten thousand battle-tested British soldiers were sailing towards the Chesapeake, he fretted. Should war arrive on the Potomac, he urged Anne to flee Alexandria for the countryside, or she would "encounter disagreeable scenes." He lamented, "Oh that I was with you and feeble as I am. But I can only pray for your safety."[27]

So far away, he now longed to play the role of provider for those he had impoverished, pined for attention from the ones he had deserted, and wished to instruct the young children in whose lives he had been but a ghost.

Henry IV, the master of Stratford Hall, who had inherited his father's dashing spirit, carried on the family's military tradition. Bringing his father great joy, he received a commission from Madison, became Major Lee, and was stationed in Washington before marching to the Canadian border as an aide to General James Wilkinson. The elder Lee relied on his son to negotiate land prices—his addiction for acquisition unending—and pleaded with him to "take care of my wife and children," knowing he would now never be able to do so himself.

Charles Carter, the oldest of Lee's children with Anne, had been sixteen when his father left Virginia. In 1816 he began college, according to his father's desires, at Harvard. Of the three youngest boys, he was the child Lee knew best, the one most often in his thoughts. Through lengthy letters, Lee hoped to inculcate not only Charles Carter with his paternal wisdom, but through him Smith and Robert as well.

The letters were long and discursive, full of advice to cultivate his son's virtue and stir his intellect. He reminded the boy of his "abhorrence to lying," saying "that it led to every vice and cancelled every tendency to virtue." He demanded to know Charles Carter's curriculum, and suggested one of his own. Carter should "read the best poets, the best orators, and the best historians; as from them you draw principles of moral truth, axioms of prudence and material for conversation." And avoid novels, he urged. The father had idolized history's heroes and great scholars, and so too should the son. "Epaminondas—Imitate this great man," he enthused. The names of Socrates, Locke, Hume, Sophocles, and of course Washington dotted the multi-paged missives.[28]

In one letter Lee expounded on religion, revealing his own Deism and reliance on reason and—shockingly for the times—casting doubt on Christ's divinity. "Whether Christ was an inspired man as some believe, or the son of god as Christians

assert and some of them believe," he wrote, "all must acknowledge the excellence of the morality he taught and wish its spread
for the good of mankind." He confessed a hatred of religion's
"two great enemies, superstition and enthusiasm," as well as a
disdain for both Evangelicalism and the pageantry of Catholi-
cism. "What I understand to be pure religion is a heart void of
offense to God and man and a belief or faith in one God who
delights in right and disproves of wrong," he explained, contend-
ing that "the forms and ceremonies of religion differ, but in
essence they all worship the almighty creator and rest on his
providence and protection here and hereafter."[29]

When the long letters went unanswered, he grew impatient
in his loneliness, pleading for any little bit of information about
his family: "will you not give me the delight in reading your letters?" he badgered Charles Carter.[30] "Although I never hear from
you nor any of my children, my dear wife, I write whenever I
can," he complained to Anne.[31]

The letters he did occasionally receive from Henry, Charles
Carter, and his wife, were read and re-read, lifting his spirits and
filling his heart. When letters to his middle daughter went unanswered, he asked incredulously, "how can my darling Anne
neglect me—Mamma's revived my drooping body, your sister's
comforted my afflictions, and your brother H[enry] and C[arter]'s
completed my victory for a while over pain."[32]

Lee wondered about the youngest children, mysteries to him.
"Smith is ever in my thoughts. I never knew him thoroughly and
I wish much to know him intimately as I did Carter—my absence
has prevented me," he lamented to his wife Anne. "I long to get
a thorough knowledge of you," he anxiously wrote to the boy,
"which I am deprived of and the most proper period of your life
will pass before I can execute my wishes.... "

Daughter Mildred, he knew "nothing about" and he wrote that he feared "I never shall." Then there was the youngest boy, just ten years old. "Robert is as good as ever I trust—it is in his nature," he wrote to Anne. Perceptively, he claimed to see glimpses of his most disciplined and pious sibling in this son: "he always seemed to me to be a copy of my brother Edmund."[33] Another letter, written to Charles Carter, concluded, "Hug my dear Robert for me...."[34]

Little gestures were proffered to fill the space left by his absence. With his letters Lee sent baskets filled with books, yards of cloth, coffee, coconuts, pineapples, shells, and ginger, along with other "trifles" such as a whale bone and a single pearl.[35] There was little more he could do. When he heard that Anne was in financial distress, forced to sell the family's horses, he could only protest impotently that her, "self privations cannot be permitted—if I ever approach you, I must alter the condition. God of heaven, how cutting to my heart the knowledge of your situation."[36]

What Lee left unexpressed in letters he poured into his diary. The little day book he carried along from destination to destination was a confessional, a conversation partner, a sounding board for a mind that remained acute while his body faltered. Its early pages documented his journey. "My previous wound received from the mob of Baltimore," he scrawled in his nearly indecipherable cursive, was "menacing me with a continuance of disease."[37] His diary celebrated those who had shown him kindness and offered him friendship: "William Oxley, always sincere and full of friendship," "Thomas Applewhaite, aged 73, but still young in body and mind." It cataloged the gifts he scavenged between the islands: a copper kettle for washing, a fish trap, a box of shells, an Indian war club, powder and shot for Charles Carter. There were details of his diet, which included roasted or boiled apples, stewed prunes, gruel, broth with spinach leeks, and rye bread.[38]

But as months, then years passed, the writing rambled, the pages filled with windy expositions on history, religion, and philosophy. Lamentations on the mortality rates in New Spain, talk of the violent volcano of Forallo, inquiries into the conquerors of India and possessors of China. Pertinent fragments from the tragedies of Philoctetes and Electra, favorite passages from Voltaire, Johnson, Gibbon, commentary on Timius Beh Tamerlance, quotations from Confucius and Cicero for "my dear son CCL and thru him to my equally dear Smith and Robert."[39]

There was also wisdom for his children from a man who had served as Lee's own mentor; Lee hoped, no doubt, that Washington's example would serve as a similar guide to future generations of Lees: "The great and good Washington once told me in a letter answering one from me suggesting a mode of conduct—to take care how I executed the proposed matter for 'a man ought not only to act from honest principles, but he ought to appear so to do.'"[40]

And there were passages in which Lee perhaps saw his own reflection. One from Sophocles: "Let mortals, hence be taught to look beyond the present time, nor dare to say, a man is happy, till the last decisive hour shall close his life without the taste of woe."[41] And another from Elijah Fenton: "Calmly he looked on either life, and here. And saw nothing to regret, or there to fear."[42] There was too an appropriate maxim nestled among musings on Tacitus: "Obligations are only acknowledged when we can requite them; if they exceed our ability, to be insolvent is painful, and gratitude turns to hatred."[43]

Lee's diary was the testament to an astonishing intellect, and a steel trap of a memory. But it was also the record of a lonely, sick man, caught in his own thoughts, struggling desperately to make terms with his failures, and using what was left of his darkening mind to create a makeshift epitaph as he stewed over his past and came to terms with the fact that he had no future.

The state of Lee's health would fall and then ascend ever so slightly. Reports of advances were often followed by complaints of agony. "I can scarcely go thro the task of writing to you my dear wife and to my H[enry], so debilitated am I and so constant are the pains I suffer," he wrote to Anne from Nassau.[44] In 1816 Lee placed himself under the care of a "celebrated" Spanish physician whose treatments were said to have cured all his patients "not actually in the arms of death." His treatments seemed to lift Lee a little; he rued not meeting him sooner, thinking perhaps he could have been cured.[45] Indeed, in time he reported that his "obstinate" disease "at last yields to the skill" of the Spaniard.[46] The pain lessened, though did not vanish. "Although I never shall (I fear) be well," he wrote, "yet as I continue as I am I shall be satisfied."[47]

The doctor placed him on a strict and unappetizing diet, forbidding meat and liquor, prescribing gruel for breakfast and peas or pea soup for dinner. "This fare so long continued puts me so low that the remedy may prove destructive to me," he whined.[48] Before this, despite his destitution, Lee had ordered beef flanks and ribs, venison hams, and gallons of pickled oysters from New York.[49]

As the years passed, he often mentioned a return from "my miserable exile."[50] Writing from Caicos, in the summer of 1816, he hoped the lessening of pain would allow for a homecoming in just a few months.[51] The following spring, in Nassau, he talked about an impending voyage to America and even asked Anne to tell both Henry Lee IV and Richard Bland Lee of his imminent arrival.[52] But there were always obstacles. He wished to continue with the Spanish doctor a few months more, "to see if the severe pain to which I am a prey 16 hours of the 24 can be mollified more if not subdued."[53] He was particular about his conveyance home, demanding a ship that would afford him the comfort of his own cabin. He also had no money.

In late 1817, Lee was lingering in Nassau, having taken refuge in a boarding house in New Providence. Its owner was an aged widow, Mrs. Baldwin, who took him in as others had done over the past five years, mothered him, cared for him, and clothed him. In the winter a young lawyer from Baltimore, James Causten, arrived on the island, pursuing a spoliation claim on naval cargo apprehended by the French, and took a room at the old woman's home.[54]

When Lee caught word of Causten's presence in New Providence, and of the ship that had brought him there, he introduced himself at once. His appearance—Lee was shabbily dressed and obviously laboring in pain—perplexed Causten, who knew the old hero's name and his Revolutionary exploits. Lee, clinging to the young man as if they were old friends, claimed he had booked passage on a ship soon to depart for the United States, but preferred to travel home in the company of Causten. Not wanting to deny a favor to an old and enfeebled patriot, he acquiesced.[55]

A date for departure was set; Baldwin opened her home to host a grand farewell turtle dinner in her ward's honor. There was a complication, though. Lee still owed money to various individuals who had offered him assistance. Naturally he had not a penny to pay any of it back. He asked for Causten's assistance, but the lawyer had only the funds necessary for their pending voyage. Lee coaxed the money from Baldwin in exchange for a promissory note from a firm in Savannah. His debts paid, Lee joined Causten onboard his small ship, the *Betsy*—destined for St. Mary's on the southeast coast of Georgia—and at last sailed home.[56]

Causten was distressed by Lee's terrible condition; the old general, sick for so long, brushed off his young friend's concerns and proceeded, even in his wretched state, to do as he had always done: mesmerize his companion with all manner of conversation, including, of course, tales from the Revolution and of Washington. He also dwelt upon the riot in Baltimore, offering up a narrative—the story that he had just happened to be in the city and by chance had paid a call at the home of Alexander Hanson— that did not square with reality.[57]

It was a typical performance, complete with attempts to involve Causten in convoluted financial schemes. Colonel Brown, the old Tory whom Lee had visited in Nassau, he said, had given him the deed to land in Florida, including a parcel on Tampa Bay. Lee wanted Causten to take the titles and sell them; they would then split the profits. But Causten didn't wish to be entangled in Lee's speculations.[58]

In the peace following the Revolutionary War, Nathanael Greene had purchased land on the southern tip of Cumberland Island off the Georgia Coast, where he had planned to construct a summer home. His death in 1786 dashed that dream, but his wife Catharine remarried, moved to the island, and built a mansion on her late husband's land.[59]

The house was a grand affair looking down on the Atlantic, four stories tall, with four chimneys at each end and sixteen fireplaces, the foundation atop an Indian burial mound supporting tabby walls. Acres of gardens, orchards, and live-oaks surrounded the house.[60] Remembering its location and nearness, Lee asked to be deposited on the island so that he could pay proper homage to his old friend. Greene, of course was long dead; his wife had followed him in 1814; their daughter Louisa, living there with her husband James Shaw, was now the mistress of Dungeness. Lee had met Mrs. Shaw fleetingly in her childhood. He did not know her or how she would receive this comrade of her father's, but he insisted on making landfall near her home.[61]

In the late afternoon of February 10, 1818, Phineas Miller Nightingale, Shaw's fifteen-year-old nephew and Greene's grandson, was playing on Dungeness's grounds when he saw a schooner heading towards the property's wharf. Growing curious, he studied the unfolding scene: The small ship anchored and then dropped a dinghy in the water. A limp old man was deposited therein, and then joined by the captain and two sailors. They rowed to land, and the sailors stood up, formed a chair with their arms and hands, lifted the old man, and carried him ashore. They then dropped off all his worldly possessions: a ragged horsehair-trunk and a cask of Madeira. After five years of absence, Henry Lee had returned to the country he had helped free and found.[62]

Spotting young Nightingale, Lee waved at him. The boy came face to face with a wraith. Lee was ghostly white, emaciated and impoverished, barely clothed, and barely able to move. Asking and discovering the boy's identity, Lee, overjoyed, threw his arms around him. Leaning on his shoulder, he walked a short distance to a log. There he sat down and asked that the boy convey a message to his aunt. General Lee had arrived. "I am come purposely to die in the house and in the arms of the daughter of my old friend and compatriot."[63]

A carriage was sent for; Lee was conveyed to the mansion and greeted warmly. The Shaws happily gave him a room. He went there at once, seeking seclusion. In the weeks that followed he rarely left it. Once a day, though, he asked for Nightingale, the direct blood descendant of the beloved Greene, and with his arms around the boy's neck strolled delicately through the gardens along a picturesque path bordered by groves of orange trees. Once returned to his room, he found relief in the serene sight of the ocean, the touch of its breeze, and the harmonies of the songbirds whose concertos had arrived with spring.[64]

He was able to write once more to Anne, telling her he was in Georgia, where he planned to "stay a short time only" and hoped that his son Henry or brother Edmund would meet him. "Do not write," he concluded, "but embrace my girls and boys with love for me."[65]

What meals Lee could digest were served in his room; he rarely had the strength to dine with the family. He was so close to home at last, but his infirmities multiplied. He grew unable to walk; he was confined to his bed, powerless to sit up, even. Soldiers stationed nearby came to pay their respects; in moments without pain, he dazzled them with old anecdotes from the Revolution, worshipful stories of Washington and Greene, and eloquent dissertations on politics, frosted with venomous attacks on Democratic-Republicans. In less lucid moments, when the depression was strong and the pain unbearable, his shrieks and agonized groans filled the house, echoing off its six-feet-deep walls.[66]

Shaw sent her maid, a woman called "Mom Sarah" to attend the ailing guest, only to have him hurl his boot at her. When she threw it right back at him, earning his admiration, Lee relented and at last permitted her to enter his room. His gallbladder was ruined—a memento from Baltimore's mob. Doctors were called for, but the few remedies within their power were useless. When a surgical procedure was suggested, Lee refused. "My dear sir, were the great Washington alive, and here, and joining you in advocating it, I would resist."[67]

The pain grew constant, his life clearly fading. On Tuesday, March 24, 1818, Lee became unable to speak. The following day, in the afternoon, he died.[68]

Immediately, news of the death spread across the sound. Military vessels docked in the Atlantic flew their colors at half-mast. Their sailors, and soldiers from neighboring bases, arrived en masse at Dungeness for the interment. Marines and infantry-men served as an escort and their commanding officers as pall-bearers; swords were sheathed and crossed atop the casket.[69]

The funeral procession had but a little way to go, to a small family cemetery half a mile from Dungeness. As it traveled, min-ute guns echoed across the ocean from the deck of the SS *John Adams*, which was docked nearby. When the body was lowered into the ground, more salutes were fired. Far from home and family, but finally free of pain, Henry Lee rested at last.[70]

∾

James Causten's brief encounter with Lee was mystifying— and archetypal in its way. Causten had happily fulfilled the vet-eran's wish, conveying him back to America. He was awed by his storied history, overcome by his charisma and conversation, but left bewildered by his inconsistences. When he left Lee at Cum-berland Island, a sailor approached Causten and inquired why he had brought "that old rascal" stateside. Appalled by such a question, Causten defended his new friend, only to hear a number of tales from other officers about Lee's misdeeds.[71]

When Causten traveled to Savannah on the widow Baldwin's behalf to redeem the note of credit Lee had given her in return for the money to clear his debts in New Providence, he was greeted by a knowing smile at the firm supposedly holding Lee's funds. Over the years, many had come there seeking redemption on promissory notes given by Lee, he was informed, though he never was entitled to a single cent in their hands. The American hero, crowned with "a halo of fame," who had entered his life with prospects so fair, had ended it by swindling a kindly old widow.[72]

Causten could not reconcile it all. He knew that Lee's few remaining belongings of value—the deed for the land in Florida and the manuscript of his memoirs—were still in that battered trunk left on Cumberland Island. He learned that Anne Lee was in Alexandria and set out to meet her, to tell her of her husband's last days and of the location of his possessions, and to reclaim the money stolen from Mrs. Baldwin.[73]

When he arrived at the red brick house on Oronoco Street, Causten was ushered into the parlor, where Mildred Lee sat, playing a piano. By the time he had arrived in Alexandria, letters had arrived from Henry IV and Richard Bland Lee bringing word of her father's fate. When he asked to speak to the girl's mother, he was told she was unwell and confined to her room. But he had come all the way from Baltimore, and he only wished for a few minutes of her time to convey the last words of her late husband. Mildred then disappeared. Moments later she returned, to explain that her mother did not wish to hear them.[74]

# EPILOGUE

In the early 1860s, Robert E. Lee received a peculiar memento. It was a slim leather-bound book, the lengths of its linen pages covered with scrawl. Flipping through the brittle pages, among the fragmented quotes and history lessons, he saw his own name.

The book was a gift from J. H. Chandler, whose own father had found it among a bundle of papers years before. The elder Chandler had treasured the artifact for some time; its author and original owner was "the right-hand man of Washington," known posthumously as "Light-Horse" Harry Lee, in homage to his now fabled revolutionary exploits.[1]

It was the diary of the father Lee had barely known, arriving amidst a war tearing apart the Union he had helped found. That Robert—Lee's youngest son, whose name would forever be linked to and overshadow his own—had by chance inherited it was incongruous.

Lee's oldest son, Henry IV, had received his namesake's love of words, command of history, and political talents. For a time, he had sat in Virginia's legislature. Carrying on another family tradition, he married well, winning the hand of Anne Robinson McCarty, the wealthy heiress of Pope's Creek Plantation.

But he flamed out spectacularly, seducing his eighteen-year-old sister-in-law and ward Betsy McCarty while his wife was mourning the death of their newborn daughter. Disgrace and poverty followed, Stratford Hall slipped through his hands, what little pride the family retained was finally humbled, and the sobriquet "Black-Horse" attached to his name. He found some use for his talents crafting rhetoric for Andrew Jackson before dying in Paris in 1837 and being laid to rest in an unmarked grave on the hill-top village of Montmartre.[2]

His younger half-brother, Charles Carter Lee, settled in Washington, DC after graduating from Harvard. Like his father, he was a bon-vivant, a storyteller, and an eager if unsuccessful entrepreneur. Carter wrote of Henry Lee admiringly and fondly, remembering his "mighty powers," describing his mellifluous voice as a "trumpet with a silver sound," and recalling their happy days together.[3] Charles Carter's casual and never-published memoirs painted a luminous and loving picture of his childhood and a happy life at Stratford Hall—an experience not shared by his parents.

As adults, the two eldest surviving sons defended their father's legacy and memory, corresponding with and picking the now failing brains of Henry Lee's friends and allies, men such as James Madison and John Marshall. These exercises ultimately formed a historical shield against the counter-narrative valorizing Thomas Jefferson. The third president's court historians had hurried to redeem his conduct as governor of Virginia during the Revolution and undermine not only Henry Lee's chronicle of the era but even his military achievements. The accusation that

Jefferson had abandoned Richmond upon Benedict Arnold's arrival had greatly angered the Sage of Monticello. In 1815, he labeled the originator of this accusation "the lying Lee" and described his memoirs as no more than a "historical novel" full of "romances" written for "the amusement of credulous and uninquisitive readers."[4]

The younger Lees' research and rebuttal culminated in a publication written by Henry IV and edited by Charles Carter that swatted away the "vague charge of malicious slander" leveled at their father. Their *Observations on the Writings of Thomas Jefferson, with Particular Reference to the Attack They Contain on the Memory of the Late Gen. Henry Lee; In a Series of Letters* combed through years of correspondence, offered pointed commentary, and argued, witheringly, that "abuse from Mr. Jefferson affords not the slightest proof of demerit, since he heaped it on the heads of the most illustrious men of his country."[5]

For the two younger boys, Sydney Smith and Robert, Light-Horse Harry Lee was a more remote figure. Though they had hardly known him in life, they had heard stories about his battlefield exploits, had glimpsed his pistol and sword, and were drawn to a soldier's life no doubt in part because of his outsized legacy.

With Smith away from home in the U.S. Navy, his sister Anne crippled by tuberculosis of the bone, and Mildred still of tender age, Robert assumed the role of companion and caretaker for his widowed and enfeebled mother. Anne Lee leaned on her youngest son for both domestic and emotional support; the boy proved to be the steadfast companion to his mother that her own husband had not been, charioting her about Alexandria, helping to keep house, mixing her medicines, and even lovingly endeavoring to cheer her during her continual bouts of depression.[6]

"How can I live without Robert?" Anne is said to have cried when the boy, succumbing to the family calling, departed for the U.S. Military Academy at West Point in 1825. "He is both son and daughter to me."[7] After graduation in the summer of 1829 Lee returned to Virginia; on July 10, Anne Lee died at Ravensworth, the Fairfax home owned by the Fitzhugh family, with Robert at her side.[8]

Robert E. Lee's professional and personal life looked nothing like his father's. At West Point he was the consummate cadet, placing second in his class. The pace of his career was slow and steady, in contrast with Light-Horse Harry's meteoric rise. Noticeably absent from his character were the stormy ambition and ego-fueled petulance that had earned the elder Lee equal numbers of admirers and enemies.

Exhibiting a gift for military engineering, Lee was given assignments in Georgia, then back in Virginia, then in Washington. In 1837 he went west to help redirect the current of the Mississippi River around the city of St. Louis, winning a promotion to captain in the process.

He acquired a modicum of glory during America's 1846–48 war with Mexico, when he tasted battle and witnessed its carnage for the first time. Lee's brilliant reconnaissance work before the battles of Cerro Gordo and Contreras endeared him to General Winfield Scott, one of that war's great heroes. What came after this was a distinguished though decidedly journeyman-like career, with postings in Baltimore and surveying work in Florida, before his 1852 appointment as superintendent of West Point.[9] After three years on the Hudson, he departed for the Texas frontier.

Robert Lee had married Mary Custis, the great-granddaughter of Martha Washington in 1831; her father, George Washington Parke Custis, had built his home, Arlington House, high on an incline overlooking the Potomac and Washington, DC. He filled its rooms with relics inherited from the nation's first first couple, his grandmother and step-grandfather who had also been his adoptive father. Upon his death in 1857, this shrine to Washington, the man Robert Lee's father had so revered, was willed to Lee.[10]

Custis had initially balked at the notion of his daughter marrying a member of the disgraced Lee clan. Robert was aware of the cloud of shame created by his father and elder half-brother, but could do little about it. "Of these no one can be more sensible than myself, or less able to devise a remedy," he wrote to Mary before their marriage. "But should I be able to escape the sins into which they have fallen, I hope the blame, which is justly their due, will not be laid to me."[11]

And in fact Robert E. Lee's conduct was starkly different from that of his disgraced father and brother. He cared tenderly for his often-ill wife and doted on their children; though during his frequent absences from home he fretted that they would never know him, as he had never known his own father. He feared and avoided debt and unwise investment—physic dreads no doubt lingering from childhood.

Where Henry had been reckless, Robert wielded nearly tyrannical self-control. The father's Deist faith, typical of many of the founders, was characterized by love of reason and inquiry and reverence for virtue, but suspicion of superstition. The son was a devout Episcopalian, praying and poring over the Bible daily.[12] The elder Lee was optimistic to the point of irrationality; Charles Carter claimed it was "a disposition to aim too high, or at too much" which "ruined my great father."[13] The youngest Lee boy was burdened by self-doubt and his own perceived failures as a soldier and as a family man.[14]

By intention or intuition, Robert E. Lee learned from Henry Lee's mistakes. He could not, though, forever outride heredity and history.

By the time Lee was stationed at West Point, the nation was in the midst of a paroxysm like those that had bedeviled his father's generation. States were pitted against one other and in opposition to the federal government. Only this struggle was over a different issue: the fate of slavery and the southern economy and way of life and, ultimately, whether the promises etched in the Constitution that Lee's father had defended passionately applied to all Americans. And it would not be settled with compromise or a strategic display of federal power.

In the fall of 1860 the badly fractured electorate made Abraham Lincoln, a moderate representative of the recently formed Republican Party, president. Finding the Illinoisan intolerable because of his opposition to the westward expansion of slavery, the southern states, starting with South Carolina that December, began to pull away from the Union. Robert Lee watched the dissolution with horror. He wondered—asking himself a question that would have pleased his father—what George Washington would have made of this budding rebellion. "How his spirit would be grieved could he see the wreck of his mighty labors!" he exclaimed to his wife, Mary.[15]

In the spring of 1861 Lincoln, now in office, labored to organize a force to oppose this southern uprising; the war had begun after Confederate bombardment of Fort Sumter in Charleston.

Winfield Scott, long in the tooth and too plump to find his way into the saddle, remained the highest-ranking general in the nation. Unable to lead men into the field, he suggested that Lee command the American forces defending the nation's capital. The offer of this assignment was tendered to Lee during an interview with Lincoln's seasoned political counsellor, Francis P. Blair, in his home adjacent to the Executive Mansion.

Secession was a sin, Robert Lee told his host. But never would he take up arms against his home country—Virginia. That business settled, he left Blair's house and reported the conversation to Scott. Two days later Lee forwarded the general a formal resignation of his commission. By April 23 he was in command of Virginia's militia forces.[16] Robert E. Lee would never again in his life be an American citizen.[17]

In the midst of the Civil War that followed, Lee received the parcel containing his father's dairy; the letter accompanying it called Henry Lee's memoirs a monument "to the memory of the gallant soldiers who pledged their lives, their fortunes, and their sacred honor in our first war independence as their descendants are doing in the second."[18]

To J. H. Chandler, who had sent the small book and accompanying letter, Robert E. Lee's destiny had finally intersected with his father's. He was leading a glorious rebel army in pursuit of a people's freedom. Indeed, in war, the spirit of Light-Horse Harry had emerged in Robert E. Lee's gallant figure, his inspiring sway over men, his tactical improvisation, and his adrenaline-fueled thrill for battle.

At the onset of the Battle of Guilford Courthouse, one Lee had stalked across the American lines, his sword covered in blood, his face full of fury. Watching the violent splendor of the unfolding Battle of Fredericksburg from Telegraph Hill nearly eighty years later, another Lee is said to have remarked, "It is well this is so terrible. Otherwise we should grow too fond of it."[19]

But their causes were discordant. Henry Lee had departed Virginia in 1794 and marched an army into Pennsylvania to extinguish an uprising against the American government. In 1863, Robert E. Lee left Virginia leading an invading rebel force into Pennsylvania, fighting against that same government.

At every instance when the embryonic Republic was threatened by rebellion or fracture—during Shays Rebellion, the Whiskey Insurrection, the introduction of the Virginia and Kentucky Resolutions—Henry Lee had resisted civil war and endorsed a central government protected by a robust standing army.

Alexander Hamilton's plans to finance the new nation had incensed the elder Lee and even provoked talk of revolt. But his pique had receded because he continually saw the fate of the nation, as well as his own fortunes, tied to a union of the states and their people, North and South. The alternative—disunion fueled by political discord—would inevitably lead, he knew all too well, to civil war, brother slaughtering brother. He had seen it and participated in it during America's Revolution and wished never to do so again.

Henry Lee had hoped to be remembered in history as a giant, like his hero Washington. He had asked his sons to study that man's life in hopes that, in his absence, Washington would guide them to the glory he had never grasped. It is not hard to imagine another scenario, where Robert E. Lee accepted Lincoln's offer of a high command of the federal force, where many of the Confederate Army's fabled military glories are erased from history, where the son of Henry Lee saves the Union and joins George Washington in the pantheon of great American heroes.

This is all conjecture. And so too is the belief that Henry Lee would have stood against Southern secession or ever contemplated taking up arms against Virginia, his family's beloved state, the home of his countrymen. It was, after all, not only Robert E. Lee who had sided with the South; Sydney Smith Lee served in the Confederate Navy. He did later regret the rebellion, though.

Henry Lee was a slave owner. And despite condemnations of slavery, common amongst plantation-owning southern founders, Lee made it clear in Congress that he viewed bondsmen as property that the government had no right to interfere with the ownership of.

In 1869, Robert, with research contributed by Charles Carter, composed a biography of his father to be appended to a new printing of his memoirs. This was a largely bland and sanitized portrait of the man, drawn from previous publications as well as some previously unseen letters, themselves abridged.

Lee did make sure, though, to include a passage seemingly aligning his father's own views with his own role in the recent war, reminding readers that Henry Lee, when governor of Virginia, had stipulated that he would accept no federal command that would construe "disregard or forgetfulness" towards his state.[20]

In 1817 Allan McLane, who had served unhappily in his Legion, described Henry Lee as "the monster."[21] Samuel Storrow, a cousin of Anne Lee, described him as a "heartless and depraved profligate" who had "died a Vagrant and Beggar."[22] A refrain supposedly fashioned by a Lee family friend went, "Light Horse Harry Lee a fool was born, a fool he lived, and a fool he died."[23]

There is no doubt that Henry Lee left behind an outrageously complicated legacy, pockmarked by scandal and self-immolation. His debt-fueled downfall, though not singular among men of his generation, was certainly stunning.

This much is clear, though: from his entrance into Virginia's dragoons at the age of twenty to his death in the home of

Nathanael Greene's descendants at sixty-two, Lee never lost faith in the nation he had helped bring into being. He never retreated from the loyalty he had expressed at the Virginia ratifying convention: "In all local matters I shall be a Virginian: in those of a general matter, I shall not forget that I am an American."[24]

Lee's faith in America never withered—even after his political fortunes declined, his dreams of wealth were dashed, and his countrymen battered his body for defending the Constitution.

On this score Henry Lee was a great, if greatly flawed, patriot and a man who deserves to be mentioned among the early heroes of the Republic, in contrast to his son Robert, whose own decisions and definition of country continue to confound and divide, even to the present day.

&#x2767;

In 1862, while inspecting coastal Confederate defenses, Robert E. Lee made a pilgrimage to the now abandoned Dungeness to visit his father's grave.[25] Eight years later, in 1870, with the Civil War settled, in the midst of his stewardship of Washington College, in Lexington, Virginia, where the old general would spend his final days, he once again traveled to Cumberland Island.

By then the mansion was no more, burned during the war. The Greene family cemetery, though, remained. Accompanied by his daughter Agnes, Lee gazed at the grave of the father whose life had only briefly crossed his own. Before they left, Agnes strewed "beautiful fresh flowers" atop the little plot. A short time later Lee detailed the visit to Mary, calling it "the last tribute of respect" he would ever be able to pay.[26] And indeed it was. He died later that same year. His grave is in the chapel in Lexington bearing the Lee name.[27]

Only weeks before the assault on Fort Sumter, Virginia's General Assembly had appropriated funds to move Henry Lee's body from its resting place on Cumberland Island back to his home state. War, however, intervened. His body remained undisturbed.

But over half a century later, in the spring of 1912, Virginia once again reconsidered reclaiming its old hero. Five hundred dollars were allocated to retrieve the body and place it in the Lee Chapel on the campus of Washington and Lee University—the school's name now amended to recognize Robert's postbellum efforts as its president.

On May 26, 1913, a state-appointed committee departed Virginia, making its way to Fernandina in northeast Florida by train. They then continued directly to Dungeness by boat to be greeted by representatives of Lucy Carnegie, now the owner of the rebuilt estate.

A small fleet of automobiles guided the party to the graveyard. A warm breeze carried the scent of oleander and jasmine. Magnolias cast their shadows in the cemetery; the moss dangling from live oaks swayed nearby. As the Atlantic waves somberly beat against the shore, the Virginians raised Lee's body and transferred it to a new casket. It was then sailed back to the mainland and subsequently put on a train for the Old Dominion, reaching the town of Lynchburg on Memorial Day.

There it was greeted by the Sons and Daughters of the American Revolution, the Colonial Dames, and a spontaneously gathered crowd. The rector of the town's Episcopal church delivered brief remarks before the old hero made his final journey, arriving in Lexington on the evening of May 30. Waiting there were students, faculty, and also cadets from the nearby Virginia Military Institute who escorted the remains to the Victorian chapel sitting in the center of campus.

That night they were placed in a crypt alongside those of his youngest son. An American flag covered the casket.[28]

# ACKNOWLEDGMENTS

I am especially grateful to Judy Hynson, the director of Research and Library Collections at Stratford Hall, for opening the doors to the duPont library, for sharing her wisdom on all things Lee, and for putting up with my very frequent queries. Thanks also go to Deborah Grosvenor for taking on the project in the first place and to Jamie Simko for enduring it. Friends and family also provided invaluable support during the writing of this book, and in many cases long before it. I'm indebted to them.

# NOTES

## 1: FREESTONE POINT

1. Paul C. Nagel, *The Lees of Virginia: Seven Generations of an American Family* (Oxford University Press, 1990), 7–20.
2. Nagel, 21–29.
3. Ludwell Montague, *The Lees of Virginia: Descendants of Richard Lee and Anna Constable, Who Came to Jamestown in 1639* (Society of the Lees of Virginia, 1967), 3.
4. Nagel, *The Lees of Virginia*, 33–44.
5. Ibid., 40–43.
6. Ibid., 40.
7. Ibid., 50–55.
8. Edmund Jennings Lee, *Lee of Virginia, 1642–1892: Biographical and Genealogical Sketches of the Descendants of Colonel Richard Lee* (Heritage Books, 2008), 133.
9. Ibid., 133. Those slaves included "Tom, Dinah, Hannah, Moll, Daniel, Frank, little Dinah, Dick and Cato, now at Xeapsco Quarter and Titus, Cain, Westminster, Eava. Harry, Joe, Sabina

her child, Joe and Harry, now at Saisbury plain Quarter and at my dwelling plantation Prue's Frank and Whiney's Moll."

10. Bernice-Marie Yates, *The Perfect Gentleman: The Life and Letters of George Washington Custis Lee* vol. 1 (Xulon Press, 2003), 23.

11. *The Virginia Magazine of History and Biography*, vol. 28 no. 1 (January 1920): 90–96.

12. George Washington, *Journal of My Journey Over the Mountains* (Joel Munsell's Sons, Albany, 1892), 59–66; Benjamin Lossing, *Lossing's Pictorial Field Book of the War of 1812* vol. 1 (New York: Harper and Brothers, Franklin Square, 1868), 110; Washington Irving, *The Works of Washington Irving: Life of George Washington* vol. 1 (New York: G.P. Putnam, 1861), 35–36.

13. John Bentley, "Smithfield" to Henry Lee, 1753, in *Edmund Jennings Lee Papers*, Virginia Historical Society.

14. Lee, *Lee of Virginia*, 297–98.

15. Nagel, *The Lees of Virginia*, 159.

16. Lee, *Lee of Virginia*, 295.

17. Prince William County Commission, 1753 April 22, Williamsburg, VA, appointing Henry Lee attorney for Prince William County, in *Edmund Jennings Lee Papers*, the Virginia Historical Society.

18. David A. Clary, *George Washington's First War* (New York: Simon and Schuster, 2011), 153–64; James Thomas Flexner, *Washington: The Indispensable Man* (New York: Back Bay Books, 1994), 24–26.

19. George Washington to Henry Lee, 8 October 1755, in Founders Online, National Archives, http://founders.archives.gov/documents/Washington/02-02-02-0083 (original source: W. W. Abbot, ed., *The Papers of George Washington*

[Charlottesville: University Press of Virginia, 1983], Colonial Series, vol. 2, 14 August 1755–15 April 1756, pp. 87–88).

20. George Washington, Memorandum respecting the Militia, 8 May 1756, in Founders Online, National Archives, http://founders.archives.gov/documents/Washington/02-03-02-0096 [original source: W. W. Abbot, ed., *The Papers of George Washington*, April 1756–9 November 1756 [Charlottesville, VA: University Press of Virginia, 1984], Colonial Series, vol. 3, 99–100).

21. Noel B. Gerson, *Light Horse–Harry: A Biography of Washington's Great Cavalryman, General Henry Lee* (New York: Doubleday and Company, 1966), 1.

22. Henry Lee, *The Revolutionary War Memoirs of General Henry Lee*, ed. Robert E. Lee (Boston: Da Capo Press, 1998), 265.

23. Nagel, *The Lees of Virginia*, 160.

24. Ibid., 159.

25. Diary entry, 19 October 1768, in Founders Online, National Archives, http://founders.archives.gov/documents/Washington/01-02-02-0003-0028-0019 (original source: Donald Jackson, ed., *The Diaries of George Washington* [Charlottesville, VA: University Press of Virginia, 1976], vol. 2, 14 January 1766–31 December 1770, 100–1).

26. Edmund S. Morgan, *The Challenge of the American Revolution* (New York: W.W. Norton Company, 1976 ), 8; Edmund S. Morgan and Helen M. Morgan, *The Stamp Act Crisis: Prologue to Revolution* (Chapel Hill: University of North Carolina Press, 1962), 96–97.

27. Pauline Maier, *From Resistance to Revolution* (New York: W.W. Norton and Company, 1991), 53.

28. Thomas S. Kidd, *Patrick Henry: First Among Patriots* (New York: Basic Books, 2011), 51–52.
29. Nagel, *The Lees of Virginia*, 83.
30. John E. Findling and Frank W. Thackeray, eds., *Events that Changed America in the Eighteenth Century* (Santa Barbara: The Greenwood Press, 1998), 74.
31. Ibid., 77.
32. Ibid., 84–92.
33. Charles Boyd, *Light-Horse Harry Lee* (New York: Charles Scribner's Sons, 1931), 2.
34. Samuel Appleton Storrow to "Sister," September 6, 1821, in *Ethel Armes Papers*, Library of Congress.

## 2: ALL SONS OF LIBERTY

1. Peter Beney, *The Majesty of Colonial Williamsburg* (Gretna, LA: Pelican Publishing, 1997), 29.
2. Thomas Jefferson Wertenbaker, *Princeton, 1746–1896* (Princeton New Jersey: Princeton University Press, 1996), p. 54; *William and Mary College Quarterly Historical Magazine* vol. 8, (Richmond, VA: Whittet & Shepperson Printers), 33.
3. Gideon Mailer, *John Witherspoon's American Revolution* (University of North Carolina Press, 2017), 13.
4. Mailer, 63.
5. Ibid., 66.
6. Ibid., 99.
7. L. H. Butterfield, *John Witherspoon Comes to America* (Princeton University Library, 1957), 58.
8. Ibid., 68.
9. David Walker Woods Jr., *John Witherspoon* (Michigan: Fleming H. Revell, 1906), 97.

10. James Madison to James Madison Sr., 30 September 1769, in Founders Online, National Archives, http://founders.archives. gov/documents/Madison/01-01-02-0005 (original source: William T. Hutchinson and William M. E. Rachal, eds. *The Papers of James Madison, 16 March 1751–16 December 1779* vol. 1, [Chicago: The University of Chicago Press, 1962], 45–48).

11. Cazenove Gardner Lee and Dorothy Mills Parker, *Lee Chronicle: Studies of the Early Generations of the Lees of Virginia* (New York University Press, 1957), 86.

12. Noll, Mark A. *Princeton and the Republic, 1768-1822: The Search for a Christian Enlightenment in the Era of Samuel Stanhope Smith* (Vancouver: Regent College Pub., 1989), 29.

13. Arthur Herman, *How the Scots Invented the Modern World: The True Story of How Western Europe's Poorest Nation Created Our World and Everything in It* (New York: Three Rivers Press, 2001), 243–45.

14. Wertenbaker, *Princeton*, 108.

15. Mark A. Noll, *Princeton and the Republic, 1768–1822: The Search for a Christian Enlightenment in the Era of Samuel Stanhope Smith* (Regent College Publishing, 1989), 29.

16. Richard A. Harrison, *Princetonians, 1769–1775: A Biographical Dictionary* (Princeton Legacy Library, 1980), xxiii.

17. Edmund Jennings Lee, *Lee of Virginia, 1642–1892: Biographical and Genealogical Sketches of the Descendants of Colonel Richard Lee* (Maryland: Heritage Books, 2008), 131.

18. Charles Boyd, *Light-Horse Harry Lee* (New York: Scribner's and Sons, 1931), 1.

19. Alexander Leitch, *A Princeton Companion* (Princeton University Press, 1978), 329–30.

20. Boyd, *Light-Horse Harry Lee*, 2–4

21. Ibid.

22. Ethel Armes, *Stratford Hall: The Great House of the Lees* (Richmond, VA: Garrett and Massie, 1936), 230.

23. John Witherspoon to Henry Lee, 20 December 1770, in John Witherspoon Collection, Princeton University.

24. Boyd, *Light-Horse Harry Lee*, 4–5; Ashbel Green, *Discourses Delivered in the College of New Jersey: Addressed Chiefly to Candidates for the First Degree in the Arts; with Notes and Illustrations, including a Historical Sketch of the College, from Its Origin to the Accession of President Witherspoon* (Philadelphia: E. Littell and R. Norris Henry, 1822), 403–04.

25. Paul C. Gutjahr, *Charles Hodge: Guardian of American Orthodoxy* (Oxford University Press, 2011), 48.

26. John MacLean, *History of the College of New Jersey, at Princeton* (Russell Creech, 2006), 334.

27. George Washington Parke Custis, *Recollections and Private Memoirs of Washington* (New York: Derby and Jackson, 1860), 356.

28. MacLean, *History of the College of New Jersey*, 372.

29. Varnum Lansing Collins, *Princeton* (Oxford University Press), 76.

30. Philip Vickers Fithian, *Journal and Letters of Philip Vickers Fithian 1773–1774: A Plantation Tutor of the Old Dominion* (Princeton University Press), 42.

31. Sheldon S. Cohen and Larry R. Gerlach, "Princeton in the Coming of the American Revolution," *Princeton Alumni Weekly*, volume 76, 9.

32. David W. Robson, *Educating Republicans: The College in the Era of the American Revolution, 1750–1800* (Santa Barbara, CA: Greenwood Press, 1985), 68.

33. Cohen and Gerlach, "Princeton in the Coming of the American Revolution," 9.

34. Ibid.

35. John Adams and Charles Francis Adams, *The Works of John Adams, Second President of the United States* (New York: Charles C. Little and James Brown, 1850), 356.

36. MacLean, *History of the College of New Jersey, at Princeton,* 317.

37. Fithian, 42–43.

38. Ibid.

## 3: THIS STRUGGLE FOR THE RIGHTS OF MANKIND

1. Charles Lee to Benjamin Rush, September 19, 1775, Papers of Charles Lee, Vol. 4, New York Historical Society Publication Fund, 1871, 207.

2. "Where, How or with Whom My Time Is Spent," in the journals of George Washington [April 1775], in Founders Online, National Archives, http://founders.archives.gov/documents/Washington/01-03-02-0005-0008 (original source: Donald Jackson, ed. *The Diaries of George Washington* vol. 3, [Charlottesville, VA: University Press of Virginia, 1978], 1 January 1771–5 November 1781, 319–23).

3. *The Century,* vol. 77, 194–95.

4. Eric Stockdale and Randy Holland, *Middle Temple Lawyers and the American Revolution* (Eagan, Minnesota: Thomson West, 2007), 148.

5. Robert W. Coakley, *The War of the American Revolution* (Stetson Conn, 1975), 87.

6. Lawrence Kaplan, *Thomas Jefferson: Westward the Course of Empire* (Lanham, MD: Rowman and Littlefield, 1999), 70.

7. Benson John Lossing, *The Pictorial Field-book of the Revolution,* vol. 2, (New York: Harper and Brothers, 1855), 280.

8. Ibid.

9. Ibid., 16.

10. Edmund Jennings Lee, *Lee of Virginia, 1642–1892: Biographical and Genealogical Sketches of the Descendants of Colonel Richard Lee* (Berwyn Heights, MD: Heritage Books, 2008), 292.

11. Robert S. Gamble, *Sully* (Chantilly, VA: Sully Foundation Limited, 1973), 14.

12. Philip Vickers Fithian, *Journal and Letters of Philip Vickers Fithian 1773–1774: A Plantation Tutor of the Old Dominion* (Princeton University Press, 1943), 96.

13. Ibid., 103.

14. Henry Lee II to William Lee, May 15, 1775, in Ethel Armes, *Stratford Hall: The Great House of the Lees* (Garrett and Massie, 1936), 133.

15. James Thomas Flexner, *Washington: The Indispensable Man* (New York: Back Bay Books, 1994), 59–61.

16. John W. Hartman, *The American Partisan: Henry Lee and the Struggle for Independence 1776–1780* (Shippensburg, PA: Burd Street Press, 2000), 9–10.

17. Henry Lee to Charles Lee, 5 July 1775, in Thomas Gage Papers, William L. Clements Library, Ann Arbor, Michigan.

18. Hartman, *The American* Partisan, 1.

19. Noel B. Gerson, *Light-Horse Harry* (New York: Doubleday, 1966), 14.

20. Peter Force, *American Archives: Consisting of a Collection of Authentick Records, State Papers, Debates, and Letters and Other Notices of Publick Affairs, the Whole Forming a Documentary History of the Origin and Progress of the North American Colonies; of the Causes and Accomplishment of the American Revolution; and of the Constitution of Government for the United States, to the Final Ratification Thereof. In Six Series.... Prepared and Published under Authority of an Act of Congress* (March 2, 1833, March 3, 1843), 1529–32.

21. Francis Barnum Culber, *Blooded Horses of Colonial Days: Classic Horse Matches in America before the Revolution* (self-published, 1922), 123.

22. Theodorick Bland, *The Bland Papers* (Edmund and Julian C Ruffin, 1840), xxv.

23. Hartman, *The American Partisan*, 12.

24. Archives of Maryland, Volume 18, 585.

25. Hartman, *The American Partisan*, 13.

26. Ibid., 14–15.

27. George Lillie Craik and Charles Macfarlane, *The Pictorial History of England: Being a History of the People, As Well as a History of the Kingdom* (New York: Harper and Bothers,1837), 282.

28. Gregory, J. W. Urwin, *The United States Cavalry: An Illustrated History, 1776–1944* (University of Oklahoma Press, 2003), 9.

29. Ibid.

30. Ibid., 9–11

31. Ibid., 11.

32. Ibid., 13.

33. Official Letters of the Governors of the State of Virginia, vol. 1, (D. Bottom, superintendent of public printing, 1926), 72.

34. Hartman, *The American Partisan*, 21.

35. Flexner, *Washington*, 95.

36. L. Edward Purcell and Sarah J. Purcell, *Encyclopedia of Battles in North America 1517–1916* (New York: Checkmark Books, 2000), 222–23.

37. Hartman, *The American Partisan*, p. 25; George Weedon, *Valley Forge Orderly Book* (New York: Dodd, Mead and Company 1802), 69.

38. Ibid., 15; Henry Banks, *The Vindication of John Banks: Of Virginia, against Four Calumnies Published by Judge Johnson, of Charleston, South Carolina, and Charles Caldwell, of Lexington, Kentucky* (self-published, 1826), 61.

39. Ibid., 27–28.

40. Ibid., 29.

41. Titus Elwood Davis, *The Battle of Bound Brook* (Washington Campground Association, 1894), 17.

42. Henry Lee to Theodorick Bland, April 18, 1777, in Bland, *The Bland Papers*, 51.

43. Hartman, *The American Partisan*, 30.

44. Bland, *The Bland Papers*, 53.

45. Journals of the Continental Congress, Tuesday 27 May 1777.

46. Willard Sterne Randall, *Alexander Hamilton, A Life* (New York: Harper Perennial, 2003), 11.

47. Ibid., 68.

48. Ron Chernow, *Alexander Hamilton* (London, England: Penguin, 2005), 63–65.

49. Michael E. Newton, *Alexander Hamilton: The Formative Years* (Phoenix, AZ: Eleftheria Publishing, 2015), 182.

50. Randall, *Alexander Hamilton*, 120; Arthur Lefkowitz, *George Washington's Indispensable Men: The 32 Aides-de-Camp Who Helped Win American Independence* (Mechanicsburg, PA: Stackpole Books, 2003), 64–66, 114, and 119–123.

51. John Richard Alden, *George Washington: A Biography* (Baton Rouge, LA: Louisiana State University Press, 1984), 154; F. A. Winyantes, ed., *The Services of Lieut.-Colonel Francis Downman in France, North America and the West Indies between the Years 1758 and 1784* (Woolwich, London: Printed at the Royal Artillery Institution, 1898), 29.

52. Hartman, *The American Partisan*, 33–34.

53. Ibid.

## 4: A REBEL CAPTAIN BY THE NAME OF LEE

1. George Washington to John Hancock, 30 August 1777, in Founders Online, National Archives, http://founders.archives.gov/documents/Washington/03-11-02-0091 (original source: Philander D. Chase and Edward G. Lengel, eds., *The Papers of George Washington, 19 August 1777–25 October 1777*, vol. 11, [Charlottesville, VA: University Press of Virginia, 2001], Revolutionary War Series, 93–94).

2. General Orders, 25 August 1777, in Founders Online, National Archives, http://founders.archives.gov/documents/Washington/03-11-02-0056 (original source: Chase and Lengel, *The Papers of George Washington, 19 August 1777–25 October 1777*, 63–64).

3. George Washington to Colonel Theodorick Bland, 30 August 1777, in Founders Online, National Archives, last modified November 26, 2017, http://founders.archives.gov/documents/Washington/03-11-02-0089 (original source: Chase and Lengel, *The Papers of George Washington, 19 August 1777–25 October 1777*, 91–92).

4. L. Edward Purcell and Sarah Purcell, *Encyclopedia of Battles in North America* (New York: Checkmark Books, 2000), 75–76.

5.  Edward G. Lengel, *General George Washington: A Military Life* (New York: Random House Publishing, 2005), 230–31; Purcell and Purcell, *Encyclopedia of Battles*, 30–31.

6.  Thomas J. McGuire, *Brandywine Battlefield Park: Pennsylvania Trail of History Guide* (Harrisburg, PA: Pennsylvania Historical and Museum Commission, 2001), 29–34.

7.  Henry Lee, *The Revolutionary War Memoirs of General Henry Lee* (Boston: Da Capo Press, 1998), ed. Robert E. Lee, 90–92.

8.  Ibid.

9.  Ibid.

10. Alexander Hamilton to John Hancock, 18 September 1777, in Founders Online, National Archives, http://founders.archives. gov/documents/Hamilton/01-01-02-0282 ([original source: Harold C. Syrett, ed., *The Papers of Alexander Hamilton, 1768–1778*, vol. 1 [(New York: Columbia University Press, 1961)], 326–27]).

11. James Thomas Flexner, *Washington: The Indispensable Man* (New York: Back Bay Books, 1994), 104–06.

12. Lee, *The Revolutionary War* Memoirs, 97–102; Henry Lee to George Washington, 31 October 1777, in Founders Online, National Archives, http://founders.archives.gov/ documents/Washington/03-12-02-0060 (original source: Frank E. Grizzard, Jr. and David R. Hoth, eds., *The Papers of George Washington, 6 October 1777–25 December 1777* vol. 12, [Charlottesville, VA: University Press of Virginia, 2002], Revolutionary War Series, 67–68).

13. Henry Lee to George Washington, 3 November 1777, in Founders Online, National Archives, http://founders.archives. gov/documents/Washington/03-12-02-0091 (original source: Grizzard and Hoth, eds., *The Papers of George Washington, 6 October 1777–25 December 1777*, pp. 104–05).

14. John W. Hartman, *The American Partisan: Henry Lee and the Struggle for Independence 1776–1780* (Shippensburg, PA: Burd Street Press, 2000), 44–46.

15. Sally Wister, *Sally Wister's Journal: A True Narrative: A Young Girl's Account of Her Experiences during the Revolutionary War* (Carlisle, MA: Applewood Books, 1995), 20.

16. Purcell and Purcell, *Encyclopedia of Battles*, 249–51.

17. Flexner, *Washington*, 109–10.

18. George Washington to Henry Laurens, 23 December 1777, in Founders Online, National Archives, http://founders.archives.gov/documents/Washington/03-12-02-0628 (original source: Grizzard and Hoth, eds., *The Papers of George Washington, 6 October 1777–25 December 1777*, 683–87).

19. Henry Lee to George Washington, 4 January 1778, in Founders Online, National Archives, http://founders.archives.gov/documents/Washington/03-13-02-011 (original source: Edward G. Lengel, *The Papers of George Washington, 26 December 1777–28 February 1778*, vol. 13, [Charlottesville, VA: University of Virginia Press, 2003], Revolutionary War Series, 141–142).

20. Henry Graham, *History of Delaware County, Pennsylvania* (Philadelphia: L.H. Everts & Co., 1884), 636.

21. Hartman, *The American Partisan*, 53–54.

22. *New Jersey Gazette*, January 14, 1778.

23. Paul Lockhart, *The Drillmaster of Valley Forge: The Baron de Steuben and the Making of the American Army* (New York: Harper Collins, 2008), 88; Gary B. Nash, *The Unknown American Revolution: The Unruly Birth of Democracy and the Struggle to Create America* (Penguin, 2005), 222.

24. Friedrich von Muenchhausen, *At General Howe's Side, 1776–1778: The Diary of General William Howe's Aide de Camp*

(Monmouth Beach, NJ: Phillip Freneau Press, 1974), trans. Ernst Kipping and ann. Samuel Smith, 47.

25. John Marshall, *Life of Washington,* vol. 3, (Philadelphia: C.P. Wayne, 1804 ), 377–78.

26. Alexander Garden, *Anecdotes of the American Revolution: Illustrative of the Talents and Virtues of the Heroes and Patriots Who Acted the Most Conspicuous Parts Therein* (Charleston, SC: A.E. Miller, 1828), 128.

27. Johann Ewald, *Diary of the American War: A Hessian Journal* (New Haven and London: Yale University Press, 1979), 12.

28. Henry Lee to George Washington, 20 January 1778, in Founders Online, National Archives, http://founders.archives. gov/documents/Washington/03-13-02-0252 (original source: Lengel, *The Papers of George Washington, 26 December 1777–28 February* 1778, 292–93).

29. General Orders, January 20, 1778, in John C. Fitzpatrick, *The Writings of George Washington from the Original Manuscript Sources 1745....* (Washington, DC: United States Government Printing Office, 1939 ), 321.

30. George Washington to Henry Lee, 20 January 1778, in Founders Online, National Archives, http://founders.archives. gov/documents/Washington/03-13-02-0254 (original source: Lengel, *The Papers of George Washington, 26 December 1777–28 February* 1778, 294).

31. Von Muenchhausen, *At General Howe's Side,* 47.

32. George Washington to William Buchanan, 7 February 1778, in Founders Online, National Archives, http://founders.archives. gov/documents/Washington/03-13-02-0385 (original source: Lengel, *The Papers of George Washington, 26 December 1777–28 February* 1778, 465–66).

33. George Washington to Anthony Wayne, 9–12 February 1778, in Founders Online, National Archives, http://founders. archives.gov/documents/Washington/03-13-02-0411 (original source: Lengel, *The Papers of George Washington, 26 December 1777–28 February 1778*, 492–93); Jared Sparks, ed., *The Writings of George Washington: Being His Correspondence....* (New York: Harper and Brothers, 1847), volume 5, 241–42.

34. George Washington to Henry Lee, February 16, 1778, The Papers of George Washington Digital Edition (Charlottesville, VA: University of Virginia Press, Rotunda, 2008).

35. Henry Lee to George Washington, 19 February 19, 1778, in ibid.

36. Henry Lee to George Washington, 22 February 22, 1778, in ibid.

37. Charles Caldwell, ed., *Memoirs of the Life and Campaigns of the Hon. Nathaniel Greene* (Philadelphia: Robert Desilver, 1819), 67–70.

38. Flexner, *Washington*, 118.

39. Alexander Hamilton to Stephan Moylan, 29 March 1779, in Harold Coffin Syrett and Jacob Ernest Cooke, eds. *Papers of Alexander Hamilton* (New York: Columbia University Press, 1961), 447.

40. Henry Lee to George Washington, 31 March 1778, in Founders Online, National Archives, http://founders.archives.gov/ documents/Washington/03-14-02-0344 (original source: David R. Hoth, ed., *The Papers of George Washington,1 March 1778–30 April 1778*, [Charlottesville, VA: University of Virginia Press, 2004], 368–69).

41. George Washington to Henry Lee, 1 April 1778, in John C. Fitzpatrick, *The Writings of George Washington from the*

*Original Manuscript Sources 1745–1799*, (Washington, DC: U.S. Government Printing Office, 1939), 198.

## 5: A MOST GALLANT AFFAIR

1. George Washington to Henry Laurens, 3 April 1778 in George Washington, *The Writings of George Washington Vol. 4:* (Boston: Russell, Odiorne and Metcalf and Hilliard, Gray and Company, 1834), 303–04.
2. Francis Bernard Heitman, *Historical Register of Officers of the Continental Army during the War of the Revolution, April 1775 to December 1783* (Rare Book Shop Publishing, 1914), 260.
3. George Washington to Henry Laurens 3 April 1778, in George Washington, *Official Letters to the Honorable American Congress: Written Between the United Colonies and Great Britain by his Excellency George Washington, Commander in Chief of the Continental Forces now President of the United States* vol. 2, (London: Printed for Cadell Junior and Davies G.G. and J. Robinson,, B. and J. White, W. Otridge and Son, J. Debrett, R. Faulder and T. Egerton, 1795), 237.
4. Henry Laurens to Henry Lee, 8 April 1778, Letter book, Papers of Continental Congress, item 13, U.S. National Archives and Records Administration, Washington, DC.
5. George Washington to Henry Lee, 12 April 1778, in John C. Fitzpatrick, ed., *The Writings of George Washington from the Original Manuscript Sources 1745....* vol. 1, (U.S. Government Printing Office, 1936), 251.
6. John W. Hartman, *The American Partisan: Henry Lee and the Struggle for Independence 1776–1780* (Burd Street Press, 2000), 67–68.

7. Journals of the Continental Congress, 1774–1789, Monday, 27 April 1778 (Washington: Government Printing Office, 1912).

8. Benjamin H. Irvin, *Clothed in Robes of Sovereignty: The Continental Congress and the People Out of Doors* (Oxford University Press, 2011), 154; C. F. William Maurer, *Dragoon Diary: The History of the Third Continental Light Dragoons* (Bloomington, Indiana: AuthorHouse, 2005), 82.

9. James Thomas Flexner, *Washington: The Indispensable Man* (New York: Back Bay Books, 1994), 121–23.

10. Ibid.; L. Edward Purcell and Sarah J. Purcell, *Encyclopedia of Battles in North America 1517–1916* (New York: Checkmark Books, 2000), 181–83.

11. Henry Lee, *The Revolutionary War Memoirs of General Henry Lee*, ed. Robert E. Lee (Boston: Da Capo Press, 1998), 115–16.

12. Henry Lee to Anthony Wayne, 24 August 1778, in the Papers of Anthony Wayne, The Historical Society of Pennsylvania, 5:80.

13. George Washington to Henry Lee, 16 October 1778, in Founders Online, National Archives http://founders.archives.gov/documents/Washington/03-17-02-0426 (original source: Philander D. Chase, ed., *The Papers of George Washington, 15 September–31 October 1778*, [Charlottesville, VA: University of Virginia Press, 2008], Revolutionary War Series, 406–07).

14. Hartmann, *The American Partisan*, 142–44.

15. Henry Lee to George Washington, 14 December 1778, Lengel, Edward, ed., *The Papers of George Washington: Revolutionary War Series, 1 November 1778 – 14 January 1779*, vol. 18, (Charlottesville and London: University of Virginia Press, 2008), 410.

16. James Thacher, *A Military Journal During the American Revolutionary War, from 1775 to 1783* (Boston: Richardson and Lord, 1823 ), 193–94.

17. George Washington to Henry Lee, 30 June 1779, in Founders Online, National Archives, http://founders.archives.gov/documents/Washington/03-21-02-025 (original source: William M. Ferraro, ed.,*The Papers of George Washington, 1 June–31 July 1779*, vol. 2, [Charlottesville, VA: University of Virginia Press, 2012], Revolutionary War Series, vol. 21, 309–10).

18. Henry Phelps Johnston, *The Storming of Stony Point on the Hudson, Midnight July 15, 1779: Its Importance in Light of Unpublished Documents* (Gastonia, North Carolina: James T. White and Co, 1900), 199–200.

19. Ibid., 50.

20. George Washington to Henry Lee, 9 July 1779, in Founders Online, National Archives, http://founders.archives.gov/documents/Washington/03-21-02-0330 (original source: Ferraro, ed., *The Papers of George Washington, 1 June–31 July 1779*, 401–03); George Washington to Henry Lee, 10 July 1779, in Founders Online, National Archives, http://founders.archives.gov/documents/Washington/03-21-02-0344 (original source: ibid., 422).

21. Ibid, 201.

22. Heitman, *Historical Register of Officers of the Continental Army*, 424.

23. George H. Farrier, ed., *Memorial of the Centennial Celebration of the Battle of Paulus Hook, August 19, 1879* (Jersey City, NJ: M. Mullone, 1879), 25–30.

24. Ibid., 71.

25. Richard Kidder Meade to Henry Lee, 28 July 1779, in Fitzpatrick, ed., *The Writings of George Washington*, vol. 15, 498.

26. Farrier, ed., *Memorial of the Centennial Celebration of the Battle of Paulus Hook*, 39–41.

27. George Washington to Henry Lee, 10 August 1779, in George Washington Papers, Series 4, General Correspondence, Library of Congress.

28. Ibid.

29. George Washington to William Alexander, 12 August 1779 in Fitzpatrick, ed. *The Writings of George Washington*, 83.

30. Farrier, ed., *Memorial of the Centennial Celebration of the Battle of Paulus Hook*, 42–43.

31. Ibid.

32. Jim Piecuch and John Beakes, *"Light Horse Harry" Lee in the War for Independence* (The Nautical & Aviation Publishing Company of America, 2013), 51.

33. Henry Barton Dawson, *Battles of the United States, by Sea and Land: Embracing Those of the Revolutionary and Indian Wars, the War of 1812, and the Mexican War, from Original Paintings by Alonzo Chappel* (New York: Johnson, Fry and Company, 1858), 545–47.

34. Farrier, ed., *Memorial of the Centennial Celebration of the Battle of Paulus Hook*, 45–55.

35. Ibid.

36. Ibid.

37. To George Washington from Major Henry Lee, Jr., 22 August 1779, in Founders Online, National Archives, http://founders. archives.gov/documents/Washington/03-22-02-0174 (Original source: Benjamin L. Huggins, ed., *The Papers of George Washington, Revolutionary War Series, 1 August–21 October*

*1779*, vol. 22, [Charlottesville, VA: University of Virginia Press, 2013], 210–224).

38. Henry Lee to George Washington, 22 August 1779, in Founders Online, National Archives, http://founders.archives.gov/ documents/Washington/03-22-02-0174 (original source: Benjamin L. Huggins, ed., *The Papers of George Washington, 1 August–21 October 1779*, vol. 22, [Charlottesville, VA: University of Virginia Press, 2013], Revolutionary War Series, vol. 22, 210–24).

39. Clinton, Henry. *The American Rebellion: Sir Henry Clinton's Narrative of his Campaigns, 1775-1782* (New Haven, CT: Yale University Press, 1954), 139.

40. Nathanael Greene to Catherine Greene, 23 August 1779, in Richard K Showman, Elizabeth C. Stevens, and Dennis M. Conrad, eds., *Greene Papers*, vol. 4, (The University of North Carolina Press, 1986), 333.

41. General orders, 22 August 1779, in Founders Online, National Archives, http://founders.archives.gov/documents/ Washington/03-22-02-0170 (original source: Huggins, *The Papers of George Washington, 1 August–21 October 1779*, 207–08).

42. George Washington to John Jay, 23 August 1779, Founders Online, National Archives, http://founders.archives.gov/ documents/Washington/03-22-02-0181 (original source: Benjamin L. Huggins, ed., *The Papers of George Washington, 1 August–21 October 1779* [Charlottesville VA: University of Virginia Press, 2013], 230–231).

43. Lafayette to Henry Lee, 12 September 1779, in Farrier, ed., *Memorial of the Centennial Celebration of the Battle of Paulus Hook*, 55.

## 6: GOLD SEVEN TIMES TRIED IN THE FIRE

1. Anthony Wayne to Sharp Delany, 24 August 1779 in Henry Barton Dawson, "The Assault on Stony Point: By General Anthony Wayne, July 16, 1779," in *Gleanings from the Harvest-Field of American History* (Riverside Cambridge: H. O. Houghton, 1863), 137–38.

2. "The Pennsylvania Germans, Lucy Forney Bittinger, 1902," *New England Magazine*, vol. 26, 511–12.

3. Henry Barton Dawson, *Battles of the United States, by Sea and Land: Embracing Those of the Revolutionary and Indian Wars, the War of 1812, and the Mexican War, from Original Paintings by Alonzo Chappel* (New York: Johnson, Fry and Company, 1858), 137.

4. Henry Lee to Anthony Wayne, 25 August 1779, in Papers of Anthony Wayne, Pennsylvania Historical Society, 7:112.

5. George Washington to William Alexander, 28 August 1779, in John C. Fitzpatrick, ed., *The Writings of George Washington from the Original Manuscript Sources, July 29, 1779–October 20, 1779* vol. 16, (Washington: United States Government Printing Office, 1937), 190.

6. Ibid.

7. Ibid.

8. George Washington to the officers Commanding Major Henry Lee's Corps, 29 August 1779, in Founders Online, National Archives, http://founders.archives.gov/documents/Washington/03-22-02-0231 (original source: Benjamin L. Huggins, ed., *The Papers of George Washington, 1 August–21 October 1779*, vol. 22, [Charlottesville, VA: University of Virginia Press, 2013], Revolutionary War Series, 296–97).

9. Henry Lee to Joseph Reed, 27 August 1779, in William Bradford Reed, ed., *Life and Correspondence of Joseph Reed*, vol. 2, (Philadelphia: Lindsay and Blakiston, 1847), 126–27.

10. Ibid.

11. Ibid.

12. Henry Lee to Charles Lee, September 8, 1779, in Virginia Historical Society, Edmund Jennings Lee Papers, Mss1L5113 a7 CA 15R204103-N01.

13. Nathanael Greene to George Weedon, 6 September 1779, in Richard K Showman, Elizabeth C. Stevens, Dennis M. Conrad, eds., *Papers of Greene*, vol. 4, (University of North Carolina Press, 1986), 364.

14. General orders, 11 September 1779, in Founders Online, National Archives, http://founders.archives.gov/documents/Washington/03-22-02-0321 (original source: Huggins, ed., *The Papers of George Washington, 1 August–21 October 1779*, 396–98).

15. George Washington to Henry Lee, 1 September 1779, in Founders Online, National Archives, http://founders.archives.gov/documents/Washington/03-22-02-0254 (original source: Huggins, ed., *The Papers of George Washington, 1 August–21 October 1779*, 29–30).

16. Jim Piecuch and John Beakes, *"Light Horse Harry" Lee in the War for Independence* (Baltimore, Maryland: The Nautical & Aviation Publishing Company of America, 2013), 54.

17. Lee's Defense August 1779, as quoted in John Beakes and Jim Piecuch, *Light Horse Harry Lee in the War for Independence*. Charleston: Nautical and Aviation Publishing Company of America, 2013, 54.

18. Josiah Quincy, ed., *The Journals of Major Samuel Shaw: The First American Consul at Canton: With a Life of the Author* (Boston: W. M. Crosby and H. P. Nichols, 1847), 69–70.

19. Henry Lee to Joseph Reed, September 9, 1779, in William Bradford Lee, *The Life and Correspondence of Joseph Reed*, vol. 2, (Philadelphia: Lindsay and Blackiston, 1847), 127.

20. George Washington to Major Henry Lee, 3 September 1779, in Founders Online, National Archives, http://founders. archives.gov/documents/Washington/03-22-02-0269 (original source: Huggins, ed., *The Papers of George Washington, 1 August–21 October 1779* [Charlottesville, VA: University of Virginia Press, 2013], 344–345).

21. John C. Fitzpatrick, ed., *The Writings of George Washington*, 264–65.

22. George H. Farrier, ed., *Memorial of the Centennial Celebration of the Battle of Paulus Hook* (Jersey City, NJ: M. Mullone, 1879), 54–55; Joseph Florimond Loubat, *The Medallic History of the United States of America, 1776–1876*, vol. 1 (self-published, 1880), 30–31.

23. Alexander Hamilton to John Laurens, 11 September 1779, in Harold C. Syrett and Jacob E. Cooke, ed., *The Papers of Alexander Hamilton, 1779–1781*, vol. 2, (New York: Columbia University Press, 1961), 165–68.

24. Henry Lee to Joseph Reed, 20 June 1780, Henry Lee, *The Revolutionary War Memoirs of General Henry Lee*, ed. Robert E. Lee (Boston: Da Capo Press, 1998), 24.

25. George Washington to Henry Lee, 30 September 1779, in Founders Online, National Archives, http://founders. archives.gov/documents/Washington/03-22-02-0473 (original source: Huggins, ed. *The Papers of George Washington, 1 August–21 October 1779*, vol. 22, [Charlottesville, VA:

University of Virginia Press, 2013], Revolutionary War Series, 563–64).

26. John W. Hartman, *The American Partisan: Henry Lee and the Struggle for Independence 1776–1780* (Pennsylvania: Burd Street Press, 2000), 163–64.

27. Nathanael Greene to George Washington, 3 April 1780, in Richard K. Showman, Robert E. McCarthy, Dennis M. Conrad, and E. Wayne Carp, eds., Papers of Nathanael Greene, vol. 5, (University of North Carolina Press, 1989), 502.

28. Henry Lee to Thomas Burke, 6 June 1780, in Papers of *Anthony Wayne.*

29. Thomas Burke to Anthony Wayne, 6 June 1780, in ibid.

30. Robert Tomes, *Battles of America by Land and Sea,* vol. 1, (New York: Patterson and Nielson, n.d.), 747–51.

31. Lee, *Memoirs,* p. 395.

32. Ibid., 396–98.

33. Ibid., 399–400.

34. Ibid., 399–401.

35. Ibid, 402–10.

36. George Washington to Henry Lee, 22 October 1780, in Fitzpatrick, ed., *The Writings of George Washington,* 240.

## 7: THE GREAT GAME

1. John Morgan Dederer, *Making Bricks without Straw* (Manahattan, Kansas: Sunflower University Press, 1983), 26–28.

2. Edward Stevens to Thomas Jefferson, 20 August 1780, in the Thomas Jefferson Papers, series 1, general correspondence, manuscript division, Library of Congress.

3. *Magazine of History, with Notes and Queries,* vol. 5, 305.

4. Gerald M. Carbone, *Nathanael Greene: A Biography of the American Revolution* (Palgrave Macmillan, 2008), 10–30.

5. George Washington to General Nathanael Greene, 22 October 1780, in Washington Irving, *Life of George Washington*, vol. 2, (New York: G.P. Putnam's Sons, 1875), 551.

6. George Washington to Nathanael Greene, 22 October 1780, in Dennis M. Conrad, Roger N. Parks, Martha J. King, and Richard K. Showman, eds., *The Papers of General Nathanael Greene*, vol. 6, (Chapel Hill, NC: Published for the Rhode Island Historical Association by The University of North Carolina Press, c. 1976–2005), 424.

7. Henry Lee to Nathanael Greene, 23 October 1780, ibid., 427.

8. Henry Lee to Nathanael Greene, 25 October 1780, in ibid., 430.

9. Stanley J. Idzerda and Robert R. Crout, eds., *Lafayette in the Age of the American Revolution: Selected Letters and Papers, 1776–1790*, vol. 3, (New York: Cornell University Press, 1981), 209.

10. Nathanael Greene to Samuel Huntington, 2 November, in ibid., 459–60.

11. Henry Lee, *The Revolutionary War Memoirs of General Henry Lee*, ed. Robert E. Lee (Boston: Da Capo Press, 1998), 30–32.

12. *South Carolina Historical Magazine*, vol. 17–18, 67.

13. Robert Bass, *Swamp Fox: The Life and Campaigns of General Francis Marion* (Sandlapper Publishing Company, 1974), 5–10, 29.

14. Ibid., 82.

15. Lee, *Memoirs*, 223; Jim Piecuch and John Beakes, *"Light Horse Harry" Lee in the War for Independence* (Baltimore,

Maryland: The Nautical & Aviation Publishing Company of America, 2013), 89–90.

16. Henry Lee to Nathanael Greene, 16 January 1781, in Conrad, et al., eds., *The Papers of General Nathanael Greene,* vol. 7, 135–36.

17. Bass, *Swamp Fox*, 130–31; Lee, *Memoirs*, 224.

18. Ibid., 224–25, Bass, *Swamp Fox*, 137.

19. Lee, *Memoirs*, 225–31.

20. *The Papers of General Nathanael Greene*, Vol VII: 26 December 1780--29 March 1781, ed., Conrad, King, Parks, Showman (Chapel Hill: University of North Carolina Press, 1994), 231.

21. Ichabod Burnet to Henry Lee, 2 February 1781, in Conrad, et al., eds., *The Papers of General Nathanael Greene*, vol. 7, 234.

22. Lee, *Memoirs*, 238–39.

23. Alexander Garden, *Anecdotes of the American Revolution: Illustrative of the Talents and Virtues of the Heroes and Patriots Who Acted the Most Conspicuous Parts Therein*, vol. 2, (Charleston, SC: A.E. Miller, 1828), 118–20.

24. Lawrence E. Babits and Joshua B. Howard, *Long, Obstinate, and Bloody: The Battle of Guilford Courthouse* (University of North Carolina Press, 2009), 36.

25. William Graham, *General Joseph Graham and His Papers on North Carolina Revolutionary History* (Raleigh, NC: Edwards and Broughton, 1904), 322.

26. Lee, *Memoirs*, 254.

27. Ibid., 256.

28. Ibid, 257.

29. Ibid., 258.

30. Lee, *Memoirs*, 256–59; Hugh F. Rankin, *The North Carolina Continentals* (The University of North Carolina Press, 2005), 290.

31. Babits and Howard, *Long, Obstinate, and Bloody*, 38–39.

32. Graham, ed., *General Joseph Graham and His Papers*, 318–22.

33. Ibid., 332.

34. Lee, *Memoirs*, 266–68.

35. Nathanael Greene to Henry Lee, 9 March 1781, in Conrad, et al., eds., *The Papers of Nathanael General Greene*, vol. 7, 415.

36. Henry Lee to Nathanael Greene, 9 March 1781, in ibid., 417.

37. Henry Lee to Nathanael Greene, 11 March 1781, in ibid., 427.

38. Lee, *Memoirs*, 273–74.

39. Pension application of David Williams S3578 f18NC, transcribed by Will Graves, 6 May 1808, Babits and Howard, 78.

40. Lee, *Memoirs*, 278–84.

41. Ibid.; Pension application of David Williams.

42. Lee, *Memoirs*, 286–87, 596.

43. Nathanael Greene to Abner Nash, 18 March 1781, in Conrad, et al., eds., *The Papers of General Nathanael Greene*, vol. 7, 448.

## 8: A FATAL STAB TO THE BRITISH TYRANT

1. Henry Lee, *The Revolutionary War Memoirs of General Henry Lee*, ed. Robert E. Lee (Boston: Da Capo Press, 1998), 327–28.

2. Ibid., 326–29.

3. Ibid., 288.

4. David Lee Russell, *The American Revolution in the Southern Colonies* (Jefferson, NC: McFarland and Company, 2000), 235.

5. Lee, *Memoirs*, (Boston: Da Capo, 1998), 320–22.

6. Nathanael Greene to George Washington, 29 March 1781, in Dennis M. Conrad, Roger N. Parks, Martha J. King, and

Richard K. Showman, eds., *The Papers of General Nathanael Greene* vol. 7, (Chapel Hill, NC: The University of North Carolina Press, c. 1976–2005), 479–80.

7. Henry Lee to Nathanael Greene, 2 April 1781, in ibid., 28–29.

8. Robert Bass, *Swamp Fox: The Life and Campaigns of General Francis Marion* (Orangeburg, SC: Sandlapper, 1974), 167–68.

9. Patrick O'Kelley, *Unwaried Patience and Fortitude: Francis Marion's Orderly Book* (Conshohocken, PA: Infinity, 2006), 525.

10. Bass, *Swamp Fox*, 167–69; Lee, *Memoirs*, 174.

11. Henry Lee to Nathanael Greene, 23 April 1781, in Conrad, et al., eds., *The Papers of Nathanael Greene*, vol. 8, 138.

12. Lee, *Memoirs*, 330–34, Bass, *Swamp Fox*, 169–80.

13. Henry Lee to Nathaniel Greene, 20 April 1781, in *The Life of Nathanael Greene: Major-General in the Army of the Revolution, Volume 3*, by George Washington Greene (New York: Hurd and Houghton, 1871), 257-258; Francis Marion to Nathanael Green, 6 May 1781, Nathanael Greene to Francis Marion, 9 May 1781, in *The Papers of General Nathanael Greene Vol VIII: 30 March-10 July 1781*, ed., Conrad, King, Parks, Showman, (Chapel Hill: University of North Carolina Press, 1995), 213.

14. Marjorie Julian Spruill, Joan Marie Johnson, and Valinda W. Littlefield, eds., *South Carolina Women: Their Lives and Times* (University of Georgia Press, 2009), 111–23.

15. Lee, *Memoirs*, 343–48; Steven D. Smith, James B. Legg, Tamara S. Wilson, and Jonathan Leader, *"Obstinate and Strong": The History and Archaeology of the Siege of Fort Motte* (University of South Carolina—South Carolina Institute of Archaeology and Anthropology, 2007), 21–29.

16. Ibid., 28–29.

17. Kathryn Keenan, *In Search of Granby: A Colonial Village of South Carolina* (masters thesis, 2016,); Lee, *Memoirs*, 349–53.
18. Ibid., 349–53.
19. Nathanael Greene to Henry Lee, 22 May 1781, in Conrad, et al., eds., *The Papers of Nathanael Greene*, vol. 8, 291.
20. Tarleton Brown, *Memoirs of Tarleton Brown, a Captain in the Revolutionary Army* (privately printed, 1862), 25.
21. Joseph Johnson, *Traditions and Reminiscences, Chiefly of the American Revolution in the South* (Charleston: Walker & James, 1851), 359-60.
22. Lee, *Memoirs*, 357–70.
23. Edward Cashin, *The King's Ranger: Thomas Brown and the American Revolution on the Southern Frontier,* (Fordham University Press, 1999), 137.
24. Lee, *Memoirs*, 371–777.
25. Ibid.
26. Francis C. Kajencki, *Thaddeus Ko ciuszko: Military Engineer of the American Revolution* (Hedgeville, WV: Southwest Polonia Press, 1998), 159–60; Lee, *Memoirs*, 373–77.
27. Robert Sears, *The Pictorial History of the American Revolution* (self-published, 1846), 379.
28. John R. Maass, *The Road to Yorktown: Jefferson, Lafayette and the British Invasion of Virginia* (The History Press, 2015), 19–21.
29. James Thomas Flexner, *Washington: The Indispensable Man* (New York: Back Bay Books, 1994), 155–64.
30. Ibid.; Conrad, et al., eds., *The Papers of General Nathanael Greene*, vol. 9, 142.
31. Nathanael Greene to Henry Lee, 25 June 1781, in, Henry Lee (IV) *The Campaign of 1781 in the Carolinas: With Remarks,*

*Historical and Critical on Johnson's Life of Greene* (Philadelphia: E. Littell, 1824), xiv.

32. Jim Piecuch and John Beakes, *"Light Horse Harry" Lee in the War for Independence* (The Nautical & Aviation Publishing Company of America, 2013), 187–93.

33. Lee, *Memoirs*, 410–11.

34. The Papers of General Nathanael Greene: 11 July 1781-2 December 1781 Vol. 9, ed. Conrad, Parks, King, University of North Carolina Press,177.

35. Bass, *Swamp Fox*, 216.

36. Ibid., 216–17; Lee, *Memoirs*, 468–69.

37. Ibid., 472.

38. Ibid., 462–75; L. Edward Purcell and Sarah J. Purcell, *Encyclopedia of Battles in North America 1517 to 1916* (Checkmark Books, 2000), 86–87.

39. Nathanael Greene to Thomas McKean, 11 September 1781, in Lee, *Memoirs*, 602.

40. Ibid.; George F. Scheer Jr., "Henry Lee on the Southern Campaign," *The Virginia Magazine of History and Biography*, vol. 51, no. 2 (April 1943), 141–50.

41. Nathanael Greene to George Washington, 7 October 1781, in George Washington Papers, Library of Congress.

42. Lee, *Memoirs*, 512–14; Flexner, 163–64.

## 9: YOU CANNOT CEASE TO BE A SOLDIER

1.  George Washington to Nathanael Greene, 31 October 1781, George Washington Papers, Library of Congress.

2.  General orders, 24 November 1781, in Dennis M. Conrad, Roger N. Parks, Martha J. King, and Richard K. Showman, eds., *The Papers of General Nathanael Greene*, vol. 9, (Chapel

Hill, NC: The University of North Carolina Press, c. 1976–2005), 617.

3. Ibid., vol. 10, 7.

4. Henry Lee, *The Revolutionary War Memoirs of General Henry Lee*, ed. Robert E. Lee (Boston: Da Capo Press, 1998), 550–51.

5. Henry Lee to Nathanael Greene, 14 December, 1781, in Conrad, et al., *The Papers of General Nathanael Greene*, vol. 10, 54.

6. Nathanael Greene to Henry Lee, 21 December 1781, in ibid., 85.

7. Gregory Massey, *John Laurens and the American Revolution* (University of South Carolina, 2000), 60–62.

8. Ibid., 22.

9. *The Papers of Henry Laurens, Vol. 11, January 5, 1776–Nov. 1, 1777* (University of South Carolina, 1988), 547.

10. Lee, *Memoirs*, 528–36.

11. Henry Lee to Nathanael Greene, 26 January 1782, in Conrad, et al., *The Papers of General Nathanael Greene*, vol. 10, 264–65.

12. Nathanael Greene to Henry Lee, 27 January 1782, in ibid., 268–69.

13. Henry Lee to Nathanael Greene, 29 January 1782, in ibid. 282–83.

14. The Papers of General Nathanael Greene Vol 10: 3 December 1781-6 April 1782, ed. Conrad, Parks, King, The University of North Carolina Press; (October 19, 1998), 379.

15. Henry Lee to Nathanael Greene, 10 February 1782, in ibid., 350.

16. Nathanael Greene to Henry Lee, 12 February 1782, in ibid., 379.

17. Charles Carter Lee, *Recollections of Stratford Hall: My Boyhood* (University of Virginia), 1–3.

18. Paul Nagel, *The Lees of Virginia: Seven Generations of an American Family* (Oxford University Press, 1990), 67–68.

19. Ibid., 65.

20. Ibid., 66–67; Alexander Purdie and John Dixon, *The Virginia Gazette*, 16 August 1770.

21. Ibid.

22. Ethel Armes, *Stratford Hall: The Great House of the Lees* (Garrett and Massie, 1936), 219.

23. Philip Vickers Fithian, *Journal and Letters of Philip Vickers Fithian 1773–1774: A Plantation Tutor of the Old Dominion* (Princeton University Press, 1943), 45–46.

24. Lee, *Recollections of Stratford Hall*, 2.

25. Henry Lee to Nathanael Greene, 18 February 1782, in Conrad, et al., *The Papers of General Nathanael Greene*, vol. 10, 391.

26. Edmund Jennings Lee, *Lee of Virginia, 1642–1892: Biographical and Genealogical Sketches of the Descendants of Colonel Richard Lee* (Berwyn Heights, MD: Heritage Books, 2008), 167.

27. Jeanne A. Calhoun, "The African American Experience at Stratford Hall: 1782," Stratford Hall: Home of the Lees of Virginia, https://www.stratfordhall.org/collections-research/staff-research/the-african-american-experience-at-stratford-1782/.

28. Armes, *Stratford Hall*, 240–41.

29. Doris Devine Fanelli, *The History of the Portrait Collection, Independence National Park* (Philadelphia: American Philosophical Society, 2001), 203.

30. The garment was possibly his field jacket, though the epaulette would signify the rank of captain, either making this uniform

an older one or indicating that the portrait was painted before the generally accepted date

31. *Freeman's Journal and Philadelphia Daily Advertiser*, 13 October 1784.

32. George Mason to Zacharia Johnston, 18 November 1791, Robert Rutland, ed., *The Papers of George Mason, 1725–1792* (Chapel Hill, NC: University of North Carolina Press, 1970), 1245.

33. Nagel, *The Lees of Virginia*, p. 165; Charles Boyd, *Light-Horse Harry Lee* (New York: Scribner's and Sons, 1931), 151.

34. Henry Lee to George Washington, 7 August 1786, in Founders Online, National Archives, http://founders.archives.gov/documents/Washington/04-04-02-0186 (original source: W. W. Abbot, ed., *The Papers of George Washington, 2 April 1786–31 January 1787*, vol. 4, [Charlottesville, VA: University Press of Virginia, 1995], Confederation Series, 200–01).

35. Richard Henry Lee to William Shippen Jr., 8 May 1785, in James Curtis Ballogh, ed., *The Letters of Richard Henry Lee, 1779–1794*, vol. 2, (New York: The MacMillan Company, 1914), 355–56.

36. Armes, *Stratford Hall*, 243–44.

37. John C. Fitzpatrick, ed., *Journals of the Continental Congress, 1774–1789, Edited from the Original Records in the Library of Congress*, by John C. Fitzpatrick, (Washington: United States Government Printing Office, 1934), 1 February 1786.

38. Henry Lee to Henry Lee II, 7 February 1786, in Leesburg Papers (8557-a), University of Virginia Library.

39. Boyd, *Light-Horse Harry Lee*, 161.

40. Fitzpatrick, *Journals of the Continental Congress*, 28 and 30 June, 1786.

41. Henry Lee to George Washington, 11 July 1786, in Founders
    Online, National Archives, http://founders.archives.gov/
    documents/Washington/04-04-02-0148 (original
    source: Abbot, ed., *The Papers of George Washington, 2 April
    1786–31 January 1787*, Confederation Series, vol. 4, 154).

42. Fitzpatrick, *Journals of the Continental Congress*, 12 July 1786.

43. Boyd, *Light-Horse Harry Lee*, 153–55.

44. Ibid.; Henry Lee to George Washington, 7 August 1786, in
    Founders Online, National Archives, http://founders.archives.
    gov/documents/Washington/04-04-02-0186 (original
    source: Abbot, ed., *The Papers of George Washington, 2 April
    1786–31 January 1787*, Confederation Series, vol. 4, pp. 200–
    01).

45. Boyd, *Light-Horse Harry Lee*, 156–58.

46. Henry Lee to Richard Bland Lee, 11 November 1786, in Ethel
    Armes Collection of Lee Papers, Manuscript Division, Library
    of Congress.

47. Armes, *Stratford Hall*, 251; Boyd, *Light-Horse Harry Lee*,
    161–62.

48. To James Madison from Henry Lee, 20 December 1786,
    Founders Online, National Archives, last modified June 13,
    2018, http://founders.archives.gov/documents/
    Madison/01-09-02-0112. [Original source:The Papers of James
    Madison, vol. 9, 9 April 1786–24 May 1787 and supplement
    1781–1784, ed. Robert A. Rutland and William M. E. Rachal.
    (Chicago: The University of Chicago Press, 1975), 219–220.]

49. Armes, *Stratford Hall*, 252.

50. Edmund Jennings Lee, *Lee of Virginia, 1642–1892:
    Biographical and Genealogical Sketches of the Descendants of
    Colonel Richard Lee* (Berwyn Heights: Heritage Books, 2008),
    295–97.

51. James Thomas Flexner, *Washington: The Indispensable Man* (New York: Back Bay Books, 1994), 200–01.

52. Ibid., 199.

53. George Washington to Henry Lee Jr., 26 July 1786, in Founders Online, National Archives, http://founders.archives.gov/documents/Washington/04-04-02-0164. (Original source: Abbot, ed., *The Papers of George Washington, 2 April 1786–31 January 1787*, Confederation Series, vol. 4, 170–71).

54. Henry Lee to George Washington, 8 September 1786, in Founders Online, National Archives, http://founders.archives. gov/documents/Washington/04-04-02-0229 (original source: Abbot, ed., *The Papers of George Washington, 2 April 1786–31 January 1787*, Confederation Series, vol. 4,. 240–41).

## 10: ONE PEOPLE

1. Hugh Blair Grigsby, *The History of the Virginia Federal Convention of 1788, with Some Account of Eminent Virginians of That Era Who Were Members of the Body*, (Richmond: the Virginia Historical Society, 1890), 25–27.

2. Norman K. Risjord, *Jefferson's America*, 1760–1815 (Lanham, MD: Rowman and Littlefield, 2009), 222.

3. Henry Lee to James Madison, 7 December 1787, in Founders Online, National Archives, http://founders.archives.gov/documents/Madison/01-10-02-0191 (original source: Robert A. Rutland, Charles F. Hobson, William M. E. Rachal, and Frederika J. Teute, eds., The Papers of James Madison, 27 May 1787–3 March 1788, vol. 10, [Chicago: The University of Chicago Press, 1977], 295–96).

4. Henry Lee to James Madison from Henry Lee, 7 December 1787, in Founders Online, National Archives, http://founders. archives.gov/documents/Madison/01-10-02-0191 (original

source: Rutland, et al., eds., The Papers of James Madison, 27 May 1787–3 March 1788, vol. 10, 295–96).

5. Henry Lee to James Madison, [ca. 20 December] 1787, in Founders Online, National Archives, http://founders.archives. gov/documents/Madison/01-10-02-0211 (original source: Rutland, et al., eds., The Papers of James Madison, 27 May 1787–3 March 1788, vol. 10, 339–40).

6. Henry Lee to James Madison, 10 June 1789, in Founders Online, National Archives, http://founders.archives.gov/ documents/Madison/01-12-02-0129 (original source: Charles F. Hobson and Robert A. Rutland, eds., The Papers of James Madison, 2 March 1789–20 January 1790 and supplement 24 October 1775–24 January 1789, vol. 12, [Charlottesville: University Press of Virginia, 1979], 212–14).

7. Jonathan Elliot, The Debates in the Several State Conventions on the Adoption of the Federal Constitution, vol. 3, (New York: Burt Franklin, 1888), 1.

8. James Madison to George Washington, 18 October 1787, in Founders Online, National Archives, http://founders.archives. gov/documents/Washington/04-05-02-0349 (original source: W. W. Abbot, ed., The Papers of George Washington, 1 February 1787–31 December 1787 vol. 5, [Charlottesville, VA: University Press of Virginia, 1997], Confederation Series, 381–83).

9. Elliot, The Debates in the Several State Conventions, 3–5.

10. Ibid., 351-52.

11. Ibid., 22.

12. Hugh Blair Grigsby, The History of the Virginia Federal Convention of 1788, 106–11.

13. Ibid., 111–12.

14. Elliot, The Debates in the Several State Conventions, 64–65.

15. Ibid., 178–87.

16. Ibid., 178–79.

17. Elliot, The Debates in the Several State Conventions, 585–86.

18. The Virginia Convention, 2–27 June 1788 (editorial note), in Founders Online, National Archives, http://founders.archives. gov/documents/Madison/01-11-02-0057. Original source: Robert A. Rutland and Charles F. Hobson, eds., The Papers of James Madison, vol. 11, 7 March 1788–1 March 1789 (Charlottesville, VA: University Press of Virginia, 1977), 72–76.

19. Henry Lee to Richard Henry Lee, 10 August 1788, Lee Family Papers, University of Virginia Library.

20. Henry Lee to George Washington, 13 September 1788, in Founders Online, National Archives, http://founders. archives.gov/documents/Washington/04-06-02-0452 (original source: W. W. Abbot, ed., The Papers of George Washington, 1 January 1788–23 September 1788, vol. 6, [Charlottesville, VA: University Press of Virginia, 1997], Confederation Series, 510–513).

21. George Washington to Henry Lee, 22 September 1788, in Founders Online, National Archives, http://founders.archives. gov/documents/Washington/04-06-02-0469 (original source: Abbot, ed., The Papers of George Washington, 1 January 1788–23 September 1788, vol. 6, [Charlottesville, VA: University Press of Virginia, 1997], Confederation Series, 528–31).

22. George Washington to Henry Lee, 30 November 1788, in Founders Online, National Archives, http://founders. archives.gov/documents/Washington/05-01-02-0109 (original source: Dorothy Twohig, ed., The Papers of George Washington, 24 September 1788–31 March 1789, vol. 1, [Charlottesville,

VA: University Press of Virginia, 1987) Presidential Series, 139–40); Virginia Journal, and Alexandria Advertiser, 24 March 1785; George Washington to Henry Lee, 12 December 1788, in Founders Online, National Archives, http://founders. archives.gov/documents/Washington/05-01-02-0131 (original source: Twohig, ed. The Papers of George Washington, 24 September 1788–31 March 1789, Presidential Series, vol. 1, 174–75).

23. John Marshall, *The Life of George Washington* (Philadelphia: James Crissy, and Thomas, Cowperthwait and Co, 1843) vol. 2, 140–41; Henry Lee, *The Revolutionary War Memoirs of General Henry Lee*, ed. Robert E. Lee (Boston, MA: Da Capo Press, 1998), 42.

24. Marshall, *The Life of George Washington*, 146.

25. Henry Lee to George Washington, 14 March 1789, in Founders Online, National Archives, http://founders.archives.gov/ documents/Washington/05-01-02-0300 (original source: Twohig, ed., The Papers of George Washington, 24 September 1788–31 March 1789, Presidential Series, vol. 1, 394–95).

26. Henry Lee to James Madison, 4 March 1790, in Founders Online, National Archives, http://founders.archives.gov/ documents/Madison/01-13-02-0059 (original source: Charles F. Hobson and Robert A. Rutland, eds., The Papers of James Madison, 20 January 1790–31 March 1791, vol. 13, [Charlottesville, VA: University Press of Virginia, 1981], 87–91).

27. Henry Lee to Alexander Hamilton, [16 November 1789], in Founders Online, National Archives, http://founders.archives. gov/documents/Hamilton/01-05-02-0313, vol. 5, (original source: Harold C. Syrett, ed., The Papers of Alexander Hamilton, June 1788–November 1789, [New York: Columbia

University Press, 1962]), 517]; Henry Lee to Alexander
Hamilton to Henry Lee, [1 December 1789], in Founders
Online, National Archives, http://founders.archives.gov/
documents/Hamilton/01-06-02-0001 (original source: Syrett,
ed, The Papers of Alexander Hamilton, December 1789–
August 1790, [New York: Columbia University Press, 1962],
vol. 6, 1).

28. Henry Lee to James Madison, 4 March 1790, in Founders
Online, National Archives, http://founders.archives.gov/
documents/Madison/01-13-02-0059. Vol. 13, (Original
source: Hobson and Rutland, eds., The Papers of James
Madison, 20 January 1790–31 March 1791, 87–91).

29. Ibid.

30. Henry Lee to James Madison, 3 April 1790, in Founders
Online, National Archives, http://founders.archives.gov/
documents/Madison/01-13-02-0099. Vol. 13, (original
source: Hobson and Rutland, eds., The Papers of James
Madison, 20 January 1790–31 March 1791), 136–38.

31. Ibid.

32. Henry Lee to James Madison, 3 April 1790, in Founders
Online, National Archives, http://founders.archives.gov/
documents/Madison/01-13-02-0099 (original source: Hobson
and Rutland, eds., The Papers of James Madison, 20 January
1790–31 March 1791, vol. 13, pp. 136–38).

33. Ethel Armes, *Stratford Hall: The Great House of the Lees*
(Richmond, VA: Garrett and Massie, 1936), 247.

34. Robert K. Headley, Genealogical Abstracts from 18th-Century
Virginia Newspapers (Baltimore, MD: Clearfield, 2007), 202.

35. Ibid., 203.

36. George Washington to Henry Lee, 27 August 1790, in the
Archives of the Robert E. Lee Memorial Foundation, Papers of

the Lee Family, Box 2, M2009.074, Jessie Ball duPont Library, Stratford Hall.

## 11: INDIFFERENT DESTINY

1. Francis Paul Prucha, *The Great Father: The United States Government and the American Indians* (Lincoln, NE: University of Nebraska Press, 1995), 63–64.

2. Henry Lee to George Washington, 28 November 1790, in Founders Online, National Archives, http://founders.archives. gov/documents/Washington/05-06-02-0337 (original source: Mark A. Mastromarino, ed., *The Papers of George Washington, 1 July 1790–30 November 1790*, [Charlottesville, VA: University Press of Virginia, 1996], 694).

3. *The Statutes at Large: Being a Collection of All the Laws of Virginia*, vol. 13, (Philadelphia: Thomas Desilver, 1823), 170–71.

4. Henry Knox to George Washington, 27 March 1791, in Founders Online, National Archives, http://founders.archives. gov/documents/Washington/05-08-02-0010 (original source: Mastromarino, ed., *The Papers of George Washington, 22 March 1791–22 September 1791*, Presidential Series, vol. 8, 14–17).

5. Henry Lee to James Madison, 29 July 1791, in Founders Online, National Archives, http://founders.archives.gov/ documents/Madison/01-14-02-0052 (original source: Robert A. Rutland and Thomas A. Mason, eds., *The Papers of James Madison, 6 April 1791–16 March 1793*, vol. 14, [Charlottesville, VA: University Press of Virginia, 1983], 59–60).

6. Henry Lee to James Madison, 6 August 1791, in Founders Online, National Archives, http://founders.archives.gov/ documents/Madison/01-14-02-0060 (original source: Rutland

and Mason, eds., *The Papers of James Madison, 6 April 1791–16 March 1793*, vol. 14, 66).

7. Russell Frank Weigley, *Philadelphia: A 300 Year History* (New York City, New York: W.W. Norton, 1982), 200.

8. Henry Lee to James Madison, 24 August 1791, in Founders Online, National Archives, http://founders.archives.gov/documents/Madison/01-14-02-0068. (original source: Rutland and Mason, eds., *The Papers of James Madison, 6 April 1791–16 March 1793*, vol. 14, 73–74).

9. Henry Lee to James Madison from Henry Lee, 24 August 1791," in Founders Online, National Archives, http://founders.archives.gov/documents/Madison/01-14-02-0068 (original source: Rutland and Mason, eds., *The Papers of James Madison, 6 April 1791–16 March 1793*, vol. 14, 73–74).

10. George Washington to Henry Lee, 7 December 1791, in Founders Online, National Archives, http://founders.archives.gov/documents/Washington/05-09-02-0156 (original source: Mark A. Mastromarino, ed. *The Papers of George Washington, 23 September 1791–29 February 1792* [Charlottesville, VA: University Press of Virginia, 2000], Presidential Series, vol. 9, 262–63).

11. Henry Lee to St. George Tucker, 10 July 1792, in photocopy at Jessie Ball duPont Library, Stratford Hall.

12. Virginius Dabney, *Richmond: The Story of a City* (Charlottesville, VA: University Press of Virginia, 1990), 78–79.

13. Samuel Mordecai, *Richmond in By-Gone Days, Being Reminisces of an Old Citizen* (George M West, 1856), 58–60.

14. Dabney, *Richmond*, 78–79.

15. Samuel Appleton Storrow to "Sister," 6 September 1821, in Ethel Armes Papers, Library of Congress.

16. Henry Lee to James Madison, 8 January 1792, in Founders Online, National Archives, http://founders.archives.gov/documents/Madison/01-14-02-0163 (original source: Rutland and Mason, eds., *The Papers of James Madison, 6 April 1791–16 March 1793*, vol. 14, 183–85).

17. "The Origins of Freneau's *National Gazette*," (editorial note), 25 July 1791, in Founders Online, National Archives, http://founders.archives.gov/documents/Madison/01-14-02-0046 (original source: Rutland and Mason, eds., *The Papers of James Madison, 6 April 1791–16 March 1793*, vol. 14, 56–57).

18. Henry Lee to Alexander Hamilton, 12 August 1791, in Founders Online, National Archives, http://founders.archives.gov/documents/Hamilton/01-09-02-0032 (original source: Harold C. Syrett, ed., *The Papers of Alexander Hamilton, August 1791–December 1791*, vol. 9, [New York: Columbia University Press, 1965], 31–32).

19. Henry Lee to Alexander Hamilton, [18 October 1791], in Founders Online, National Archives, http://founders.archives.gov/documents/Hamilton/01-09-02-0291 (original source: Syrett, ed., *The Papers of Alexander Hamilton, August 1791–December 1791*, vol. 9, 404–05).

20. Henry Lee to James Madison, 4 April 1792, in Founders Online, National Archives, http://founders.archives.gov/documents/Madison/01-14-02-0251 (original source: Rutland and Mason, ed., *The Papers of James Madison, 6 April 1791–16 March 1793*, vol. 14, 278–79).

21. Henry Lee to James Madison, 8 January 1792, in Founders Online, National Archives, http://founders.archives.gov/documents/Madison/01-14-02-0163 ([original source: Rutland and Mason, eds., *The Papers of James Madison, 6 April 1791–16 March 1793*, vol. 14, 183–85]).

22. Ibid.

23. Henry Lee to James Madison, 29 January 1792, in Founders Online, National Archives, http://founders.archives.gov/documents/Madison/01-14-02-0182 (original source: Rutland and Mason, ed., *The Papers of James Madison, 6 April 1791–16 March 1793*, vol. 14, 203–05).

24. Ibid.

25. James Curtis Ballagh, *The Letters of Richard Henry Lee, 1779-1794*, vol. 2, 547–49.

26. Memorandum of Consultation on Indian Policy, 9 March 1792, in Founders Online, National Archives, http://founders.archives.gov/documents/Jefferson/01-23-02-0205 (original source: Charles T. Cullen, ed., *The Papers of Thomas Jefferson, 1 January–31 May 1792*, vol. 23, [Princeton: Princeton University Press, 1990], 239–44).

27. Alan Gaff, *Bayonets in the Wilderness: Anthony Wayne's Legion in the Old Northwest* (Norman, OK: University of Oklahoma Press, 1996), 24–25.

28. Henry Lee to James Madison, 18 April 1792, in Founders Online, National Archives, http://founders.archives.gov/documents/Madison/01-14-02-0264 (original source: Rutland and Mason, ed., *The Papers of James Madison, 6 April 1791–16 March 1793*, vol. 14, 291).

29. Calendar of Virginia State Papers and Other Manuscripts...., vol. 5 (Richmond, VA: Rush U. Derr, Superintendent of Public Printing,1885), 199, 211, 455, 595, and 644; vol. 7 (Richmond, VA: J. H. O'Bannon, Superintendent of Public Printing, 1888), 142.

30. Henry Lee to Alexander Hamilton, 23 June 1792, in Founders Online, National Archives, http://founders.archives.gov/documents/Hamilton/01-11-02-0461 (original source: Syrett,

ed., *The Papers of Alexander Hamilton, August 1791–December 1791*, vol. 11, 550–51).

31. Douglas Egerton, *Rebels, Reformers, and Revolutionaries: Collected Essays and Second Thoughts* (London, England: Routledge, 2002), 168; Charles Boyd, *Light-Horse Harry Lee* (New York City, NY: Scribner's and Sons, 1931), 206–07.

32. Calendar of Virginia State Papers and Other Manuscripts…, vol.7 (1888), 239.

33. Charles Royster, *Light-Horse Harry Lee and the Legacy of the American Revolution*, (Baton Rouge, LA: Louisiana State University Press, 1994), 126.

34. Boyd, *Light-Horse Harry Lee* (New York City, NY: Scribner's and Sons,1931), 207.

35. Headley, *Genealogical Abstracts from 18th-Century Virginia Newspapers*, 203.

36. Henry Lee to Alexander Hamilton, [10 September 1792], in Founders Online, National Archives, http://founders.archives.gov/documents/Hamilton/01-12-02-0270 (original source: Syrett, ed., *The Papers of Alexander Hamilton, July 1792–October 1792*, vol. 12, 352–53).

37. Henry Lee to James Madison, 10 September 1792, in Founders Online, National Archives, http://founders.archives.gov/documents/Madison/01-14-02-0327. (Original source: Rutland and Mason, eds., *The Papers of James Madison*, vol. 14, *6 April 1791–16 March 1793*, vol. 14, 363–64).

38. Henry Lee to Alexander Hamilton, 23 June 1792, in Founders Online, National Archives, http://founders.archives.gov/documents/Hamilton/01-11-02-0461. (original source: Syrett, ed., *The Papers of Alexander Hamilton, July 1792–October 1792*, vol. 12, 550–51).

39. Francisco de Miranda, *Archivo del General Miranda*, (Editorial Sur-America, 1938), 147.

40. Henry Lee to George Washington, 29 April 1793, in Founders Online, National Archives, http://founders.archives.gov/documents/Washington/05-12-02-0393 (original source: Christine Sternberg Patrick and John C. Pinheiro, eds., *The Papers of George Washington, 16 January 1793–31 May* [Charlottesville, VA: University of Virginia Press, 2005], Presidential Series, vol. 12, 493–495).

41. Samuel Appleton Storrow to "Sister," 6 September 1821, Ethel Armes Papers, Library of Congress.

42. Henry Lee to George Washington from Henry Lee, 29 April 1793, in Founders Online, National Archives, http://founders.archives.gov/documents/Washington/05-12-02-0393 (original source: Christine Sternberg Patrick and John C. Pinheiro, eds., *The Papers of George Washington, 16 January 1793–31 May 1793* [Charlottesville, VA: University of Virginia Press, 2005], Presidential Series, vol. 12, 493–95).

43. George Washington to Henry Lee, 6 May 1793, in Founders Online, National Archives, http://founders.archives.gov/documents/Washington/05-12-02-0428 (original source: Patrick and Pinheiro, eds., *The Papers of George Washington, 16 January 1793–31 May 1793*, Presidential Series, vol. 12, 532–534).

44. Henry Lee to George Washington, 15 May 1793 in Ethel Armes, *Stratford Hall: The Great House of the Lees* (Richmond, VA: Garrett and Massie, 1936), 277.

45. Henry Lee to George Washington, 14 June 1793," in Founders Online, National Archives, http://founders.archives.gov/documents/Washington/05-13-02-0059 (original source: Patrick and Pinheiro, eds., *The Papers of George Washington,*

*16 January 1793–31 May 1793*, Presidential Series, vol. 12, 532–34).

46. Henry Lee to Alexander Hamilton, 6 May [1793], in Founders Online, National Archives, http://founders.archives.gov/ documents/Hamilton/01-14-02-0278 (original source: Harold C. Syrett, ed., *The Papers of Alexander Hamilton, February 1793–June 1793*, vol. 14, [New York: Columbia University Press, 1969], 416–17).

47. Charles Carter to Henry Lee, 20 May 1793, in Lee-Jackson Collection, Leyburn Library.

48. George Washington to Henry Lee, 21 July 1793, in Founders Online, National Archives, http://founders.archives.gov/ documents/Washington/05-13-02-0176 (original source: Christine Sternberg Patrick, ed., *The Papers of George Washington, 1 June–31 August 1793*, [Charlottesville, VA: University of Virginia Press, 2007], 260–62).

49. Armes, *Stratford Hall*, 277–78.

## 12: POINTING THE BAYONET AGAINST THE HEARTS OF OUR COUNTRYMEN

1. Henry Lee to George Washington, 14 June 1793, in Founders Online, National Archives, http://founders.archives.gov/ documents/Washington/05-13-02-0059 (original source: Christine Sternberg Patrick, ed., *The Papers of George Washington, 1 June–31 August 1793*, vol. 13, [Charlottesville, VA: University of Virginia Press, 2007], Presidential Series, 77–80).

2. Henry Lee to Alexander Hamilton, 15 June 1793, in Founders Online, National Archives, http://founders.archives.gov/ documents/Hamilton/01-14-02-0381 (original source: Harold C. Syrett, ed., *The Papers of Alexander Hamilton, February*

*1793–June 1793*, vol. 14, [New York: Columbia University Press, 1969], 549–50).

3. Henry Lee to George Washington, 14 June 1793, in Founders Online, National Archives, http://founders.archives.gov/documents/Washington/05-13-02-0059 (original source: Patrick, *The Papers of George Washington, 1 June–31 August 1793* Presidential Series, vol. 13, pp. 77–80).

4. Calendar of Virginia State Papers and Other Manuscripts...., vol. 6 (Richmond: A.R. Micou, 1866), 384.

5. Ibid., 406.

6. Papers of the Wayne County, Indiana, Historical Society, Indiana State Library vol. 1, no. 1 (1903), 3–11.

7. David V. Baker, *Women and Capital Punishment in the United States: An Analytical History* (Jefferson, NC: McFarland and Company, 2016), 302.

8. Calendar of Virginia State Papers, vol. 6 (1792–93).

9. Albert Jeremiah Beveridge, *The Life of John Marshall*, vol. 2, (Boston and New York: Houghton and Mifflin Company, 1916), 203–04.

10. Henry Lee to George Washington, 17 September 1793, in Founders Online, National Archives, http://founders.archives.gov/documents/Washington/05-14-02-0071 (original source: David R. Hoth, ed., *The Papers of George Washington, 1 September–31 December 1793*, vol. 14, [Charlottesville, VA: University of Virginia Press, 2008], Presidential Series, 108–11).

11. Calendar of Virginia State Papers, vol. 6 (1792–93), 510.

12. Ibid., 642.

13. Henry Lee to George Washington, 17 September 1793, in Founders Online, National Archives, http://founders.archives.gov/documents/Washington/05-14-02-0071 (original source: Hoth, ed., *The Papers of George Washington, 1*

*September–31 December 1793*, Presidential Series, vol. 14, 108–11).

14. Norman K. Risjord, *Chesapeake Politics, 1781–1800* (New York City: Columbia University Press, 1978), 431–32.

15. James Madison to Thomas Jefferson, 24 November 1793, in Founders Online, National Archives, http://founders.archives. gov/documents/Madison/01-15-02-0096 (original source: Thomas A. Mason, Robert A. Rutland, and Jeanne K. Sisson, eds., *The Papers of James Madison, 24 March 1793–20 April 1795*, vol. 15, [Charlottesville, VA: University Press of Virginia, 1985], 143).

16. Charles Royster, *Light-Horse Harry Lee and the Legacy of the American Revolution*, (Baton Rouge, LA: Louisiana State University Press, 1994), 140–41.

17. Calendar of Virginia State Papers, vol. 7 (Richmond: J. H. O'Bannon, Superintendent of Public Printing, 1888), 233.

18. Ibid.

19. Calendar of Virginia State Papers, vol. 7 (1794–95), 240.

20. Thomas P. Slaughter, *The Whiskey Rebellion: Frontier Epilogue to the American Revolution* (Oxford University Press, 1986), 113.

21. George Washington to Thomas Jefferson, 15 September 1792, in Founders Online, National Archives, http://founders.archives. gov/documents/Jefferson/01-24-02-0352. Vol. 24, (original source: John Catanzariti, ed., *The Papers of Thomas Jefferson, 1 June–31 December 1792* [Princeton: Princeton University Press, 1990], 383–85).

22. William Hogeland, *The Whiskey Rebellion: George Washington, Alexander Hamilton, and the Frontier Rebels Who Challenged America's Newfound Sovereignty* (New York City, NY: Simon and Schuster Paperback, 2006), 145–48.

23. Ibid., 145–48.

24. Slaughter, *The Whiskey Rebellion*, 179.

25. Ibid., 185–189.

26. Proclamation, 7 August 1794, in Founders Online, National Archives, http://founders.archives.gov/documents/Washington/05-16-02-0365 (original source: David R. Hoth and Carol S. Ebel, eds., *The Papers of George Washington, 1 May–30 September 1794*, vol. 16, [Charlottesville, VA: University of Virginia Press, 2011], Presidential Series, 531–37).

27. Henry Knox to Bartholomew Dandridge Jr., 16 May 1794, in Founders Online, National Archives, 2018, http://founders.archives.gov/documents/Washington/05-16-02-0066 (original source: David R. Hoth and Carol S. Ebel, eds., *The Papers of George Washington, 1 May–30 September 1794*, vol. 16, [Charlottesville, VA: University of Virginia Press, 2011], Presidential Series, 78–79).

28. Tully No. I, [23 August 1794], in Founders Online, National Archives, http://founders.archives.gov/documents/Hamilton/01-17-02-0102 (original source: Harold C. Syrett, ed., *The Papers of Alexander Hamilton, August 1794– December 1794*, vol. 17, [New York: Columbia University Press, 1972], 132–135).

29. Richard Beeman, *The Old Dominion and the New Nation: 1788–1801* (Lexington, KY: University Press of Kentucky, 1972), 135.

30. Calendar of Virginia State Papers...., vol. 7, 1794-1795, (Richmond: J.H. O'Bannon, 1888), 266–67.

31. Henry Lee to George Washington, 3 September 1794, in Founders Online, National Archives, http://founders.archives.gov/documents/Washington/05-16-02-0438 (original source: Hoth and Ebel, eds., *The Papers of George Washington,*

*1 May–30 September 1794*, Presidential Series, vol. 16, 636–37).

32. George Washington to Henry Lee, 26 August 1794, in Founders Online, National Archives, http://founders.archives.gov/documents/Washington/05-16-02-0418 (original source: Hoth and Ebel, eds., *The Papers of George Washington, 1 May–30 September 1794*, Presidential Series, vol. 16, 600–05).

33. Henry Lee to George Washington, 17 August 1794, in Founders Online, National Archives, http://founders.archives.gov/documents/Washington/05-16-02-0391(original source: Hoth and Ebel, eds., *The Papers of George Washington, 1 May–30 September 1794*, Presidential Series, vol. 16, 572–73).

34. Henry Lee to George Washington, 3 September 1794, in Founders Online, National Archives, http://founders.archives.gov/documents/Washington/05-16-02-0438 (original source: Hoth and Ebel, eds., *The Papers of George Washington, 1 May–30 September 1794*, Presidential Series, vol. 16, 636–37).

35. John B. Linn and William H. Egle, *Pennsylvania Archives*, vol. 4, (Harrisburg, PA:, 1890), 95.

36. Beeman, *The Old Dominion and the New Nation*, 134.

37. Alexander Hamilton to Henry Lee, 3 September 1794, in Syrett, ed., *The Papers of Alexander Hamilton, August 1794–December 1794*, vol. 17, 191.

38. Don Higginbotham, *Daniel Morgan: Revolutionary Rifleman* (Chapel Hill, NC: University of North Carolina Press, 1961), 189–90.

39. Calendar of Virginia State Papers. . . ., vol. 7, 1794–1794 (Richmond: J.H. O'Bannon, 1888), 204–05.

40. Henry Lee to James Madison, 23 September 1794, Founders Online, National Archives, http://founders.archives.gov/documents/Madison/01-15-02-0271 (original source: Thomas

A. Mason, Robert A. Rutland, and Jeanne K. Sisson, eds., *The Papers of James Madison, 24 March 1793–20 April 1795*, [Charlottesville, VA: University Press of Virginia, 1985], 359).

41. Richard H. Dillon, *Meriwether Lewis* (Lafayette, CA: Great West Books, 2003), 19.

42. Slaughter, *The Whiskey Rebellion*, 212–14.

43. Calendar of Virginia State Papers...., vol. 7 (Richmond: J. H. O'Bannon, 1888), 334.

44. Ibid., 334.

45. Mark Plus, *Henry Knox: Visionary General of the American Revolution* (London, UK: Palgrave Macmillan, 2008), 218–19.

46. Slaughter, *The Whiskey Rebellion*, 214.

47. Ibid., 205.

48. Donald Jackson, ed., *The Diaries of George Washington*, vol. 1, (Charlottesville, VA: University Press of Virginia, 1976–79), 6 vols., 170–98.

49. Harold C. Syreet, ed., The Papers of Alexander Hamilton Digital Edition, (Charlottesville, VA: University of Virginia Press, Rotunda, 2011).

50. From George Washington to Henry Lee, 20 October 1794, Founders Online, National Archives, last modified June 13, 2018, http://founders.archives.gov/documents/Washington/05-17-02-0061. [Original source: The Papers of George Washington, Presidential Series, vol. 17,1 October 1794–31 March 1795, ed. David R. Hoth and Carol S. Ebel. (Charlottesville: University of Virginia Press, 2013), 91–94.]

51. "Diary of Robert Wellford," *William and Mary College Quarterly Historical Magazine*, vol. 11, 1903, 11.

52. Ibid, 13.

53. General Henry Lee to the Inhabitants of the Four Western Counties, 8 November 1794, Virginia Historical Society.

54. Henry Lee to John Fitzgerald, 9 November 1794, in Jessie Ball duPont Library, Stratford Hall.

55. *The Magazine of History, with Notes and Queries.* Extra numbers, vol. 3, 26–27.

56. Hugh Henry Brackenridge, *Incidents of the Insurrection* (New Haven, CT: College and University Press, 1972), 202.

57. Leland Baldwin, *Whiskey Rebels: The Story of a Frontier Uprising* (Pittsburgh, PA: University of Pittsburg Press, 1967), 36.

58. Ibid., 35–47.

59. Brackenridge, *Incidents of the Insurrection*, 196–200.

60. William Findley, *History of the Insurrection: In the Four Western Counties of Pennsylvania in the Year MDCCXCIV; with a Recital of the Circumstances Specially Connected Therewith, and an Historical Review of the Previous Situation of the Country* (Samuel Harrison Smith, 1794), 218.

## 13: CRACKED

1.  Jefferson's Notes on the History of the Medals, [ca. 8 July 1792], in Founders Online, National Archives, http://founders.archives.gov/documents/Jefferson/01-16-02-0039-0005 (original source: Julian P. Boyd, ed. *The Papers of Thomas Jefferson, 30 November 1789–4 July 1790*, vol. 16, [Princeton, NJ: Princeton University Press, 1961], 77–79); William A. Burwell to Thomas Jefferson, 29 December 1809, in Founders Online, National Archives, http://founders.archives.gov/documents/Jefferson/03-02-02-0075 (original source: J. Jefferson Looney, ed., *The Papers of Thomas Jefferson, 16 November 1809 to 11 August 1810*, vol. 2, [Princeton, NJ: Princeton University Press, 2005], J. Retirement Series, 104–06).

2. Henry Lee to Alexander Hamilton, 5 January 1795, in Founders Online, National Archives, http://founders.archives.gov/documents/Hamilton/01-18-02-0014 (original source: *The Papers of Alexander Hamilton, January 1795–July 1795*, vol. 18, [New York: Columbia University Press, 1973], 11–12).

3. Richard Beeman, *The Old Dominion and the New Nation: 1788–1801* (Lexington, KY: University Press of Kentucky, 1972), 135.

4. George Washington to Henry Lee, 21 July 1793, in Founders Online, National Archives, http://founders.archives.gov/documents/Washington/05-13-02-0176, vol. 13, (original source: Christine Sternberg Patrick, ed., *The Papers of George Washington, 1 June–31 August 1793*, [Charlottesville, VA: University of Virginia Press, 2007], Presidential Series, 260–62).

5. Charles Royster, *Light-Horse Harry Lee and the Legacy of the American Revolution*, (Baton Rouge, LA: Louisiana State University Press, 1994), 133–34.

6. Noble E. Cunningham Jr., *In Pursuit of Reason: The Life of Thomas Jefferson* (Manhattan, NY: Random House, 1988), 198–99.

7. From Thomas Jefferson to James Madison, 28 December 1794, in Founders Online, National Archives, http://founders.archives.gov/documents/Jefferson/01-28-02-0171 (original source: John Catanzariti, ed., *The Papers of Thomas Jefferson, 1 January 1794–29 February 1796*, vol. 28, [Princeton, NJ: Princeton University Press, 2000], 228–30).

8. Henry Lee to George Washington, 17 August 1794, in Founders Online, National Archives, http://founders.archives.gov/documents/Washington/05-16-02-0391 (original source: David R. Hoth and Carol S. Ebel, eds., *The Papers of George*

*Washington, 1 May–30 September 1794*, vol. 16, [Charlottesville, VA: University of Virginia Press, 2011], Presidential Series, 572–73).

9. From George Washington to Henry Lee, 26 August 1794, Founders Online, National Archives, last modified June 13, 2018, http://founders.archives.gov/documents/ Washington/05-16-02-0418. [Original source: The Papers of George Washington, Presidential Series, vol. 16,1 May–30 September 1794, ed. David R. Hoth and Carol S. Ebel. (Charlottesville: University of Virginia Press, 2011), 600–605.]

10. Thomas Jefferson to George Washington, 19 June 1796, in Founders Online, National Archives, http://founders.archives. gov/documents/Jefferson/01-29-02-0091, vol. 29, (original source: Barbara B. Oberg, ed., *The Papers of Thomas Jefferson, 1 March 1796–31 December 1797* [Princeton, NJ: Princeton University Press, 2002], 127–30).

11. William B. Giles to James Madison, 12 April 12, 1795, in Manuscript/Mixed Material, James Madison Papers, Library of Congress.

12. Henry Lee to George Washington, 17 July 1795, in Founders Online, National Archives, http://founders.archives.gov/ documents/Washington/05-18-02-0263, vol. 18, (original source: William M. Ferraro, David R. Hoth, and Jennifer E. Stertzer, eds., *The Papers of George Washington, 1 April–30 September 1795* [Charlottesville, VA: University of Virginia Press, 2015], Presidential Series, 351–52).

13. George Washington to George Lewis, 27 July 1795, in Founders Online, National Archives, http://founders.archives.gov/ documents/Washington/05-18-02-0297 (original source: William M. Ferraro, David R. Hoth and Jennifer E. Stertzer, eds., *The Papers of George Washington, 1 April–30*

*September 1795* [Charlottesville, VA: University of Virginia Press, 2015], Presidential Series, vol. 18, 430–32).

14. Timothy Pickering to Alexander Hamilton, 17 November 1795, in Founders Online, National Archives, http://founders. archives.gov/documents/Hamilton/01-19-02-0086, vol. 19, (original source: Harold C. Syrett, ed., *The Papers of Alexander Hamilton, July 1795–December 1795* [New York: Columbia University Press, 1973] 435–41).

15. Memorandum for Henry Lee, 18 February 1793, in Founders Online, National Archives, http://founders.archives.gov/ documents/Washington/05-12-02-0123, vol. 12, (original source: Christine Sternberg Patrick and John C. Pinheiro, eds., *The Papers of George Washington, 16 January 1793–31 May 1793* [Charlottesville, VA: University of Virginia Press, 2005], Presidential Series, 173–74).

16. George Washington to Henry Lee, September 8, 1797, in John C. Fitzpatrick, ed., *The Writings of George Washington from the Original Manuscript Sources 1745–1799*, vol. 36, (Washington, DC: U.S. Government Printing Office), 28–30.

17. Charles Page Smith, James Wilson: Founding Father, 1742-1798. Published for the Institute of Early American History and Culture,1956, 374.

18. Charles Boyd, *Light-Horse Harry Lee* (New York City, New York: Scribner's and Sons, 1931), 245–46.

19. Robert S. Gamble, *Sully: The Biography of a House* (Sully Foundation, 1973), 40, 197.

20. James Madison to George Washington, 20 June 1792, in Founders Online, National Archives, http://founders.archives. gov/documents/Madison/01-14-02-0294 (original source: Robert A. Rutland and Thomas A. Mason, eds., *The Papers of James Madison, 6 April 1791–16 March 1793*, vol. 14,

[Charlottesville, VA: University Press of Virginia, 1983], 319–24).

21. George Washington to Robert Lewis, 26 June 1796, Founders Online, National Archives, http://founders.archives.gov/documents/Washington/99-01-02-00648 (original source: John C. Fitzpatrick, ed., *The Writings of George Washington from the Original Manuscript Source, March 30, 1796–July 31, 1797* [Washington, DC: U.S. Government Printing Office, 1940], 99).

22. James Thomas Flexner, *Washington: The Indispensable Man* (New York City, New York: Back Bay Books, 1994), 356.

23. Virginia Resolutions, 21 December 1798, Founders Online, National Archives, http://founders.archives.gov/documents/Madison/01-17-02-0128 (original source: David B. Mattern, J. C. A. Stagg, Jeanne K. Cross, and Susan Holbrook Perdue, eds., *The Papers of James Madison, 31 March 1797–3 March 1801 and supplement 22 January 1778–9 August 1795*, vol. 17, [Charlottesville, VA: University Press of Virginia, 1991], 185–191).

24. *The Virginia Report of 1799–1800, Touching on the Alien and Sedition Laws, of December 21, 1798, the Debates and Proceedings Thereon in the House of Delegates of Virginia* (Richmond, VA: J.W. Randolph, 1850), 105–08.

25. Ibid.

26. Charles F. Hobson, ed., *The Papers of John Marshall: Correspondence, Papers, and Selected....* vol. 12, (Chapel Hill, NC: University of North Carolina Press, 2006), 516.

27. Henry Lee to George Washington from Henry Lee, Jr., 28 September 1798, Founders Online, National Archives, http://founders.archives.gov/documents/Washington/06-03-02-0024 (original source: W. W. Abbot and Edward G. Lengel, eds., *The*

*Papers of George Washington, 16 September 1798–19 April 1799*, vol. 3, [Charlottesville, VA: University Press of Virginia, 1999], Retirement Series, 55).

28. Armes, 285–86.

29. George Washington Alexander Hamilton from George Washington, 10 April 1799, in Founders Online, National Archives, http://founders.archives.gov/documents/ Hamilton/01-23-02-0021 (original source: Harold C. Syrett, ed., *The Papers of Alexander Hamilton, April 1799–October 1799*, vol. 23, [New York: Columbia University Press, 1976], 31–32); Alexander Hamilton to Henry Lee, 18 February 1799, in Founders Online, National Archives, http://founders. archives.gov/documents/Hamilton/01-22-02-0289 (original source: Harold C. Syrett, ed., *The Papers of Alexander Hamilton, July 1798–March 1799*, vol. 22, [New York: Columbia University Press, 1975], 486–87).

30. Albert Jeremiah Beveridge, *The Life of John Marshall*, vol. 2, (Boston, MA: Houghton Mifflin Co, 1919), 415. Biographies of Lee and histories of the Lee family, including those by Noel B. Gerson, Charles Boyd, and Ethel Armes, state that George Washington rode to the polls to cast his vote for Lee, but in fact Washington's home, Mount Vernon, was in the boundaries of what was then Virginia's 17th Congressional District. Washington's diaries do record a journey to Alexandria on April 24, 1799 to vote for a "Representative from the District to Congress." This would most likely have been Leven Powell, a Federalist who was elected to Congress to represent the 17th. Washington had, however, voted for Lee's younger brother Richard Bland Lee, for Congress a decade before and recorded doing so. See Washington's diary entry for 24 April 1799, in Founders Online, National Archives, http://founders.

archives.gov/documents/Washington/01-06-02-0008-0004-0024, vol. 6, (original source: Donald Jackson and Dorothy Twohig, eds., *The Diaries of George Washington, 1 January 1790–13 December 1799* [Charlottesville, VA: University Press of Virginia, 1979], 344).

31. Henry Lee to William Sullivan, 30 April 30, 1799, in Jessie Ball duPont Library, Stratford Hall.

32. Thomas Jefferson to Archibald Stuart, 14 May 1799, in Founders Online, National Archives, http://founders.archives.gov/documents/Jefferson/01-31-02-0094 (original source: Barbara B. Oberg, ed., *The Papers of Thomas Jefferson, 1 February 1799–31 May 1800* [Princeton, NJ: Princeton University Press, 2004], 109–111).

33. Norman K. Risjord, *Chesapeake Politics 1781–1800* (New York: Columbia University Press, 1978), 546–47; John Edward Oster, ed., John Marshall, *The Political and Economic Doctrines of John Marshall, Who for Thirty-Four Years Was Chief Justice of the United States. And Also His Letters, Speeches, and Hitherto Unpublished and Uncollected Writings,* (Clark, NJ: The Lawbook Exchange, 2006), 173.

## 14: FAREWELL GREAT AND NOBLE PATRIOTS

1. John Ragosta, *Patrick Henry: Proclaiming A Revolution* (New York, New York: Routledge, 2017), 142.

2. George Washington Parke Custis, Mary Randolph Custis Lee, and Benson John Lossing, *Recollections and Private Memoirs of Washington* (New York: Derby and Jackson, 1860), 362; Levi Carroll Judson, *The Sages and Heroes of the American Revolution, in Two Parts,* (New York, New York: Lee and Shepard, 1875), 159–60.

3.  Ethel Armes, *Stratford Hall: The Great House of the Lees* (Richmond, VA: Garrett and Massie, 1936), 287.

4.  James Thomas Flexner, *Washington: The Indispensable Man* (Boston, MA: Back Bay Books, 1994), 396–402.

5.  Benjamin Franklin Hough, *Washingtoniana; or, Memorials of the Death of George Washington*, vol. 1, (Elliot Woodward, 1865), 25–26.

6.  John Marshall, *The Life of George Washington*, vol. 2, (Philadelphia: James Crissy, 1843), 441.

7.  Hough, *Washingtoniana*, 26.

8.  Ibid., 29.

9.  Ibid, 29–30, 40.

10. James D. Kornwolf and Georgina Wallis Kornwolf, *Architecture and Town Planning in Colonial North America* vol. 2, (Baltimore, MD: Johns Hopkins, 2002), 1195; Henry D. Biddle, ed., *Extracts from the Journal of Elizabeth Drinker from 1759 to 1807* (Philadelphia, PA: J.B. Lippencott, 1889), 354.

11. Hough, *Washingtoniana*, 40–41.

12. Ibid., 33.

13. Russell Frank Weigley, *Philadelphia: A 300 Year History* (New York City, New York: W.W. Norton and Company, 1982), 203.

14. Hough *Washingtoniana*, 48.

15. Ibid., 49–51.

16. Ibid., 51–54.

17. Bird Wilson, *Memoir of The Life of the Right Reverend William White, D.d.: Bishop of The Protestant Episcopal Church in the State Of Pennsylvania* (Philadelphia, PA: James Kay Jun, & Brother, 1839), 351.

18. Henry Lee, "A Funeral Oration on the Death of General Washington," in Custis, Lee, and Lossing, *Recollections and*

*Private Memoirs of Washington* (New York: Derby and Jackson, 1860), 615.

19. Ibid., 615.
20. Ibid. 616.
21. Ibid., 617.
22. Ibid.
23. Henry Lee, "A Funeral Oration on the Death of General Washington," in *Harper's Encyclopedia of United States History from 458 A. D. to 1906, Based upon the Plan of Benson John Lossing, LL.D.* (New York City: Harper and Brothers, 1906), 344.
24. Ibid., 344.
25. Ibid., 345.
26. Ibid., 346.
27. Ibid.
28. Hough, *Washingtoniana*, 127.
29. "Eulogies at the Death of Washington," *The Bookman, An Illustrated Literary Journal*, vol. 10 (September 1899– February 1900), 575.
30. Hough, *Washingtoniana*, 58–59.
31. John Fanning Watson, *Annals of Philadelphia and Pennsylvania, in the Olden Time*, vol 1, (Elijah Thomas, 1857), 181.
32. Annals of the Congress of the United States, vol. 10, (Washington: Gales and Seaton, 1851), 273–74.
33. Ibid., 275.
34. Ibid.
35. Ibid., 231–32.
36. Ibid.

37. William Cox, *Celebration of the One Hundredth Anniversary of the Establishment of the Seat of Government in the District of Colombia* (Government Printing Office, 1901), 104.

38. Edward J. Larson, *A Magnificent Catastrophe: The Tumultuous Election of 1800* (New York: Free Press, 2007), 98–111.

39. Fawn McKay Brodie, *Thomas Jefferson: An Intimate History* (New York City: W.W. Norton and Company, 1974), 324–25.

40. Timothy Pickering, *A Review of the Correspondence Between Hon. John Adams and William Cunningham* (Salem, Massachusetts: Cushing and Appleton, 1824), 71.

41. "Catalogue of Henry Lee III's Financial Transactions," compiled by Judy Hinson, director of Research and Collections at Stratford Hall, Stratford Hall.

42. Armes, *Stratford Hall*, 294.

43. Ibid., 295.

44. Howard Montagu Colvin, *Architecture and the After-Life* (New Haven, CT: Yale University Press, 1991), 357–58.

45. Annals of the Congress, 801–02.

46. William Edward Dodd, *The Life of Nathaniel Macon* (Raleigh, NC: Edwards and Broughton, 1903), 56–57, 263, 398, 410.

47. Annals of Congress, 803.

48. Thomas Hart Beonton, *Abridgment of the Debates of Congress, from 1789 to 1856*, (New York City, NY: D. Appleton and Company, 1857), 505.

49. Ibid., 504.

50. Alexander Hamilton to Oliver Wolcott Jr., 16 December 1800, in Founders Online, National Archives, http://founders. archives.gov/documents/Hamilton/01-25-02-0131 (original source: Harold C. Syrett, ed., *The Papers of Alexander*

*Hamilton, July 1800–April 1802*, vol. 25, [New York: Columbia University Press, 1977], 257–59).

51. Ron Chernow, *Alexander Hamilton* (London: Penguin, 2005), 422.

52. Henry Lee to Alexander Hamilton, 6 February 1801, in Founders Online, National Archives, http://founders.archives. gov/documents/Hamilton/01-25-02-0176 (original source: Syrett, ed., *The Papers of Alexander Hamilton, July 1800–April 1802*, vol. 25, 331–32).

53. Ibid.

54. George Mifflin Dallas, ed. *Life and Writings of Alexander James Dallas* (Philadelphia, PA: JB Lippincott, 1871), 112–13.

55. Henry Lee to Harrison Gray Otis, 6 April 1801, in Harrison Gray Otis Papers, Massachusetts Historical Society.

## 15: UNCEASING WOE

1. Paul Leicester Ford, *The True George Washington* (Philadelphia, PA: J.B. Lippincott, 1896), 272.

2. John James Maund to Robert Carter, 3 January 1801, in Kate Mason Rowland, ed., "Letters of John James Maund," 1790–1802, *William and Mary Quarterly*, 1912.

3. Paul C. Nagel, *The Lees of Virginia: Seven Generations of an American Family* (Bethesda, MD: Oxford University Press, 1990), 178.

4. Robert Morris to Henry Lee, 27 August 1801, in Manuscripts, Virginia Historical Society.

5. Charles Carter Lee, *Recollections of Stratford Hall: My Boyhood* (University of Virginia), 9.

6. Nagel, *The Lees of Virginia*, 203–04.

7. Ibid.

8. "Financial Transactions of Henry Lee III," compiled by Judy Hinson, director of Research and Collections at Stratford Hall, Stratford Hall.

9. Nagel, *The Lees of Virginia*, 179.

10. Robert S. Gamble, *Sully: The Biography of a House*, (Sully Foundation, 1973), 51.

11. Henry Lee to unknown, Nov. 8, 1800, Huntington Library.

12. Charles Royster, *Light-Horse Harry Lee and the Legacy of the American Revolution*, (Baton Rouge, LA: Louisiana State University Press, 1994), 175.

13. Deposition of Ransdell Pierce, 1 January 1806, photocopy in Jessie Ball duPont Library, Stratford Hall.

14. Nathaniel Pendleton to George Deneale, November 1803, photocopy in Jessie Ball duPont Library, Stratford Hall.

15. Nagel, *The Lees of Virginia*, 179.

16. Henry Lee to George Deneale, 20 October 18--, George Deneale Papers, Virginia Historical Society.

17. Armes, Stratford Hall, 304-05.

18. Ethel Armes, *Stratford Hall: The Great House of the Lees* (Richmond, VA: Garrett and Massie, 1936), 306–07.

19. Nagel, *The Lees of Virginia*, 180.

20. Armes, *Stratford Hall*, 308–09.

21. Fawn McKay Brodie, *Thomas Jefferson: An Intimate History* (New York City: W.W. Norton and Co., 1974), 76.

22. Ibid.

23. Dumas Malone, *Jefferson and His Time: Jefferson the Virginian* (New York City, NY: Little, Brown, 1948), 448.

24. Thomas Jefferson to John Walker, 13 April 1803, in Founders Online, National Archives, http://founders.archives.gov/documents/Jefferson/01-40-02-0140 (original source: Barbara B. Oberg, ed., *The Papers of Thomas Jefferson, 4 March–10*

*July 1803*, vol. 40, [Princeton, NJ: Princeton University Press, 2013], 187–89).

25. Henry Lee to Thomas Jefferson, 24 February 1806, in Thomas Jefferson Papers, Founders Online, National Archives, http://founders.archives.gov/documents/Jefferson/99-01-02-3294.

26. Henry Lee to Thomas Jefferson, 17 January 1807, in Thomas Jefferson Papers, Founders Online, National Archives, http://founders.archives.gov/documents/Jefferson/99-01-02-4894; Thomas Jefferson to Henry Lee, 1 February 1807, in Founders Online, National Archives, http://founders.archives.gov/documents/Jefferson/99-01-02-4995.

27. Henry Lee, *A Cursory Sketch of the Motives and Proceedings of the Party Which Sways the Union....* (Philadelphia: self-published, 1809), 3.

28. Ibid., 4–7.

29. Ibid., 7–9.

30. Ibid, 22.

31. Henry Lee, "Fourth Division—You Are Called Upon by Your Governor," 1807, in Virginia Historical Society.

32. Charles Boyd, *Light-Horse Harry Lee* (Scribner's and Sons, 1931), 290.

33. Ibid, 290.

34. To James Madison from Henry Lee, 11 February 1809, Founders Online, National Archives, last modified June 13, 2018, http://founders.archives.gov/documents/Madison/99-01-02-4016.

35. Elizabeth Brown Pryor, *Reading the Man: A Portrait of Robert E. Lee Through His Private Letters* (London: Penguin, 2007), 14–15.

36. Henry Lee to Robert G. Harper, 20 September 1808, in Manuscripts, Virginia Historical Society.

37. Oren Frederic Morton, *A History of Rockbridge County, Virginia* (New York City: The Mclure Co, 1920), 239.

38. Henry Lee to James Breckinridge, 4 March 1809, in Manuscripts, Breckinridge Family Papers, Virginia Historical Society.

39. Boyd, *Light-Horse Harry Lee*, 291.

40. Henry Lee to Robert G. Harper, 12 March 1809, in Jessie Ball duPont Library, Stanford Hall.

41. Boyd, *Light-Horse Harry Lee*, 297.

42. Henry Lee IV to Henry Lee, 3 July 1809, New York Historical Society, quoted in Royster, *Light-Horse Harry Lee*, 184.

## 16: WHEN FUTURE GENERATIONS SHALL INQUIRE

1. Henry Lee to Bernard Carter, 7 March 1810, in Henry Lee Papers, Library of Virginia, Richmond.

2. William Brock to William A. Washington, 5 December 1809, in Beverley Family Papers, Virginia Historical Society.

3. Henry Lee to Charles Simms, 6 January 1809, in Library of Congress, in Charles Simms Papers, Peter Force Collection.

4. John Mercer to Henry Lee, 16 November 1809, photocopy in Jessie Ball duPont Library, Stratford Hall.

5. W. R. Davie to Henry Lee, 1810, photocopy in Jessie Ball duPont Library, Stratford Hall.

6. William Goddard to Henry Lee, 2 April 1810, in Jessie Ball duPont Library, Stratford Hall.

7. Christopher Greene to Henry Lee, 1809, photocopy in Jessie Ball duPont Library, Stratford Hall.

8. Charles Royster, *Light-Horse Harry Lee and the Legacy of the American Revolution*, (Baton Rouge: Louisiana State University Press, 1994), 190.

9. Ibid., 111.

10. William R. Davie to Henry Lee, 21 February 1810, in Jessie Ball duPont Library, Stratford Hall.

11. Henry Lee, *The Revolutionary War Memoirs of General Henry Lee*, ed. Robert E. Lee (Boston, MA: Da Capo Press, 1998), 81.

12. Ibid., 512.

13. Ibid., 116.

14. Ibid., 371.

15. Ibid., 215.

16. Ibid., 198.

17. Ibid., 259.

18. Ibid., 299.

19. Michael Kranish, *Flight from Monticello: Thomas Jefferson at War* (Bethesda, MD: Oxford University Press, 2010), 278.

20. Fawn M. Brodie, *Thomas Jefferson: An Intimate History* (W.W. Norton, New York, London, 1998), 146; Royster, 216.

21. Lee, *Memoirs*, 299–300.

22. Lee, *Memoirs*, 107.

23. Henry Lee to Charles Simms, 6 January 1810, in Library of Congress.

24. Henry Lee to Bernard Carter, 7 March 1810, in Virginia State Library.

25. Royster, *Light-Horse Harry* Lee, 231.

26. Ethel Armes, *Stratford Hall: The Great House of the Lees* (Richmond, VA: Garrett and Massie, 1936), 324.

27. Robert S. Gamble, *Sully: The Biography of a House* (Sully Foundation, 1973), 51.

28. R. B. Lee to William Goddard, 23 May 1810, in the Papers of the Lee Family, Archives of the Robert E. Lee Memorial Foundation. The modern edition of Lee's *Memoirs*, which I cite throughout, was published under a different title: *The*

*Revolutionary War Memoirs of General Henry Lee*, ed. Robert E. Lee (Boston, MA: Da Capo Press, 1998).

29. Charles Boyd, *Light-Horse Harry Lee* (New York: Scribner's and Sons, 1931), 301.

30. William A. Burwell to Thomas Jefferson, 29 December 1809, in Founders Online, National Archives, 2017, http://founders. archives.gov/documents/Jefferson/03-02-02-0075 (original source: J. Jefferson Looney, ed., *The Papers of Thomas Jefferson, 16 November 1809 to 11 August 1810*, vol. 2, [Princeton, NJ: Princeton University Press, 2005], Retirement Series, 104–06).

31. Elizabeth Brown Pryor, *Reading the Man: A Portrait of Robert E. Lee Through His Private Letters* (London: Penguin, 2007), 33; Gamble, *Sully*, 52–53.

32. Amy Bertsch "Out of the Attic," *Alexandria Times*, April 23, 2015.

33. Douglas Southall Freeman, *Lee: An Abridgment by Richard Harwell* (New York City, NY: Touchstone, 1991), 7; Henry Alexander White, *Robert E. Lee and the Southern Confederacy 1807–1870* (New York City, New York: G.P. Putnam's Sons, 1897), 130; Boyd, *Light-Horse Harry Lee*, 303.

## 17: THE SAD CATASTROPHE OF BALTIMORE

1. *Proceedings of the Massachusetts Historical Society: The Rev. John Piece's Memoirs,* (Boston: Massachusetts Historical Society, 1905), 377; Jonathan Dayton to James Madison, 21 March 1812, in Founders Online, National Archives, http:// founders.archives.gov/documents/Madison/03-04-02-0274 (original source: J. C. A. Stagg, Jeanne Kerr Cross, Jewel L. Spangler, Ellen J. Barber, Martha J. King, Anne Mandeville Colony, and Susan Holbrook Perdue, eds., *The Papers of James*

*Madison, 5 November 1811–9 July 1812 and Supplement 5 March 1809–19 October 1811*, vol. 4, [Charlottesville, VA: University Press of Virginia, 1999), Presidential Series, 257–58).

2. Norman K. Risjord, *Jefferson's America, 1760–1815* (Lanham, MD: Rowman & Littlefield, 2009), 361–70.

3. Spencer C. Tucker, James R. Arnold, Roberta Wiener, Paul G. Pierpaoli Jr., John C. Fredriksen, eds., *The Encyclopedia of the War of 1812: A Political, Social, and Military History*, (ABC-CLIO, 2012), 747.

4. Edwin Emerson and Marion Mills Miller, *1800–1821* (New York, NY: P.F. Collier and Son, 1906), 259–60; John Clark Ridpath, *Downfall of the Federalists*, The New Complete History of the United States of America (New York, NY: Elliot-Madison, 1912), 3971–78.

5. Potts-Fitzhugh House, National Register of Historic Places Inventory, United States Department of the Interior, National Park Service.

6. Charles Boyd, *Light-Horse Harry Lee* (New York: Scribner's and Sons, 1931), 304. Henry Lee to James Madison, 11 February 1809, James Madison Papers, Library of Congress.

7. Henry Lee to James Madison, 11 February 1809, James Madison Papers, Library of Congress.

8. Ibid.

9. Ibid.

10. Henry Lee to James Madison, 21 June 1812, in Founders Online, National Archives, http://founders.archives.gov/documents/Madison/03-04-02-0523 (original source: Stagg, et al., eds., *The Papers of James Madison, 5 November 1811–9 July 1812 and Supplement 5 March 1809–19 October 1811*, 494).

11. J. Jefferson Looney, ed. *The Papers of Thomas Jefferson, November 1812–September 1813*, vol. 7, (Princeton, NJ: Princeton University Press, 2010), Retirement Series, 289.

12. C. B. Richardson, *The Historical Magazine, and Notes and Queries Concerning the Antiquities, History and Biography of America* vol. 2 (New York), 1858.

13. Henry Lee to James Madison, 24 April 1812, Founders Online, National Archives, http://founders.archives.gov/documents/Madison/03-04-02-0367 (original source: Stagg, et al., eds., *The Papers of James Madison, 5 November 1811–9 July 1812 and Supplement 5 March 1809–19 October 1811*, Presidential Series, vol. 4, 348–49).

14. Frank A. Cassell, "The Great Baltimore Riot of 1812," *Maryland Historical Magazine*, vol. 70, no. 3 (1975), 242.

15. Ibid., 243; John Thomas Scharf, *History of Western Maryland: Being a History of Frederick, Montgomery, Carroll, Washington, Allegany, and Garrett Counties from the Earliest Period to the Present Day including Biographical Sketches of their Representative Men*, vol. 4, (Berwyn Heights, MD: Clearfield Company and Willow Bend Books, 1995), Presidential Series, 403.

16. Thomas John Scharf, *The Chronicles of Baltimore: Being a Complete History of "Baltimore Town" and Baltimore City from the Earliest Period to the Present Time* (Baltimore, MD: Turnbull Bros, 1874), 310.

17. Ibid.

18. Charles Royster, *Light-Horse Harry Lee and the Legacy of the American Revolution*, (Baton Rouge, LA: Louisiana State University Press, 1994), 159; Report of the Committee of Grievances and Courts of Justice of the House of Delegates of

Maryland, on the Subject of the Recent Mobs and Riots, in the City of Baltimore, 1813, 3, 110.

19. Scharf, *The Chronicles of Baltimore*, 310.

20. Report of the Committee of Grievances, 4.

21. Scharf, *The Chronicles of Baltimore*, 311.

22. Michael Ingrisano, *The First Officers of the United States Customs Service: Appointed by President George Washington in 1789*, Department of the Treasury and Customs Services, 1987, 4; Scharf, *The Chronicles of Baltimore*, 337.

23. *An Exact and Authentic Narrative of the Events Which Took Place in Baltimore, on the 27th and 28th of July Last. Carefully Collected from Some of the Sufferers and Eyewitnesses. To Which is Added a Narrative of Mr. John Thomson, one of the Unfortunate Sufferers*, (N.P. Printed from the Purchasers, September 1, 1812, Library of Congress Online Catalogue), 5.

24. *Proceedings of the Massachusetts Historical Society*, 378.

25. Henry Lee to A. C. Hanson, 20 July 1812, in *Niles' Weekly Register, Written, Edited and Published by Hezekiah Niles, March 1812–September 1812* (The Franklin Press, 1812), vol. 2, 378.

26. Cassell, "The Great Baltimore Riot of 1812," 246.

27. Ibid., 247.

28. Ibid., 248.

29. Report of the Committee of Grievances, 235.

30. Ibid., 248.

31. Cassell, "The Great Baltimore Riot," 248–50.

32. Report of the Committee of Grievances, 267–68.

33. Ibid., 250–51.

34. Scharf, *The Chronicles of Baltimore*, 319–20.

35. Cassell, "The Great Baltimore Riot of 1812," 251.

36. Ibid., 251–52.

37. Scharf, *The Chronicles of Baltimore*, 320–22.

38. *An Exact and Authentic Narrative of the Events Which Took Place in Baltimore*, 17–18.

39. Scharf, *The Chronicles of Baltimore*, 322–23; Cassell, "The Great Baltimore Riot of 1812," 352–54.

40. Royster, *Light-Horse Harry Lee*, 162.

41. *An Exact and Authentic Narrative*, 21.

42. Scharf, *The Chronicles of Baltimore*, 324.

43. Royster, *Light-Horse Harry Lee*, 163.

44. *An Exact and Authentic Narrative*," 24; Cassell, "The Great Baltimore Riot of 1812," 254.

45. Ibid., 256.

46. *An Exact and Authentic Narrative*, 27.

47. Cassell, "The Great Baltimore Riot," 256.

48. *Proceedings of the Massachusetts Historical Society*, 384.

49. Scharf, *The Chronicles of Baltimore*, 328.

50. Scharf, *The Chronicles of Baltimore*, 326.

51. "Narrative of John E. Hall," *Maryland Gazette*, 27 August, 1812.

52. Scharf, *The Chronicles of Baltimore*, 328.

53. "Narrative of John E. Hall."

54. Scharf, *The Chronicles of Baltimore*, 328–29; Report of the Committee of Grievances, 91.

55. *An Exact and Authentic Narrative*, 32–33.

56. James C. Boyd to James McHenry, 2 August 1812, quoted in Cassell, "The Great Baltimore Riot," 256.

57. "Soldier of 76," "To the Citizens of Maryland," *Maryland Gazette*, 13 August 1812.

58. *National Intelligencer*, 6 August 1812.

59. "Baltimore Mob," *Maryland Gazette*, 30 July 1812.

60. Royster, *Light-Horse Harry Lee*, 165.

61. Henry Lee IV to William E. Williams, 4 August 1812, in Calendar of the General Otho Holland, Williams Papers, The Maryland Historical Records Survey, 1940, 351.

62. Lucy Lee Carter to Alice Lee Shippen, 22 August 1812, in Jessie Ball duPont Library, Stratford Hall.

63. Alice Lee Shippen to Lucy Lee Carter, 17 September 1812, in Jessie Ball duPont Library, Stratford Hall.

## 18: MY MISERABLE EXILE

1. Anna Modigliani Lynch and Kelsey Ryan, eds., *Antebellum Reminiscences of Alexandria, Virginia, Extracted from the Memoirs of Mary Louisa Slacum Benham*, Office of Historic Alexandria/Alexandria Archaeology City of Alexandria, 2009, 3; Philip Slaughter, *A Memoir of the Life of the Right Rev. William Meade* (Cambridge: John Wilson and Son, 1885), 64.

2. *Proceedings of the Massachusetts Historical Society: The Rev. John Piece's Memoirs* (Boston: Massachusetts Historical Society, 1905), 378.

3. Thomas J. Rogers, *A New American Biographical Dictionary: Or, Rememberancer of the Departed* (Easton, PA: T.J. Rogers, 1824), 306.

4. Charles Boyd, *Light-Horse Harry Lee* (Scribner's and Sons, 1931), 328–29.

5. Robert Walsh, *The American Review of History and Politics, and General Repository of Literature and State Papers, 1812*, vol. 4, (London: Forgotten Books, 2018), 212.

6. Ibid., 230.

7. Boyd, *Light-Horse Harry Lee*, 331.

8. Henry Lee to James Madison, 15 January 1813, in Founders Online, National Archives, http://founders.archives.gov/documents/Madison/03-05-02-0495 (original source: J. C. A. Stagg, Martha J. King, Ellen J. Barber, Anne Mandeville

Colony, Angela Kreider, and Jewel L. Spangler, eds., *The Papers of James Madison, 10 July 1812–7 February 1813*, vol. 5, [Charlottesville, VA: University of Virginia Press, 2004], Presidential Series, 585).

9. James Monroe to Robert B. Taylor, 1 March 1813, in War of 1812, Papers of the Department of State, 1789–1815.

10. Ibid.

11. Henry Lee to Ferdinand O'Neal, 4 May 1813, in Archives of the Robert E. Lee Memorial Foundation, Papers of the Lee Family, Box 2, M2009.121, Jessie Ball duPont Library, Stratford Hall.

12. Henry Lee to Bernard Carter, 4 February 1813, Special Collections, Washington and Lee University.

13. Charles Royster, *Light-Horse Harry Lee and the Legacy of the American Revolution*, (Baton Rouge, LA: Louisiana State University Press, 1994), 232–33

14. "Letter of Introduction for Henry Lee, [April] 1813," in Founders Online, National Archives, http://founders.archives. gov/documents/Madison/03-06-02-0161 vol. 6. (original source: Angela Kreider, J. C. A. Stagg, Jeanne Kerr Cross, Anne Mandeville Colony, Mary Parke Johnson, and Wendy Ellen Perry, eds., *The Papers of James Madison, 8 February–24 October 1813* [Charlottesville, VA: University of Virginia Press, 2008], Presidential Series, 169–70).

15. George Beckwith to Earl Bathurst, 26 November 1813, in "Major General Henry Lee and Lieutenant General George Beckwith on Peace in 1813," *American Historical Review*, Volume 32, January 1927, 284–92; Henry Lee to George Beckwith, 10 November 1812, in ibid.

16. George Beckwith to Henry Lee, 18 November 1813, in ibid.

17. Henry Lee to Rufus King, 19 November 1813, in Charles R. King, ed., *The Life and Correspondence of Rufus King, Comprising His Letters, Public and Official, His Public*

*Documents, and His Speeches*, vol. 5, (New York, NY: G.P. Puntam's Sons, 1898), 352–55.

18. Henry Lee to James Madison, 17 November 1813, Founders Online, National Archives, http://founders.archives.gov/documents/Madison/03-07-02-0040 (original source: Angela Kreider, J. C. A. Stagg, Mary Parke Johnson, Anne Mandeville Colony, and Katherine E. Harbury, eds., *The Papers of James Madison, 25 October 1813–30 June 1814*, vol. 7, [Charlottesville, VA: University of Virginia Press, 2012], Presidential Series, 44–45).

19. Henry Lee to Rufus King, 19 November 1813, in King, ed., *The Life and Correspondence of Rufus King*, vol. 5, 352–55.

20. Henry Lee to James Madison, 4 August 1813, in Founders Online, National Archives, http://founders.archives.gov/documents/Madison/03-06-02-0469 vol. 6, (original source: Angela Kreider, et al., eds., *The Papers of James Madison, 8 February–24 October 1813*, Presidential Series, 497–98).

21. Henry Lee to James Madison, 17 November 1813, Founders Online, National Archives, 2018, http://founders.archives.gov/documents/Madison/03-07-02-0040 (original source: Angela Kreider, J. C. A. Stagg, Mary Parke Johnson, Anne Mandeville Colony, and Katherine E. Harbur, eds., *The Papers of James Madison, 25 October 1813–30 June 1814*, vol. 6, [Charlottesville, VA: University of Virginia Press, 2012], Presidential Series, 44–45).

22. George Beckwith to Earl Bathurst, 25 November 1813, *American Historical Review*, vol. 32, no. 2 (January 1927), 284–92.

23. Henry Lee to James Madison, 17 November 1813, in Founders Online, National Archives, http://founders.archives.gov/documents/Madison/03-07-02-0040 (original source: Angela

Kreider, et al., eds., *The Papers of James Madison, 25 October 1813–30 June 1814*, Presidential Series, vol. 7, 44–45).

24. Henry Lee, Diary of Henry "Light-Horse" Lee, Special Collections, Washington and Lee University, 11.

25. Henry Lee to Anne Lee, undated, Washington and Lee University; Henry Lee to -- 29 August 1816, Virginia Historical Society.

26. James Causten, General Henry Lee Narrative Written Circa 1865, Manuscripts, Virginia Historical Society, 3.

27. Henry Lee to Ann Lee, 12 September 1816, Virginia Historical Society.

28. Henry Lee to Charles Carter Lee, 26 June 1816, in Henry Lee, *The Revolutionary War Memoirs of General Henry Lee*, ed. Robert E. Lee (Boston, MA: Da Capo Press, 1998), 57.

29. Henry Lee to Charles Carter Lee, 15 August 1813, quoted in R. David Cox, *The Religious Life of Robert E Lee* (Grand Rapids: William Eerdmans Publishing, 2017), 29.

30. Henry Lee to Charles Carter Lee, 30 September 1816, in Lee, *The Revolutionary War Memoirs*, 59.

31. Henry Lee to Anne Lee, 29–30 August 18--, in Special Collections, Washington and Lee University.

32. Henry Lee to Anne Kinloch Lee, no date, in Special Collections, Washington and Lee University.

33. Henry Lee to Anne Lee, 6 May 1817, in Virginia Historical Society.

34. Henry Lee to Charles Carter Lee, 15 August 1813, in Cox, *The Religious Life of Robert E. Lee*, 279.

35. Henry Lee to Anne Lee, 29–30 August 18--, in Washington and Lee University, Special Collections.

36. Henry Lee to Anne Lee, 6 May 1817, in George Bolling Lee Papers, Virginia Historical Society.

37. Lee, Diary, 3.

38. Ibid., 73, 74, 69–70, 79.

39. Ibid., 25, 19.

40. Ibid., 19.

41. Ibid., 38.

42. Ibid., 71.

43. Ibid., 208.

44. Henry Lee to Anne Lee, 27 December 1817, Special Collections, Washington and Lee University.

45. Henry Lee to Anne Lee, 29–30 August, in Special Collections, Washington and Lee University.

46. Henry Lee to unknown, 25 April 1817, in Jessie Ball duPont Library, Stratford Hall.

47. Henry Lee to Anne Lee, 6 May 1817, in George Bolling Lee Papers, Virginia Historical Society.

48. Henry Lee to Anne Lee, 27 December 1817 in Special Collections, Washington and Lee University.

49. Henry Lee to Nicholas Fish, 4 November 1816, in Nicholas Fish Papers, Library of Congress.

50. Henry Lee to unknown, 25 April 1817, in Jessie Ball duPont Library, Stratford Hall.

51. Ibid.

52. Henry Lee to unknown, 25 April 1817, in Jessie Ball duPont Library, Stratford Hall; Henry Lee to Anne Lee, 22 June 1817, in Special Collections, Washington and Lee.

53. Henry Lee to Anne Lee, 29–30 August, in Washington and Lee.

54. Causten, General Henry Lee Narrative, 1–2.

55. Ibid.

56. Ibid.

57. Ibid., 3–5.

58. Ibid.

59. Ibid, 5.

60. Roulhad Toledano, *The National Trust Guide to Savannah, Architectural and Cultural Treasures* (Washington, DC: Preservation Press, 1997), 52–53.

61. Causten, General Henry Lee Narrative, 5.

62. Charles G. Jones Jr., *Reminisces of the Last Days, Death and Burial of General Henry Lee* (John Munsell, 1870).

63. Ibid., 20.

64. Ibid., 21–29.

65. Henry Lee to Anne Lee, 1818, in Special Collections, Washington and Lee University.

66. Jones, *Reminisces*, 24–27.

67. Ibid., 28–31.

68. Ibid., 33.

69. Ibid., 33–36.

70. Ibid.

71. Causten, General Henry Lee Narrative, 5.

72. Ibid., 1, 6.

73. Ibid., 7.

74. Ibid.

**EPILOGUE**

1. J. H. Chandler to Robert E. Lee, 1863, in Special Collections, Washington and Lee.

2. Paul C. Nagel, *The Lees of Virginia: Seven Generations of an American Family* (Bethesda, MD: Oxford University Press, 1990), 206–15, 226–27.

3. Elizabeth Brown Pryor, *Reading the Man: A Portrait of Robert E. Lee Through His Private Letters* (London: Penguin, 2007), 23.

4. Thomas Jefferson to James Monroe, 1 January 1815, in Founders Online, National Archives, http://founders.archives.gov/documents/Jefferson/03-08-02-0150 (original source: J. Jefferson Looney, ed., *The Papers of Thomas Jefferson, 1*

*October 1814 to 31 August 1815*, vol. 8, [Princeton, NJ: Princeton University Press, 2011], Retirement Series, 176–79).

5. Henry Lee IV, *Observations on the Writings of Thomas Jefferson, with Particular Reference to the Attack They Contain on the Memory of the Late Gen. Henry Lee. In a Series of Letters*, 1832.

6. Thomas Forehand Jr., *Robert E. Lee's Softer Side* (Gretna, LA: Pelican Publishing, 2007), 46–47.

7. Edmund Jennings Lee, *Lee of Virginia, 1642–1892: Biographical and Genealogical Sketches of the Descendants of Colonel Richard Lee* (Berwyn Heights, MD: Heritage Books, 2008), 413.

8. Douglas Southall Freeman, *Lee: An Abridgment by Richard Harwell* (Touchstone, 1991), 21.

9. Ibid., 36–37, 61–62, 79–81, 89–91.

10. Pryor, *Reading the Man*, 45–46.

11. William, C. Davis, *Crucible of Command: Ulysses S. Grant and Robert E. Lee—the War They Fought, The Peace They Forged* (Boston, MA: Da Capo Press, 2014), 37; Pryor, *Reading the Man*, 79.

12. David, R. Cox, *The Religious Life of Robert E. Lee* (Grand Rapids, MI: William B. Eerdmans Publishing, 2017), 28–31.

13. Ibid.

14. Thomas Lawrence Connley (Baton Rouge, LA: Louisiana State University Press, 1977), xii.

15. Fitzhugh Lee, *General Lee: A Biography of Robert E. Lee* (Enhanced Media, 2017), 46.

16. Ibid., 46–47.

17. In 1865 Lee applied to reestablish his citizenship and swore the necessary amnesty oath to have it restored. The State Department, apparently intentionally, never processed the

request. It was not until 1975, several years after an archivist discovered the application, that his citizenship was restored. See "General Robert E. Lee's Parole and Citizenship, Pieces of History," *Prologue* vol. 37, no 1 (spring 2005).

18. J. H. Chandler to Robert E. Lee, 1863, in Special Collections, Washington and Lee.

19. Pryor, *Reading the Man*, 336.

20. Henry Lee, *The Revolutionary War Memoirs of General Henry Lee*, ed. Robert E. Lee (Boston, MA: Da Capo Press, 1998), 45.

21. Allan McLane to George Handy, 25 February 1817, Society of Cincinnati Library, Anderson House, Washington, DC.

22. Samuel Appleton Storrow to "Sister," 6 September 1821, Ethel Armes Papers, Library of Congress.

23. Nagel, *The Lees of Virginia*, 163.

24. Jonathan Elliot, *The Debates in the Several State Conventions on the Adoption of the Federal Constitution* (Burt Franklin, 1888), vol. 3, 179.

25. Robert E. Lee to Mary Lee, 18 January 1862, in Robert Edward Lee, *Recollections and Letters of General Robert E. Lee* (New York: Doubleday, 1904), 61.

26. Robert E. Lee to Mary Lee, 18 April 1870, in Lee, *Recollections and Letters of General Robert E. Lee* (New York: Doubleday, Page and Company, 1904), 398.

27. Mary Lee to Charles Carter Lee, 1 August 1870, in Ethel Armes Papers, Library of Congress.

28. Journal of the Senate of Virginia, 42–45.

# INDEX